In Their Own Best Interest

In Their Own Best Interest

A History of the U.S. Effort to Improve Latin Americans

LARS SCHOULTZ

Harvard University Press

Cambridge, Massachusetts & London, England

First Harvard University Press paperback edition, 2020
First printing

Library of Congress Cataloging-in-Publication Data

Names: Schoultz, Lars, author.

Title: In their own best interest : a history of the U.S. effort to improve Latin Americans /
   Lars Schoultz.

Description: Cambridge, Massachusetts : Harvard University Press, 2018. | Includes
   bibliographical references and index.

Identifiers: LCCN 2017061473 | ISBN 9780674984141 (cloth : alk. paper) |
   ISBN 9780674244924 (pbk.)

Subjects: LCSH: United States—Foreign relations—Latin America. | Latin America—Foreign
   relations—United States. | United States—Foreign relations—Moral and ethical aspects. |
   United States—Foreign relations—Philosophy. | Politicians—United States—Attitudes. |
   Economic assistance, American—Latin America—History. | Progressivism (United States politics)

Classification: LCC F1418 . S395 2018 | DDC 327.7308—dc23 LC record available at
   https://lccn.loc.gov/2017061473

For Jane

Contents

Introduction

Altruists and Realists

In Honduras, USAID programs strengthen the participation of marginalized groups in local and national governance; increase food security for the poorest sectors of society; support renewable energy and environmental conservation; expand basic education and skills training for at-risk youth and adults; and improve decentralized health care in terms of quality and access for local citizens and civil society. Efforts also address citizen security through community-based crime prevention activities. USAID projects work to spur economic growth, advance social justice, improve education and health, and engage the poorest members of Honduran society in the country's development.[1]

This book is an effort to understand the people who wrote that paragraph.

They had been working on it for over a century, and in 2016, a quarter-century after the disintegration of the Soviet Union, the U.S. Agency for International Development, created in 1961 to stop the spread of communism, was strengthening, increasing, supporting, expanding, improving, addressing, working, spurring, engaging, and advancing solutions to most of the socio-economic-political problems Hondurans might have, except communism.

And helping with all this was the National Endowment for Democracy, the NED, created in 1983 to realize Cold War President Ronald Reagan's "hope for the long term—the march of freedom and democracy which will leave Marxism-Leninism on the ash-heap of history." That is where communism had been put to rest a quarter-century ago, but the NED was not resting; here in 2016 it had seven verbs' worth of its own projects in Honduras, from "fostering youth participation in local accountability" to "evaluating efforts to fight corruption and impunity."[2] Of the seven, one was being implemented by the Democratic Party's nominally independent National Democratic Institute (NDI). When asked how the Institute was spending $575,000 of the NED's money, its Latin America specialist replied, "NDI maintains a small office in Tegucigalpa to provide technical assistance to support all the political parties represented in the Congress on transparency and political participation issues."[3]

Several other uplifting institutions were working closely alongside both AID* and the NED, including the State Department's Bureau of Democracy, Human Rights and Labor, which is responsible for producing an annual assessment of human rights in every member of the United Nations, except the United States. As always, Honduras did not fare well: "The most serious human rights problems were corruption, intimidation, and institutional weakness of the justice system leading to widespread impunity; unlawful and arbitrary killings and other criminal activities by members of the security forces; and harsh and at times life-threatening prison conditions."[4]

---

*In the early 1990s Agency officials decided that AID should be rebranded as USAID, even though its birth certificate (Executive Order 10973, November 3, 1961, 27 F. R. 10469) says it is the "Agency for International Development," or AID, just as the Federal Bureau of Investigation is the FBI, not the USFBI. The pages that follow stick with the Agency's legal title, in part for economy and in part as a nod in the direction of everyday usage beyond AID's offices. Economy: USAID is spoken and read as three syllables ("you ess aid"), whereas AID is a one-syllable proper noun and acronym spoken and read as the common noun, "aid," unless there would be some confusion. Usage: After a full quarter-century, USAID has not managed to replace AID in everyday Washington conversations, and AID is especially common as an adjective—"an AID administrator" or "an AID vendor." The Conclusion offers a more significant reason to make an issue of AID's rebranding.

None of this was new. U.S. policy toward Honduras began building to AID's ten-verb crescendo in 1911, when Secretary of State Philander Knox told Congress that Hondurans were "bankrupt, famished, and discouraged" and his assistant secretary informed the press that Honduras "has politically, financially and economically about as bad a record for stability as could be found on the face of the earth." So, Secretary Knox continued, "There is no hope for peace and prosperity for Honduras except through the United States."[5]

What did he propose to do? Ask Wall Street to loan Hondurans some money, with repayment ensured by his State Department, which would provide a U.S. citizen to collect and disburse Honduras's taxes, and by the U.S. Navy, which would provide a contingent of Marines to protect the U.S. citizen. This arrangement was used so often that critics gave it a name: Dollar Diplomacy.

Now jump ahead a half-century to 1961, when U.S. foreign policy was devoted to the containment of communism in the "underdeveloped" world, many of whose less-prosperous residents were said to be caught up in a worrisome Revolution of Rising Expectations. It was two years after Fidel Castro had led a group of revolutionaries down from Cuba's mountains, ousted a Washington-friendly dictator, nationalized U.S. investments, befriended the Soviet Union, and prompted everyone to wonder whether a second shoe might drop. The State Department's Bureau of Intelligence and Research worried that it might occur in Honduras, with its "almost universal poverty [and] serious obstacles to advancement," which included "dishonest and inefficient administration, poor transportation and difficult terrain, and extremely low educational levels. About two-thirds of the 2 million population is illiterate."[6] The Kennedy administration responded with the first mega-uplift since the Marshall Plan: the Alliance for Progress.

Fast-forward another half-century, from 1961 to 2016, when AID was providing Hondurans with those ten verbs' worth of assistance. Entering the White House in 2009, President Barack Obama had inherited the 2008 Central America Regional Security Initiative (CARSI), which had five "pillars," one of which was the creation of "Strong, Capable, and Accountable Central American Governments."[7] Then in 2010 the new administration added the Caribbean Basin Security Initiative, a collection of five additional foreign assistance schemes, not all of them from AID, including the "Nonproliferation, Antiterrorism, Demining, and Related [to narcotics trafficking] Programs" (NADR, pronounced "nadir").[8] A year after that, in 2011, President Obama announced a new Central American Citizen Security Partnership, with an initial U.S. contribution of $200 million, and in 2014, with tens of thousands of Central Americans headed toward the United States, fleeing poverty and violence, the presidents of Honduras, El Salvador, and Guatemala selected Washington as the site to launch their Alliance for Prosperity, for which the U.S. Congress contributed $750 million in FY2016. The Obama administration may have been disappointed (it had requested $1 billion under its new U.S. Strategy for Engagement in Central America), but the $750 million more than doubled the $317 million in FY2014 and was a third more than the $560 million in FY2015. Buried by this funding avalanche was the Obama administration's Caribbean Energy Security Initiative, launched in 2015 "to help countries achieve a more sustainable and cost effective energy matrix." It relied heavily on the U.S. private sector, with subsidized financing available through the U.S. government's Overseas Private Investment Corporation.[9]

In Honduras, so far the peak price for one year of this uplifting has been $162,950,000 in 2015, which included the cost of about one hundred Marines but not their expensive ($25 million each) CH-53E Super Stallion heavy-lift helicopters. Also excluded was the cost of maintaining Tegucigalpa's cramped embassy, where 476 people were working cheek by jowl in offices that even a professor would scorn. From its creation in 1961 through 2017, AID alone spent well over $3 billion to improve Hondurans—an average of about $55 million each year for over half a century.[10]

HONDURAS HAS TRADITIONALLY been portrayed as an especially needy case, but in one sense it is far from exceptional: the United States has been trying to improve Latin Americans for over a century.[11]

Although this effort will be examined in the chapters that follow, it is not the purpose of this book; rather, its purpose is to explore a special culture that guides Washington's effort to improve other peoples around the globe. This culture serves as the foundation supporting institutions with tens of thousands of government employees and private contractors who preach and teach everything from oral hygiene to representative democracy and show no sign of slowing down, let alone stopping. No longer is the United

States a passive City on a Hill, an example for others. It has become a nation of uplifters.*

YOU WILL FIND six distinct definitions of "culture" in the *Oxford English Dictionary.* As employed here, it is conceived as a "cult," with nothing negative intended by the use of that word; it simply identifies any group with distinctive norms that produce distinctive group behavior. Students of culture—ethnographers—explore how norms regulate the thinking of groups of people when they hunker down around a campfire to discuss their problems and decide what to do about them.

There are campfires on almost every corner in Washington, D.C. They are called "meetings."

The existence of these meetings explains why observation has always been a popular research method among students of foreign policy. It is a simple-minded but enormously time-consuming method of collecting data—in our case, data about the behavior of U.S. officials committed to improving other peoples. The goal, wrote Bronislaw Malinowski, a pioneering ethnographer, is "to grasp the native's point of view, his relation to life, to realize his vision of the world."[12]

The "natives" in this book are U.S. policymakers. They are broadly defined to include those who influence the policymaking process, even if they are not on the government's payroll and even if their aggregated views are inserted into the process via public opinion polls. The purpose of observing their meetings is to grasp their point of view, which is another way of saying *the constellation of beliefs* that serve as the foundation of their culture.[13] As beliefs become broadly accepted, they produce the norms that guide what people decide at their meetings.

When first observed as commuters on Washington's Metro or as neighbors living down the street, the people who wrote the paragraph that opens this Introduction look and act as if they have a standard constellation of

---

*As employed here, "uplifting" is defined as helping others improve their values or their behavior or their institutions—or all three. This effort to improve other peoples—to help them "develop"—should not be confused with relief and recovery from famines, earthquakes, civil wars, and the like. Clearly there can be some overlap, but nothing that follows is about what is commonly known as *humanitarian* assistance; this book is about *development* assistance, about making others less underdeveloped.

beliefs, blending in with the rest of us. But it does not take much observation to discover that they share a unique group culture, a distinctive constellation of beliefs. The authors of that paragraph are not simply people who go to work every morning; as they push open the door of their office building, they step into a world apart, entering what another cultural anthropologist, Clifford Geertz, would have called an "imaginative universe." This makes it difficult to understand what the natives are up to.[14]

The problem, of course, is that the beliefs underlying any culture cannot be seen, although they can be heard if you listen carefully at their meetings. A common alternative is simply to ask policymakers about their beliefs and why they hold them, but they may not want to tell you the truth. They may not know what the truth is. To overcome this rather significant problem of interviewing, the observation of behavior provides the raw data that you can use to infer beliefs.

Getting started is the difficult part; every observer of an unfamiliar culture initially encounters a babel of voices, each providing play-by-play commentary upon what appears to be a beehive of random behavior, as policymakers return to the hive from a meeting, tap out a memo to tell colleagues (and future researchers) what happened, then dart off to another meeting. But as with real bees, this is anything but random. Gradually, one meeting at a time, observers come to see patterns. Until the patterns crystalize, keep asking yourself this: When they wrote that paragraph about Honduras, what could they have been thinking?

THIS BOOK FOCUSES upon the beliefs that underlie the effort to improve other peoples. Why not conquer and enslave these less-"developed" peoples, which has been considered normal in so much of history? Or is uplifting a mechanism of conquest, an alibi for power, soft subjugation? Or did today's avalanche of uplifting activities simply begin with a tentative step taken atop a slippery slope, then gather momentum as it picked up one verb after another?

Two prominent theories offer two different answers. One is that today's uplifting activities reflect a humane impulse. It has been captured best by Adam Smith:

> How selfish soever man be supposed, there are evidently some principles in his nature, which interest him in the fortune of others, and render their happiness necessary to him, though he derives nothing from it except the pleasure of seeing it.[15]

Adding heft to this human-nature theory is the fact that nearly all other wealthy nations are currently doing the same, shouldering the Rich Man's Burden. Adam Smith's theory travels far beyond American exceptionalism.

An equally prominent competing theory is that today's uplifting activities serve as a useful mechanism to protect and promote selfish interests. It has been captured best by Cold War realist Hans Morgenthau:

> Foreign aid is no different from diplomatic or military policy or propaganda. They are all weapons.[16]

A reasonable working hypothesis is that the opening paragraph about improving Hondurans is best understood as an amalgam, as a united effort by Adam Smith altruists and Hans Morgenthau realists.

Pure altruists and pure realists are ideal types, however, and rarely observed in Washington, where the goal is to come out of a meeting with the best possible deal, which rarely is anyone's best imaginable deal. Close-to-pure altruists are required to indicate at least a minimal concern for U.S. interests; if they refuse, they are not invited to the next meeting. On the other side, close-to-pure realists generally believe that what is good for the United States is also in the best interest of the targets of U.S. policy—that is, most Washington realists consider themselves altruistic, especially when it comes to dealing with Latin Americans. They believe today what President Theodore Roosevelt believed about his 1903 takeover of Panama: "We in effect policed the Isthmus in the interest of its inhabitants and our own national needs, and for the good of the entire civilized world."[17]

So think not of rigid either/or categories but of policymakers arrayed along an altruism-to-selfishness continuum, the most important feature of which is that everyone at every point on the continuum believes the United States should do something to improve underdeveloped peoples. They differ only about why.

WHILE SEVERAL OTHER regions of the world could have been chosen as a focus, Latin America has been the proving ground for all the uplifting mechanisms currently used by the United States around the world. Along with the Hawaiians (who needed little uplifting) and the Filipinos (who initially needed a lot), Latin Americans were the first people under the control of the United States who were not enslaved or moved onto reservations.

And Latin Americans were also first when the United States began to focus less on economic and more on political uplifting. As that transition was getting under way, late in the twentieth century, an experienced AID contractor wrote that "with programs that date from the late 1960s, the Latin America and Caribbean Bureau has the longest, most in-depth involvement in democratic institution building." At about the same time the first annual report of the National Endowment for Democracy noted that "the bulk of our support has gone to grantees in Latin America. This is due, in large part, to the fact that our fellow Americans to the south have been first to become acquainted with the Endowment and its work; they have sought our help and we have been honored to assist in appropriate ways."[18]

Only Latin Americans have lived on the cutting edge of Washington's uplifting for more than a century.

After selecting Latin America as a focus, the next step is to make a list of all the decisions since the early nineteenth century that appear to have had a significant impact on U.S. policy toward Latin America, even if they were not taken with a mind to improving Latin Americans—the 1934 Reciprocal Trade Agreements Act is a good example. Then each decision needs to be examined as a separate case, working backward, meeting by meeting, searching for evidence of beliefs. For example, one especially important be-lief, now part of today's large constellation of beliefs, can be traced back to the early nineteenth century, when the first U.S. envoys to newly indepen-dent Latin America identified the people they encountered as backward—it was not merely their weak economies or their chaotic governance—those were indicators that the people themselves were inferior, a mélange produced by two stunted branches of the human species, Hispanic and indigenous.

This belief was broadly accepted in Washington by the final decades of the century, when the leaders of both major political parties began to hold meetings about an unrelated issue: how to reduce the boom-and-bust con-sequences of dramatic but unregulated economic growth. One solution that emerged from their meetings was to acquire more customers, starting with conveniently located Latin Americans. In 1889 they were invited to visit the United States for the first government-sponsored trade show in U.S. history.

This was commerce, pure and simple; the uplifting began a decade later, at the turn into the twentieth century, and was not the result of this economic interest. Rather, it occurred after an accident involving Cuba's decades-long struggle for independence from Spain, at the tail end of which the battleship *Maine* exploded in Havana's harbor. Once the *Maine* was avenged and Spain was gone, officials in Washington began to argue about what to do with the territory the United States had seized—Cuba, Puerto Rico, the Philippines, and Guam. These arguments occurred atop one of those slippery slopes, and the United States slid into an entire generation of uplifting, the first in U.S. history, nearly all of it in the nearby Caribbean, Central America, and Mexico.

Then came World War I, and the uplifting fervor of the Progressive era, already much diminished by disappointing results, was now being challenged by southern Latin Americans opposed to the subjugation of northern Latin Americans. This led to an ever-so-slow retrenchment. As a capstone, Latin Americans demanded a formal commitment to nonintervention, which they received in the 1930s—no more uplifting, at least in the primitive manner Progressives had uplifted, with military takeovers to create "protectorates."

That was followed during the Depression by Washington's creation of a new set of tools aimed at resuscitating the U.S. economy. Although none of these tools was designed with Latin America in mind, many had a remarkably powerful influence upon the region's economies. Among those effects was the creation of a generation of Latin American leaders who by the late 1940s were standing in line to request Washington's help with their economic problems.

These requests came at a time when U.S. policy toward Latin America was being made in an anticommunist trance, which dictated that Latin Americans, largely detached from the Cold War, were ineligible for intensive uplifting. Then in the late 1950s Fidel Castro's Cubans converted Latin America into a battleground, and the United States began to take its uplifting seriously—the idea was to improve the lives of Latin Americans who might otherwise be inclined to move their chips to the Soviet side of the table. But the intensity of Latin American uplifting could not be sustained during a divisive war in Vietnam, and soon a transition began to today's relentless low-intensity uplifting.

AFTER OBSERVING ALL this, a remarkably large number of researchers have come to the same conclusion: Washington's uplifting culture is based upon two primary beliefs. Across the mental continuum, from the purest altruist to the purest realist, nearly every policymaker uses these beliefs to some extent in order to interpret stimuli from the environment.

First and foremost is a belief about the need to protect and promote U.S. interests, real and imagined. These are primarily security and economic interests, plus domestic political interests that have become all but dominant in the twenty-first century as globalization continues to wring the "foreign" out of foreign policy.

Then there is another primary belief, albeit one that is somewhat less important until officials begin to design specific policies to protect U.S. interests. This belief is that the citizens of a large number of other countries would benefit by developing beyond the point to which they have already developed. Flip your globe 180 degrees so that North is where South has traditionally been placed, and the typical U.S. policymaker, like the typical U.S. citizen, will identify the Global South, including all of Latin America, as beneath the United States—developing, to be sure, so perhaps not as far down civilization's ladder as in days of yore, but still substantially beneath.

Although the presence of this belief in Latin Americans' inferiority will be obvious in the pages that follow, the purpose of this book is not to examine either it or the other primary belief—the one about protecting and promoting U.S. interests. That work has been done, but with an unsatisfying outcome: data were collected about these two primary beliefs and then books were written to highlight their combined influence upon policy decisions. That may have been useful in its day, but these two beliefs are constants, while the policy decisions were variable. Obviously, something more was needed. Now after much re-searching by a generation of competent scholars, one secondary belief almost shouts for attention: *a belief that the United States should seek to improve underdeveloped peoples,* to help them become more developed, less backward. Over the course of a century, this belief has slowly elbowed its way into the center of most explanations of U.S. policy toward a majority of the world's peoples, beginning with Latin Americans. Although its strength fluctuates over time and varies from issue to issue, this belief consistently guides the thinking of both Adam Smith altruists and Hans Morgenthau realists.

The variation is easiest to observe at those moments when policymakers, having perceived a threat to primary interests, set up meetings to determine what to do about it, only to discover that the old way of addressing the problem is no longer useful. At one time it was common to believe in the efficacy of Dollar Diplomacy, a policy driven initially by a security concern. Specifically, well-armed European governments were threatening to send gunboats into the Caribbean to collect what was owed to their citizens, and that could easily lead to a new era of colonization—to a violation of the Monroe Doctrine. And as it turned out, keeping the Europeans at arm's length required compensating European bondholders sooner rather than later, and that led to refinancing loans from Wall Street, which created an economic interest in being repaid. In turn, that economic interest required the U.S. tax collectors protected by the Marines. The result would be the elimination of a threat to U.S. security *and* the improvement of bottom lines on Wall Street *and* the uplifting (the solvency) of whatever Latin American country was being targeted at the time.

This crude policy was selected by early twentieth-century Progressives because, obviously, they believed it would produce the most satisfactory results, given the scant options. But as we will see in Chapter 4, Dollar Diplomacy eventually became prohibitively expensive, both in economic opportunity costs (pushback from Latin Americans) and in domestic political costs (pushback from voters). Soon no one believed in it any longer.

The acceptance and then the rejection of the beliefs underlying Dollar Diplomacy is simply an era's worth of variation. The most important recent variation has been away from a belief that Latin Americans need economic improvement to a belief that Latin Americans need political improvement— better "governance" in today's parlance.

As for timing, the intensity of beliefs about uplifting varies at a pace and in a fashion that is difficult to predict because it is impossible to control for changing circumstances, for changing personalities, and especially for Latin Americans' stubborn refusal to be passive. But any book that examines the belief in Latin Americans' need for improvement will point out that today's uplifting culture did not develop in a linear fashion. Rather, it is the product of two bursts engineered by two generations. The Progressive generation set the uplifting mold, cementing into Washington's foreign policy culture a belief that the United States should help improve underdeveloped peoples. Then after a quarter-century interlude the Cold War generation created the institutions that compose today's uplifting industry. The Agency for International Development, the National Endowment for Democracy and their brethren represent the transformation of uplifting from an ad hoc activity—a money doctor here, a few Marines there—into a deeply entrenched bureaucracy. Institutionalization.

This uplifting industry employs tens of thousands of direct-hire individuals and contractors, every one of whom has a personal interest in uplifting. Acting in concert through their component institutions, they have solidified the belief that "development assistance" (yesterday's "foreign aid") is both a humane obligation and a useful tool to promote U.S. interests. Dismissed with contempt by many and subject to criticism by most, this industry has the uncommon distinction of having captured both the altruistic hearts and the realistic minds of just about everyone in Washington. It is a marvel to observe.

CHAPTER I

Establishing the Need for Improvement

In taking them cordially by the hand we may lead them upward.
—William Churchwell, Special Agent to Mexico, 1859

NO ONE KNOWS exactly when the United States began to think about improving Latin Americans. There was no hint of uplifting in 1781, when the Continental Congress sent its first envoy to the region—a consul assigned to colonial Havana and instructed simply "to assist American traders with his advice, and to solicit their affairs with the Spanish government."[1] Nor did leaders of the following generation have an interest in uplifting Latin Americans; instead, early nineteenth-century Washington was concerned about protecting a modest handful of whalers and traders who were having difficulty coping with the region's newly independent governments, many of which were not yet in full control of their territories, some of which were predatory, and several of which were unfamiliar with the norms governing international commerce. A few were all of the above. And so in 1817 President James Monroe ordered the U.S. Navy to patrol the west coast of South America, and soon additional cruisers were stationed along the continent's east coast and in the Caribbean, sailing from port to port, discouraging piracy and suggesting there was a price to be paid for mistreating U.S. citizens and their property.[2]

The reports of these first few Navy officers, consuls, and special agents established Latin Americans' need for improvement. None could equal the lyrical talent of Alexis de Tocqueville, who wrote that the seas of pre-European Latin America "sparkled with the fires of the tropics; for the first time the extraordinary transparency of the water disclosed the ocean's depths to the navigators. Here and there little scented islands float like baskets of flowers on the calm sea. Everything seen in these enchanted islands seems devised to meet man's needs or serve his pleasures." Then came the Spanish, and several centuries of colonial mismanagement had left Latin America in disarray. "May not revolution be the most natural state for the Spaniards of South America?" Tocqueville wondered. "The people dwelling in this beautiful half continent seem obdurately determined to tear out each other's guts; nothing can divert them from that objective." His summary judgment: "There are no nations on earth more miserable than those of South America."[3]

Tocqueville had never set foot in Latin America. His views were largely based on a series of lengthy conversations in the United States with Joel Poinsett, an early U.S. envoy to both the Southern Cone and Mexico who softened his legendary pessimism by suggesting to Tocqueville (who in turn suggested to his readers) that "one must not judge the Spaniards of the New World too severely. When the Revolution caught them, they were still living in the sixteenth century [and] you could not imagine a more complete unawareness of all the discoveries of modern civilization."[4]

Most early envoys shared Poinsett's appraisal. "They call this a Republic," reported a consul in Buenos Aires. "I assure you there is not on earth a more despotic Monarchy," which was also a view of the U.S. chargé in Lima: "The Supreme power is generally in the hands of some military chief, who, looking only to his personal aggrandisement, tramples upon the rights of all." That was also the message from Caracas, where there was "a breaking up of all the foundations of law and order—all guaranties for civil liberty and personal security—a letting down of all hope of future progress in civilization and material prosperity."[5]

Many of these early envoys found it difficult to withhold their comments from the people they were criticizing, and that posed a problem: diplomats are posted abroad in order to protect and promote the interests of their country, a task that can be rendered more difficult by commenting upon the shortcomings of one's hosts, especially if this criticism is accompanied, as it often was, by suggestions regarding the steps needed for improvement. These earliest offers of advice were strongly discouraged by John Quincy Adams, secretary of state during the years when much of Latin America was becoming independent: "Wherever the standard of freedom and Independence has been or shall be unfurled, there will her heart, her benedictions and her prayers be. But she goes not abroad, in search of monsters to destroy. She is the well-wisher to the freedom and independence of all. She is the champion and vindicator only of her own."[6]

This was repeated four years later, in 1825, when Spanish authorities were largely gone and a U.S. minister reported that he was having difficulty convincing Chileans to change their ways—"very much opinionated, it is difficult to administer them, any salutary advice." At that time there were so many similar dispatches coming from the rest of Latin America that Adams's successor, Henry Clay, issued a general order: "All expressions of contempt for their habits, civil or religious, all intimations of incompetency on the part of their population, for self Government, should be sedulously avoided."[7]

This policy continued into the next generation, with a typical mid-nineteenth-century secretary of state, James Buchanan, warning a typical U.S. envoy, this one in Lima, that "it is impossible that you can reform either the morals or the politics of Peru, and as this is no part of your mission, prudence requires that you should not condemn them in public conversations. You ought to take its institutions and its people just as you find them and endeavor to make the best of them for the benefit of your own country."[8]

But unlike secretaries Adams and Clay in the 1820s, the generation taking over in the late 1840s encouraged U.S. envoys to point out "the example of our own country where all controversies are decided at the ballot box."[9] This was probably nothing more than State Department boilerplate, sanctified by the City-on-a-Hill pedigree, but some mid-nineteenth-century envoys followed this "ballot box" instruction, only to find their hosts uninterested in the U.S. example. Often miffed, these envoys then began suggesting that Latin Americans' incessant squabbling "should be restrained by the strong hand of a great civilized nation," or that Washington should "force these Spanish American Republics to keep the peace."[10]

Meanwhile the United States had seized the northern half of Mexico, and a series of envoys to what was left of that country was convinced that "the present Government of Mexico, is as useless for any good to the country, and as vicious & tyrannical as it is possible to conceive." So reported U.S. minister John Forsyth, who appears to have been the first to suggest providing Latin Americans with military assistance—in this case, a "thousand Americans, picked, true, well paid and ably officered, and to be distributed throughout the Corps of the Mexican Army."

Washington refused to consider the idea, and eventually Forsyth threw in the towel, allowing Secretary of State Lewis Cass to send Mexico a less-demanding diplomat who recommended patience: "In taking them cordially by the hand we may lead them upward."[11]

IN ASSESSING THIS pre–Civil War era, it is only fair to recognize the difficulties faced by Washington's early envoys, who found themselves among an unfamiliar people, few of whom seemed capable of speaking or even listening in English. In 1831 one such early envoy to Mexico confessed to being "totally unacquainted with the language of the people amongst whom my duties were to be discharged," while another in Argentina wrote about needing an aide to translate any document before he could read it, and a late nineteenth-century U.S. envoy to Chile reported this when his ship stopped en route at Callao: "The government's tugboat came off to the steamer and a gorgeously arrayed official presented himself at my cabin, addressing me in Spanish, with profound bows and great deference. I returned the bows in kind and even amplified their impressiveness. But I was totally unable to understand the gentleman and therefore totally unable to respond."[12]

These early emissaries reported what they saw, with their vision filtered, as it always will be, through their own cultural lens. In this case the lens was masculine, white, Anglo, and consistently Protestant. Looking at Latin America, they saw Catholic societies mired in deep poverty, plagued by weak economies, led by corrupt warlords, and still suffering from a hangover of the Inquisition. In general, the longer they stayed at a post, the more these emissaries found to criticize.[13]

Now, still in the 1850s at the tail end of the era of Manifest Destiny, many U.S. envoys saw acquisition as the ideal form of uplifting, and they were often encouraged by Washington. "It is beyond question the destiny of our race to spread themselves over the continent of North America," President James Buchanan told the Senate in 1858, and that no longer meant westward: "The tide of emigrants will flow to the south, and nothing can eventually arrest its progress." Eager to add slave states, a few Southerners were already taking independent action with filibustering expeditions, but most simply urged Washington to act. Seize control of the fledgling Central American confederation, insisted one member of the House of Representatives, a Southern sympathizer, and "wave upon wave of immigration will roll in upon that country, until, ere long, its internal wars, ignorance, superstition, and anarchy, will be supplanted by peace, knowledge, Christianity, and our own Heaven-born institutions."[14]

Then the South fired on Fort Sumter, and for a season there was little thought of Latin America.

THE POST-CIVIL WAR decade saw some continuation of the debate about acquiring nearby territory—particularly the Dominican Republic, whose leaders had petitioned Washington for annexation—but the soldiers who had shed their uniforms in 1865 were not interested in expansion. Instead they turned inward, modernizing and expanding agriculture, developing heavy industry, building the world's most extensive transportation infrastructure, centered upon railroads, and replacing small workshops with large factories. Commenting upon two decades of astounding growth, in 1885 steel magnate Andrew Carnegie boasted that "America already leads the civilized world."[15]

A quite different assessment came from the less-lofty reaches of the economic pyramid, where the trickle down had been modest and where a series of deep recessions had turned dreams into nightmares. "We have had no steady growth and prosperity," observed a Gilded Age economist during one of the several post–Civil War downturns; "no immunity from industrial ills, but rather a constant succession of heats and chills, industrial convulsions, strikes, combinations, suspensions of industry, and irritation between classes."[16]

"Overproduction" was the most common explanation for these ups and downs: basically, the nation's ever-more-efficient factories were churning out more widgets than the domestic market could absorb, triggering layoffs until inventories had been reduced. As in industry, even more so in agriculture, where the 1862 Homestead Act had opened up some of the planet's most productive acreage, and it was not long before another economist was pointing out what every farmer already knew: "There is no sufficient market for our surplus agricultural products except a foreign market."[17]

As is to be expected in any agrarian democracy, the concern of these farmers quickly led to meetings in Washington, most of them on the floors of Congress, where a senator from flour-exporting Minnesota told his colleagues, "We will be compelled to seek new markets for the surplus or close our factories and let a portion of our harvests rot upon the ground."[18]

As Congress was taking that under consideration, U.S. envoys were submitting reports similar to one from Lima, which conformed to pre–Civil War assessments ("annexation would be hailed with delight") but now added a new enticement: once Peru had been annexed, "large markets would be opened to our productions and manufactures."[19] Soon a presidential commission was on its way to explore these markets. Its 1885 report recommended "that our representatives to these Republics be charged to respond to that feeling that is so often expressed by them as that of a child to a mother."[20]

Understandably offended, a sarcastic Argentine journalist complained that the commission had been sent to inform the local residents that they "might be thankful to be allowed to exist at all on the same hemisphere as the star-spangled Republic." The fact that the commission had spent only forty-eight hours in Buenos Aires (and one of those two days a Sunday) simply confirmed that "the people of the United States know little about us and care no more. They have a vague notion that we are a cross between Indians, whites and wild horses and that when we hear that an American Drummer comes the natives line the shore in scant costume loaded with crude gold waiting for Yankee notions." His conclusion: "So long as Europe comes here with its millions and Americans come here with itinerating commissions, the business supremacy of Europe in this country will be seen."[21]

In this case the offended journalist was an Anglo-Argentine, no doubt relieved to see that the United States would be too clumsy to challenge British economic supremacy in that faraway market. There was more than Argentina to Latin America, however, much of it a conveniently located outlet for the overproduction of U.S. goods, and the 1880s saw a continuous stream of statements proposing closer ties—"more intimate commercial and political relations with the fifteen sister Republics," as the Democrats phrased it in their 1884 platform, matched by the Republicans' endorsement of a policy that sought "peace and trade with all powers, but especially with those of the Western Hemisphere."

This vague talk—a mood more than a movement—continued to percolate through Washington until 1889, when the United States invited every Latin American country except black Haiti to attend a conference to discuss ways to increase trade. It was the first such initiative in U.S. history, and the gathering turned out to be less of a conference in Washington than a trade show involving a forty-two-day, six-thousand-mile excursion to visit factories from Maine to Missouri.[22] The idea was for the visitors to see for themselves what U.S. producers had to sell.

Like the earlier trade commission, the conference produced few immediate results: in 1850 Latin Americans had taken 14 percent of U.S. exports; in 1900 they took 9 percent, which was about average for the intervening half-century.[23] But the post–Civil War generation can take credit for focusing attention on the importance of international trade to the health of an industrializing economy, while the trade commission and the Washington conference helped direct this attention toward the millions of potential customers in nearby Latin America.

AS THIS WAS occurring in the Western Hemisphere, a wave of European colonial expansion had been sweeping up what was left of the globe's potential consumers. "The islands and the continents have already been divided," lamented former president Benjamin Harrison in 1899, but nothing was yet set in stone, and "the United States is not, I am sure, ambitious to take the crumbs that remain." A year later he pointed out what everyone could see: "The battle of the markets is at its fiercest."[24] Note this was not a contest to build a better mousetrap; it was to capture the market for mousetraps, and the United States was not winning.

This was long after Alexander Hamilton had indicated the route to victory: "If we mean to be a commercial people," he had advised a full century earlier, "we must endeavor, as soon as possible, to have a navy."[25] Focused upon internal development, Hamilton's eighteenth-century compatriots had thought otherwise, and so now, here in the late nineteenth century, President Grover Cleveland lamented that "we have not a single vessel of war that could keep the seas against a first-class vessel of any important power."[26] The recent trade commission had pointed out that this weakness "seriously impaired our national influence in South America," hinting that the United States should do what Europeans were already doing: securing foreign markets with intimidating displays of military power.[27] Gunboats opened ports and kept them open to goods from the mother country.

Soon Washington began discussing which party had been responsible for dismantling the Navy—from seven hundred to only fifty ships in the five years after Appomattox. One Democrat observed that the Republicans had been in power almost continuously and "we are now the most helpless of the great nations on the water." The best a defensive Republican could do on that day was admit that the Navy "is not very large; but we have a considerable number of excellent vessels."[28]

As these discussions continued, generally to the Republicans' disadvantage, the GOP began advocating "restoration of our navy to its old-time strength and efficiency," but that only encouraged the Democrats to up the ante. "Old-time" would not be enough, they sneered; times had changed, and if the United States wanted to fan its feathers in a face-off with one of the major powers, it would require a type of warship these rivals already had—something called a "battleship."[29]

There was a reason the Navy had none: with the United States still isolated from global conflicts, the Navy's modest post–Civil War mission had been to protect U.S. ports (with monitors) and U.S. traders (with cruisers). Both were far less powerful than late nineteenth-century battleships, which were designed to take command of the high seas. They were the "ships of the line"—originally, the "line-of-battle ships"—that a major power deployed against a rival's line-of-battle ships, with the winner taking control not simply of the seas but also of the surrounding foreign ports where traders bought and sold.

Meanwhile, the U.S. Navy was up to its scuppers in lobbying. In 1876 the secretary of the Navy reported that "there is no navy in the world that is not in advance of us with regard to ships and guns." In 1882 his successor added that the nation's "reputation, honor, and prosperity require that such naval vessels as it possesses should be the best which human ingenuity can devise and modern artificers can construct. Our present vessels are not such, and cannot be made such." So should a confrontation occur, an admiral warned, "the sight may be the reverse of pleasant." "We have no navy either for offense or defense," complained Navy Secretary William Chandler in 1883, and his final annual report two years later was no less pessimistic. "It is questionable whether we have a single naval vessel finished and afloat at the present time that could be trusted to encounter the ships of any important power. . . . We have nothing which deserves to be called a navy, . . . [not] a single vessel that has either the necessary armor for protection, speed for escape, or weapons for defense."[30]

With this prodding, by the late 1880s the leaders of both major parties were willing to agree that if all the major powers had battleships, then the United States must have them as well. Congress began a series of appropriations to construct a first generation of six battleships, and within a decade a prominent journalist would write that "almost as if by magic, the importance of naval power as the advance agent of commercial supremacy has flashed upon the mind of the country. The irresistible tendency to expansion, which leads the growing tree to burst every barrier, which drove the Goths, the Vandals, and finally our Saxon ancestors in successive and irresistible waves over the decadent provinces of Rome, seems again in operation, demanding new outlets for American capital and new opportunities for American enterprise."[31]

Congress eventually appropriated funds for not six but sixteen battleships, soon to be used in concert for perhaps the most elaborate feather-fanning in U.S. history: the Great White Fleet, sent in 1907–1909 on a circumnavigation of the globe to introduce the world's new ostentation of peacocks.

THE ACQUISITION OF this weapon required personnel who knew how to use it, and for that the Navy needed a new school. In 1885 the Naval War College opened its doors in Newport, Rhode Island, where its initial class of nine promising midcareer officers (not novices, as at Annapolis) were instructed by a faculty focused upon both tactics and strategy.[32] Their principal professor of naval strategy was Alfred Thayer Mahan, whose lectures outlined how gunboat diplomacy had worked over the centuries.

First came the traders: "The merchant seaman, seeking for trade in new and unexplored regions, made his gains at risk of life and liberty from suspicious or hostile nations, and was under great delays in collecting a full and profitable freight. He therefore intuitively sought at the far end of his trade route one or more stations, to be given him by force or favor, where he could fix himself or his agents in reasonable security, where his ships could lie in safety." Over time these safe havens "grew until they became colonies."

Mahan glossed over the transition from safe haven to colony, but "by force or favor" suggested gunboat diplomacy. Intimidating warships helped traders establish a safe haven, and once such a haven was established, the most effective way to maintain it was to keep a warship close at hand. This encouraged the locals to keep their doors open and discouraged rival traders from dropping anchor. "It is only a step from commercial control to territorial control," wrote the secretary of the Navy, and to this Mahan added the punch line: these colonies provided the mother country with "a new outlet for what it had to sell, a new sphere for its shipping, more employment for its people, more comfort and wealth for itself."[33]

With their instruction complete, the War College students were almost ready to take command of their new battleships; only one thing was missing: a better justification to use them, something less selfish or more noble than a pot of gold.

That was provided by the secretary of the Navy, Benjamin Tracy. In 1891, a year after Mahan published his lectures, Tracy pointed out that Latin America was not simply the only remaining uncolonized region—given its proximity, Latin America was also the region where U.S. security could not permit colonization by others. "The establishment of complete commercial supremacy by a European power in any state of the Western Hemisphere means the exclusion of American influences and the virtual destruction as far as that state is concerned, of independent existence."[34] Powerful rivals would then be at the nation's doorstep and, trade or no trade, that would violate the bedrock principle of U.S. foreign policy, announced by the 1811 No-Transfer resolution and the 1823 Monroe Doctrine, both of which were based upon a commonsense principle that anyone can understand: Keep anyone who might harm you as far away as possible.

That helps explain today's gated communities, and it also helps explain what happened here at the turn into the twentieth century. Latin American customers were attractive, to be sure, but the exclusion of foreign powers was essential.

THIS THINKING WAS especially congenial to the rising generation, who had been too young to participate in the Civil War. The most prominent figure of that generation, Theodore Roosevelt, born in 1858, appeared to regret having missed out on the *frisson* of a fight to the death. Speaking as the assistant secretary of the Navy, he told an early cycle of War College students that "no triumph of peace is quite so great as the supreme triumph of war," and he said more or less the same thing as president a decade later: "A just war is in the long run far better for a man's soul than the most prosperous peace." One of Roosevelt's biographers found that "similarly wild utterances could be counted indefinitely."[35]

This was more than wild talk. Secretary of State John Hay saw "unchained energy" in Roosevelt, "ferocious in the pursuit of his objects, undeterred by the considerations which ordinarily influence men." Secretary of War William Howard Taft was convinced that "he has the spirit of the old Berserkers." And he really did lead a charge up the San Juan Heights.[36]

A peculiar logic lay behind this. Most students of international relations conceptualize war as a mechanism for resolving disputes, and not a particularly desirable one; Roosevelt saw war as an indicator of superior character. "All the great masterful races have been fighting races, and the minute that a race loses the hard fighting virtues, then, no matter what else it may retain, no matter how skilled in commerce and finance, in science or art, it has lost its proud right to stand as the equal of the best. . . . Cowardice in a race, as in an individual, is the unpardonable sin." That was said in 1895, the year the United States decided to serve as Venezuela's champion in a boundary dispute with Great Britain. Roosevelt turned it into a test of his rising generation's manhood. "I rather hope the fight will come soon," he told a friend; "the clamor of the peace faction has convinced me that this country needs a war."[37]

Theodore Roosevelt was not a reflection of his generation's opinions; he created the opinions of the country's provincial citizenry—many if not most of whom would soon call themselves Progressives. Their initial focus had been upon domestic reform, and most, like midwestern newspaper editor William Allen White (b. 1868), had never given much thought to foreign affairs. At the age of twenty-eight White had achieved a certain level of prominence with a bitterly sarcastic editorial arguing that the bankruptcy law of his home state was driving out investors.[38] But except for the tariff question, which affected Kansas farmers, White's early editorials in the Emporia *Gazette* rarely ventured into foreign policy, and when they did, he was cautious. In 1898, when the battleship *Maine* was destroyed in Havana's harbor, White editorialized that "the American people should thank Heaven that in this crisis they have a president [William McKinley] who is too big a man to be a jingo"—a war over the incident would be "ruinous and perhaps unnecessary."[39]

Then he came to know Roosevelt, and in his autobiography he recalled that the young leader "sounded in my heart the first trumpet call of the new time that was to be. . . . I had never known such a man as he, and never shall again. He overcame me . . . , he poured into my heart such visions, such ideals, such hopes, such a new attitude toward life and patriotism and the meaning of things as I had never dreamed men had." "No one can be about him without feeling an excess of devotion," added Secretary of State John Hay; and historian William Leuchtenburg captured perfectly the use to which Roosevelt put his charisma: "It is impossible to understand the acquiescence of many Progressives in the imperialist movement without realizing the remarkable hold that Theodore Roosevelt had on his followers."[40]

Roosevelt was to influence U.S. policy toward Latin America as no other citizen ever has. He did so by convincing William Allen White's generation that the world would be a better place if the United States had more control over what was happening overseas, beginning with Latin America. And so the Kansas newspaper editor who a year earlier had opposed the looming Spanish-American War now wrote that "it is the Anglo-Saxon's manifest destiny to go forth as a world conqueror. He will take possession of all the islands of the sea. He will exterminate the peoples he cannot subjugate. This is what fate holds for the chosen people. It is so written." Another member of this rising generation, Senator Albert Beveridge (b. 1862), told his colleagues that "self-government and internal developments have been the dominant notes of our first century; administration and the development of other lands will be the dominant notes of our second century."[41]

This was not the talk of their parents, sobered by the Civil War; rather, it was the talk of their pre–Civil War grandparents, who had pushed aside the indigenous Americans and Mexicans who stood in the way of the nation's obvious ("manifest") destiny. Praising that earlier generation, Roosevelt argued that "it was inevitable, as well as in the highest degree desirable for the good of humanity at large, that the American people should ultimately crowd out the Mexicans."[42]

This chauvinism dismayed the aging generation of Civil War veterans, and one of them, President William McKinley, promised another aging leader, Senator Carl Schurz, that "there will be no jingo nonsense under my Administration." Seeing where Roosevelt's Progressives were heading, Schurz had already warned his Senate colleagues not to take a bite of the forbidden fruit. "The incorporation of the American tropics in our national system would . . . be fraught with incalculable dangers to the vitality of our democratic institutions."[43]

Alfred Thayer Mahan had already replied: The British "did not find, and have never found, that the possession of and rule over barbarous, or semi-civilized, or inert tropical communities were inconsistent with the maintenance of political liberty in the mother country." Senator Beveridge agreed: "The rule of liberty, that all just governments derive their authority from the consent of the governed, applies only to those who are capable of self-government." Asked by a skeptical colleague if governments derived their power from the consent of the governed, Senator Orville Platt replied: "From the consent of some of the governed."[44]

And so it went, as the post–Civil War generation's simple quest for foreign markets evolved into the next generation's effort to administer government among semicivilized people living in inert tropical communities—an effort that one of Roosevelt's closest colleagues believed "makes for civilization and the advancement of the race."[45] It was time for Progressives to launch Washington's first concerted effort to improve Latin Americans.

CHAPTER 2

Uplifting Begins

The War of 1898

First. We do not want to take them for ourselves.
Second. We do not want any foreign nations to take them for
themselves.
Third. We want to help them.

—Secretary of State Elihu Root, 1907

WHAT NEEDED TO be done to capture Latin American markets and to exclude outside competitors? For an answer, this rising generation turned to
the nineteenth-century Positivists, who emphasized the need for order and
progress—and, given what U.S. envoys had been reporting for decades, in
Latin America it would have to be order first, then progress. Porfirio Díaz's
Mexico and the southern part of Latin America were coming along
nicely—Brazil even had "Ordem e Progresso" emblazoned on its flag—but
for every success story "there remain a number of minor countries wherein
the right of revolution is cherished," explained Herbert Croly, an influential Progressive-era writer. "Just what can be done with such states is a
knotty problem. In all probability no American international system will
ever be established without the forcible pacification of one or more such
centers of disorder."[1] Forcible pacification would be Step 1 on the ladder of
Progressive uplifting.

Cuba was the premier center of disorder in the late 1890s. A declining
power, Spain had long had difficulty controlling its last major Latin American possession, and Cuban rebels were making their final push for inde-

pendence when Progressives decided to help—"firm action on behalf of the wretched Cubans" was Theodore Roosevelt's proposal, offered as an application of his broader belief that "it is for the interest of civilization that the United States themselves, the greatest branch of the English-speaking race, should be dominant in the Western Hemisphere." Or simply look at a map, wrote the Navy's Alfred Thayer Mahan, urging his readers to think ahead about the approaches to a canal across Central America. Cuba had "a position that can have no military rival among the islands of the world except Ireland."[2]

As President McKinley was finding it increasingly difficult to resist the pressures coming from these surging jingoes, Spain offered limited autonomy to Cuba's increasingly effective rebels, a move that prompted Spanish loyalists to take to the streets in protest. "Excitement and uncertainty predominates everywhere," cabled the U.S. consul, requesting gunboats to protect U.S. citizens and their property. McKinley responded with one of the nation's first battleships (actually, a beefed-up heavy cruiser), and within a month it had exploded and was sitting on the bottom of Havana's harbor, a total wreck. Even a rock-ribbed anti-imperialist such as William Jennings Bryan, the Democrats' nominee for president in 1896, agreed that "the time for intervention has arrived. Humanity demands that we shall act."[3]

IT WAS NOT much of a fight. An already exhausted Spain quickly sued for peace and handed over Cuba, the Philippines, Puerto Rico, and Guam. Now the McKinley administration had to figure out what to do with them. Forced to improvise, Washington assigned the first three acquisitions to the Army and Guam to the Navy. Neither service had much experience in administering anything beyond its own barracks, which it did, as all militaries do, through a rigid command structure that presumed obedience and punished insubordination. The learning curve for governing civilians—foreign civilians—was going to be steep, probably close to perpendicular.

"I hope they may prove more orderly and less likely to plunge into civil war and brigandage than has been expected," an apprehensive assistant secretary of state confided to President McKinley, while the U.S. minister in Spain worried that "acceptance of a practical protectorate over Cuba seems to me very like the assumption of the responsible care of a madhouse." A caution flag was also waved by Germany's aging iron chancellor, Otto von Bismarck: "The Creole and the West Indian half-breeds are difficult to manage," he warned in an interview; "the Americans will find them, later on, a hard nut to crack."[4]

That said, nutcracking should not have been difficult, at least in Cuba. The 1898 congressional war resolution had simply stipulated that the United States would (1) expel the Spanish and then (2) "leave the government and control of the island to its people."

The first step had been taken in a blink, but the second took nearly four years, largely because many Progressives were searching for a way to avoid taking it. Among them was the infinitely malleable William Allen White, now convinced that "what has to be will be. It was probably intended in the beginning that the Anglo-Saxon should conquer the Latin." A month later White added his view that "only Anglo-Saxons can govern themselves," which was also the view of one of the Army's occupying generals, who wrote that the Cubans were "no more capable of self government than the savages of Africa." White's opinion was that "the Cubans will need a despotic government for many years to restrain anarchy until Cuba is filled with Yankees."[5]

Because someone had to govern them, Progressive jingoes argued that it should be the United States, and the Army's governor-general assured Washington that Cubans would jump at the opportunity, particularly if it involved some uplifting: "Clean government, quick decisive action and absolute control in the hands of trustworthy men, establishment of needed legal and education reforms and I do not believe you could shake Cuba loose if you want to." Having already predicted that "in two or three years they will insist on being part of us," Roosevelt needed no convincing. Nor did former president Grover Cleveland, a Democrat and hardly a jingo, who now believed that "Cuba ought to be submerged for awhile before it will make an American state or territory of which we will be particularly proud."[6]

President McKinley insisted until his death that the commitment to Cuban independence must be kept, but he also warned against "a hasty experiment bearing within itself the elements of failure"—a warning against immediate withdrawal that reflected the advice coming from Havana: "We have got to infuse new life, new principles and new methods of doing things," wrote Cuba's governor-general, Leonard Wood, and "this is not the work of a day or of a year, but of a longer period."[7]

Perhaps General Wood was right, but officials in Washington accepted his reports too readily. "He was very unscrupulous," complained one of his colleagues, "meaning that he would manufacture facts when he didn't have them. That's a hell of a thing to say about a distinguished person. Well, it's so." Wood was "an intensely ambitious, aggrandizing man," continued this colleague, future Supreme Court justice Felix Frankfurter, "but a man of force, of decisive action, dynamic. . . . He is very attractive and superficially charms people."[8]

This charm probably helped Wood convince Secretary of War Elihu Root, who joined the chorus advocating patience while the uplifting continued. "The Cubans must necessarily acquire some new ideas and new methods," Root wrote, but he appeared to differ from Wood by adding that this "cannot be done by having outsiders preach at them. It is something they have to do themselves." Root may have believed that, but no sooner had he mailed that letter to mollify one of the nation's leading anti-imperialists, Harvard president Charles Eliot, than he picked up his pen to draft the well-known compromise between colony and independence—the Platt Amendment. It gave the United States the right to retake the island whenever Washington felt it was needed "for the protection of life, property, and individual liberty."[9]

Cubans protested to no avail, and only after they agreed to become a U.S. protectorate were they allowed to elect their first president, in a U.S.-supervised one-candidate contest won by a longtime Cuban patriot who happened to be a naturalized U.S. citizen who had been living in upstate New York for the past quarter-century. Tomás Estrada Palma returned to Cuba only after the votes had been counted. Although future president William Howard Taft would dismiss him as "honest, but a good deal of an old ass," Governor-General Wood pointed out to Roosevelt, now president,* that "there is, of course, little or no independence left Cuba under the Platt Amendment." Jingo Senator Albert Beveridge was pleased: "The United States has given her our permanent counsel, aid, and comfort."[10]

THE SPANISH-AMERICAN WAR resulted in the creation of Washington's first formal protectorate. Its second major effect was to convince the final hold-

---

*The war's principal hero, Roosevelt had been elected governor of New York in November 1898. Then in 1900 McKinley chose him as his running mate, and when McKinley was assassinated in September 1901, Roosevelt became president after serving as vice president for only six months.

outs that it was time to build a canal across Central America. That, too, would require a substantial amount of uplifting.

European colonizers had recognized the value of a canal since 1513, when Vasco Núñez de Balboa first crossed Panama on foot, and Thomas Jefferson was among the early U.S. leaders who mused about a canal's economic value.[11] But a firm commitment was made only after the war with Spain, when U.S. security interests, having already expanded to include Hawaii, now had expanded further to the far western Pacific. The Navy needed the ability to quickly move its warships from one ocean to another.

After a final flurry of debates over alternative routes, Congress settled on Colombia's department of Panama, despite the fact that several generations of U.S. envoys had been filing reports capable of giving pause to even the most committed canal enthusiast. Entirely typical was an early report that "Spanish customs prevail which are at war with every thing which would add to their prosperity." That was in 1834. A midcentury envoy saw some hope for improvement when U.S. entrepreneurs completed a railroad across the Isthmus (Panamanians "are now brought into connection with a race whose motto is progress") but cautioned that no one should anticipate rapid improvement—the locals were "accustomed to live like hogs upon what they could root out of the bowels of the earth without labor. They ate their plantain, and slept their lives away with as little mental concern or ambition as the beasts of the field." The same envoy warned that "nothing withholds the Native parties there from cutting each others throats, but the presence of our Naval force," so here, too, it would have to be order first, then progress.[12]

Whatever the situation, the United States was determined to build a canal, and Roosevelt was telling a Minnesota audience that "it is our duty toward the people living in barbarism to see that they are freed from the chains."[13] The question was not whether but how to keep Panamanians as far as possible from any canal.

After helping Panamanians detach themselves from Colombia, the Roosevelt administration negotiated a treaty with Panama's representative in Washington, a French citizen who gave the United States everything it could ever dream of having. Secretary of State John Hay described the 1903 Hay-Bunau-Varilla Treaty as "vastly advantageous to the United States, and we must confess, with what face we can muster, not so advantageous to Panama." It provided the United States with a lease in perpetuity on a broad ocean-to-ocean strip where Panamanians were legally foreigners and where the

United States would have sovereign rights "to the entire exclusion of the exercise by the Republic of Panama of any such sovereign rights, power or authority."[14]

Not everyone agreed that President Roosevelt had acted honorably, but he insisted that the Senate's anti-imperialists stop blocking the treaty's ratification so that he could start digging: "If ever a government could be said to have received a mandate from civilization, . . . the United States holds that position with regard to the interoceanic canal."[15] That argument carried the day, and the steam shovels set to work.

At the same time, the United States began helping newly independent Panama onto its feet, with a visiting Secretary of War William Howard Taft promising to provide electricity, sewers, clean water, and a concerted attack on tropical diseases. Subsequent administrations would do all of this and more—an extraordinary improvement of the country's physical infrastructure. All Panamanians had to do to receive this assistance was to be orderly; but—and here came Taft's central point—disorder would continue "unless there is implanted in the breasts of all your people [a] profound respect for the law and the constitution." For this, too, "you can count on the assistance of the Government of the United States."[16] Panamanians did not even have to ask, because the canal treaty had made Panama another protectorate, giving the United States the right to intervene "at all times and in its discretion" in the part of Panama it did not control.

AS THE CANAL was nearing completion in 1914, a new president, Woodrow Wilson, commented that "the center of gravity of the world has shifted." Indeed it had. No longer a cul-de-sac, the Caribbean was now a major international thoroughfare, and the approaches to the canal needed to be guarded. That turned many eyes to the Caribbean's other countries—to "these strange, turbulent little half-caste civilizations," as President Roosevelt had referred to them in 1906 while sailing through Caribbean waters.[17]

Debt was the principal problem. It had its origin in the mid-nineteenth century, when European bankers had begun helping Latin American governments to issue bonds, marketing them to investors by offering high interest rates and by downplaying the high risks. These bonds did exactly what they do now—they kicked the can down the road, allowing governments to have their cake today and pay for it tomorrow. Then as now, this road sometimes reached a dead end, and that—if mixing metaphors is still only a misdemeanor—that is when the chickens came home to roost: at the turn of the century several countries in the Caribbean region had fallen deeply into arrears on their repayments.

Because everyone reasoned that the defaulting countries must have some money, the question became whose bonds would be serviced, and Europe's gunboats were being sent to provide the answer. The norm at the time allowed any government with sufficient power, acting on behalf of its citizen-investors, to seize a bankrupt government's assets, which in practical terms meant seizing its customs houses, the principal source of revenue for every nineteenth-century Latin American government. Once the gunboats had collected what was owed, they were supposed to sail away, but now, as canal construction was getting under way, President Roosevelt warned that "it is very inadvisable to permit any foreign power to take possession, even temporarily, of the custom houses of an American Republic in order to enforce the payment of its obligations; for such temporary occupation might turn into a permanent occupation."[18]

This warning came at a moment when no fewer than nine European countries were threatening such takeovers, and one of them was especially worrisome: "Of all the nations of Europe it seems to me Germany is by far the most hostile to us," Roosevelt had written before the war with Spain. "We may at any time have trouble if she seeks to acquire territory in South America." He was more concerned three years later, after the war: "In a few years [the Germans] will be in a position to take some step in the West Indies or South America which will make us either put up or shut up on the Monroe doctrine."[19]

Venezuela had been the principal problem for decades. A solution first proposed by the State Department in 1869 was for the United States to take control of Venezuela's customs houses and distribute the receipts among European and U.S. claimants. That proposal was stillborn, but the Garfield administration revived the idea in 1881, at a time when U.S. cities had begun to replace their cobblestone streets with Venezuelan asphalt, and the resulting increase in investors had led to numerous claims for damages of every imaginable sort; most accused the government of breach of contract. Meanwhile, European bondholders' hopes had also been raised, anticipating repayment from asphalt revenues that never quite lived up to what had been promised.[20]

Understandably focused on the disputes involving its own citizens, the Roosevelt administration convinced Venezuela to set up a bilateral commission to determine which claims were legitimate and in what amount, leaving European bondholders to worry that U.S. claimants would walk away with whatever cash Venezuela might have in its treasury. They turned to their governments for help, and in late 1902 the combined gunships of Germany, Great Britain, and Italy blockaded Venezuela's ports and bombarded Puerto Cabello.

NOW IT WAS Washington's turn to worry, and not only about European gunboats but also about domestic U.S. politics.

Since 1898 the principal focus of foreign policy debates been not Cubans or Panamanians or anyone else in the Caribbean region but the faraway Filipinos, a significant number of whom saw little difference between the Spanish and U.S. armies and declined to call an end to their pre-1898 struggle for independence. As the death toll began to mount, in 1899 President McKinley reluctantly boarded the jingo bandwagon, arguing, "If we can benefit these remote peoples, who will object?" In the same month in which McKinley made his comment, Rudyard Kipling published *The White Man's Burden,* which can be read as an ironic comment on the perils of empire and whose original subtitle was "The United States and the Philippine Islands." Three months later Theodore Roosevelt, now governor of New York, assured a Chicago audience, "We will play our part well in the great work of uplifting mankind."[21]

The rival Democrats' 1900 platform insisted that imperialism was "the paramount issue of the campaign," while the Republicans' platform insisted that the Filipino imbroglio was an effort "to confer the blessings of liberty and civilization upon all the rescued peoples." Uplifting was now a political football, with President McKinley telling a Boston audience about "a people redeemed from savage indolence and habit, devoted to the arts of peace, in touch with the commerce and trade of all nations, enjoying the blessings of freedom, of civil and religious liberty, of education, and of homes, and whose children and children's children shall for ages bless the American republic because it emancipated and redeemed their fatherland, and sent them in the pathway of the world's best civilization."[22] Round One went to the Republicans—a 1900 electoral victory.

When Filipinos continued to demonstrate their unwillingness to accept the blessings of liberty and civilization, a dramatic escalation occurred both in the military struggle to establish order and in the pathway-of-civilization rhetoric coming from the White House, especially after McKinley was felled by an assassin's bullet and Theodore Roosevelt took over the task of reassuring an increasingly skeptical public. "History may safely be challenged to show a single instance in which a masterful race such as ours, having been forced by the exigencies of war to take possession of an alien land, has behaved to its inhabitants with the disinterested zeal for their progress that our people have shown in the Philippines." That was what Roosevelt told Congress in his first annual message, two months after he became president.[23]

Try as they might, the Republicans found it impossible to shake off their Philippine albatross. Month after month, newspapers and magazines published alarming reports about almost every imaginable type of physical abuse, which led many of the nation's opinion leaders, including more than a few prominent Republicans, to conclude that the United States was acting not as the champion of oppressed peoples but as just another imperial power. "We have debauched America's honor," argued Mark Twain; "we have crushed a deceived and confiding people; . . . we have robbed a trusting friend of his land and his liberty; we have invited our clean young men to shoulder a discredited musket and do bandit's work under a flag which bandits have been accustomed to fear, not to follow." His question for the jingoes: "Shall we go on conferring our Civilization upon the peoples that sit in darkness, or shall we give those poor things a rest?"[24]

Then Andrew Carnegie took up his pen: "The American people are at last learning the truth about the Philippine situation. At this moment, they are shocked at the perpetration of such atrocities as have rarely appalled civilized man." Here was the wealthiest man in the country, now its premier philanthropist, arguing that the United States had been "engaged in work which requires suppression of American ideals hitherto held sacred" and had spent "years of killing these people and burning their homes."[25]

Carnegie's article was published in the same month that Senator George Hoar stood up to speak his mind: "We are talking about torture, torture— cold-blooded, deliberate, calculated torture." Then for two hours this widely respected Republican, now completing his thirty-third year in Congress, never let his eyes shift from the chamber's jingoes as he asked them what they could be thinking.

> You have sacrificed nearly 10,000 American lives—the flower of our youth. You have devastated provinces. You have slain uncounted thousands of the

people you desire to benefit. You have established reconcentration camps. Your generals are coming home from their harvest, bringing their sheaves with them, in the shape of other thousands of sick and wounded and insane to drag out miserable lives, wrecked in body and mind. You make the American flag in the eyes of a numerous people the emblem of sacrilege in Christian churches, and of the burning of human dwellings, and of the horror of the water torture.

Three years of attempting to establish order and progress had converted the Filipinos "into sullen and irreconcilable enemies, possessed of a hatred which centuries can not eradicate."[26]

IT WAS IN this anti-imperialist context that President Roosevelt set out to solve the problem of debt-collecting European gunboats. Soon after they had bombarded Venezuela's Puerto Cabello, the administration offered to take over the country's customs houses, to bundle together U.S. claims with those of the nine European creditors plus Mexico, another claimant, and to distribute Venezuela's payments in proportion to the amount owed.

Not so fast, insisted the three blockading powers, demanding preferential treatment because they had gone to the expense of forcing the issue. After some back-and-forth, the claimants were unable to identify an international precedent to serve as guidance, and so they referred the question to the Hague Permanent Court of Arbitration, which in 1904 ruled in favor of the blockading powers.[27] Claimants now had a strong incentive to be first with their country's gunboats.

By this time the Venezuela dispute had receded into the background, in part because Roosevelt was busy fending off charges that he had engineered the takeover of Panama, stealing it from Colombia, but largely because another debt crisis had arisen, this one in the Dominican Republic. Given the scandal brewing over Panama, President Roosevelt was going out of his way to express disinterest in acquiring a Caribbean colony, but he was also determined to keep Europeans out of the area.

The only practical way to do that was for the United States to take preemptive action before Europe sent more gunboats, and for that the president needed Congress's approval. So once again the altruistic uplifting card was pulled out of the pack and placed face-up on the table: "It is our duty, when it becomes absolutely inevitable, to police these countries in the interest of order and civilization." And Roosevelt quickly added, as any altruist would, that "the attitude of men like myself toward the weak and chaotic governments and people south of us is conditioned not in the least upon the desire for aggrandizement on the part of this Nation." Roosevelt said this not once, but often.[28]

The evidence left behind in the archives suggests that Roosevelt really meant what he said, but the problem of assessing his sincerity is that most such comments were made in 1904, another election year. Domestic politics mandated restraint, as this unelected president clearly recognized. On the Dominican debt question, "I should want action deferred until the election," he instructed his secretary of state not once but twice: "We do not want to act in the closing weeks of the campaign."[29]

Meanwhile, Roosevelt had sent three fact-finding commissioners to the Dominican Republic. They reported that the country was approaching anarchy, with no effective central government and most of the country "in the grasp of desperately selfish, irresponsible political brigands . . . little better than savages." As a remedy, they recommended that the United States force Dominicans to accept a takeover of the bankrupt country's finances—a receivership—and the commissioners were supported by Albert Dillingham, commander of the Navy's Caribbean squadron: "As the great civilizing power of the world, we will be obliged . . . to control the finances of the country until every cent of the debt, both internal and external, had been paid."

That was couched in national security language—the U.S. interest in keeping European gunboats at bay—but then Dillingham pushed the envelope to the altruists' side of the table: "Govern the country, control its finances, use native police force well organized, employ the unemployed in building roads, etc., revise the tariff, and we will give the world and in no very long time, another prosperous and orderly Republic." Dillingham assured Washington that "the people of Santo Domingo are ready to be taught."[30]

Then in his December 1904 annual message, almost immediately after his election victory, President Roosevelt announced what came to be known as the Roosevelt Corollary to the Monroe Doctrine, a first-of-its-kind declaration: If a nation "keeps order and pays its obligations, then it need fear no interference from the United States," but countries that do not "may finally require intervention by some civilized nation, and in the Western Hemisphere the United States cannot ignore this duty."[31]

Three weeks later, the U.S. minister in Santo Domingo was instructed to "ascertain whether the Government of Santo Domingo would be disposed to request the United States to take charge of the collection of duties and effect an equitable distribution of the assigned quotas among the Dominican Government and the several claimants." Facing the possibility of a European takeover, Dominican leaders found themselves so disposed, and a treaty was promptly negotiated, with the administration instructing its negotiator to "put in anything the Dominicans want about our not annexing the Islands—the stronger the better." President Roosevelt could not have been more adamant in a special message to Congress: "It can not be too often and to emphatically asserted that the United States has not the slightest desire for territorial aggrandizement at the expense of any of its southern neighbors, and will not treat the Monroe doctrine as an excuse for such aggrandizement on its part. We do not propose to take any part of Santo Domingo, or exercise any other control over the island save what is necessary to its financial rehabilitation."[32]

That said, the treaty's scope was unprecedented, bordering on a takeover. The first of its eight articles committed the United States to "the adjustment of all the obligations of the Dominican government, foreign as well as domestic; the adjustment of the payment and of the conditions of amortization; the consideration of conflicting and unreasonable claims, and the determination of the validity and amount of all pending claims." A separate article stipulated that the U.S. government would help "to restore the credit, preserve the order, increase the efficiency of the civil administration, and advance the material progress and welfare of the Dominican Republic."[33]

Convinced that these commitments went several steps beyond what was needed to keep European gunboats out of the Caribbean, anti-imperialist senators insisted upon a protracted discussion of every word in every sentence—two full years of questioning, for example, whether the treaty's pledge to respect the territorial integrity of the Dominican Republic meant that it would guarantee its integrity, as it had done with the protectorates in Cuba and Panama.

AS THE SENATE was throwing up one traffic cone after another to slow the treaty's path, the U.S. consul in Havana threw in another: *"Absolutely confidential,"* he cabled, "Secretary of state, Cuba, has requested me, in name of President Palma, to ask President Roosevelt [to] send immediately two vessels; one to Habana [Havana], other to Cienfuegos; they must come at once. Government forces are unable to quell rebellion."[34]

President Roosevelt's initial reaction was mildly anti-interventionist, writing a friend, "I loathe the thought of assuming any control over the island," but that was superseded four days later with another letter to another friend: "I am so angry with the infernal little Cuban republic that I would like to wipe its people off the face of the earth." Then he calmed down and sent Secretary of War William Howard Taft to investigate. With one eye on the Dominican treaty, still languishing in the Senate, and the other eye on the 1906 off-year election, six weeks away, Roosevelt warned him to "avoid, so long as it is possible, the use of the word 'intervention.'" "Remember, we have to do not only what is best for the island but what we can get public sentiment in this country to support, and there will be very grave dissatisfaction here with our intervention."[35]

Once he had looked over the situation, Taft did not see how another takeover could be avoided, and a reluctant Roosevelt sent six thousand U.S. soldiers to occupy the island. The problem was that President Estrada Palma wished to serve for a second term, and to that end his Conservative Republican (or Moderate) party apparently had held an unfair election, prompting the Liberals' protest. And fraud was only the tip of the causal iceberg, or so Taft concluded in his final report; the nine-tenths lying just beneath the surface was cultural. Cubans were hotheads, and the insurrection "could not have occurred in a country in which the common and ignorant people are not as easily aroused."[36]

"After all we did for them," groused the president's closest congressional ally, "to find them fighting and brawling at the end of four years furnishes a miserable picture of folly and incompetency." An equally disappointed Senator Albert Beveridge wrote that "no such cleansing, uplifting, civilizing work was ever done by any people for another as the American people did for the Cubans," and he insisted the United States had no alternative but to build anew: "Our duty of administration of orderly government to weaker peoples will not be abandoned." Taft believed that "the proper solution of the present difficulties would be annexation," but he also understood the opposition that a permanent takeover would face at home. "The circumstances are such that the United States can not take this course now."[37]

The takeover probably did not affect the November election, where Roosevelt's Republicans lost twenty-eight seats in the House but gained four in the Senate.

WITH U.S. TROOPS back in Cuba, some serious fence-mending became essential if the administration had any hope of winning Senate approval of the Dominican receivership. So President Roosevelt was soon visiting Senator Hoar's home state, standing before a Harvard audience that included several of the nation's most prominent anti-imperialists, insisting that he was only trying to help—"I am doing my best to persuade the Cubans that if only they will be good they will be happy; I am seeking the very minimum of interference necessary to make them good." And he could hardly have been more direct in his instructions to Taft: "Establish peace and order on a satisfactory basis, start the new government, and then leave the island." Meanwhile, Secretary of State Root had told a Washington audience, "Our efforts should be towards helping them to be self-governing. That is what we are trying to do now." The administration's policy was simple: "First. We do not want to take them for ourselves. Second. We do not want any foreign nations to take them for themselves. Third. We want to help them."[38]

Thus assuaged, the Senate stopped picking nits out of the proposed Dominican treaty and ratified a newly negotiated replacement that deleted any reference to uplifting and the right to intervene but allowed the United States to collect the Dominican Republic's customs revenues, hand 45 percent to the Dominican government, and disburse the rest to creditors.[39]

Given this responsibility, the United States set out to determine which creditors were owed what. Nobody knew. The debts included bonds that had undergone complex multiple renegotiations and were now a nightmare for the accountants, one of whom reported that an "original bond of 1869 was in 1888 scaled down to 20 percent; in 1893 it was reduced from a 6 percent to a 4 percent bond; in 1897 from a 4 percent to a 2¾ percent bond; in 1901 the option was given for redemption at 50 percent of the scaled nominal value."

To that confusion over bonds was added a large number of foreigners' claims for damages, many of which were excessive, if not fraudulent, especially those for breeches of contract. Nonetheless, each claim had to be examined and either dismissed or acknowledged as legitimate and, if so, in what amount. Equally perplexing was the status of an undetermined number of concessions, "sometimes improvidently granted," Roosevelt lamented.[40] Among the most worrisome had been the sale of rights to manage and maintain several ports; thinking of the Germans, Roosevelt wanted to arrange for their repurchase by the Dominican authorities.

Until all this had been sorted out, a receivership could collect but not disburse, and so the State Department needed to create an accurate debt/claims/concessions database. That task was outsourced to Jacob Hollander, the first of the Progressive era's so-called "money doctors."[41] Still in his early thirties, in 1905 Hollander took leave from his position as professor of political economy at Johns Hopkins University and sailed for Santo Domingo, where he calculated the government's liabilities, assessed its revenues, and then told the creditors, claimants, and concessionaires what they probably already knew: it would be impossible to pay everyone. This led to a renegotiation of the country's debt, in the course of which the amount due foreigners was reduced by half, from $31 million to $15 million.[42]

Paying even that amount would take decades, leaving open the prospect of European intervention, so the State Department encouraged a New York investment bank to provide the Dominican government with a $20 million loan, most of which would be used to cancel concessions and to pay off European bondholders. For security, the bankers required Washington's promise that the Army's Bureau of Insular Affairs would collect the country's customs receipts. This, a major innovation in U.S. foreign policy, was marketed at home as simple charity: "Poor Santo Domingo!" lamented Secretary Root, himself a prominent New York lawyer. "She has come to us for help."[43]

Holding to one of his discipline's less admirable characteristics, Professor Hollander then returned to Johns Hopkins and prepared a glowing self-assessment: his effort in the Dominican Republic had led to "little short of a revolution [and] not a revolution of the old type, involving waste and ruin, but a revolution in the arts of peace, industry and civilization. The people of the island, protected from rapine and bloodshed, free to devote themselves to earning a livelihood, are fairly on the way to becoming a decent peasantry, as industrious and stable as sub-tropical conditions are likely to evolve" or, as he had written several years earlier, "at least to the extent possible in Latin-American countries."[44]

THE ADMINISTRATION WAS also doing its best to improve Cubans. Taft had soon returned to Washington, leaving control over the island to Charles

Magoon, who until this transfer had been governor of the Panama Canal Zone. Like Taft, he soon concluded that Cubans were "hot blooded, high strung, nervous, excitable and pessimistic." Recognizing that "we cannot change these racial characteristics," he recommended that the United States focus instead upon constraining the behavior that accompanies these characteristics—an early type of assistance that is a major feature of twenty-first-century U.S. policy toward Latin America.[45] But here in 1906 there were no uplifting bureaucracies such as a National Endowment for Democracy or an Agency for International Development; the closest Magoon could find was an Army attorney, Enoch Crowder, who was called in to design a series of reforms for Cuba's election procedures. He was the first democracy doctor to treat Latin American patients.

Meanwhile, Magoon focused upon Taft's wish that "the next government will have sense enough to lay the foundation of an army that will suppress future resorts to violence." Until now, Washington had insisted that a well-trained police force and Rural Guard would be sufficient to control Cuba's excitable people—the McKinley administration had flatly rejected Governor-General Wood's 1901 proposal to create an army, and also his fallback request for a U.S. military detachment to remain as "the moral force to hold these people up to their work until the decent element assumes its normal position in the government."[46] The Platt Amendment was a compromise: when needed, the U.S. military would return.

Because it was now obvious that a simple police force was inadequate, and because no one wanted to repeat this 1906 takeover every time the hot-headed Cubans threatened life, property, and individual liberty, here was another first: the United States created the army of a foreign country. Once the army had been trained, the second U.S. takeover of Cuba ended in early 1909, only days before William Howard Taft became president and just after Roosevelt had sent his final message to Congress. In it he warned Cubans "to remember the great truth that the only way a people can permanently avoid being governed from without is to show that they both can and will govern themselves from within."[47]

THEODORE ROOSEVELT LEFT behind a policy unimaginable to his parents' generation, whose attention had turned to Latin America only when it began to search for new customers to empty the farmers' bulging silos and to clear the manufacturers' overstocked shelves. In the face of substantial criticism,

Roosevelt cobbled together a fragile consensus that the United States had the right to maintain order in the entire Caribbean region, both islands and mainland in an arc from Venezuela to Central America. (Progressive Woodrow Wilson would add Mexico.) Unlike pre–Civil War leaders, only a few prominent Progressives asserted the right to acquire this territory; instead, they claimed the right to control the residents' behavior—"to infuse new life, new principles and new methods of doing things," as Governor-General Wood had said of Cubans in 1900.

This right was considered a responsibility, and grew naturally out of the nineteenth-century belief that Latin Americans, and inferior branch of the human species, would benefit from Washington's assistance. Anchoring their policy upon this altruistic foundation, Progressives created protectorates. Roosevelt left most of the details to the succeeding administrations of William Howard Taft and especially Woodrow Wilson. Those two would set the mold, but Roosevelt designed it, and no one has ever described its contours better than Senator Albert Beveridge: "Common sense in the management of our dependencies means practical administration of government until our wards are trained in continuous industry, in orderly liberty and in that reserve and steadiness of character through which alone self-government is possible. Such administration of government is nature's method for the spread of civilization."[48]

Until this training was complete, the United States would insist upon order, and then, once that was achieved, it would promote progress. The principal roadblock? Unfortunately, governor-general Leonard Wood told Roosevelt, "it is next to impossible to make them believe that we have only their own interests at heart."[49]

CHAPTER 3

Money Doctors, Democracy Doctors, and Marines

> The aim has been to help such countries as Nicaragua and
> Honduras to help themselves.
>
> —President William Howard Taft, 1912

> Our object, of course, is not to subordinate them, but to help
> them.
>
> —President Woodrow Wilson, 1915

WILLIAM HOWARD TAFT did not have Teddy Roosevelt's energy, but the two men thought alike. A month after his 1909 inauguration, he wrote that his predecessor's policy "has contributed much to the cause of peace by assisting countries weak in respect to their internal government so as to strengthen in them the cause of law and order. This relationship of guardian and ward as between nations and countries, in my judgment, helps along the cause of international peace and indicates progress in civilization."[1] Roosevelt never said it better.

For the Caribbean region, Mexico excluded, the question during the Taft years was which countries needed to be strengthened in the cause of law and order. That determined into which harbor the Navy's gunboats should sail. Once the ships had dropped anchor, the Marines provided order, the money doctors provided plans, and the bankers provided cash whose repayment was guaranteed by U.S. customs collectors protected by U.S. Marines. Progress was supposed to follow via a process of trickle-down development, much of it flowing from U.S. investors responding both to Latin America's budding demand for goods and services and to the rising U.S. demand for tropical foods and raw materials.

But whereas Roosevelt had sprinted, Taft ambled along. He tried to convince Elihu Root to continue as secretary of state; "when I declined," Root recalled, "he asked me to find a man for him and I recommended [Philander] Knox." Although the full-time Pittsburgh attorney and part-time U.S. senator needed some convincing, eventually "Knox consented but on a condition. He said that he did not want to keep his nose to the grindstone . . . wanted to take things a little easy."[2] For the next four years Knox would golf in Palm Beach and the bureaucracy would take over. The second-ranking State Department official commented at the end of Taft's term, "I have frequently been in charge of the Department for months at a time."[3]

Alas, this particular assistant secretary, Francis Mairs Huntington Wilson, was described by Elihu Root as "suspicious and egotistical and sensitive and took offense readily," "full of suspicion of everybody," and guided by a strong commitment to the social Darwinism Roosevelt had popularized: "The march of civilization brooks no violation of the law of the survival of the fittest," this assistant secretary wrote, and the peoples living near the United States should consider themselves fortunate that "Nature, in its rough method of uplift, gives sick nations strong neighbors." This uplifting "takes its inexorable course with private enterprise and diplomacy as its instruments. And this course is the best in the long run, for all concerned and for the world."[4] For everyone's best interests.

Written in retirement, those words have a polished quality not seen in the memoranda Huntington Wilson typically wrote during his State Department service, including this 1913 briefing memo for President-elect Woodrow Wilson: "Rotten little countries down there run heavily into debt to Europe. They wont [sic] pay. Europe comes along and demands payment. The United States must either let Europe land marines and hold custom houses for security, and so open the way for further penetration and for flagrant violation of the Monroe Doctrine, or else the United States must compel the little republics to be decent and to pay up." That was the thinking of the man who held primary responsibility for Washington's policy toward Latin America during the Taft years, from 1909 to 1913, and that is why one U.S. diplomat, returning from a 1910 inter-American conference, urged Secretary Knox to take a more active interest. "If they could only see you instead of your subordinate."[5]

While most of Huntington Wilson's 1913 memo to President-elect Wilson was simply a crude restatement of the Roosevelt Corollary—preemptive control to prevent challenges to the Monroe Doctrine—he added something that Roosevelt-era jingoes had not necessarily opposed but had rarely considered important: "the political and economic advantage of the American taxpayer, the American nation." Specifically, "if the United States lends a helping hand and helps Central America get on its feet and keeps the peace long enough for it to begin to develop, we shall soon have immediately at the doors of our southern states a great and valuable commerce."[6]

To the extent that the Roosevelt administration had given attention to expanding opportunities for the U.S. private sector, it was generally to employ it as a civilizing influence. Touching on this topic just before becoming president, Roosevelt had told a Minnesota audience that "we must raise others," which was in character, but then had added "while we are benefitting ourselves," which was not. And so with his next breath Roosevelt backtracked, adding: "It is our duty toward the people living in barbarism to see that they are freed from their chains." His point was that Washington could not do this unassisted. "The missionary, the merchant, and the soldier may each have to play a part in this destruction, and in the consequent uplifting of the people."[7]

Those merchants had been selling in Latin America for over a century, but they had been few in number until the Spanish-American War, which opened a floodgate, especially in Cuba. As Fidel Castro would comment a half-century later, "I do not believe that such an incredibly rapid economic penetration ever occurred in any other country." Certainly he knew that Yankee traders had been sailing into the island's harbors since the eighteenth century, but this early commerce had been modest—initially the exchange of salted cod (*bacalao*) for whatever human ingenuity could coax out of a stalk of sugarcane; molasses was one favorite, rum was another. This trade had grown slowly, but then Spain's 1818 decision to open Cuba to foreigners permitted U.S. merchants to establish a foothold in an emerging market, and by the 1840s about half the ships entering Havana were coming from the United States. By 1899 more than six thousand U.S. citizens were permanent residents. Some were missionaries and some were landowners, but most were merchants.[8]

Then the U.S. occupation created a once-in-a-lifetime opportunity for investors, protected first by the U.S. Army and then by the Platt Amendment.

Investors "came with bulging pockets to a people who had been impoverished by thirty years of struggle," Fidel Castro continued, "to buy up the best lands in this country," acquiring "all our mines, our natural resources; they exploited public services, took over most of the sugar industry, the most productive industries, the electrical industry, the telephone, the railroad, the main businesses, and also the banks."[9]

Inclined to sweeping generalizations, Castro would always argue that this occurred throughout Latin America, but Cuba was unique because of the four-year U.S. occupation and because a 1902 trade agreement lowered the U.S. tariff on Cuban sugar, making it the least-expensive foreign source at a time when the nation's sweet tooth was being pushed above the gum line by John Pemberton, whose Coca-Cola hit the market in 1885; by William Wrigley Jr., who in 1893 began selling his wildly popular Juicy Fruit; by Clarence Crane, who only a few years earlier had introduced the original Life Saver, Pep-O-Mint; and by Milton Hershey, who turned to Cuba for sugar to sweeten bitter cacao, eventually acquiring sixty thousand acres of land plus five *centrales* and a 251-mile railroad.

And this 1902 tariff agreement was reciprocal, with U.S. producers granted favored access to Cuban consumers.[10] Add to that the very substantial advantage of physical proximity, and one need not be an admirer of Fidel Castro to agree with him on one point: "They progressively took over this country." Although the canal made Panama a close competitor, no other Latin American economy has ever been so securely tied to the United States.

With its vast mineral wealth and its open-door policy during the *porfiriato*, Mexico also had a claim to runner-up. A new mining code in 1884 had proven to be especially attractive, triggering foreign investments in gold, silver, lead, and especially the copper needed to conduct the electricity flowing into the millions of homes that until now had been illuminated by kerosene lamps. Then in 1913 the company that came to be known as Kelvinator began to market the first home refrigerator, using copper condensing coils. After that, the dam simply burst; everyone in the United States wanted to be on the grid, and the grid was made with minerals Mexico had in abundance.

U.S. investors quickly strung a necklace of major mines across northern Mexico, from Baja California (Santa Rosalía) to Sonora (Cananea) to Chihuahua (Batopilas) to Coahuila (Sierra Mojada). And as mining grew, so did the need for railroads to carry the ore, most of which tied Mexico to the United States: the central line from Mexico City to El Paso was flanked by an eastern line from Mexico City to Laredo and a shorter western line from Guaymas to Nogales, and Colis Huntington's line ran from the heart of Mexican mining in Durango to Piedras Negras on the border. All were the product of Mexican labor and U.S. capital and materials, from rails to rolling stock.[11]

Then in 1901 Edward Doheny, a Rockefeller partner, brought in the first major Mexican gusher near Tampico, just six years before the Model T, "a car for the great multitude," as Henry Ford liked to say.[12] He and his Detroit competitors set off an oil boom of monumental proportions among an entirely new set of investors who, like those who were already in Mexico, deeply appreciated Porfirio Díaz's ability to maintain order while they increased production.

There would be no interest in uplifting Mexico during the Taft years, only commerce. In 1909, when word reached Washington of Mexicans' growing opposition to Díaz, Taft became the first U.S. president to visit Mexico, crossing the international bridge from El Paso to Cuidad Juárez. President Díaz "is very anxious to strengthen himself with his own people by a picturesque performance in which we show our friendship for him and his government," Taft wrote his wife. "And I am glad to aid him in the matter for the reason that we have two billions American capital in Mexico that will be greatly endangered if Díaz were to die and his government go to pieces. . . . I can only hope and pray that his demise does not come until I am out of office."[13]

That letter was written a day after the two leaders had met, and for the next two years the administration watched the Díaz government go to pieces and the Mexican Revolution unfold, doing little more than beefing up the border patrol and saying little more than how sad it was to see Mexicans fighting among themselves.

Meanwhile, other U.S. investors had been slowly moving into the rest of Latin America. As Roosevelt's secretary of state, Elihu Root, had pointed out in 1906, "the people of the United States have for the first time accumulated a surplus of capital beyond the requirements for internal development. That surplus is increasing with extraordinary rapidity. We have paid our debts to Europe . . . and have entered the ranks of the investing nation." Investing where? "Great opportunities for peaceful commercial and industrial expansion to the South are presented."[14]

That said, Progressive-era investments were heavily concentrated in the northern part of Latin America, and only modest trade existed beyond Cuba,

Mexico, and southern Brazil, whose coffee accounted for a quarter of early twentieth-century imports from Latin America. The truly dramatic expansion of trade and investment would occur during the 1920s, after World War I.

"DOLLAR DIPLOMACY" IS the label critics would soon give to the Taft administration's policy toward these northern Latin Americans, underscoring their conviction that Wall Street had seized control of the Taft State Department. Administration officials responded that neither side dominated the other—"'Dollar Diplomacy' simply means intelligent teamwork," insisted Huntington Wilson, and the team's captain lived in Washington, not on Wall Street.[15]

Framing the question as one of U.S. security interests, Secretary Knox asked this: "Shall the Government of the United States make American capital an instrumentality to secure financial stability, and hence prosperity and peace, to the more backward republics in the neighborhood of the Panama Canal?" The question was being raised in regard to Honduras. It "has defaulted its foreign debt for 40 years and has politically, financially and economically about as bad a record for stability as could be found on the face of the earth."[16] So wrote Huntington Wilson a few weeks after Knox posed his question. Unlike Knox, he appeared not to worry about Honduras's proximity to the canal and noticeably did not argue, as Roosevelt had, that debt-collecting European gunboats would threaten U.S. security interests.

So why, then, did this impoverished Central American country receive an inordinate amount of the State Department's attention during the Taft years? The hypothesis favored by the administration's critics was that Taft was pushed into action by an assortment of U.S. investors, most of whom were involved in providing U.S. consumers with bananas. Here was a delicacy, to be sure, offering ample vitamins and minerals plus a desirable amount of roughage, but bananas were not petroleum or even sugar, and Samuel Zemurray's Cuyamel Fruit Company was not even remotely comparable to the Mexican enterprises owned by politically potent investors with names like Rockefeller and Guggenheim.

Many Zemurrays were active in Honduras, however, which since independence had been a weak state with fragile governments—the original Banana Republic, so named by O. Henry while he was living in Honduras to avoid prosecution for embezzlement in the United States. But the Taft administration insisted there was another reason for the U.S. gunboat anchored offshore: "The *Tacoma* is not in Honduranean waters on banana-police duty, but to exert a moral influence toward political tranquility at this juncture when we are after bigger game than bananas."[17]

The bigger game surely had something to do with Washington's ongoing concern over continuous bickering among five unstable governments. These disputes—most minor, a few highly destabilizing—had already prompted the Roosevelt administration, working in tandem with Mexico's Porfirio Díaz, to invite the five to attend a conference in Washington, at the end of which they signed a Treaty of Peace and Friendship. That led to the creation of the Central American Court of Justice, which Secretary Knox called "the first perfect type of international court."[18]

Words spoken too soon, for the experiment was disbanded after only a few years. The truly important product of this 1907 conference was to convince State Department officials that they, already responsible for Cuba, Panama, and the Dominican Republic, were also responsible for order and progress in Central America. It appears that the Canal, now under construction, had turned Washington's eyes to Central America. It now seemed reasonable for the United States to police this part of the Caribbean region.

For whatever reason, in 1911 Secretary Knox told Congress "there is no hope for peace and prosperity for Honduras except through the United States," pointing out that the government's annual revenue was less than $2 million, nearly all of it from customs receipts, while its foreign debt amounted to at least $100 million and perhaps $124 million—the product of four loans totaling $27 million and now "swelled inordinately by the long accumulation of defaulted interest." Hondurans were "bankrupt, famished, and discouraged."[19]

With that as its justification, the Taft administration reached into the policy cupboard, pulled out the recipe that seemed to be working well in the Dominican Republic, and popped its essential ingredients into the Honduran oven. At Washington's request, a consortium of four New York banks drew up a loan contract while the State Department negotiated a treaty guaranteeing repayment from customs receipts collected by an official chosen by the president of Honduras from a list of individuals created by the bankers and approved by President Taft.[20]

This, the 1911 Knox-Paredes treaty, was promptly rejected by the Honduran Congress, which complained that it would convert "a free country into an administrative dependency of the United States."[21] Undeterred, the Taft administration sought ratification by the U.S. Senate, with Secretary Knox providing a highly skeptical Congress with an altruist's justification: the State Department "has, from first to last, been mindful of the traditional policy of friendly aid and assistance to the sovereign commonwealths of the northern continent and has been animated by a sense of the moral obligation to promote their wellbeing."[22]

Washington's anti-imperialists had been hearing that for more than a decade, and they refused to listen further. The administration could barely secure approval from the Senate Committee on Foreign Relations. With ratification already rejected by the Honduran Congress and questionable by the full U.S. Senate, the bankers withdrew their offer to lend and Hondurans were left with nothing more than a brief speech by Secretary Knox during a 1912 goodwill trip to Central America and the Caribbean. It emphasized Washington's respect and affection.[23]

KNOX HAD TRAVELED in his Navy cruiser from equally bankrupt and equally unstable Nicaragua, where he had repeated exactly what Huntington Wilson had said a year earlier: "prosperity means contentment and contentment means repose." The Taft administration's goal was "to create a material prosperity which should wean the Central Americans from their usual preoccupation of revolution," and to that end the State Department had sent money doctor Ernest Wands to sort out Nicaragua's finances and to prepare a plan to revitalize the economy.[24]

As in Honduras, this plan used the Dominican Republic template: a loan from New York bankers secured by a customs receivership. It was formalized as the 1911 Knox-Castrillo treaty, and the State Department pulled out all the stops in an effort to secure Senate ratification. Abandoning the altruism that had failed him in Honduras, Secretary Knox marketed his Nicaragua treaty as "of vast commercial advantage."[25] Unconvinced, anti-imperialist senators balked at ratification. Undeterred, the State Department asked Wall Street to go ahead with a modest loan and Nicaragua to go ahead with its part of the agreement, which consisted of appointing a U.S. citizen as the nation's customs collector. Arriving in Nicaragua in late 1911 after similar work in the Philippines, Clifford Ham would serve until 1928. Meanwhile, the bankers sent two money doctors to Nicaragua, and they produced a currency stabilization plan that serves as an excellent example of Progressive-era prescriptions.[26]

To ensure that Nicaraguans not interfere with Ham's work, about three thousand Marines were landed during the Taft years, coming and going in small batches as conditions dictated. Among them was Major Smedley Butler, who wrote frequently to his mother and his father, a member of the House of Representatives. His letters dismissed the locals as a "useless lot of vermine," and he regularly offered his opinion that Nicaraguan politics reflected "simply a sordid desire on the part of one dog to take from another cur a good picking bone." He was equally harsh in his assessment of U.S. investors: "*renegade swine* from the slums of our race. . . . The whole game of these degenerate Americans down here is to force the United States to intervene and by so doing make their investments good."[27]

A mixed-claims commission proposed in the never-ratified Knox-Castrillo treaty attempted to clear the slate by processing 7,911 claims, totaling $13.8 million, including one from the bishop of Nicaragua, who insisted that the government had violated an 1861 agreement to pay his salary. The most vexing cases involved concessions that had been sold to an astounding array of entrepreneurs; one had purchased the exclusive right to produce ice for the entire country.

If the commission erred, it did so in favor of Nicaragua, awarding claimants $1.8 million, only 13 percent of what they had wanted. U.S. claimants received an even lower percentage: $539,000 of the $7.6 million they requested, or 11 percent. The lead U.S. commissioner wrote that the commission was "more interested in the adjustment of claims on terms favorable to Nicaragua . . . than it was to collecting money for American claimants."[28]

The low payout suggests that President Taft should be taken at his word: "In Central America the aim has been to help such countries as Nicaragua and Honduras to help themselves." The protection of U.S. economic interests appears to have been a minor concern, and the security of the Panama Canal of even lesser importance, pulled off the shelf when useful during a discussion with a member of Congress or a journalist. William Howard Taft simply felt obliged to help Central Americans "to rehabilitate their finances, to establish their currency on a stable basis, to remove the customshouses from the danger of revolution by arranging for their secure administration, and to establish reliable banks."[29] It was the right thing to do, in their own best interests.

HONDURAS AND NICARAGUA—these were the highlights of the Taft administration's policy toward Latin America, although some might argue that Cuba needs to be added.

It will be recalled that in 1906 Secretary of War Taft had declared himself provisional governor, inaugurating a takeover that continued until a few weeks before President Taft's 1909 inauguration. Not much happened between then and April 1912, when Secretary Knox arrived at the end of his Central American–Caribbean goodwill trip.

"When we landed at the Caballería wharf, there was no band, no soldiery, not even police, not a committee or a single member of a committee—not a soul." So began the report of an accompanying journalist.

> We scrambled into automobiles while curious longshoremen idlers and a few photographers looked on. Then we went to the hotel which had been set aside for us, through a couple miles of streets, including the Prado, and not a single American flag was to be seen. This was the reception which the land that the United States had freed from Spanish subjection, at the cost of much treasure and not a few lives, the land that the United States had unselfishly refused to add to her own domain, the land whose chief city she had redeemed from pestilence—this was the reception which Cuba gave the highest diplomatic official of the United States, visiting her with a suite, on friendly mission, conveyed, for greater honor, on a naval cruiser.[30]

The frosty welcome may have reflected some lingering resentment of the 1906–1909 takeover, but it also may have stemmed from the instructions given to U.S. minister John Jackson a year before Knox's arrival: "You are to endeavor, by friendly representations and advice, to deter the Cuban Government from enacting legislation which appears to you of an undesirable or improvident character."[31] That is what Jackson had been doing when Secretary Knox sailed into Havana's harbor.

President José Miguel Gómez eventually got around to acknowledging the presence of the U.S. secretary of state, giving Knox an opportunity to demonstrate that he was hopelessly tone deaf. Replying to a welcoming toast, he pointed out that "the United States stands firmly as the true, wholehearted friend of Cuba, glad of the work we have done for the Cuban people and ready to aid them to conserve the civic and material benefits which it was our good fortune to be instrumental in helping them to win."[32]

No sooner had Secretary Knox left for his next stop than the Gómez government found itself with a genuine crisis. It began when Cuba's Partido Independiente de Color launched a strike by dockworkers as part of a broader agitation for reforms that would allow for the party's unfettered participation in the upcoming 1912 election. The stoppage was initially interpreted by the U.S. legation in economic terms: "Present strike seriously damages horticultural interests, almost entirely American, and important American shipping interests."[33] Then the prominence of race increased with each passing day.

> *May 21:* "Armed negro bands near Habana and in Oriente and Santa Clara Provinces and possibly elsewhere. Leaders threaten to destroy foreign property."
> *May 23:* "Negroes are avoiding encounters, their first object being the destruction of property."
> *May 24:* "The negroes now in revolt are of a very ignorant class, and, although it may or may not be the intention of their leaders to attack foreigners and destroy their property, it would at any time require only a well-conceived appeal to their prejudices or cupidity to precipitate serious disorders."

At this point a U.S. warship sailed into Havana's harbor.

An angry President Gómez protested that the ship's presence "injures the feeling of a people loving and jealous of their independence, above all when such measures were not even decided upon by previous agreement between both Governments, which places the Government of Cuba in a humiliating inferiority." The U.S.S. *Nashville* stayed, the reports continued:

> *June 1:* "Persistent and consistent rumors of concerted negro uprising in Habana."
> *June 2:* "Negroes have bought large quantities of knives and other arms."
> *June 4:* "Whites throughout the Republic continue to grow more apprehensive."[34]

On June 5 President Gómez invited the United States to position troops on a less-conspicuous part of the island—"that we take over the protection of foreign property thus leaving the Cuban Government free to prosecute campaign against negroes." A thousand U.S. soldiers moved into central and eastern Cuba and, as President Taft would soon report to Congress, "the Cuban Government was thus able to use all of its forces in putting down the outbreak."[35]

BY THIS TIME—mid-1912—the Taft administration was fighting for its life, a slugfest that began at the Republicans' nominating convention, when the credentials committee refused seats to hundreds of Theodore Roosevelt's supporters. Then those few who had been seated refused to vote—their walkout handed Taft a first-round nomination but prompted the creation of a Progressive ("Bull Moose") Party, which nominated Roosevelt, splitting the GOP and handing both houses of Congress to the Democrats and the White House to Woodrow Wilson.

Wilson's Democrats had spent over a decade branding Republicans as imperialists, and in his final campaign speech candidate Wilson had dismissed Dollar Diplomacy as "mere commercial exploitation"; Latin Americans "have had harder bargains driven with them in the matter of loans than any other peoples in the world."[36] Then early in his presidency he added, "Interest has been exacted of them that was not exacted of anybody else, because the risk was said to be greater; and then securities were taken [customs collectors backed by the Marines] that destroyed the risk—an admirable arrangement for those who were forcing the terms! I rejoice in nothing so much as the prospect that they will now be emancipated from these conditions." The new president's central point was that "you cannot be friends upon any other terms than upon terms of equality."[37]

That said, President Wilson's second secretary of state would argue that "the equality of American republics and, in a measure, their independence are legal rather than actual," and his first secretary of state thought the same. As Wilson's most careful student noted, "The years from 1913 to 1921 witnessed intervention by the State Department and the navy on a scale that had never before been contemplated."[38]

Setting aside the pursuit of Pancho Villa, a unique event, every one of these interventions flowed from a commitment to improve Latin Americans, and the amount of uplifting during the Wilson administration would far exceed that of the Taft years. Of course Wilson had eight years and Taft only four, and of course the circumstances were different—especially in Mexico, where the revolution reached its full fury just as Woodrow Wilson was being elected. Wilson's focus in Mexico and elsewhere in the Caribbean region was upon promoting democracy, as befits a political science professor who had written that the expansion of literacy was activating "imperative forces of popular thought [that] promise to reduce politics to a single pure form by excluding all other governing forces and institutions but those of wide suffrage and a democratic representation."[39] Writing in the late 1880s, Professor Wilson cautioned that this was going to take time, because democracy was "a form of state life which is possible for a nation only in the adult age of its political development."[40]

There was still much of Professor Wilson in President Wilson a quarter-century later, only now he had the ability to help others reach the adult age. A week after his inauguration he announced that democracy would be "the basis of mutual intercourse, respect and helpfulness between our sister republics and ourselves." After a year in office he asserted what no predecessor ever had: "We are the friends of constitutional government in America; we are more than its friends, we are its champions." After four years he reaffirmed that "the Government of the United States will refuse to extend the hand of welcome to any one who obtains power in a sister republic by treachery and violence." After eight years Wilson's final undersecretary of state recalled that "it was with him a matter of principle . . . that recognition would not be extended to governments in Latin America which had come to power through revolution or through a *coup d'état* until after the people concerned had evidenced their approval."[41]

The prerequisite of democracy is independence, of course, and self-determination had long guided the thinking of Wilson's initial secretary of state, William Jennings Bryan, one of the nation's most ardent anti-imperialists and a three-time Democratic nominee for the presidency. In late 1898, as the McKinley administration was deciding what to do with the territory acquired from Spain, Bryan had insisted upon withdrawal: "This nation can not endure half-republic and half-colony—half free and half vassal." And like Wilson, Bryan was firmly committed to the promotion of democracy. "If we have occasion to go into any country," he advised the new president, "our only object must be to secure to the people an opportunity to vote."[42]

Unfortunately, the new secretary of state had a hopelessly disorganized mind, as evidenced by the yawning gap between his speeches and writings, on the one hand, and his behavior, on the other. Unlike predecessor Philander Knox, legendary for his protracted absences, the difficulty with Bryan was "his apparent inability when present to give consecutive thought or really intelligent consideration to anything brought before him." So wrote the State Department's legal adviser, who added that "he never seems to have a reasoned judgment on anything or any real appreciation of what he was doing."[43]

The new administration's policy toward Latin America was a case on point: after spending a decade criticizing Republican paternalism, the new secretary of state was reported to have told one of his first audiences that "those Latin republics are our political children, so to speak. We little know just how much they look to us. Because our country fought for freedom they fought for freedom; because we created a great Constitution they designed constitutions. They not only look to us but pattern after us."[44]

Here there would be full agreement between the president and his secretary of state. "Bryan and Wilson were both fundamentally missionaries of democracy," concluded Arthur Link, "driven by inner compulsions to give other peoples the blessings of democracy and inspired by the confidence that they knew better how to promote the peace and well-being of other countries than did the leaders of those countries themselves."[45]

TAKE MEXICO, WHERE a civil war was under way when Wilson entered the White House. Unwilling to appoint an ambassador because it would indicate recognition of Victoriano Huerta, who had seized power and murdered his predecessor only three weeks before Wilson's inauguration, the president instead sent a personal representative: "We are seeking to counsel Mexico for her own good," read the message he carried, which then laid out a plan for Mexicans to follow. It began with an armistice among the warring factions and concluded with an election in which Huerta would not be a candidate. Never before had the United States identified a specific individual whom the citizens of a foreign country should not elect as their leader. Huerta's foreign secretary brushed off the suggestion as "humiliating . . . hardly admissible even in a treaty of peace after a victory."[46]

Thus rebuffed, President Wilson felt the issue was of sufficient importance to go before a joint session of Congress. "Every instinct of neighborly interest and sympathy is aroused [by] the deplorable posture of affairs in Mexico," he began. "All the world expects us under such circumstances to act as Mexico's nearest friend and intimate adviser." He promised to be cautious, however—to "wait for a further opportunity to offer our friendly counsels," confident that "the steady pressure of moral force will before many days break the barriers of pride and prejudice down, and we shall triumph as Mexico's friends."[47]

The notes taken at President Wilson's first cabinet meeting by Secretary of the Navy Josephus Daniels indicate the administration's hopelessly misguided belief that "the chief cause of this whole situation in Mexico was a contest between the English and American Oil Companies."[48] But the British had interests to protect—their supply of Mexican petroleum—and so Prime Minister Asquith sent a special envoy to inquire about the Wilson administration's intentions. He reported back to Asquith that President Wilson began their conversation by emphasizing the need to protect U.S. security interests: "With the opening of the Panama Canal it is becoming increasingly important that the Governments of the Central American Republics should improve, as they will become more and more a field for European and American enterprize: bad government may lead to friction and to such incidents as Venezuela affair under [Cipriano] Castro. The President is very anxious to provide against such contingencies by insisting that those Republics should have fairly decent rulers and that men like Castro and Huerta should be barred."[49]

The conversation then turned to how, exactly, Latin Americans were to acquire fairly decent rulers, and here is where the professor in President Wilson was alleged to have said that his goal was "to teach the South American Republics to elect good men."[50] This mystified the British, who were not known for promoting democracy overseas: "The foremost duty of the United States is declared to be,—the internal reform of this unhappy neighbor," reported the baffled British envoy. "Since the days of the Holy Alliance it is doubtful if any government has thus declared its mission to reform the moral shortcomings of foreign nations."[51]

As Wilson was holding this conversation, Secretary Bryan was telling U.S. diplomats abroad to announce that the first step was for the United States "to force Huerta's retirement, peaceably if possible but forcibly if necessary."[52] This kicked off a season of intimidating gunboat diplomacy, culminating in a clash at Veracruz that left at least two hundred Mexicans and nineteen U.S. soldiers dead. But Huerta was soon gone. Washington was not convinced that his replacement was much of an improvement, but a major war had broken out in Europe. Encouraged by the need to place a higher priority on Europe and, it appears, sobered by the death toll at Veracruz, President Wilson told one startled audience, "It does not lie with the American people to dictate to another people what their government shall be." He said the same thing to another gathering: "If the Mexicans want to raise hell, let them raise hell."[53] At least in Mexico, there now was a difference between demanding democracy and promoting democracy.

Pancho Villa's raids and Pershing's punitive expedition notwithstanding, President Wilson's policy now evolved away from improving Mexican politics to protecting U.S. economic interests, especially after 1917, when Article 27 in Mexico's new Constitution threatened foreign ownership of land and of the mineral and petroleum deposits that lay beneath the soil. This required patient diplomacy, and Secretary Bryan's replacement, Robert Lansing, complained to the president that his meetings with Mexican authorities involved "long discussions upon abstract subjects, such as the nature of sovereignty, liberty, etc., which delights the Latin mind." He also confided to a friend that "it was no easy matter to swallow one's pride and to keep ladling out soothing syrup to those Greasers."[54]

But Lansing's willingness to swallow and ladle helped steer the Wilson administration through the war years and into the early 1920s, leaving to succeeding administrations the task of developing a workable relationship with Mexico, and leaving to the wife of a U.S. diplomat the task of writing an appropriate epitaph for relations with Mexico during the eight years a political science professor occupied the White House: "We can but express the pious hope that, with the help of god, no foreign nation will ever have a chance to serve us to the same extent."[55]

IN HIS 1990 volume about the Progressive era, historian John Milton Cooper called President Wilson's policy toward Mexico's Huerta government "the most extensive effort yet mounted by any president to bring down a regime in the Western Hemisphere." He should have stopped right there, but Cooper's 2009 biography of Woodrow Wilson added that the death toll at Veracruz "marked the end of that part of the Rooseveltian tendency in his foreign policy thinking"; President Wilson "would never again seem so caviler and enthusiastic about military intervention."[56] Cooper could not have been more wrong. The clash at Veracruz came early, in 1914, and

Woodrow Wilson had only begun to teach Latin Americans to elect good leaders. As with his two Progressive predecessors, this effort would focus on Central America and the Caribbean, where secretaries Bryan and Lansing would come to rely upon Boaz Long, a deserving Democrat from New Mexico whose party loyalty won him a State Department appointment.

Assigned to the Division of Latin American Affairs because he spoke Spanish, Long needed a crash course in diplomacy before being sent as minister to El Salvador, and during his Washington training he was visited by Minor C. Keith, who in 1899 had merged his various Central American banana companies with Andrew Preston's Boston Fruit Company to create the aptly named United Fruit Company. Now Keith was building two railroads to transport the bananas growing on United Fruit's 388,000 acres in Honduras, and its government had refused to live up to its agreements; hence Keith's visit to the State Department.

Long used Keith's information to compose a briefing memo for Secretary Bryan: in Honduras "there is no hope of improvement and every prospect of worse conditions unless the country is afforded decided help from without." Because the Honduran government had no credit and almost no revenue, it needed "some proper arrangement for refunding the foreign debt and providing for internal development," with "internal development" likely an oblique reference to money that the Honduran government would use to fulfill its promises so that Keith could complete his railroads.[57]

Inheriting from the Taft administration the problems of bankruptcy and investor squabbling, Bryan had sent his first gunboat to Honduran waters only six weeks after taking office, and he had authorized a second deployment four months later. Then came Long's memorandum, and the deployments continued: September 1915, October 1916, April 1919, and September 1919.[58] All were modest in size and brief in duration; in general, one or more U.S. warships would simply drop anchor close to shore, where they served as reminders that the United States was watching to see how its citizens were being treated—classic gunboat diplomacy from an administration that campaigned against gunboat diplomacy.

As had occurred during the Taft years, a "proper arrangement" for Honduras's external financing was never made, probably because the Wilson administration had no time to spare on this fairly insignificant problem. In addition to a remarkably ambitious domestic agenda, which included creating the Federal Reserve system and instituting an income tax, the president's limited time for Latin America was focused upon Mexico, while Bryan's was focused upon unfinished business in Nicaragua, where the Marines had landed in 1911 and the Taft administration had left a small contingent (125 to 150 soldiers) to sustain the fragile U.S.-installed government of Adolfo Díaz. Money doctor Charles Conant noted that Díaz was best known for his cooperation with U.S. investors.[59]

Because Nicaragua had been a convenient example used by the Democrats to attack Dollar Diplomacy, a reporter asked President Wilson why, after four months in office, he had not said anything about withdrawing the Marines. Nicaragua was a troubled country, the president responded. "We are sincerely desirous of finding some way by which we can render them some assistance"; indeed, for all of Central America, he said, "we are trying to deal in as helpful and friendly a way as we can . . . to help in every legitimate way."[60] That was reinforced a month later by Bryan's assurance that his State Department was acting as "a Good Samaritan and helping those who have fallen among thieves."[61]

The mention of "thieves" was a not-so-oblique reference to U.S. bankers. It will be recalled that a Wall Street loan accompanied by an informal U.S. receivership had been established after the Senate's anti-imperialists rejected the 1911 Knox-Castrillo treaty. Two years had passed, Nicaragua was still mired in bankruptcy, and the Wilson administration decided to keep the receivership but also try something new: the U.S. Treasury was to give Nicaragua $3 million in exchange for exclusive rights to a canal route—not because anyone in Washington wanted to build another canal and not to preclude another power from doing so (although that was sometimes mentioned), but because the Wilson administration wanted to provide President Díaz with financial assistance and it was not going to ask the thieves on Wall Street for help.[62]

A first version of the proposed Bryan-Chamorro treaty contained language making Nicaragua a U.S. protectorate, exactly like Cuba under the Platt Amendment, which Bryan had once decried as "a scheme of injustice." One chiding senator commented, "I am very much surprised that Secretary Bryan could have subscribed to the principles contained in this treaty"; a second wondered "why Secretary Bryan should come forward at such a time with a dollar diplomacy policy that goes far beyond the limits of Root or Knox"; and a third added that "'dollar diplomacy,' which was so strenuously denounced by Secretary Bryan, looks like the proverbial 30 cents alongside of the proposed treaty with Nicaragua." Summarizing for its readers, a London newspaper reported that "the Democrats have adopted bodily the foreign policy of the Republicans."[63]

Under pressure from their anti-imperialist colleagues, the Democrat-controlled Senate Committee on Foreign Relations rejected the Democratic administration's proposed treaty by an embarrassing 2-to-1 margin, prompting the administration to remove the Platt Amendment and try again. A number of senators remained opposed, but unlike the opposition to Taft's treaties, which focused upon the allegedly unfair terms imposed by allegedly rapacious Wall Street bankers, the opponents to Bryan's revised treaty, which involved no bankers, complained instead that "we are dealing with the puppets which we put in power; we are making a treaty with those who do not represent the Nicaraguan people."[64] Was not popular consent the keystone of President Wilson's policy?

After expressing its concern, the Senate ratified the treaty, largely because the administration had placated those whose primary dislike was Wall Street bankers. So for a brief moment the Díaz government had some breathing room, able to meet its payroll with $3 million from the U.S. taxpayers, few of whom noticed this significant policy innovation. Although it was billed as a simple purchase of the right to build a canal and to acquire naval bases along Nicaragua's coasts, it was in fact a new condiment in Washington's larder—a transfer of cash.[65]

The Marines remained in Nicaragua throughout the Wilson administration, serving as a deterrent to any group that might challenge the authority of the country's Conservative governments. One such group was the Liberal party. As a State Department official from the 1920s would eventually acknowledge, "the policies which the Taft administration inaugurated, and which the Wilson administration continued, were unfair to the Nicaraguan Liberals and caused distrust and resentment in other American countries. The intervention left the United States committed to the support of a minority in Nicaragua."[66]

THEN IT WAS back to the Dominican Republic, where the immediate goal of President Roosevelt's 1907 customs receivership had been to keep debt-collecting European gunboats out of the Caribbean. The debt had not yet been repaid when Woodrow Wilson entered the White House in 1913, so the customs houses were still under U.S. control. Nor had the country's warring political factions been put out of business, so Secretary Bryan instructed his minister in Santo Domingo to express "the profound displeasure that is felt by this Government at this pernicious revolutionary activity." He also offered to help: "Say to any who may feel aggrieved, or who may be disposed to resort to violations, that the good offices of this Government can be counted upon at all times to assist in the establishment of justice, in the remedying of abuses, and in the promotion of the welfare of the people." Specifically, he offered to help Dominicans "join together in securing justice through law and in the election by free and fair ballot of officials whom the people desire."[67]

The administration waited a year, during which time the Dominicans failed to hold a free and fair election, and so Bryan presented them with an ultimatum—the Wilson Plan, it came to be called: the United States would conduct the election, would count the ballots, and "would feel at liberty thereafter to insist that revolutionary movements cease."[68]

With U.S. gunboats anchored in several of the country's harbors, the Dominicans accepted this assistance, then waited until the Navy had sailed away before renewing their disputes. An exasperated Secretary Bryan instructed the U.S. minister to tell the country's conspirators that "this Government meant what it said when it declared that it would tolerate no more insurrections in Santo Domingo and it will furnish whatever force may be necessary to put down insurrections and to punish those guilty of exciting or supporting insurrections." An equally exasperated commander of the U.S. Atlantic Fleet reported "that the only way to handle them is by force," even though more than a decade of intimidation had produced this: "I have never seen such hatred displayed by one people for another, as I notice and feel here. We positively have not a friend in the land."[69]

Five months later (and, more to the point, three weeks after his 1916 reelection), President Wilson ordered the Navy to return to Santo Domingo with a full complement of Marines, whose commander was instructed to announce that he, Captain Harry Knapp, "acting under the authority and by the direction of the Government of the United States, declare and announce to all concerned that the Republic of Santo Domingo is hereby placed in a state of Military Occupation by the forces under my command."

As the Navy explained, with "endeavors to induce the Dominican authorities to conduct the government in a manner satisfactory to the United States Government having proved fruitless and with the intention of restoring order and prosperity to the country, the Military Government was established." Captain Knapp told Dominicans that the purpose of the takeover was "to give aid . . . in returning to a condition of internal order." A month later he announced that no elections would be held until further notice.[70] So began an eight-year military occupation.

SHORTLY BEFORE THE Dominican takeover, President Wilson had told Edith Bolling Galt, whom this widower would soon marry, that political unrest on the western side of Hispaniola required much the same assistance. "We are just now necessarily in armed control of Haiti, the present congress and president of the dusky little republic depending entirely on our marines to keep the peace. . . . Our object, of course, is not to subordinate them, but to help them in the most practical and most feasible way possible."[71]

Seven months earlier, in 1915, President Wilson had told Secretary Bryan that "it is our duty to take immediate action," but other pressing issues had intervened. Then Bryan had been replaced by Robert Lansing, who also was told by the president that "there is nothing for it but to take the bull by the horns and restore order . . . to insist upon constitutional government there."[72] The takeover occurred three days later, with Wilson instructing U.S. forces to "lose no opportunity and spare no means to impress upon the people of Hayti the sincerity of the beneficent intentions of the United States." Secretary Lansing also assured Haiti's Washington minister "of our entirely unselfish motives"—the Marines were being sent "in the interest of humanity."[73]

Superimposed upon disorder was bankruptcy, and to address this problem the president told Edith Galt that "we have just rushed a treaty down [to Haiti] for ratification by the congress which will, if ratified, give us practically complete control of the finances of the Haitian government." Secretary Lansing admitted that "this method of negotiation, with our marines policing the Haytien Capital, is high handed [but] it is the only thing to do if we intend to cure the anarchy and disorder which prevails."[74]

This treaty stipulated that the president of Haiti would, first, appoint a customs receiver and a financial advisor, both nominated by the president of the United States, and that to maintain order the government of Haiti would, second, "create without delay an efficient constabulary . . . organized and officered by Americans." Then, third, "should the necessity occur, the United States will lend an efficient aid for the preservation of Haitian independence and the maintenance of a government adequate for the protection of life, property and individual liberty." Fourth and finally was a promise of development assistance: the United States "will, by its good offices, aid the Haitian Government in the proper and efficient development of its agricultural, mineral and commercial resources." One of the occupying Marines captured the underlying mentality: "What we wanted was clean little towns, with tidy thatch-roofed dwellings."[75]

With progress painfully slow, a disillusioned Secretary Lansing wrote that "the experience of Liberia and Haiti show[s] that the African race are devoid of any capacity for political organization and lack genius for government. Unquestionably there is in them an inherent tendency to revert to savagery and to cast aside the shackles of civilization which are irksome to their physical nature."[76]

After more than two years of training, in 1919 the Gendarmerie was still not prepared to take over the duties being performed by the Marines, so "for the present and until political conditions become much more stable, it would be decidedly detrimental to the interests of both Haiti and the United States to withdraw the Occupation, to abolish the existing martial law or modified form of military government." So wrote Colonel John Russell, the Marine commander, as he dismissed a suggestion that his force be reduced to a small legation guard. Perhaps nothing more was needed in somnolent Nicaragua, but here in Haiti, where the locals had "an inherent tendency to revert to savagery," the nominal president "is anti-American, a man of no integrity, a schemer, a Vaudou believer, and he will only work for the good of Haiti when it is to his own personal interests or he is forced to do so by the Occupation."

Martial law was therefore more important than ever. "One restraint that is today placed upon the Haitien and makes him walk the righteous path is the fear of the [U.S. military's] Provost Judge," Colonel Russell insisted. "If the Provost Court was abolished all the good work of the Occupation during the past three years would be greatly nullified. The Haitien would soon slip back to the old methods, scheming, grafting, intriguing, with perhaps even assassination, and attempts at revolutions would again become a part of Haitien life. . . . The time would truly be opportune for the Haitien politician to gather his friends together and by use of money and lies about the Americans and all whites, to undermine the Gendarmerie and start serious trouble." That would not be difficult, because "the uneducated Haitien who lives in the country is more or less an animal, who will do whatever he is told."[77]

Meanwhile, one of the occupying Marines, Smedley Butler, had provided his father with an example of military supervision: "The Haitian National Legislature became so impudent that the Gendarmerie had to dissolve them, which dissolution was effected by genuinely Marine Corps methods. If I ever get to the States, I shall . . . give you a mouth to ear account of this dissolution, [but] am afraid to write it, for fear the Department of State might get hold of the letter." A few months later Butler was commended for building a highway at exceptionally low cost, apparently with forced labor—he told the Navy's assistant secretary, Franklin Roosevelt, that "it would not do to ask too many questions as to how we accomplished this." That probably helps explain what the Marine commander reported: "They simply will not cooperate, and in the bottom of their hearts practically all are equally opposed to us." "Just the same old tiresome grind," Butler complained to his parents.[78]

THEN THERE WAS Cuba. The Taft administration's assistance in quelling the 1912 race-based turmoil had provided Washington with yet another opportunity to help Cubans address the problem of government corruption— at the height of the insurrection the U.S. legation had cabled Washington for permission to take "some more or less active fiscal control, which would protect the Cuban treasury against the wholesale looting of which it has hitherto been subjected."[79]

That 1912 opportunity had not been seized—as noted, the Marines simply backstopped the Gómez government—but the seed had been planted. In early 1917, not long before the United States entered World War I, it sprouted in Woodrow Wilson's White House when the administration sent Marines to the central and eastern parts of the island to protect U.S. investors. They were still there two years later, when the war was over and Major General Enoch Crowder was available to work on the problem of corruption.

Crowder was already familiar with Cuba. During the 1906–1909 takeover he had been charged with designing and implementing a second code of electoral procedures because the 1901 code, also designed by U.S. Army personnel, had been unable to withstand manipulation. Then this Crowder-authored second code had failed in the 1916–1917 election, and now, in 1919, with another election on the horizon, Crowder was being sent to try again. The task of the U.S. minister, William Gonzales, was to convince

Cubans to welcome the envoy's arrival: "Endeavor to obtain from the President of Cuba a request that the United States should send a commission to Cuba to aid in the supervision of the elections."

Gonzales failed. "President Menocal would not agree to having the United States send a commission to Cuba to aid in the supervision of the elections, as this would wound Cuban pride, and that some means could surely be found to accomplish the desired end without such humiliation." Instructed to make another attempt, he reported another failure: "the President regrets not being able to accept [because] acceptance would seem to indicate a lack of confidence in the reasonableness and good sense of the Cuban public."

A third try found the delicate wording needed for success, and the embassy released the following statement: "As the existing election laws of Cuba were partly drawn under the direction of that eminent lawyer and devoted friend of Cuba Major-General E. H. Crowder," President Menocal had decided "to invite General Crowder to come to Cuba at an early date to advise with the legal experts of the Cuban Government in the labor of preparing such amendments to the election laws of Cuba as will meet the needs of the present and future."

It did not take Crowder long to identify the principal problem: "grotesquely fraudulent registration," including 264,396 fictitious names on the list of registered voters in the single province of Santa Clara. An accurate list required the United States to help conduct a census, and soon the U.S. legation could report that "the Ortiz Census Bill, in the amended form which General Crowder has drafted," authorized a census "guided by an American Advisor and six technical experts from the United States." This same report offered an early assessment: "The work of General Crowder and his staff cannot fail to be regarded as epoch making."[80]

Crowder hoped the next step in Cuba's improvement would be "a measure of supervision over electoral administration," and so Minister Gonzales was instructed to wrangle another invitation. After all, "what would be more natural than for Cuba to invite General Crowder . . . to interpret and apply the new law?"[81]

Although he was told to frame the invitation as simply "another effort to help Cuba to solve her own problems," Gonzales again found President Menocal unreceptive, this time adamantly. "He would retire from office before consenting to the humiliation." Then Gonzales added, perhaps too brazenly, "at no time have I concurred in the desirability of supervising elections." His view was that "if Cuba cannot hold fairly honest elections under the new electoral laws, it would be much preferable frankly to take over the Government for a long period and institute the many reforms possible under such conditions, than to undertake the doubtful, endless and thankless task of guaranteeing honest elections. That form of invasion of sovereignty promises little for the future of this country."[82]

Having thus identified himself as less than a team player, Gonzales was soon moved to Peru, making way in Havana for Boaz Long, earlier the minister to El Salvador, who had already laid out his view of an appropriate region-wide policy: "Extending our influences over these less favored people with the idea of educating them and regulating and improving their agricultural and commercial development, and making them good citizens of a democracy involves a colossal task but one not unworthy of an enlightened American policy."[83]

That was written in 1918; now, in 1920, his assignment was to succeed where Gonzales had failed, and so he delicately approached President Menocal: "Some of the officials of our Government had been wondering whether it would not be an excellent thing all around for General Crowder to be invited to come to Cuba to perform this work of observation." Menocal's response was equally delicate. "He would be delighted to have the General come down as his guest," but after the election, not before.[84]

And so an election was held without U.S. assistance on November 1, 1920, but at year's end the results had not yet been announced, apparently because they were unfavorable to the incumbent. This obvious fiasco was superimposed upon an extraordinary collapse of the Cuban economy, with sugar prices plummeting from record highs to almost-record lows, as post–World War I European beet sugar reentered the market. In the second half of 1920 the world price of a pound of sugar fell from an astronomical twenty-two cents to less than two cents, bankrupting almost everyone who had borrowed during the bubble, which in turn bankrupted most of Cuba's banks.[85]

With the economy in free-fall and the election an obvious farce, General Crowder was ordered once again to proceed to Cuba. He still had no invitation, so the Wilson administration sent him aboard a battleship.

"President Menocal invited me to Palace," Minister Long reported, and "explained that he could not receive General Crowder because of the manner in which he has been [sent]. President Menocal appeared deeply aggrieved and asserted that he had endeavored to work in harmony with our Government and he could not understand General Crowder's being sent on a warship."

The State Department replied that "it has not been customary, nor is it considered necessary, for the President of the United States to obtain the prior consent of the President of Cuba to send a special representative to confer with him." Then came what may stand as the most thinly veiled threat in U.S. diplomatic history: "You may state to President Menocal that it is the earnest desire of this Government to avoid the necessity of taking any measures which could be construed as intervention in Cuba or as supervision of the domestic affairs of that Republic, which we still feel confident can be avoided, provided President Menocal assumes a receptive attitude in respect to the advice and just recommendations which the President has instructed General Crowder to convey to him."[86]

With push close to shove, President Menocal welcomed Washington's proconsul, who began several months of arm-twisting, leading to new elections in several provinces and then to the inauguration of President Alfredo Zayas.

BY THIS TIME the tenure of the third and final Progressive was over. Although Woodrow Wilson was considered an unusually complex man, his policy toward Latin America showed neither complexity nor subtlety. Indeed, what historian Robert Quirk wrote about Wilson's policy toward Mexico could have been written of his administration's policy in general: the president "never lost his magisterial air in dealing with those he considered his inferiors."

Almost everyone saw this. "In a way it was a species of overlordship," Secretary Lansing recalled, "an assumption by the President of a right to determine who should not rule another country." A future secretary of state commented on President Wilson's "curious character—a blend of high idealism with absolute inability to foresee the reaction which his views and efforts would produce on other people."[87]

One of those presidents who died before he could defend himself with a memoir, Woodrow Wilson surely would have replied that he was only trying to be helpful. He might have conceded that his uplifting advice could have been offered more diplomatically, with fewer gunboats, but to any such suggestion he could have pointed out that he was a very busy man, confronted by a World War, then Versailles and the League of Nations, to which was added a debilitating stroke, leaving little time or energy for coaxing anyone to do anything, and certainly not anything related to Latin America.

Instead, this starchy moralist simply handed Latin Americans a series of nonnegotiable demands, all designed in their own best interests, presenting them as tablets coming from the Washington mountaintop. Then he went to his grave without indicating either satisfaction or disappointment with the outcome. Although he surely would not have considered Latin America a highlight of his foreign policy, we will never know if he could see from Washington what Marine Smedley Butler saw from Haiti: that all the well-intentioned intimidation did not come close to having its desired effect. "These wretched politicians do not intend to fall in with our American plans and ideas for their betterment."[88]

CHAPTER 4

Latin American Opposition and the Retreat from Protectorates

> We have been withdrawing our marines as rapidly as possible from Santo Domingo, Haiti, and Nicaragua, completing in the last-named country, amid the grateful recognition of all of its parties, a successful educational experiment in the fundamentals of self-government.
>
> —Secretary of State Henry Stimson, 1933

IN 1920, AN election year, the incumbent Democrats did not say a word in their platform about how they had spent the last eight years bringing order and progress to the peoples of northern Latin America—a sure sign of their assessment of public opinion. But then, out of the blue, the party's vice presidential candidate, Franklin Delano Roosevelt, flubbed his effort to explain why the United States would not be at a disadvantage in the new League of Nations when compared to the British, who would have six votes, assuming that the Commonwealth countries would vote as the mother country. FDR reassured a campaign audience that the United States had its own commonwealth: "Does anyone suppose that the votes of Cuba, Haiti, San Domingo, Panama, Nicaragua and of the other Central American States would be cast differently from the vote of the United States? We are in a very true sense the big brother of these little republics. We are actually acting as trustee at the present time for many of them."

Then he dug his hole a bit deeper by joking about his work as assistant secretary of the Navy: "You know, I have had something to do with the running of a couple of little republics. The facts are that I wrote Haiti's constitution." That would have been two years earlier, in 1918, after which the occupying Marines held a plebiscite to determine if Haitians approved of what FDR claimed as his handiwork—99.2 percent of them did: 98,294 to 759.[1]

Helping as a big brother was still perfectly acceptable here in 1920, but the Republican standard-bearer, Warren Harding, insisted that running a couple of little republics was going too far. He characterized Roosevelt's comments as "the first official admission of the rape of Haiti and Santo Domingo by the present Administration." "Thousands of native Haitians have been killed by American marines," he continued, promising that, if elected "I will not empower an Assistant Secretary of the Navy to draft a constitution for helpless neighbors in the West Indies and jam it down their throats at the point of bayonets."

Harding then took advantage of FDR's gaffe to generalize about eight Democratic years of "repeated acts of unwarranted interference in the domestic affairs of the little Republics of the Western Hemisphere." These, he said, "have not only made enemies of those who should be our friends but have rightfully discredited our country as their trusted neighbor."[2] And candidate Harding did not appear to be speaking only for himself—he hit an attractive note with his post–World War I campaign slogan, "A Return to Normalcy." Anti-imperialists appear to have created among the war-weary public a vague opposition to Washington's gunboat intimidation. Voters who had read Edward Gibbon were now nodding in agreement with his conclusion that "there is nothing perhaps more adverse to nature and reason than to hold in obedience remote countries and foreign nations, in opposition to their inclination and interests."[3] Warren Harding received 60 percent of the popular vote. Two decades of Progressives had collected a set of responsibilities that only a minority now wanted.

Yet the U.S. military was still running the Dominican Republic, and it also held complete control of occupied Haiti, even if a facade of self-government existed. And since 1917 two companies of Marines had been stationed in central Cuba, protecting U.S. sugar interests, while in Nicaragua the military presence consisted of a "legation guard" of U.S. Marines, a euphemism for propping up the Conservative governments favored by the United States. "The success of the official ticket in 1912, 1916, and 1920 was made possible only by the presence of the American Legation Guard in Managua," wrote one young State Department official. "The presence of the Legation Guard has been regarded in Nicaragua as an indication that the United States would again intervene by force in the event of a revolution."[4] In turn, Nicaragua's Conservatives allowed U.S. civilians to collect and disburse the country's taxes, exactly as they were doing in the Dominican Republic and Haiti, but with fewer Marines.

DESPITE THE FDR-HARDING kerfuffle, Washington's management of its Latin American protectorates was not a central issue of the 1920 campaign. Ten million soldiers and perhaps as many civilians had been killed between 1914 and late 1918, when an armistice halted the Great War. Then President Wilson had sailed for Europe, where he would spend several months helping to draw up the Treaty of Versailles.

Paris had seen U.S. peacemakers before—it was where John Adams, Benjamin Franklin, and John Jay had negotiated with Great Britain to end the war for independence, and it was also where the McKinley administration had imposed its peace upon a defeated Spain, but this third time was different. This time more than two dozen countries were involved, this time the United States was one of the "Big Four," and this time a U.S. president's Fourteen Points were being used as the principal girder for a global architecture centered upon a League of Nations. Woodrow Wilson received the 1919 Nobel Peace Prize.

If all this had been baseball, the war would have marked the moment when the United States moved up to the majors after a quarter-century of minor league play, primarily in the Single-A Caribbean and Central America, where care had been taken not to quarrel with any of the world's heavy hitters—with anyone who might swing back. For two decades there had been enough swagger to please even the most demanding jingo, beginning with Secretary of State Richard Olney's 1895 pronouncement that "today the United States is practically sovereign on this continent, and its fiat is law."[5] But the Progressives' macho wing had managed to avoid confronting any significant power, preferring instead to keep European gunboats out of the Caribbean by collecting their debts for them, a service for which Washington charged not a penny.

And the Progressives had dropped their effort to teach Mexicans how to elect good leaders once a few Yankee noses had been bloodied at Veracruz in 1914: Woodrow Wilson had gone from "all the world expects us . . . to act as Mexico's nearest friend and intimate adviser" (before Veracruz) to "if they want to raise hell, let them raise hell" (after Veracruz). And, not coincidentally, 1915 was the year the State Department spun Mexico off from the rest of Latin America, giving this rambunctious neighbor its own Division of Mexican Affairs, separate from the Division of Latin American Affairs. Only the weak countries of Central America and the Caribbean had found themselves on the receiving end of the Progressives' Big Stick.

Then came that Great War, and in its wake came vastly enlarged global responsibilities. Convinced that the League of Nations was the best hope for avoiding another catastrophe, President Wilson launched a speaking tour to generate support for U.S. participation, and the effort consumed him—a collapse in Colorado, followed by a major stroke a week later. Severely disabled, Wilson eventually regained enough strength to make decisions, but his disability, when combined with new postwar responsibilities, reduced to the barest minimum the attention that could be given to Latin America.

YET SOMEONE HAD to manage the Progressives' accumulated commitments, so it was fortunate that the State Department personnel now included a substantial cadre of career Latin Americanists who had been posted in the region and then rotated back to Washington. They had been exposed to Latin American opinion and often did more than simply report on these opinions— they served as Latin Americans' voice.

Aside from the facts that they were white males and that so many of them were in line to inherit a family fortune, these diplomats were difficult to categorize. A young Sumner Welles would eventually become the most prominent member of this group, dominating U.S. policy toward Latin America in the 1930s and early 1940s, but now he was setting out to build his career. The scion of a well-connected New York family, he had joined the Diplomatic Service after graduating from Harvard in 1914 and been posted first to Tokyo and then to Buenos Aires before being brought back to Washington in 1920 to serve as deputy chief and soon as chief of the State Department's Division of Latin American Affairs—this at the tender age of twenty-seven and after only two years in only one Latin American capital.

Well connected he obviously was, but the youngster had talent. "I had the invaluable assistance of Sumner Welles," recalled the Harding administration's secretary of state, Charles Evans Hughes. "I recognized at once his exceptional ability, his poise and force of character."[6]

Welles never criticized the Progressive-era takeovers; the problem, he would later write, was that "all sense of proportion was lost." Progressives "became so imbued with the role of evangel, that there soon became apparent an earnest desire not only to reform the conditions of life and government of the peoples inhabiting the insular possessions of the United States [such as Puerto Rico], but likewise the conditions of life and government of the independent peoples inhabiting the sovereign Republics of the American hemisphere."

That was written in the late 1920s. Now, in the early part of the decade, Welles's principal contribution was to emphasize what Secretary of State Robert Lansing had told President Wilson about Mexico in 1916: U.S. intervention "is extremely distasteful to all Latin America." Welles had seen in Buenos Aires that the Progressives' policy toward northern Latin America was damaging relations with southern Latin America.[7]

Welles and several like-minded colleagues had their opponents, one of whom was the Harding administration's initial undersecretary of state and a Teddy Roosevelt–style jingo. After fighting with the Rough Riders and serving with the forces occupying the Philippines, Henry Fletcher had spent four years as ambassador to Chile and two more as ambassador to Mexico, where he taught his German shepherd to growl whenever it heard the word "Greaser." But he was of an older generation, on its way out, and "not a philosopher or even a man given to very deep contemplation of political issues." That was the conclusion of the poor soul who selected Fletcher's career as her dissertation topic; she found nothing in his record to suggest the slightest concern for Latin American opinion.[8]

He was chopped liver for Welles and his allied coworkers, one of whom, Dana Munro, eventually would write several semiautobiographical studies of Caribbean policy in the 1920s and 1930s. He had earned a doctorate in economics from the University of Pennsylvania after two years of research in Central America, where he came away with a positive assessment, relatively speaking. His 1925 notes for a lecture to junior Foreign Service officers describe Central Americans as a "rather higher type of people than in D[ominican] R[epublic], far in advance of Haitians. Inhabitants mixed Spanish Indians, and Indians of good stock. Also more pure white. More possibilities for advancement."[9]

After his Central American dissertation research came service as an aviator in World War I, then Munro joined the State Department and was sent to

Valparaiso as a consul, where he saw among Chileans what Welles was seeing among Argentines. He would later recall, "Our efforts to help the Caribbean states had done us a great deal of harm in other parts of the hemisphere." Fortunately, "some officers in the State Department [such as himself] were beginning to doubt whether insisting that political conflicts be settled in a way that seemed most proper to us and officiously opposing measures that we considered unwise was the best way to improve political conditions in the Caribbean." But Munro believed that any withdrawal had to proceed at an orderly pace along a route laid out in Washington: "We certainly had no desire to see the United States take control permanently of any of the Caribbean states, but we saw nothing wrong in exercising a measure of control to stop disorder and bring about needed reforms."[10] This is what was considered fresh thinking in the early 1920s.

Nodding in agreement was another exemplar of the era's career diplomats, Francis White, who soon would be Sumner Welles's successor as the State Department's principal Latin Americanist, and then hold that post (with different titles) for a full decade. Heir to a Baltimore real estate fortune, he had rounded off the rough edges of his Yale education with two years in Paris and Madrid. In 1915 he joined the Diplomatic Service at a salary of $1,200 a year, supplemented by a trust fund allowance of $3,000 a year. Sent first to China, then to Persia and briefly to Havana (eleven months) and Buenos Aires (fourteen months), he was brought back to Washington in 1922. A year later, at the age of thirty, White became chief of the Division of Latin American Affairs; Dana Munro was thirty-one when he became White's principal deputy.[11]

"The Latin American mind does not work along the same groove as the Anglo-Saxon mind," White explained to the undersecretary of state. "Constitutional principles mean little to them . . . [but] by this I of course do not mean that we should not use our efforts to bring about constitutional government." How? The appropriate policy was patiently to "help them and coach them and advise them."[12] Another good example of fresh thinking.

THIS THINKING WAS being encouraged by dramatic economic changes. The wartime U.S. economy had required unprecedented quantities of industrial raw materials and petroleum, far more than could be extracted from known domestic deposits and from nearby but unstable Mexico. And demand had not dropped when the fighting ended, in large measure because the middle class had taken to motoring. Hence the Democrats' 1920 campaign platform had emphasized "the importance of the acquisition by Americans of additional sources of supply of petroleum and other minerals." Although the Republicans sidestepped the topic (unsettled postwar conditions "preclude the formulation of a definite program"), after its November victory the GOP would vigorously implement the policy proposed by its rivals, assigning this task to its up-and-coming star, Herbert Hoover, secretary of commerce at a time when that was a far more important cabinet position than it is today.

The U.S. private sector's focus was moving southward with investments in Chile and Peru (copper) and Colombia and Venezuela (oil). They even invested in Bolivia, betting on an increase in the popularity of convenience foods—first soup in tin cans, soon followed by tuna in tin cans (1909), orange juice in tin cans (1921), and then the product that alone made the Bolivia bet a good one: in 2007 Hormel packed its *billionth* can of Spam. And U.S. payments for these raw materials meant that Latin Americans had dollars to spend on capital goods for infrastructure and consumer durables, everything from electricity and telephones to automobiles and refrigerators.

To that add Wall Street's newly gained ability to assist these miners and merchants. Until the Woodrow Wilson years, an 1863 law had prohibited national banks from operating foreign branches, forcing U.S. exporters and importers to pay European bankers to handle their transactions. In addition to the lost commissions, a National City Bank vice president pointed out, this prohibition worked to the competitive disadvantage of every U.S. exporter, who "suffers from the lack of intimate contact and confidential relations with the business life of other countries, which can best be supplied by resident American bankers."[13]

Never immune to Wall Street's influence, in 1914 Congress had repealed the 1863 law, then quickly jumped aside to avoid being trampled by a stampede. National City literally flew out of the gate, immediately opening its first foreign office in Buenos Aires, and there were 181 foreign branches of U.S. banks when the 1920s began, the lion's share belonging to National City, whose Latin American network of forty-eight branches stretched from the Santiago in Cuba to the Santiago in Chile.[14]

1914 was also the year war broke out among Europeans. A few months later the Wilson administration hosted a Pan-American Financial Conference, something of a repeat of the 1899 effort. Treasury Secretary William

McAdoo wrote that "forty-three delegates came from Latin America. At the conference they met one hundred and fifty American delegates, representing the banking and commercial interests of the United States, [and] the foreign delegates, as guests of the nation, were conducted by special train on a tour of the principal cities east of the Mississippi and north of Ohio."[15]

Because Europeans were focused on killing one another, the conference was more successful than it might have been under other circumstances. That first U.S. branch bank had opened its doors in Buenos Aires just as the fighting began on the Continent, and a few months later came Wall Street's $15 million loan to Argentina, the first dollar-denominated U.S. bank loan to that country. The European war raged for nearly three years before the United States joined in, and Treasury Secretary McAdoo would recall that "the South Americans were like the customers of a store that had burned down; they were looking for a place to spend their money."[16]

When the guns fell silent in late 1918, a war-torn continent needed rebuilding, but Europeans, having squandered their wealth on bombs and bayonets, had little money and less self-confidence. Meanwhile, U.S. soldiers were returning to ticker-tape parades up their unscathed avenues, and the vaults at Fort Knox were bulging with the treasure Europe had transferred to pay for its food and armaments. That made the United States the only one of the Big Four that could be relied upon to maintain the free convertibility of its currency into gold; as the incumbent Democrats bragged in their 1920 platform: "The Federal Reserve note is the unit of value throughout all the world."[17]

All this occurred without a single shot from one of Alfred Thayer Mahan's gunboats—Europeans had simply propped open the door to South America as they were leaving, allowing U.S. producers to stroll in and make themselves comfortable.

SO NOW IT was time to ensure that the United States would be on good terms with Latin America's consumers, and if they were upset by Washington's Caribbean protectorates, perhaps they could be accommodated.

In Cuba there were only about five hundred Marines out in the boondocks protecting U.S. sugar interests that no longer seemed to need protection. But a U.S. proconsul, Enoch Crowder, was living on a battleship in Havana's harbor while working on his "Moralization Program," Washington's latest effort to straighten Cubans out. "The success of General Crowder's mission has undoubtedly been facilitated because of his arrival on the *Minnesota* and because of her continued presence in Cuban waters," wrote Undersecretary of State Norman Davis, pleading with the Navy not to order Crowder to find a hotel. "His residence on the vessel has added prestige to his mission, which is desirable at this time."[18]

But the Navy needed its ship for something other than a floating hotel, and General Crowder soon moved into the Hotel Sevilla, from which he continued sending Washington a steady stream of reports on his progress in "this very difficult task of reconstructing or, better said, building anew the institutional life of this country," almost always adding something like "you would be pleased with the progress made and with the new National conscience that is awakening." By this time, 1923, he wrote that it "can be truthfully said that I have eliminated large graft from the *National* administration."

With that mission accomplished, Crowder moved on to the improvement of local government:

> It is a part of my plan to seek a constitutional amendment authorizing a change in the form of municipal government. When I secure this I have the gigantic task of writing the new municipal law for the Islands [*sic*] and putting it into execution. I have got to make a survey of municipal, provincial, and national public utilities which at present are exploiting the people of Cuba; I have got to make an educational survey of the Islands with a view to checking the alarming growth of illiteracy of children of school age; I have got to make a survey of sanitary conditions with a knowledge that the Treaty stipulations between the two countries are being violated by Cuba and that sanitation is non-existent outside of the City of Havana; and I have got to reform the municipal tax system of the country and refund the municipal debts of one hundred and sixteen municipal districts.[19]

Here is where General Crowder claimed his place as the most ambitious individual uplifter in the history of U.S. policy toward Latin America, and it was too much for the new generation of fresh thinkers. The Marines were called home a few months later, and Crowder became a plain-vanilla diplomat, the first U.S. ambassador to Cuba and no longer a Personal

Representative of the President. He now was an envoy reporting to the State Department, with no mandate to "moralize" Cubans.

EXITING THE OTHER protectorates would be more difficult, consuming all of the 1920s and the early 1930s.

Washington's fresh thinkers had no one to blame but themselves. They wanted to withdraw but felt an obligation to ensure against a resurgence of disorder, which almost everyone still interpreted as little more than wrestling over who would loot the treasury. As Francis White phrased it, "With certain exceptions general characteristic of most Governments in Latin America, especially those in tropics and having very small pure white population, is that great dishonesty exists among public officials."[20]

The solution was to continue the Progressives' effort to create apolitical militaries to guard against disorder, now twinned with an effort to teach the locals how to select their leaders in free and fair voting. And then, third, the United States would need to create an efficient bureaucratic apparatus to collect taxes, pay bills, reassure lenders, and attract investors. These three improvements (a competent apolitical military, a democratic pathway to power, and an efficient state apparatus) became the focus of the U.S. withdrawal process. The idea was to increase the level of assistance so that the United States could stop assisting.

THE FIRST ATTEMPT to implement this model was in the Dominican Republic, where the size of the Marine detachment peaked at 3,007 in early 1919, a few months after the European armistice. With Europe neutered, a U.S. consul had written that "such reasons as may have justified the occupation of the country no longer exist," and a deputy collector of customs agreed: "If there was ever a time in the history of the world when Europe was not thinking of interfering in the Western Hemisphere, it is the present."[21]

When the U.S. takeover began in 1916, Admiral Harry Knapp had told Dominicans that it was "designed to assist the country to return to a condition of internal order." Upon their arrival the Navy's Marines concluded that the country's army had become an instrument of oppression, and so it had been replaced by a new Guardia Nacional Dominicana.[22] A Marine trainer recognized that "there was, at this time, still a slight feeling of resentment against the occupation," but soon "a new generation trained in American ideas and standards of personal honor and morals, will succeed in steering the ship of state without further wreck."[23]

Until that occurred, the focus of the Dominican Republic's military governor, Admiral Thomas Snowden, was to keep Dominicans from slipping back into the bedlam of rival groups seeking to seize the treasury.[24] And there were development projects to complete. Operating with a bare minimum of supervision by war-distracted Washington, the Marines under Snowden's command had been working "to spread education, both literacy and vocational, throughout the country, to provide communications and other modern facilities, together with improved harbor facilities, and while leaving the Dominican Judiciary intact, to improve the laws and economic condition of the country."

Completing all this was going to take time, and in the meantime Admiral Snowden reported that "the country is tranquil and all the citizens thereof, except the former political factions, accept and have expressed . . . the hope that the existing government will continue to work until the objects of the occupation are fully accomplished."[25] That early 1920 report was only the first of several similar messages during this U.S. election year, and little different from the one Admiral Snowden sent a few days before the voting: "During a recent inspection throughout the Republic, . . . everywhere was manifest the contentment of the masses of the people under the existing Government."[26]

But there was a complication. In early 1919 the U.S. consul in Santo Domingo had warned about "the very active and rather wide spread propaganda in behalf of the restoration of independence" and, more specifically, about the activities of the president whom the Marines had removed in 1916, Francisco Henríquez y Carvajal. Like Woodrow Wilson, he had also set out for Paris, "with the purpose of bringing to the attention of the peace conferees the present political status of the Dominican Republic, its right to the consideration of the world and to the restoration of its independence."[27]

No one wanted Henríquez working the conference corridors, buttonholing delegates to discuss the fifth of President Wilson's Fourteen Points (decisions about colonial possessions must give equal weight to the wishes of the colonized people), but that is what Henríquez was doing until a member of the U.S. delegation suggested he present his views directly to the State Department in Washington. Henríquez jumped at the invitation, pausing only long enough to present the U.S. delegate with a lengthy memorandum politely explaining why the Marines should get out of his country.[28]

His first stop was New York, where he participated in the creation of the Comisión Nacionalista Dominicana, which would link the views of Dominican nationalists to the anti-imperialist media. Then it was on to Washington and the State Department's Division of Latin American Affairs, where his reception by two low-level officials was an indicator of the Wilson administration's low level of interest. At the first of two polite discussions, Henríquez pulled out another memorandum requesting that the Marines pack their bags; at the second he received the Paris treatment—told that Washington was not the appropriate venue and urged to consider "taking up the matters contained in his memorandum directly with the Military Governor," Admiral Snowden.[29]

That would be a waste of time, Henríquez replied, leaving instead to join the Dominican exile community in Cuba and probably not recognizing his achievement: State Department officials began to challenge Admiral Snowden. Not all Dominican politicians were wild-eyed troublemakers, they wrote; Henríquez, for one, was a calm, responsible leader with whom they could negotiate. The U.S. delegation had already reported from Paris that "Dr. Henríquez y Carvajal is not rabidly anti-American," and now officials in Washington saw the same thing, even if they could not get his name straight: "Carvajal appears to be well disposed and ready to cooperate with the Military Government."

And so the State Department decided to concede a bit: an internal memorandum summarizing the discussions indicates that at their second meeting "Mr. [Hallett] Johnson informed Senor Carvajal that the State Department had found room for some agreement." Specifically, "the suggestion as to reducing the actions of the Provost [military] Courts in Santo Domingo, seemed reasonable."[30]

Accordingly, the State Department sent a cable expressing this view to its principal official in the Dominican Republic, William Russell, with instructions that it be given to Admiral Snowden, the country's military governor. Snowden replied that "it is not practicable at the present time to suspend entirely . . . military law and provost courts." Additional suggestions were dismissed almost before they were made: the end of censorship "cannot be permitted," and "not the founding of political parties, as Dr. Carvajal says, but the effacement of them, is necessary for the good of the country." As for any thought of withdrawal, Admiral Snowden repeated that the removal of U.S. forces "would result in anarchy and early ruin."

That had been followed a day later by yet another of the admiral's reassuring quarterly reports, which presented the same message but from a positive perspective: "Quiet and good order have continued to prevail throughout the quarter, broken only by the intermittent and trivial activities of a small number of bandits." No doubt wondering how many times he had to say the same thing, the admiral once again insisted that "the best people in all parts of the republic have repeatedly assured me that they did not want any other government." The State Department's Russell agreed that "chaos will prevail" if the Marines were to be withdrawn.[31]

Faced with this opposition, the Wilson State Department backed off. Its only victory was to insist that Admiral Snowden soften his military dictatorship by creating a Junta Consultiva of leading Dominican citizens. Appearing to concede, Snowden grudgingly assembled a junta, but it took only two months for its members to see they would be informed rather than consulted. Handing Snowden their resignations, they joined with others to create the Unión Nacional Dominicana, whose sole purpose was independence; in the meantime, they pledged not to cooperate in any way with the foreigners who occupied their country.[32]

Nothing more occurred until some months later, when Sumner Welles arrived in Washington from Buenos Aires and began to voice his concern about South American opinion. The first clear sign of his influence came in September 1920 when the outgoing secretary of state, Bainbridge Colby, convinced the Navy to commute the sentence of poet Fabio Fiallo, who had become a *cause célèbre* throughout Latin America, jailed for publishing articles calling for independence. Welles drafted the memo Secretary Colby used to explain to the secretary of the Navy why freeing Fiallo was important, emphasizing that it "will prove most helpful to our interests throughout Latin America."[33] This was the argument of a realist with an interest in improving the image of the United States in South America.

Once Navy Secretary Josephus Daniels had ordered Admiral Snowden to release his prisoner, Fiallo traveled to New York, where the Comisión Nacionalista helped him establish ties with sympathetic opinion leaders. Offered the pages of *Current History* to express the views of Dominican nationalists, Fiallo wrote that "99 per cent, if not a full 100 per cent, wish the Americans to leave." His thinking was congruent with that of a U.S. salesman with private-sector interests to protect: "In my sojourn of two months, covering the entire island as an American commercial traveler, I did not meet a single Dominican who did not want the Americans out, bag and baggage."[34]

All this occurred at the same time Warren Harding's Republicans were waging their campaign to retake the White House. Then, a few weeks after their victory, a lame duck Woodrow Wilson startled everyone by unveiling a withdrawal plan. Common courtesy mandated consultation with the nation's incoming leaders, but President Wilson had clearly been stung by Harding's campaign criticism. He told his son-in-law, "I have been part of this record from the first, and there is nothing in it to be ashamed of at any point." He had started it, he would end it. "I don't care a damn what the Republicans do."[35]

Tit for tat is often an adequate explanation of human behavior, but in this case President Wilson's timing is better explained by South American opinion on the eve of Secretary of State Colby's goodwill trip to South America, a much-delayed courtesy call that included thanking Brazilians for their wartime support. When Colby gave prior notice of the withdrawal to the secretary of the Navy (once again, drafted by Welles's Latin American division), he noted in his first paragraph "the anxiety expressed by the governments of other American republics as to our intentions in Santo Domingo," and he repeated in his final paragraph that the withdrawal announcement "will, I feel certain, have a most beneficial effect upon our relations with all the Latin American Republics."[36]

Secretary Colby sailed for South America seven days later, and it could hardly have been a coincidence that the withdrawal announcement was made during his first stop in Rio de Janeiro.

"The local [U.S.] officials knew nothing of this decision," reported a sociologist visiting Santo Domingo, while a surprised Admiral Snowden complained that "the sudden change of policy by the Home Government deciding to turn over the government to the Dominican people struck the Military Government at a most unfortunate period," when plummeting postwar sugar prices had triggered a severe recession. But the *New York Times* applauded the decision, editorializing that the four-year military occupation, preceded by a decade-long financial receivership, had "made the republic solvent, and educated the people in the principles of self-government."[37]

IT TOOK ALMOST four years to withdraw from the Dominican Republic, largely because the Department of State and the Department of the Navy had difficulty determining how much help Dominicans needed with the transition, while many Dominicans were determined that the United States help not at all—just go. Discarded almost immediately was General Crowder's advice that a Cuba-style Platt Amendment be added to any departure agreement; discarded soon thereafter was Admiral Snowden, replaced by an admiral who understood that the train was leaving the station and the Navy needed to hop aboard.[38]

Once settled into office, President Harding and Secretary Hughes modified President Wilson's withdrawal plan with a more detailed plan of their own and then sent Sumner Welles to implement it. Backed by two thousand Marines, Welles convinced Dominicans to do it Washington's way: select a provisional government, which would then conduct an election using a process "closely modeled upon the Cuban electoral Code, which had been elaborated with the utmost care by the Cuban Congress, and which had in turn been based upon a draft presented at the request of the Cuban Government by Major-General Enoch H. Crowder."[39]

Dominicans then cast their ballots, inaugurated their new president, and watched the Marines sail for home.

The list of Dominican leaders who assumed power in 1924 was similar to the list of those who were removed from power in 1916, but the State Department was confident that the Marine-trained Guardia would be able to halt any relapse into pre-takeover disorder—one of the Marine trainers wrote that the Guardia had become "an honorable profession instead of a harbor of last resort for natives who were too lazy to earn their living in any other way."

A problem lingered. "The Dominican soldiers are fierce fighters, inclined to be merciless, and will follow their leaders anywhere, but cannot be trusted with responsible duties or independent posts. They will act with great credit when directly under the supervision of a superior officer [most of whom were U.S. Marines], but, when 'out on their own' are inclined to slack, and loaf away the time." Race was the principal problem. "As a general rule, the degree of intelligence increased with the decrease of the ebony tinge. The blacker recruits were generally simple-minded giants who did what they were told simply from the habits of discipline, and lacked sense of responsibility and initiative. Those who were of clearer complexion usually were more intelligent, and could be trusted with responsible jobs."[40]

One of the soldiers with a clearer complexion was Rafael Trujillo, who slowly encroached upon civilian authority until he formally seized power in 1930 via an election in which the U.S. minister reported that Trujillo received 223,851 votes and, "as the number given greatly exceeds the total number of voters in the country, further comment on the fairness of the elections is hardly necessary." Two months after Trujillo's inauguration, Secretary of State Henry Stimson told his diary that the country's new leader "is panning out to be a very good man."[41]

So began a three-decade policy of overlooking almost any depredation, as Trujillo hounded even his mildest critics, jailing those who did not flee the country and murdering those he considered especially threatening. Writing several decades later, Dana Munro's defense was to plead ignorance: "We could hardly foresee at the time that his regime would develop into one of the most atrocious dictatorships in the history of Latin America."[42]

PRESIDENT HARDING WAS dead by the time the Marines finally left the Dominican Republic, felled by a stroke in mid-1923 and entering the history books as a parochial midwestern politician with an administration marred by corruption.

After his 1920 campaign criticism, Harding had given Secretary of State Hughes the responsibility for dismantling the protectorates, a task Hughes accepted with limited enthusiasm. But he happened to be secretary of state on the hundredth anniversary of the 1823 Monroe Doctrine, and so was obliged to give two major speeches about U.S.–Latin American relations. The goal of U.S. policy, he said, was to have "prosperous, peaceful and law abiding neighbors with whom we can cooperate to mutual advantage." There was only a bit more substance in what he told his second audience: "It is the policy of this Government to make available its friendly assistance to promote stability in those of our sister Republics which are especially afflicted with disturbed conditions." Beyond that, Hughes had no big ideas for Latin America and no visible interest in acquiring any.[43]

Although policy changed very little when Vice President Calvin Coolidge took charge and then was elected for a full term in 1924, the tone changed dramatically when the urbane Hughes turned the State Department over to Frank Kellogg, a Minnesota lawyer who had gained admirers for his work on major antitrust cases, including Standard Oil. Kellogg had been elected to the Senate in 1916, and when he lost his seat in 1922, President Harding had named him ambassador to Great Britain; in early 1925 Coolidge brought him back to lead the State Department.

That was when insiders became acquainted with what one close colleague characterized as the secretary's "hasty and explosive temper." "On his desk was a sort of keyboard with buttons which summoned the various officers of the Department. If Mr. Kellogg had read something irritating in the paper before he reached his office he would strike the keyboard like a piano concertmaster, all fingers at once, and summon everybody he could think of. As we entered his room one after the other we were greeted with a storm of rage. An immediate council was held, Mr. Kellogg still sputtering, and out of that conference would come a calm and reasoned decision on the part of the Secretary of State. I never understood how it worked, but it seemed to."[44]

Undersecretary Joseph Grew was less certain about it working: "Kellogg often did behave like a petulant child and in those moods it was quite useless to try to argue or talk logic with him." His generous interpretation was that Kellogg was simply venting some of the pressure that builds up in any intense job, confiding to his diary, "The Secretary has been under a terrible strain lately" and "A day or two ago he said to me rather pathetically that he had altogether too much to do."

Whatever the cause, these eruptions would worsen over time, so policy was tethered to reality by lower-level officials—by the Dana Munros and the Francis Whites, who were "well trained, eminently cautious, and hardly likely to tilt at windmills or to take long jumps in new and untried directions"—fresh voices but not too fresh. That was the conclusion of Kellogg's biographer, who also wrote the best one-sentence summary of the Coolidge-Kellogg years: "The shop was kept running, but few new goods were put on the shelves."[45]

What the Kellogg State Department could not ignore were the goods already awaiting attention on the unloading dock. Secretary Hughes and his subordinates had completed the heavy lifting in the Dominican Republic; now responsibility for withdrawal from Nicaragua belonged to Kellogg, and here is where South American opinion, already involved in the Dominican Republic, became a truly important force.

SHOULD THEY EVER be brought back from the grave to cast a vote, past U.S. diplomats will hand Cuba the title of Most Consistently Annoying

Latin American Country, but Nicaragua would be a strong runner-up. In 1909 President Taft's secretary of state had called the country's president "a blot upon the history of Nicaragua," and his assistant secretary had referred to him as "an unspeakable carrion." Then in 1911 they had sent in the Marines, and now, here in the 1920s, Washington's simple goal was to withdraw the 107 who were left.[46]

It should not have been difficult. At the time there were 2,291 troops in the Dominican Republic, and Nicaragua, unlike the Dominican Republic, already had a government, albeit one imposed by the United States, which preferred a government composed of Conservatives. That understandably upset the country's Liberals, whom Washington had dealt out of the game because of the Taft administration's experience with Liberal president José Santos Zelaya, the unspeakable carrion who had been openly hostile after the United States jilted Nicaragua and placed its canal in Panama.

Thereafter the small U.S. military presence had facilitated the Conservative electoral victories of Emiliano Chamorro in 1916 and of his uncle Diego Chamorro in 1920. Before the 1916 voting, for example, Admiral William Caperton had sat down with Liberal presidential candidate Julián Irías to explain the facts of life. After he had done so, the admiral reported that "Mr. Irias was so well convinced that he would not make a good candidate that he announced at that time that he would withdraw from the candidacy, and also would not allow any one of his party to run." (Caperton explained that Irías was "a general disturber and agitator, and a man of not very enviable reputation.")[47]

A few years earlier, in 1922, Dana Munro had told Secretary Hughes that "because of the presence of the Marines the party in power has been able in three successive presidential elections to compel the election of its own candidate without regard to the fact that the opposition party probably had the support of a majority of the voters." And like in the Dominican Republic, here in Nicaragua Munro emphasized that "the intervention of the American Government has aroused suspicion and alarm in other Caribbean countries and has subjected the United States to vicious attacks throughout Latin America." The proper course for Washington, he advised, was to arrange for "the installation of a government which will no longer be weakened by the fact that it is maintained in power by a foreign armed force."[48]

That would require eleven years of improving Nicaraguan politics. As historian Bryce Wood would gently comment, "The Department had trouble in fulfilling its announced intention of helping the Nicaraguans to learn how to run their country."[49]

One major complexity not seen in the Dominican Republic was the long-standing tension among Central Americans, where almost a century of boundary disputes and a miscellany of other conflicts and personal ambitions had led to fairly frequent cross-border meddling and regional turmoil. As noted in Chapter 3, in 1907 the Roosevelt administration and Porfirio Díaz's Mexico had jointly invited the five governments to iron out their differences in Washington, and that meeting had produced the Central American Court of Justice to adjudicate government-to-government disputes. Unable to serve that purpose, it had been disbanded in 1918.

Then in late 1922 the State Department's fresh thinkers convinced Secretary Hughes to try again—to invite Central American leaders to Washington for a "Conference on Central American Affairs." With State's officials looking over their shoulders, the delegates produced a General Treaty of Peace and Amity, the second article of which stipulated that none of the five governments would "recognize any other Government which may come to power in any of the five Republics through a *coup d'etat* or a revolution against a recognized Government." While not a signatory, the United States announced it would abide by this stipulation as well.[50]

Meanwhile, Nicaragua's fiscal stability had been achieved thanks to the strong international demand for coffee and tropical lumber, and a decade of government frugality had been assured by the U.S. customs collector (to provide income) and the U.S.-dominated "High Commission" (to control expenses). But Nicaragua was still deeply impoverished. Two-thirds of the country's 640,000 inhabitants remained illiterate, with an estimated per capita annual income of $40, which would be about $450 in 2018 dollars.[51]

It was in this context that the State Department set out to create a legitimate government that could stand on its own two feet, without the Marines. Such a government would have to be the product of a fair election, and helping Nicaraguans hold one was about to become a memorable lesson in the frustrations of uplifting.

THERE WAS TROUBLE from the beginning. The withdrawal process had begun in late 1920, after outgoing president Emiliano Chamorro had supervised the election won by his uncle, Diego Chamorro. The president-elect was informed that the United States considered his victory to have been fraudulent and would not recognize his government without a firm promise to enact a new fraud-proof electoral law and use it to conduct a fair election in 1924. Diego Chamorro provided the requested assurance and agreed to hire a U.S. expert to write the required law.[52]

The State Department had in mind Harold Dodds, then secretary of the National Municipal League, who had already helped conduct two earlier Nicaraguan elections, neither of them fair. Now he returned to prepare more detailed legislation stipulating how the 1924 contest should be conducted, step by step, from voter registration to ballot counting. Although Nicaragua's Conservative-dominated Congress preferred the existing law, which from its perspective had yielded satisfactory results, U.S. pressure led to its replacement by Dodds's proposal.[53]

Then came implementation, and the Hughes State Department believed Nicaragua needed help with that also. This was made clear in September 1923, when Secretary Hughes spoke with Nicaragua's ambassador in Washington, former president Emiliano Chamorro. He had come to bid Hughes farewell before returning home to campaign for another term. Hughes suggested to Chamorro "that it might be well to ask Mr. Dodds [to] assist the authorities of Nicaragua in putting the law into effect," emphasizing that "it was the desire of the United States to aid the Nicaraguan Government in having an election which would be so fair and free that the people would be contented with the result." Hughes also offered U.S. assistance with "establishing an efficient constabulary to maintain order after the marines had withdrawn."[54]

The story about the 1924 election and what followed need only be summarized here. The trouble began when the U.S. minister, John Ramer, reported that President Bartolomé Martínez (uncle Diego Chamorro had died) had decided to be a candidate and "will not want American observers here at the time of elections." However, he would not object to a preelection visit so that Dodds and a few of his associates could teach poll workers how to implement the new law, nor would he object to the creation of an apolitical constabulary, but at the moment Nicaragua could not afford to do so. That early 1923 response triggered a full year of nudging, which became significantly more vigorous when Washington instructed one of the legation's junior officers, Walter Thurston, to devote full-time to ensuring a fair election.[55]

Here was the beginning of a distinguished career; one of the diplomatic reception rooms on the State Department's eighth floor eventually was named in Thurston's honor. Determined to prove his mettle, Thurston nudged on every issue, but in the end he reported that the election "was preceded by such sustained governmental pressure and violence . . . as to render the published statements of the result unworthy of acceptance."[56] "Astonishing" is how he described abuses such as occurred in San Juan del Norte, where the defeat of President Martínez's candidate prompted another election in which a 25-to-70 loss was turned into a 41-to-27 win. Forwarding to Washington what may be the most comprehensive set of election reports ever sent from Latin America, Thurston concluded that "the election just held constitutes merely another example of the inevitable triumph of the Central American official candidates."[57]

He initially advised Washington not to recognize the putative winner, Conservative Carlos Solórzano, who had run on a coalition ticket with Liberal vice president candidate Juan Sacasa, and had been opposed by a purely Conservative ticket led by former President Emiliano Chamorro. Then the young envoy reconsidered: "Unfortunately, the fundamental political and other defects of the Central American made the elaboration of an electoral law to be applied by the Nicaraguans almost a hopeless task, since no matter what agency for its execution should be chosen that agency undoubtedly would be viciously partisan."[58]

In other words, Nicaraguans had done as well as could be expected, and division chief Francis White agreed: the 1924 election "was probably in fact as fair as any which has occurred in Nicaragua during the last thirty years." If Nicaragua was to have a truly fair election, it would have to be conducted by the United States, and lame-duck Secretary Hughes quickly ruled that out because it would require armed intervention, which "is not to be contemplated."[59]

AS AN ALTERNATIVE, Francis White recommended recognition of the Solórzano government on the condition that it allow the United States to conduct the next election, in 1928. In the meantime, Secretary Hughes demanded that "immediately upon assuming office he will form a constabulary . . . for which he will request the assistance of this Government in its training and organization." The president-elect agreed.

Minister Ramer then attended Solórzano's inauguration, signifying recognition, and within six months a Guardia Nacional had been formally authorized and a U.S. Marine had signed a contract to serve as "Chief of the Constabulary and of the School of Instruction of the National Guard," assisted by four additional Marines. The first of the five arrived in early July and Washington's legation guard left two months later, in August 1925.[60] So did Minister Ramer, replaced by Charles Eberhardt, a career official.

The new envoy had only three weeks to unpack his bags before the commander of Managua's garrison, a Conservative ally of Emiliano Chamorro, "forcibly carried off to the [military garrison at La] Loma as prisoners Doctor Román y Reyes, Minister of Hacienda, two editors and several other men of alleged strong Liberal tendencies who were further alleged to be unduly influencing and coercing President Solórzano."[61] The besieged president asked the U.S. legation for a show of counterforce, and a Navy warship promptly dropped anchor at Corinto. Its captain and a few aides traveled inland to Managua, and Eberhardt reported that their presence was all it took to stop "temporarily at least the tendency toward anarchy and revolution."[62]

Temporary it was. Apparently convinced that if he wanted something done right he had to do it himself, former president Emiliano Chamorro then launched his own rebellion. Minister Eberhardt warned him that "any government assuming power by force would not be recognized," only to learn that Chamorro had found a way around this threat by establishing himself as the power behind the throne: "President Solórzano has agreed to virtually all the demands of General Chamorro," Eberhardt reported, and that "included purging offensive Liberals from Congress and designating Chamorro as 'General in Chief of the Army.'" Shed of eighteen Liberals, the Conservative Congress promptly impeached the Liberal vice president, Sacasa, who had violated the constitution by fleeing for his life without congressional approval. All the while Chamorro increased pressure upon Solórzano until he handed over the presidency.[63]

As it had threatened, the Coolidge administration refused to recognize Chamorro, but it also refused to help Vice President Sacasa, Solórzano's constitutional successor, who twice traveled to Washington in search of support. "I received him," Secretary Kellogg said, but told Sacasa that "they themselves must work out their own destiny." When Sacasa tried again three months later, he was told that the United States would not approve of any military activity aimed at the overthrow of the Chamorro government.[64]

Assailed by Nicaragua's Liberals and unrecognized by the United States, Chamorro held out until late 1926, then sailed for France, replaced by another Conservative, former president Adolfo Díaz, whom the United States had placed in office from 1912 to 1916. Now, a decade later, he was slipped into office by a Congress purged of its Liberals and encouraged by U.S. Minister Eberhardt. A special envoy, Henry Stimson, would soon write that "we know no other Nicaraguan whom we could trust to so cooperate."[65]

Obviously uncomfortable when left to his own devices, Díaz waited fewer than twenty-four hours before inviting the Marines to return. Meanwhile, Juan Sacasa, having turned to Mexico for assistance after Washington's refusal, was setting up a rival government on Nicaragua's Atlantic coast. "Intervention is absolutely necessary," cabled the local U.S. consul. "If the Díaz Government is overthrown American interests and the people of Nicaragua have to face several years of revolution degenerating into banditry. . . . I cannot emphasize too strongly that unless action is taken immediately foreign interests will face certain ruin."[66]

The Marines were back in Managua and Washington was back where it had been in 1911. "It took me from 1922 to 1926 to get the Marines out of Nicaragua," complained State's Francis White; "I then went to Spain for a few months and some incident arose and whoever was handling the matter . . . sent the Marines back again and it took me from 1927 to 1933 to get them out again."[67]

VIEWED FROM A twenty-first-century perspective, it is difficult to understand this high level of U.S. involvement. Why not simply send a ship, load the Marines, and sail away? Why did anyone care who governed Nicaragua, or how that leader had been selected?

Critics at the time argued that the Marines had landed to protect U.S. investors, and President Coolidge made these critics appear correct. "The obligations flowing from the investments of all classes of our citizens in Nicaragua, place us in a position of peculiar responsibility [and] it has always been and remains the policy of the United States in such circumstances to take the steps that may be necessary for the preservation and protection of the lives, the property, and the interests of its citizens."[68]

That said, it is still difficult to understand why President Coolidge risked lives, spent money, and invested political capital to protect a few dozen small businesses. A 1927 State Department estimate was that U.S. citizens had invested about $7 million in "tangible property" in Nicaragua, plus $3 million in government bonds. The $7 million represented 0.1 percent of an estimated $5.671 billion in U.S. investments in all of Latin America, and in Nicaragua that small amount was spread out among dozens of small businesses.[69]

Yet each of the several dozen investors had at least three members of Congress to contact, many of whom asked the State Department to respond to their constituents' pleas for assistance. There are State Department files about the J. S. Otis Mahogany Company, the Astoria Importing and Manufacturing Company, and the A. W. Tedcastle Company, a Bluefields-based shoemaker. Entirely typical was the problem of Bonanza Mines, whose president complained to rebel leader Juan Sacasa (with a copy to the local U.S. military commander) that "we have lost in operation several thousand dollars through the closing down of the mines." Supplies valued at $325 had been removed from the company store, cattle theft and other depredations had cost the company $3,810, and forced conscription was driving his workers into hiding—"to absent themselves from our work for days at a time."[70]

"They are a pampered lot of people," complained the Hoover administration's secretary of state in 1931. "The American interests on the east coast [of Nicaragua] have got to be so that they feel they have a right to call for troops whenever any danger apprehends." In his view, "the threat of the bandits there was exaggerated."[71]

IT IS WORTH noting that the $3 million in bonds involved the bigger fish from Wall Street. In 1933 the U.S. customs receiver would calculate that two decades of Washington's cooperation had helped U.S. banks realize a $2 million profit in Nicaragua, which was hardly an insignificant amount.[72] But unlike the small investors, there is little evidence of bondholders asking for Washington's assistance—after all, a U.S. citizen was still collecting the country's taxes and a U.S.-dominated High Commission was still controlling the revenue's distribution, and it appears that Wall Street had independently decided the Marines were more trouble than they were worth. "In the overwhelming majority of business transactions, we rely upon the ability and the willingness of the debtor to pay. On no other principle could modern business be conducted," wrote banker Dwight Morrow in 1927. "When we need the sheriff to help collect a loan, we recognize that our venture has turned out a failure."[73]

To appreciate the change reflected in that comment, we need to go back a decade to 1916, just before the United States entered World War I. That was when Wall Street, still becoming comfortable with foreign sovereign debt, asked the State Department to inspect a proposed loan contract with the government of Argentina. The State Department had replied that "it will be happy to examine such a contract and to express, by reason of the information at its disposal, its approval or disapproval." But by 1922 the Harding / Hughes State Department had decided not to promote or even to evaluate U.S. bank loans to foreign governments, and that pleased the most influential banker in the United States: "If our government undertakes to pass upon the goodness of a loan, even in a minute degree, does it not inaugurate a system of responsibility to which there may be no termination except by the assumption of full responsibility? Once regulation, supervision, or control is attempted, there is no limit to which it may develop and no limit to the responsibility which our government may ultimately be called upon to assume."[74]

A year later, in 1923, the State Department began to say "no objection" to any proposed loan, and when failure to object came to be interpreted as approval, in 1929 State switched to new boilerplate: "The Department is not interested in the proposed financing."[75]

Perhaps most important, some extremely influential U.S. voices no longer thought of forcible debt collection as an issue of making or losing money, but an ethical issue of right and wrong. In 1927, when banker Dwight Morrow published his article about "the immorality of putting human lives to the hazard of modern war where the sole issue is a pecuniary claim," Morrow's partner, Thomas Lamont, the managing director of J. P. Morgan, was asked if he agreed. He did: "The theory of collecting debts by gunboats is unrighteous, unworkable and obsolete. While I have, of course, no mandate to speak for my colleagues of the investment banking community, I think I may safely say that they share this view with Mr. Morrow and myself."[76]

Taking this cue from Wall Street, during the Depression the State Department would encourage bankers to create a private organization, the Foreign Bondholders Protective Council, to negotiate debt relief and to revise payment schedules. Any bondholder who requested State Department assistance during the Franklin Roosevelt years received a form letter in response: "It is the long-established policy of this Government to consider difficulties in regard to foreign securities as primarily matters for negotiation and settlement between the parties directly in interest, acting through agencies of their own." The Department emphasized that the Protective Council "functions entirely independently of the Government" and directed bondholders to the Council's offices at 10 Wall Street.[77]

Back to 1927: "Don't blame the bankers," insisted democracy doctor Harold Dodds; "they have acted, oftimes reluctantly, at the request of the State Department. And don't believe that the United States marines are in Nicaragua to protect bankers' investments."[78]

SO IF NEITHER a vocal handful of small investors nor a collection of powerful bankers was driving U.S. policy, what motivated President Coolidge to say the following in a special message to Congress? "I have deemed it my duty to use all powers committed to me to insure the adequate protection of all American interests in Nicaragua, whether they be endangered by internal strife or by outside interference in the affairs of that Republic."[79] The answer was that American interests were being threatened not by internal strife but by outside interference. That meant Mexico.

Two years earlier, in 1925, the Mexican government of Plutarco Calles had seized Washington's full attention as it began to write the implementing legislation called for in Article 27 of its 1917 Constitution—legislation related to the ownership of natural resources of major importance both to powerful U.S. economic interests and to the overall U.S. economy.[80] This property conflict would now dictate the Coolidge administration's policy toward Nicaragua, and it had the effect of stirring up a hornet's nest of anti-imperialists who until now were focused on U.S. policy toward Mexico.

Before Mexico, the anti-imperialists' opposition had focused on the Progressives' protectorates, first almost exclusively on the Philippines. But by 1920, presidential candidate Warren Harding had tapped into this lingering anti-imperialism by criticizing FDR's comments about Haiti. That probably explains why Haiti was the early focus in the Harding years, when the Senate Committee on Foreign Relations created a special subcommittee to examine U.S. policy toward that country and the neighboring Dominican Republic. It visited both countries in 1922 and produced a mildly critical report that one member of the committee, anti-imperialist Senator William King, considered too weak to sign; instead, he introduced a resolution to cut off the Navy's funds for the occupation of the Dominican Republic, Haiti, and Nicaragua. It was defeated by a margin of 43 to 9, but the battle line was clearly drawn by Senator William Borah, who insisted that "we ought to get out of Haiti and out of every place where we have no right."[81]

Now it is important to emphasize that many Progressives who called themselves anti-imperialists also had a long history as "trust busters," known for their insistence that the government break up near-monopolies in major industries, especially steel and petroleum. As a result, some anti-imperialists were almost automatically prepared to applaud Mexico's Article 27. They especially applauded the fact that it threatened their *bête noir,* Standard Oil, by far the largest investor in Mexican oil fields. They saw Standard as the leader of a band of greedy capitalists who were draining Mexico of its natural resources, not much different from the greedy Spanish who had walked off with the Aztecs' gold.

At the center of this Mexico-focused opposition in the 1920s was the anti-imperialist Committee on Cultural Relations with Latin America, which invented the idea of doing in Mexico what the leaders of Witness for Peace would do in Central America in the 1980s—taking U.S. citizens on "people-to-people" exchanges so that they could see for themselves how the Mexican government was committed to using its revenues, including those from petroleum, to help the poor. "A Cooperative Study of Mexican Life and Culture" is what they called each delegation, most of whose participants were extremely active members of mainstream Protestant denominations who would write op-eds and visit their members of Congress. (The Committee's director was Hubert Herring, a Congregational minister.) Many brought back to the United States a strong sympathy with the reformist goals of the Mexican revolution.[82]

So when Mexico became involved in Nicaragua, supporting Liberal Juan Sacasa while the United States supported Conservative Adolfo Díaz, the Mexico-focused anti-imperialists shifted their attention to Nicaragua, and took on an entirely unprecedented role in U.S. policy toward Latin America.

NOW HERE IN 1927, when President Coolidge was speaking about ensuring "the adequate protection of all American interests in Nicaragua," Washington's two-decades-long disapproval of Nicaragua's Liberals was ancient history; no one cared which party held power. Instead, the administration cared about Mexico.

Just before President Coolidge delivered his message, which had been drafted by the State Department, Undersecretary of State Robert Olds warned Secretary Kellogg that "the main thing we have at stake in this controversy is our prestige. . . . We must decide whether we shall tolerate the interference of any other power (i.e. Mexico) in Central American affairs, or insist upon our own dominant position. If this Mexican maneuver succeeds it will take many years to recover the ground we shall have lost. The tangible evidence of our influence will have disappeared and notice will have been conveyed to all Central America, and to the rest of the world, that recognition and support by this Government means nothing." And, Olds added, "to all intents and purposes we are practically at war with Mexico now."[83]

The policy of withdrawing 107 Marines after helping Nicaraguans conduct a fair election was being transformed into a test of the worldwide credibility of U.S. foreign policy.

UNDERSECRETARY OLDS NEVER explained how he came to think as he did, but he was a Minnesota lawyer (one of Secretary Kellogg's partners) and knew little about foreign affairs and next to nothing about Latin America. So he had to have been influenced by someone. One bet would be James Sheffield, the cantankerous U.S. ambassador to Mexico (1924–1927) who was carrying on a running Article 27 battle with President Calles, but Sheffield was far away and not considered especially astute. A much better wager would be that Olds was reflecting the views of the State Department's career officers, fresh thinkers on many topics but clearly exasperated by the seemingly endless renegotiation of the U.S.-Mexican relationship, especially Mexico's recent abrogation of its 1923 Bucareli agreement, which they had labored to negotiate. It had addressed, if not resolved, most of the major problems posed by the Mexican Revolution and its 1917 Constitution.[84]

The renegotiation had begun years before Bucareli, when these fresh thinkers were not yet adults. In 1910 the otherwise friendly government of Porfirio Díaz had been perceived as a troublemaker in Central America. "Possibly we can do something to straighten things out by means of a financial control, such as that in San Domingo," diplomat Henry White had told Secretary of State Knox, "but I am afraid that Mexico, whose conduct towards us is not easy to understand, except on the basis of aspiration to territorial extension in those parts, may be counted upon as hostile and likely to thwart, as far as she can, any efforts of ours in that direction."[85] Then the Revolution began, and Mexicans could pay little attention to Central America.

In late 1926, a few weeks before Undersecretary Olds warned Secretary Kellogg that Mexico was undermining the credibility of U.S. foreign policy, an assistant chief of the Latin America division, Stokely Morgan, sent a warning memo that triggered the undersecretary's concern: "There is good reason to believe that the Mexican Government now hopes to set up Governments in the five Central American countries which will be not only friendly but subservient to Mexico and completely under Mexican domination."[86] It appears that once these midlevel officials had seen Mexico's support of Nicaragua's Juan Sacasa, they ballooned that fact into a test of U.S. credibility, and apparently deputized Morgan to serve as the link between their Latin America division and senior State Department officials. And they tweaked the information he passed along. One memo downplayed fraud in the most recent Nicaragua election (the one Thurston had observed in 1924), telling Olds that "the elections were orderly but not as free as could have been wished." The takeaway for any uninformed reader: suboptimal but acceptable. Similarly, Morgan wrote that in 1912 Adolfo Díaz had "assumed the presidency," without writing what Olds may not have known: that Díaz had been imposed by Washington and, lacking a domestic constituency, had been kept in office by the Marines. Morgan's key point now: the ouster of Adolfo Díaz by Sacasa's forces "will be looked upon throughout Latin America as a back-down inspired by fear of Mexico."[87]

That is exactly what Undersecretary Olds then told Secretary Kellogg.

OLDS ALSO CALLED in reporters from the three major wire services for an off-the-record explanation of why the Marines were returning to Managua: the side supported by Mexico was challenging the side supported by the United States. That made Nicaragua immensely important because "the Mexican government today is a Bolshevist government."

After dropping this bombshell, Olds quickly added that "we cannot prove it, but we are morally certain that a warm bond of sympathy, if not actual understanding, exists between Mexico and Moscow." When the three reporters asked permission to attribute Olds's assertion to the State Department or to any administration official, named or unnamed, Olds replied: "Surely you must realize why the department cannot afford to be in the position of directing such a serious statement against a government with which it is officially on friendly terms."

Olds's gambit did not simply fail—it also shifted the focus from Nicaragua and Mexico to the Coolidge administration's attempt to manipulate the media. "The press was in a fury," reported the State Department's principal press officer, as complaints "poured in from all sides. . . . It took weeks of the most careful work before the clamor aroused by these episodes had died away."[88]

The reference to "these episodes"—a plural—is because Olds's off-the-record statement to the press was only the beginning. Next came a thirty-three-page primer, written by the no-longer-fresh thinkers in the Latin America division and intended for use in public statements by administration officials. It featured a section titled "The Radical Tendencies of President Calles," who "has been called a bolshevist, a follower of Carl [sic] Marx, and the most dangerous man in the future of Mexico. He and [his predecessor Álvaro] Obregón have been accused of ambition to annihilate wealth, put the state in the hands of red organization, destroy property rights, and socialize all the economic resources of the country. . . . In fact, it has been stated of him that he is a much redder bolshevist than Lenin ever was."[89]

Next President Adolfo Díaz fired off a letter to the New York Times: "We need the cooperation and aid of foreign experts and enterprise for our financial, economical and cultural development, [and] for these elements, unlike the Liberals, we [Conservatives] do not look to Mexico, now in a state of chaos, but to the United States, the foremost nation in the world."[90]

This was published a day before President Coolidge sent his special message to Congress, formally outing Mexico: "I have the most conclusive evidence that arms and munition in large quantities have been on several occasions since August, 1926, shipped to the revolutionists in Nicaragua [and] some of the munitions bear evidence of having belonged to the Mexican Government." Mexico City's Excelsior, a semiofficial voice of the Calles government, did not deny the charge; instead it asked, "Can only the United States legitimately provide aid to the government of another nation, and is Mexico prohibited from doing the same thing?"[91]

President Coolidge's statement was followed two days later by Secretary Kellogg's appearance before the Senate Committee on Foreign Relations, where he conceded that the United States "can, of course, withdraw its marines and let the revolutionists run over the country receiving help of Mexico and destroying American property and lives and endangering the lives of American citizens but, so far as I am concerned, I am not in favor of such a policy." He left committee members with a memorandum, "Bolshevist Aims and Policies in Mexico and Latin America."[92]

This blitz only intensified Washington's already-tense relationship with Mexico, while doing little to reduce domestic U.S. opposition to the Marines' redeployment. Instead, the press was now giving Nicaragua close attention. And, of course, once President Coolidge had sent his special message to Congress, every subsequent move had become a question of the president's personal credibility at home, plus the broader question of the credibility of U.S. foreign policy abroad. Was the administration going to prevail or not?

Pushing from below, the State Department's Latin Americanists insisted that senior officials had no choice but to hold firm, even when Mexico's ally, Juan Sacasa, offered to discuss the selection of a new interim president who would be neither himself nor Adolfo Díaz, to be followed by the election of a new president. Any such discussion "will be looked upon throughout Latin America as a back-down inspired by fear of Mexico and forced by anti-American criticism throughout the world.[93] So wrote Stokely Morgan.

HERE IS THE only time in U.S. history that a problem involving Latin America appears to have unhinged a secretary of state, who was seeing his effort to withdraw 107 Marines mushroom into Heaven only knows what. "I fear a complete nervous breakdown," begins the diary entry of one of Kellogg's closest advisers, William Castle, shortly after Olds's bombshell and two weeks before Kellogg's testimony to Congress. "The Secretary is wildly inaccurate, intolerably rude, unwilling to read memoranda or to listen to an oral statement. . . . He thinks he bears on his shoulders the whole burden of the Department, complains that no one gives him any support or assistance and totally fails to grasp the fact that we are the only people who accomplish things by getting him, often with difficulty, to sign what we have prepared."

"This place is really just a mad house," Castle continued after Kellogg's appearance before the Senate. "The Secretary is in a continual state of temper, can decide nothing, take no reasonable action, at least by his own volition. He is in the opposition no matter what question is brought up." Castle's fear was that "he is in danger at any time of making an awful blunder and getting us really into hot water. I talked over the situation very earnestly with [White House aide] Ted Clark this morning and he promised to urge the President to *order* Mr. Kellogg to go away for a rest. He tells me that Mrs. Kellogg says life at home is almost intolerable." Meanwhile, "a ship without any rudder" is how Castle described the State Department. "Yesterday morning he behaved like a wild man."

"Shortly after this," wrote Kellogg's biographer, "the President practically ordered Kellogg out of Washington."[94]

Then in what should be interpreted as a slap on the wrist of the State Department's Latin Americanists, President Coolidge dipped into the private sector and asked the Taft administration's secretary of war, Henry Stimson, to serve as a special representative to Nicaragua. A few months later the Senate unanimously approved a resolution urging the administration to arbitrate the dispute with Mexico.[95] Seeing the political handwriting on the wall—the unanimity—the president tapped another outsider, Wall Street investment banker Dwight Morrow, to resolve the Article 27 property dispute with Mexico.

It did not take long for the low-keyed Morrow to earn his reputation as one of the most effective negotiators ever sent to Latin America.[96] But Mexico was not Nicaragua, where Stimson simply blurted out an ultimatum:

> I am authorized to say that the President of the United States intends to accept the request of the Nicaraguan Government to supervise the elections of 1928; that the retention of President Díaz during the remainder of his term is regarded as essential to that plan and will be insisted upon; that a general disarmament of the country is also regarded as necessary for the proper and successful conduct of such an election; and that the forces of the United States will be authorized to accept the custody of the arms of those willing to lay them down including the government and to disarm forcibly those who will not do so.

Facing sixteen hundred Marines and more if needed, most Nicaraguan leaders agreed to proceed as Stimson directed.[97]

Leaving others to implement this agreement, Stimson returned home and almost immediately published *American Policy in Nicaragua,* a slender book emphasizing that "the United States, ever since we recognized their independence, has in many ways endeavored to lend its assistance to the five Central American countries in their progress along the difficult road to orderly self-government." In a chapter titled "Efforts of the United States to Assist in the Purification of Elections and the Discouragement of Revolution," Stimson noted that in 1920 the State Department "began to use its influence to try to reach the root of the evil and assist the Nicaraguans to purify their elections," and he predicted that U.S. supervision of the upcoming 1928 election "would assist that country in maintaining in the future an orderly and independent government."[98]

Meanwhile, the forces led by Liberal chieftain Augusto César Sandino continued fighting the Díaz government and began fighting the Marines. "A few months should see the end of the revolution," predicted Stokely Morgan; "it is not likely that we shall be compelled to keep twenty-five hundred men in Nicaragua during the entire two years" before the next election. Henry Stimson agreed: "While there will probably be resistance by small irreconcilable groups and scattered bandits, I believe that there will be no organized resistance to our action." The number of Marines grew, peaking at 5,673 in 1928, and historian Bryce Wood described the box into which the Coolidge administration had placed itself: for the next few years "the United States found itself engaged in a wide range of unexpected activities, from studying tax revenues and the interest rate on paving bonds to the dropping of bombs on bandits who were called Nicaraguan patriots elsewhere than in Washington."[99]

SANDINO WAS NEVER apprehended, but the hunt for him raised the anti-imperialists' ire to a level equaled only during the pacification of Filipinos at the turn of the century, and it rose to unseen levels when the Marines began aerial bombardments, widely condemned as indiscriminate attacks upon uninvolved peasants.

The left-leaning press was all but obsessed. After interviewing Sandino, Carleton Beals wrote several exceptionally critical articles for the *Nation,* and his book-length *Banana Gold* condemned "the apologists who drip greasy platitudes to oil the gun-carriages of our target-practice in Latin America."[100] Meanwhile, the Washington police were arresting protesters for picketing the White House without a parade permit, while the U.S. Post Office was banning the All American Anti-Imperialist League from placing stickers ("Protest Against Marine Rule in Nicaragua") on the envelopes of its mailings.

Back at his desk for a final year in office, Secretary Kellogg cabled Frank McCoy, the Army general now serving as the president's personal representative in Nicaragua: "There is a great deal of criticism in this country about the way in which these operations are being dragged out with constant sacrifice of American lives and without any concrete results. . . . People cannot understand why the job cannot be done, and frankly I do not understand myself."[101]

Meanwhile, members of Congress were raising the roof. Senator William King: "In the case of those poor, defenseless people in Nicaragua we send our armies down there and our airplanes, and we drop bombs upon their little villages and hamlets and destroy and kill and wound and burn." Then Senator George Norris: "They love their little children. They love their homes. We would call them hovels, but they are the best they have. We have burned them and destroyed them and killed some of their little children, killed some of their wives, killed some of their women, every one of whom was unarmed and not a single one of whom had ever raised a finger against us." And Senator Clarence Dill: "We, as a nation, have no legal or moral right to be murdering those liberty-loving people in a war of aggression."[102] Tiny Nicaragua had become a public relations nightmare.

Certainly there were senators who supported the administration, but the tide appeared to have turned by early 1929, when the Senate voted 38 to 30 to prohibit the Navy from deploying its Marines in Nicaragua, a sharp reversal of the 9-to-43 defeat of a similar proposal in 1922. That victory was brief—the Senate reversed itself the next day, with some of the initial 38 agreeing that it would be a good idea to allow President-elect Herbert Hoover some time to solve the problem.[103] Hoover had visited Nicaragua in a post-election trip to Latin America, and had already made clear his view: it was time to bring the Marines home.

AS ALL THIS was occurring in Washington, Nicaragua's small existing army—a jumble of forces but primarily the U.S.-trained constabulary—was being replaced by a National Guard, also to be organized and trained by U.S. officers. Soon a U.S. envoy reported that "there is a nucleus of an organization in Nicaragua in which the United States can take great satisfaction. It is the *Guardia Nacional*. Colonel E. R. Beadle is an officer of unusual ability."[104] Beadle could not stay in command forever, and during his 1927 assignment Henry Stimson had identified Beadle's replacement: "Somoza is a very frank, friendly, likable young Liberal and his attitude impresses me more favorably than almost any other."[105]

The uplifting continued amid chaos. In mid-1927 the Coolidge administration announced that "it will be necessary to establish a commission to supervise the elections [to be held in 1928]" and that "it has been agreed [with puppet President Adolfo Díaz] that the chairman of this commission should be an American nominated by the President of the United States." Two additional members would be Nicaraguans, one Conservative and one Liberal, but the two could not meet without the chairman, Army general Frank McCoy.[106] The State Department also contracted with democracy doctor Harold Dodds to draw up yet another electoral law. It would replace temporarily the law Dodds had drawn up in 1923–1924.

An election was held with the Marines supervising the voting and with the U.S.-approved Board of Elections counting and certifying the ballots. On January 1, 1929, Conservative Adolfo Díaz handed the presidential sash to Liberal José María Moncada. Two months later, Calvin Coolidge handed the White House to Herbert Hoover, who asked Henry Stimson to serve as his secretary of state. The Marines were not brought home until early 1933, a few weeks before the end of President Hoover's term and a few weeks after President Moncada had handed the presidential sash to Juan Sacasa. That was when Secretary of State Henry Stimson wrote the words that are quoted in the epigraph for this chapter.[107]

AS A RESEARCHER sifts through the documents from the 1920s, trying to identify a pattern, it eventually becomes obvious that the State Department's fresh thinkers never had much of a commitment to normalize relations with the countries of the Caribbean region. Their commitment was to overcome an obstacle to good relations with the rest of Latin America and a commitment to mollify public opinion in the United States.

In the process, the fresh grew stale. The original plan for a policy more in tune with the times was voiced best by Francis White in 1924, soon after returning from his post in Argentina: "We will get better results if we do not make long pronouncements but let the natives work out their solution as best they can with of course help and assistance from our diplomatic representatives." Then came the dreary slog, a full decade of Washington's help and assistance, and by 1930 White had forgotten what he had learned in Buenos Aires: "As soon as South America realizes that our Central American policy is not a South American one, it will cease to care what we do in Central America. True, Central America may object, but I think they simply have got to lump it."[108] Herbert Hoover and Franklin Roosevelt had their work cut out for them.

CHAPTER 5

Pledging to Be a Good Neighbor

> Our duty is plain as the Ten Commandments. Kindness,
> beneficence, assistance, aid, help, protection, all that is implied in
> good neighborhood.
>
> —Senator Charles Sumner, 1870

THE OTHER FRANKLIN beat Franklin Roosevelt to the punch, and by about eight decades. "In regard to the American Republics," President Pierce had told Congress, "it has been my constant aim strictly to observe all the obligations of political friendship and good neighborhood."

Presidents have a penchant for such statements, but as expressions of ideals rather than as descriptions of practice, and this particular president's biographer wrote that the policies of Franklin Pierce, a devout expansionist, "were but a fragment of a longer period"—the period of Manifest Destiny, to which the term "good neighbor" has never been applied. "The policy of my administration will not be controlled by any timid forebodings of evil from expansion," Pierce had promised in his 1853 inaugural address. "Indeed, it is not to be disguised that our attitude as a nation, and position on the globe render the acquisition of certain possessions, not within our jurisdiction, eminently important for our protection."[1]

When Progressives had expanded the definition of "neighbors" to include the weaker peoples of the Caribbean and Central America, they had provided their helping hand with the conviction of missionaries, never doubting that these neighbors would welcome their assistance, perhaps not immediately but certainly once they saw how U.S. tutelage could improve their lives. With that belief guiding their behavior, they had created protectorates.

Then in 1920 a post–World War I electorate had selected a president who promised a return to "normalcy," and to Warren Harding, at least, it no longer seemed normal to hold the citizens of another country in semicaptive limbo, and the State Department was reporting that the Progressives' protectorates were damaging relations with the rest of Latin America. But except for exiting the Dominican Republic, which took a full four years, the glacier-slow dismantling of these protectorates was still under way in early 1929, when Calvin Coolidge left office after boasting, "No Congress of the United States ever assembled, on surveying the state of the Union, has met with a more pleasing prospect than that which appears at the present time. The country is in the midst of an era of prosperity more extensive and of peace more permanent than it has ever before experienced." Nodding in agreement was Coolidge's successor, Herbert Hoover, who selected "Four More Years of Prosperity" as his 1928 campaign slogan. His party's platform bragged that "never has the soundness of Republican policies been more amply demonstrated and Republican genius for administration been better exemplified than during the last five years."

One of the unluckiest of presidents, Hoover ranks just behind those who were shot. Apparently he never said "prosperity is just around the corner," as the Democrats claimed, but in his first annual message, six weeks after the October 1929 stock market panic, he told Congress that "the problems with which we are confronted are the problems of growth and of progress." Still upbeat six months later, he assured another Washington audience that "we have now passed the worst."[2] Six weeks later Congress passed the trade-smothering Smoot-Hawley tariff.

IN ADDITION TO his "we have now passed the worst" reassurance, President Hoover's first annual message provided Congress with the customary roundup of foreign policy issues, including an observation that U.S. Marines were still in charge of Haiti and Nicaragua but "we do not wish to be represented abroad in such manner."

In Nicaragua, 1,600 Marines were into their third year of chasing Sandino, training the Guardia Nacional, and serving as election monitors. That number was down significantly from 5,673 only a few months earlier, and

Hoover insisted, "We are anxious to withdraw them further as the situation warrants."[3]

The Coolidge administration had set the stage for an accelerated withdrawal by sending another money doctor, William Cumberland, who reported that "the financial condition of the Nicaraguan government is relatively satisfactory." Then he clearly wanted to get something off his chest: "The measure of intervention which has been exercised by the United States has even weakened the ability and the desire of Nicaraguans to solve their own problems; they choose to look to the United States for those things which they should do for themselves." Sixteen years of U.S. political and economic control had not simply been unproductive; they had been counterproductive. "The Nicaraguans should have the opportunity of making something of themselves."[4]

And if that was not possible, Cumberland continued, "the Department must contemplate a rather complete change of American personnel"—the people who still held Nicaragua's purse strings. The U.S.-controlled High Commission was "little more than a formality and performs almost no work," and the High Commissioner, Roscoe Hill, "is not one of which to be proud. He has little competence in finance, is contentious, interests himself in questions of local politics and does not properly represent the United States. He enjoys neither respect nor the confidence of the Nicaraguan government. In addition, he is grossly overpaid." The other U.S. financial supervisor, customs collector Clifford Ham, "has long passed the height of his usefulness and should be relieved. . . . It is general knowledge that Colonel Ham is overpaid, that he takes excessively long vacations and that his health is such that he performs comparatively little work."[5]

Atop that withering criticism came the problems that often accompany occupying armies, with the chief surgeon of the U.S. Red Cross hospital at Bluefields writing, "I am ashamed of the attitude that certain of the officials of our Navy have taken, apparently because of strongheadedness or from the effects of imbibing too freely of spirituous drinks, which have been far too commonly seen among officers and enlisted men." Another U.S. doctor submitted a formal complaint that "Lt. Commander Richardson was drunk while in uniform and on duty, and not only drunk, but disorderly and insulting." Additional messages to Washington included one asserting that a second Marine officer was "a boozer," another "was seen jumping the back fence of the residence of a married woman so he wouldn't be seen by her husband who had returned home unexpectedly," and an uncounted number of "Naval officers under the influence of drink, had been in the habit of taking young girls for walks along dark streets in the more sparsely settled parts of town."[6]

Because there were no opinion polls and Nicaraguans were never asked to cast a ballot expressing their view of the United States, we cannot know to what extent these bad apples spoiled the entire barrel. Nor do we know the extent to which Nicaraguans approved of anything else done by the United States during its two-decade occupation, where development assistance had been extremely modest—generally there had been only a handful of Marines in Nicaragua, whereas several thousand were available to organize and supervise infrastructure projects in both Haiti and the Dominican Republic.

As for that handful, General Frank McCoy had suggested that the Marines should remain for a brief period after the 1928 election, but only "to give the Guardia opportunity to develop into a thoroughly disciplined impartial body which will eschew politics and keep order."[7] Yet two years later Henry Stimson, now serving the new Hoover administration as secretary of state, was dismayed by the Guardia's inability to end Sandino's insurgency, telling President José María Moncada that "if reports are to be believed, they [the Guardia] have accounted for in killed, wounded and captured far more than the original force which Sandino led away three years ago. Yet . . . a new group of bandits seems to step into the shoes of the old . . . and the problem remains as difficult as ever."

President Moncada gently responded that Secretary Stimson "had not received all the pertinent information relating to the subject under discussion." Funding an army large enough to suppress Sandino's rebels "would mean the temporary suspension of public instruction and the temporary conclusion of all road building which would create a most aggravated unemployment problem and would cause untold discontent and unrest." Given President Hoover's position, Stimson had no choice but to concede and simply urge President Moncada to assign a high priority to paying the salaries of the Guardia, for "if troops are not regularly paid there is a possibility of mutiny and other disorders."

Although he ended this 1930 exchange with "my sympathetic desire to render you every possible assistance within my power," Stimson was already aware that the United States no longer had a line in its budget for Nicaraguans.[8] There had barely been enough money to grant President Moncada's request for another U.S. citizen to supervise Nicaragua's 1930 election for members of the legislature. With 767 U.S. military personnel serving as poll watchers, Navy captain Alfred Johnson reported that the election had been "free, fair and honest."[9]

All this seemed like 1920s business as usual, but the fact that U.S. troops were chasing Sandino made Nicaragua a special case, and a better flavor of Washington's Depression-era mood could be obtained in the Dominican Republic, which in 1930 was also preparing for an election. It was understood that General Rafael Trujillo would enjoy a landslide victory, given that he would be counting the ballots, but the Hoover administration's fear of walking into another quagmire led to this preemptive cable to the U.S. minister: "You are not authorized to suggest any United States participation in or even supervision of the elections. The last thing we want is to get in a situation where that would result."[10]

With Nicaragua an exception to that rule, President Hoover agreed to supervise one final election, the 1932 voting to select a president, with another Navy officer, Admiral Clark Woodward, serving as chair of Nicaragua's Board of Elections. The contest was won by Liberal Juan Sacasa, reviled in the 1920s because of his support by Mexico, but now perfectly acceptable. On the day of Sacasa's inauguration the Guardia was turned over to its first "Jefe Director," Anastasio Somoza, handpicked by the United States, and the last Marines were withdrawn in early 1933, two months before President Hoover left the White House. Admiral Woodward's final report ended with this advice: "That the Government of the United States seek, by every means possible, to avoid again becoming involved in a commitment of the nature of the three recent Supervisions of Elections in Nicaragua."[11]

THE SITUATION IN Haiti was different. There "we have about 700 marines," President Hoover had continued in his 1929 annual message. Saying that "it is a much more difficult problem the solution of which is still obscure," the new president asked Congress to fund a commission to identify an exit strategy. Its members visited Haiti for sixteen days, wrote a report that pointed with satisfaction at "notable material progress," including eight hundred miles of new roads, but also pointed with dissatisfaction at "the lack of appreciation on the part of the educated and cultured Haitians of the services rendered them by the Occupation." In fact, "out of many dozen witnesses only one or two made favorable mention of the achievements."[12]

President Hoover also appointed a second commission, this one to examine Haiti's educational system. It was chaired by Robert Moton, president of Tuskegee Institute, and reported on an impressive list of improvements, as did a delegation of six citizens who had visited Haiti in 1926 as representatives of organizations that "favor the restoration of the Independence of the Negro Republic." Separate chapters outlined progress in agriculture, health and sanitation, education, and public works. But at what cost? "In order to get roads built cheaply and quickly, the military authorities, in 1917, revived the legal but obsolete Haitian practise [*sic*] of forced labor." Workers "were sometimes manacled like slaves, compelled to work for weeks with little or no pay and inadequate food and shot down if they attempted to escape."[13]

Add up the pluses, subtract the minuses, and judge as you will. President Hoover judged that the Marines should be withdrawn, and the State Department responded by sending Dana Munro to Haiti. Munro's instructions were clear: "The President desires to reduce or withdraw the Marine brigade when such action can be taken without jeopardizing the peace. Meanwhile, in the exercise of your duties you will bear constantly in mind the fact that the primary purpose of the Government of the United States in its relations with Haiti is to assist the people of that country through friendly advice and through cooperation in administrative matters to eliminate political and financial instability." Munro was instructed to "avoid so far as possible any interference with the freedom of action of the Haitian Government," and, specifically, not object to any law it might produce "simply because you are not in full accord as to its wisdom."[14]

Here was an uncommonly good example of assigning a fox to guard the henhouse. A few days before leaving for Haiti, the new envoy spoke with Secretary of State Stimson, who wrote in his diary that Munro believed "it was vitally important that we should not leave Haiti, but that we should, through a new treaty after 1936, keep up the continuity of occupation and influence." Stimson added, "I am inclined to agree with Munro."[15]

That was the gist of a private conversation between two professional foxes who saw their prey disappear a month later, when President Hoover used his annual message to announce that the Marines would be out by the end of 1935. So Munro took only a few months to negotiate a transition accord, and he would later acknowledge that "the most important factor in the decision to withdraw from Haiti was President Hoover's dislike of military intervention. 'Anti-imperialist' criticism of our Caribbean policy in the United States had of course been influencing the policies of the State Department ever since 1921, but I don't believe that it had so much effect on Mr. Hoover as did his own personal convictions."

The last of the Marines would leave Haiti a year ahead of schedule, in 1934, but a U.S. "Financial Adviser–General Receiver" would remain to supervise the economy until the bonds had been repaid in 1941. Hans Schmidt's 1971 judgment has so far survived the test of time: "Haiti profited little from almost twenty years of direct and complete American control."[16]

OTHER THAN ATTENDING to the Nicaragua and Haiti protectorates, there is not much more to report about the Hoover administration's Latin America policy, uplifting or otherwise, and the Depression helps explain why.[17] In late 1932, soon after President Hoover had been defeated by Franklin Roosevelt, Secretary Stimson began preparing an end-of-term wrap-up. "During the years through which we have labored the task has been made infinitely more difficult by the world's economic distress, which many times and in many places has brought bitterness of spirit and destroyed hopefulness and good will." Among those many places was the White House. "How I wish I could cheer up the poor old President," Stimson had told his diary two years earlier, lamenting "the ever present feeling of gloom that pervades everything connected with the administration."[18]

And that was written a few days before Hoover's Republicans lost eight Senate seats and 52 House seats in the 1930 off-year election, the first of four consecutive contests in which Democrats gained 170 House seats—by 1937–1938 they would hold an astonishing 331 to 89 majority. After the votes had been counted, Stimson had walked over to the White House and assured a depressed Hoover that he would continue to do whatever he could to be helpful. "Almost pathetically he expressed his appreciation." A diary entry sixteen months later, in mid-1932: "The President is so absorbed with the domestic situation that he told me frankly that he can't think very much now of foreign affairs."[19] So with the 1932 presidential election just around the corner, Hoover's Republicans limited their platform's comment about Latin America to a promise of "frank and friendly understanding."

Franklin Roosevelt's rival Democrats promised "cooperation with nations of the Western Hemisphere to maintain the spirit of the Monroe Doctrine." Nobody seemed sure what that meant, and the absence of Latin America from the campaign suggests that inter-American relations was at or near the bottom of the electorate's list of things to worry about. But then in his inaugural address Roosevelt upped Hoover's nonintervention ante by pledging to "dedicate this nation to the policy of the good neighbor, the neighbor who resolutely respects himself and, because he does so, respects the rights of others." While that sentence was meant to characterize the new administration's foreign policy generally, Latin America is where the term "Good Neighbor" came to roost, perhaps because it had bipartisan appeal: in 1928 president-elect Hoover had used the term frequently during his preinauguration trip around Latin America—three times during the brief speech he had given at his first stop in Honduras.[20]

Regardless of its origin, "Good Neighbor" clearly hit a note Roosevelt liked. He would claim the seed had been planted in 1914, when he was serving as Woodrow Wilson's assistant secretary of the Navy and had been shocked by the bloodshed at Veracruz. Dictating to an aide (and using the third person when referring to himself), in 1942 FDR lamented that "many were killed on both sides and the bad feeling throughout Latin America created by this action lasted for a generation. The President has always believed that the germ of the Good Neighbor Policy originated in his mind at that time."[21]

If so, the germ had been slow to germinate. In 1917, three years after Veracruz, FDR had handed Smedley Butler a Medal of Honor for killing two hundred Haitian *cacos,* and as the Democrats' 1920 vice presidential candidate he had joked about writing Haiti's constitution, which his Navy had crammed down the throats of these neighbors. But by 1928 FDR was arguing that "single-handed intervention by us in the internal affairs of other nations must end," and in 1931, while Roosevelt was preparing a run for the presidency, an article written at his request insisted about Latin America in general what Hans Schmidt had insisted about Haiti: "None of the military interventions undertaken by the United States in the republics to the south has resulted in any permanent benefit either to the people of the state in question or to the people of the United States." That said, it was still the duty of the United States "to extend a friendly and helpful hand to its sister republics."[22]

THE MARINES' WITHDRAWAL from Latin America was all but complete when FDR began to draft his inaugural address, so there was no reason to dwell upon that. Far more important was evidence that the peoples of South America had joined the peoples of northern Latin America to seek assurance that the withdrawal was permanent. Here in early 1933 it was obvious to everyone that the United States versus Cuba or Haiti or Nicaragua or Mexico or Colombia or Panama or Venezuela or the Dominican Republic had now become the United States versus Latin America.

How different 1933 was from 1910, when the leader of the U.S. delegation to the Fourth International Conference of American States returned from Buenos Aires to report that the "representative men" from Brazil, Argentina, and Chile "have a contempt for the Central American countries, which they consider a disgrace to the very name of America, and anything which we can do, whether by occupation, protection or otherwise, to improve existing conditions in those countries will meet with their sympathy and approval."[23]

The fresh thinkers of the 1920s—the Sumner Welleses, Dana Munros, and Francis Whites—were not surprised when the "representative men" of those three South American countries were voicing a quite different position in 1923, when the Fifth International Conference of American States convened in Santiago, Chile. This meeting featured the first real debate in the history of these inter-American conferences, focusing on two issues. One was the right of the United States to dominate the Washington-based Pan American Union, which had choreographed the conference. (The U.S. secretary of state had always chaired the governing board, and its director had always been a U.S. citizen.) The second issue was far more significant: the right of Latin American countries to adjudicate investment disputes within their borders—the right to be sovereign.

Both issues had been triggered by South America's sympathy with a country of northern Latin America—Mexico—which was absent here in Santiago because it was engaged in a bitter dispute with U.S. investors. These investors had enlisted Washington's support, and here in 1923 the Harding administration was attempting to force Mexico to accept diplomatic negotiations to resolve a dispute Mexicans insisted on resolving in their courts. The tactic was to refuse to recognize the government of Álvaro Obregón; hence, Mexico had no ambassador in Washington when the governing board of the Pan American Union, which consisted of the Latin American ambassadors to the United States, drew up the agenda for the Santiago conference. As a matter of principle, Mexico refused to participate.

Although the conferees tinkered with the issue of reducing Washington's control over the Pan American Union, in 1923 the key resolution at Santiago was about U.S. intervention on behalf of its investors. Even though it was understood to be a divisive issue, Secretary of State Charles Evans Hughes

had instructed the chief of the U.S. delegation to say at the opening ceremony that "there are happily no controversies among us that can not be settled by the process of reason." But over the course of thirty-nine days, from
inaugural ceremony to closing session, the United States insisted on the right
of a government to intervene in another country on behalf of its citizens,
including its investors. Latin Americans were equally intransigent in their
support of a resolution that "every individual is subject to the laws and authorities of the State in which he resides [and] in no case may he pretend to
obtain other rights or exercise them in any other way than that determined
by the constitution and laws of the country."[24] Rather than destroy the
meeting, Latin Americans agreed to table their proposal.

This startling change between 1910 and 1923 can be explained in several
ways.

Perhaps Henry White's 1910 report had been based upon a skewed sample
of "representative men," when a more representative sample would have revealed the existence of South American hostility.

Or perhaps the change reflected Latin Americans' 1919 experience at Versailles, where the Big Four wrote the treaty ending World War I. Although
none of the Latin America countries qualified as what came to be known
technically as "effective participants," eight had declared war and five more
had severed relations with Germany. (The remaining seven, including Argentina, Chile, and Mexico, had been neutral.) All were welcome to attend
the 1919 conference at Versailles, because it was more than a meeting to stipulate the losers' punishment. It was also to create the League of Nations.

Most Latin American governments sent delegations, which had largely
been ignored.[25] That might have been expected, of course, because only
Brazil had participated in the war (and that in a modest way—patrolling
the South Atlantic), but Sumner Welles, who had been serving in Buenos
Aires during the Versailles negotiations, recalled that "those Latin American
countries which had joined the United States in the First World War were
profoundly resentful because of their exclusion from any real participation."
It was not even clear which conference participants were to attend the treaty's signing ceremony. When President Wilson insisted that all be included,
"the Latin-American delegates came up to me one at a time and expressed
their gratitude in very effusive terms." So wrote Secretary of State Lansing.
"It was almost pitiful to see how happy they were."[26]

For the neutrals, the formal signing turned out to be a statement about where they stood in the international pecking order. The Peace Conference produced a single document serving two purposes. The first 26 substantive articles of the Treaty of Versailles constituted the Covenant creating the League of Nations; the next 414 articles focused on Germany's punishment. Those Latin American countries that had not declared war could not sign the entire treaty, so after the twenty-six Covenant articles came an Annex for signatures of the "Original Members of the League of Nations," with two classes: the first class was "Signatories of the Treaty of Peace," followed by a second category of "States Invited to Accede to the Covenant."[27]

From the perspective of Latin America's neutrals, there should have been two separate treaties. As it was, several Latin American delegations, particularly those of Argentina and Chile, left Versailles with a bitter taste in their mouths. Rather than accept their status, they would use future conferences to insist upon their sovereign equality, and the first opportunity after Versailles was the 1923 inter-American conference at Santiago.

A third cause of the change in South American opinion between 1910 and 1923 appears to have been South Americans' belief that the United States had been abusive of northern Latin Americans during the intervening Taft and Wilson years, and now, here in 1923, the United States was twisting Mexico's arm on an issue, foreign investment, that ran counter to South American thinking—to the Calvo and Drago doctrines.

The situation had been much different in 1910, when the Marines had recently been withdrawn from Cuba, when the Dominican Republic still had an independent government, as did Haiti, and when there were no Marines in Nicaragua. Then after the 1910 meeting came the armed invasions of the Dominican Republic, Haiti, and Nicaragua, plus the series of disputes with Mexico, including the armed occupation of Veracruz. All of this appears to have affected the thinking of southern Latin Americans, who may have felt disrespected at Versailles but had never felt the sting of U.S. power. So in addition to the specific concern about Mexico's absence from the 1923 meeting at Santiago, South Americans were now voicing their opposition to U.S. Marines patrolling Latin American streets, to U.S. citizens collecting Latin Americans' taxes, and to U.S. uplifters "protecting" Latin Americans. It had become a question of Anglos bullying Hispanics.

PERHAPS MOST IMPORTANT, the opposition that surfaced between 1910 and 1923 was the product of a much longer gestation that had created an underlying theme of distrust. Many decades earlier, the 1836 Spanish translation of Tocqueville's *Democracy in America* had made this prediction about the northern borderlands where Anglo met Hispanic: "The people of the United States will penetrate into these solitary regions even sooner than those who have a right to occupy them. They will appropriate the soil and establish a society, so that when the legitimate owner finally arrives, he will find the wilderness cultivated and strangers quietly settled in his heritage. . . . Even the lands already peopled will have some difficulty in warding off invasion."[28]

Within a decade the United States had scooped up half of Mexico.

This was followed almost immediately by a small but prominent set of freelance filibusters intent upon seizing control of several countries in the Caribbean region, including more of Mexico, while U.S. politicians sympathetic to slavery were making no secret of their ambitions. In 1848, when the ink was not yet dry on the Treaty of Guadalupe Hidalgo, Mississippi senator Jefferson Davis demanded even more of Mexico. "I am ready, for one, to declare that my step will be forward, and that the cape of Yucatán and the island of Cuba must be ours." Davis had his eye on even more territory a decade later, in 1859: "We will advance our eagles until the tread of our columns shall be heard upon this whole continent, and the shadow of their wings shall be seen in all its parts."[29]

Mississippi representative George Brown was even more candid: "If I go for the acquisition of Cuba, or for any other territory in the South, let it be distinctly understood now, and through all time, that I go for it because I want an outlet for slavery." And when he moved up from the House to the Senate, he also moved on to more territory. "I want Tamaulipas, [San Luis] Potosí, and one or two other Mexican States; and I want them all for the same reason—for the planting or spreading of slavery."[30]

Brown was no anomaly; that is the way pre–Civil War Southerners talked, and Latin Americans heard them. In 1856, the year Tennessee's William Walker seized Nicaragua, Colombian José María Torres Caicedo drew a line between his people and the imperial ambitions of his Anglo neighbors:

La raza de la América Latina,
    Al frente tiene la sajona raza.

An unpoetic translation: "Confronting Latin Americans are the Anglo-Saxons." Apparently that was the first use of the term "Latin America." Us versus Them.[31]

While Tocqueville appears to have helped set the mood, and while the actions taken under the doctrine of Manifest Destiny had confirmed every word he had written, this was only the beginning. Then came the protectorates of the Progressive era, and Latin America's reaction was *arielismo,* a major force in the evolution of Latin Americans' view of the United States. Many Latin American intellectuals and their students began to think of their people as modern-day avatars of Ariel, the high-minded "airy spirit" in Shakespeare's *Tempest,* who was juxtaposed with the materialistic Caliban (the U.S.), son of an evil witch.

In May 1898, only days after the United States had declared war on Spain, Nicaraguan poet Rubén Darío, visiting the Southern Cone, published *El triunfo de Calibán* in Buenos Aires. It began:

> No, no I cannot be on the side of those buffaloes with silver teeth. They are my enemies, they are the haters of Latin blood. They are the barbarians. . . . From Mexico to Tierra del Fuego here is an immense continent where the old seed is fertile and prepares in its vital sap the future greatness of our race. Arriving from Europe, from the universe, is a cosmopolitan breath of fresh air which helps to invigorate our own forest. But here from the north come the railroads' tentacles, with steel arms and consuming maws. . . .
>
> There are people who say to me: Don't you see that they are the strong ones? Don't you know that by an inescapable law we ought to perish, swallowed or flattened by the colossus? Don't you recognize its superiority? Of course I see the mountain which forms the hump of the mammoth. But I am not going to put my head on the rock in front of Darwin and Spencer so that the great beast can smash my brains.[32]

Six years later, in 1904, shortly after the seizure of Panama, Darío wrote *To Roosevelt:*

> You are the United States
>   you are the future invader
>   of the naive America that has indigenous blood
>   that still prays to Jesus Christ and that still speaks Spanish.

Meanwhile, in 1900 Uruguayan essayist José Enrique Rodó had published his *Ariel*. Using the conceit of an academic lecture by Prospero, he warned Latin America's youth not to be swept up by the utilitarianism and material accumulation that characterized the United States—*nordomanía*. Prospero urged the rising generation to instead embrace "spiritual idealism."

Rodó's essay was a best-seller throughout Latin America, and two decades later, in the 1920s, Prospero's turn-of-the-century students were becoming the intellectual and political leaders encountered by U.S. envoys throughout Latin America—the type of people young diplomats such as Sumner Welles and Dana Munro would encounter at social gatherings in Argentina and Chile. These young Foreign Service Officers began arguing, as Dana Munro did, that "our efforts to help the Caribbean states had done us a great deal of harm in other parts of the hemisphere." In particular, the two-decade U.S. occupation of Nicaragua had "caused distrust and resentment in other American countries." Sumner Welles was saying the same thing about the eight-year takeover of the Dominican Republic. Any benefit to either the Dominicans or the United States had been "of infinitesimal importance when compared to the suspicions, fears, and hatred to which the Occupation gave rise throughout the American continent."[33]

The ideas of Latin America's Rodós and Daríos were spread to this emerging generation via the era's social media, particularly extended newspaper essays, and also via the original social medium, face-to-face contact. Nicaragua's Darío, for example, wrote and published his *Triumph of Caliban* during a stay in the Southern Cone, but a better example of this personal contact came two decades later, during Secretary of State Colby's 1920 goodwill trip to South America. The *New York Times* reported that the Dominican Republic's Francisco Henríquez y Carvajal had set out in advance, "heading a propaganda commission charging that the United States has committed atrocities in Haiti and Santo Domingo."

Henríquez y Carvajal had already established contact with South American delegations at the 1919 Versailles peace conference, and now, a year later, the *Times* continued, he was attempting "to persuade the South American republics to champion the islanders against the United States. Carvajal has just reached Buenos Aires, following trips to Rio [de] Janeiro and Montevideo, leaving his declarations fresh in the minds of each capital before Secretary Colby's arrival. Carvajal's mission has added to Latin hostility toward the United States."[34]

That was when presidential candidate Warren Harding was arguing that two decades of efforts to improve Latin Americans "have not only made enemies of those who should be our friends but have rightfully discredited our country as their trusted neighbor."

THOSE OFFICIALS WHO were not convinced at Santiago in 1923 simply had to observe the simmering hostility displayed by Latin American delegates in 1928 when they gathered in Havana for the Sixth International Conference of American States.

It came at the worst possible moment for the United States, when several thousand Marines were scouring Nicaragua for Sandino's forces and only a few months after President Coolidge had made no friends among Latin Americans by announcing that "the person and property of a citizen are a part of the general domain of the Nation, even when abroad. . . . The fundamental laws of justice are universal in their application. These rights go with the citizen. Wherever he goes these duties of our government must follow him."[35] Understandably, many Latin Americans translated Coolidge's "duties of our government" to mean "deployment of the Marines."

With an interpretation of Anglo-Hispanic relations stretching back to Tocqueville, personalized for Latin Americans by Darío and Rodó, and now verified both by the Marines chasing Sandino and by President Coolidge's policy announcement—with all that, Latin Americans arrived in Havana intent upon securing a formal prohibition of intervention. The U.S. delegates were instructed to respond that "the United States desires to assist the Latin American countries in every possible way acceptable to and desired by them, but it does not desire to urge its assistance upon them." While uplifting was available, "in no sense can it be contemplated that any of the American peoples should be in a state of tutelage."

Was the United States therefore prepared to accept a resolution prohibiting armed intervention? No. Stretching for a justification, the Coolidge-Knox State Department instructed its delegates to reply that any such commitment would infringe upon Congress's constitutional authority to declare war. The delegation was also prepared for another effort to reduce the U.S. dominance of the Pan American Union, probably with a resolution to move its headquarters from Washington to a site in Latin America. In response, U.S. delegates were told to point out "the advantages which the United States offers as a center of information on all subjects connected with the advancement of human knowledge and welfare."[36]

As it turned out, an "Exit Washington" movement never surfaced, leaving uninterrupted the advancement of human knowledge and welfare, and the U.S. delegation also believed it had fought off the effort to ban intervention, only to find the issue raised at the closing ceremony, when the chair of the committee on international law unexpectedly proposed a resolution that "no state has the right to intervene in the internal affairs of another." That forced the delegation chief, former secretary of state Charles Evans Hughes, to explain his government's opposition: "We do not wish to intervene in the affairs of any American Republic," he insisted, but "what are we to do when government breaks down and American citizens are in danger of their lives? Are we to stand by and see them butchered in the jungle?"[37]

It is difficult to conceive of a better example of two ships passing on a moonless night, with Latin Americans laser-focused upon Washington's armed intervention and with the U.S. delegation determined to send in the Marines should Latin American butchers point the cleavers at U.S. citizens. There was only agreement that a closing ceremony should not be the place for the ships to collide, and the resolution was withdrawn, exactly as at Santiago in 1923.

Then came the 1928 U.S. election, won by Herbert Hoover, who had been secretary of commerce from 1921 to 1928. Given a green light by Wall Street plus his own preferences drawn from a Quaker background, the new president waited only a few weeks to speak as if the Coolidge policy had never existed. Choosing an audience that included by special invitation all of Latin America's ambassadors, he insisted, "It never has been and ought not to be the policy of the United States to intervene by force to secure or maintain contracts between our citizens and foreign States or their citizens."[38]

Soon Secretary of State Henry Stimson was telling the press, "It is a matter of discretion with a government how far it will protect property when it is in danger in another country." The United States might not do so if protection clashes with "broader international or governmental policies." And, to take the current concern, the Hoover administration "will hesitate long before becoming involved in any general campaign of protecting with our forces American property throughout Nicaragua."[39] Obviously, the Stimson of 1932 was not the same Stimson sent by President Coolidge to Nicaragua in 1927.

On his list of the Hoover administration's achievements, Stimson placed "our national policy against the use of military pressure to collect business debts in foreign countries."[40]

IN 1923 THE delegates at Santiago had agreed to hold these conferences at five-year intervals—in 1928 at Havana and now at Montevideo in 1933, nine months after FDR's inauguration. This was the seventh such meeting, but the first where the U.S. delegation was led by the secretary of state, Cordell Hull, and everyone understood that the Good Neighbor would be asked to agree to the resolution the United States had twice opposed: "No state has the right to intervene in the internal or external affairs of another."

"I desire most heartily to second the motion to report this resolution favorably," Secretary Hull told the committee handling the proposal. "The people of my country strongly feel that the so-called right of conquest must forever be banished from this hemisphere," and at a plenary session a few days later he reiterated that "no government need fear any intervention on the part of the United States under the Roosevelt Administration." But then he added a disappointing reservation: the United States would follow "the law of nations as generally recognized and accepted." That provided all the wiggle room Washington might ever need, and the conference ended with delegates wondering what they had accomplished.[41]

They were reassured two days later, when FDR, speaking from Washington, pledged that "the definite policy of the United States from now on is one opposed to armed intervention," a commitment he seemed to broaden a few days later in his first State of the Union address: "We have, I hope, made it clear to our neighbors that we seek with them future avoidance of territorial expansion and of interference by one nation in the internal affairs of another." After that, few could disagree with what FDR told a 1935 audience: "I am a good neighbor."[42]

And even the unconvinced few had to concede a year later, when the president sailed for Buenos Aires to attend the first of several special inter-American meetings focused on the war clouds gathering in Europe. The Argentines gave FDR a regal reception, and the ensuing 1936 Buenos Aires conference tied down Cordell Hull's conditional commitment at Montevideo while also substantially broadening the definition of intervention beyond the use of armed force: "The High Contracting Parties declare inadmissible the intervention of any one of them, directly or indirectly, and for whatever reason, in the internal or external affairs of any other of the Parties." The U.S. delegation signed, the Senate ratified, and that was that.[43]

And that was also a first, as a rising Foreign Service star pointed out in the early 1950s: nonintervention "is not a United States doctrine; it was imposed on us by the unanimous will of the Latin states as the price of their participation in the inter-American system and is directed solely at us." A 1950s assistant secretary would agree: "We made our solemn agreement of non-intervention at the insistent demand of our sister republics."[44]

BUT THE TRUE test of FDR's commitment to nonintervention came not at conferences but in day-to-day bilateral relations, and the new administration had already come perilously close to failing its first Good Neighbor examination. The subject was Cuba, where after three decades of continual U.S. intervention in almost every imaginable way, some Cubans now considered Washington the arbitrator of the island's domestic disputes. This had been underscored during the Hoover years, in 1930, when an opposition leader had asked the U.S. ambassador to mediate with President Gerardo Machado to restore Cuba's lost political liberties—liberties that "they [the opposition] believed the United States had an obligation to protect," reported Ambassador Harry Guggenheim. He replied that the Hoover policy "was not to interfere in the internal affairs of Cuba."

Guggenheim was aware of the Cuban president's faults, but initially reported that Machado's ends justified his means. "President Machado has probably administered the country better than it has ever been administered before. He has also made some serious mistakes. He has succeeded in stamping out brigandage and in greatly modifying graft and corruption, and he has accomplished notable public works. He has used high-handed methods, justifying himself by the undoubted fact that it would have been impossible to accomplish reforms against political enemies and grafters in the face of a corrupt press without using strong measures."[45]

Then as opposition grew and the government responded by becoming more repressive, in early 1932 Guggenheim reported that the country was under martial law, that the schools had been closed for over a year, and that the jails were full of political prisoners. A few months after that he added that Cuba's docile Congress had extended the suspension of constitutional guarantees for a year and authorized President Machado to extend that extension for another two years. Shootings and bombings "have recently become not only more frequent, but more reckless," and almost-daily assassinations "have inspired feelings of horror and terrified apprehension to a degree which it would be difficult to exaggerate."[46]

All this was corroborated by others, including a U.S. postal agent in Havana, who reported that 75 percent of the population now opposed Machado. "They feel that they have no voice in any thing, no freedom of speech, no freedom of press, no civil rights by trial[,] every offense, imagined or real, being tried by military court. No man's house is free from entry and search, many good people being arrested and jailed for the least word spoken to a friend against the Government or any acts of the military." And "the opinions given are from real high class Cubans who love their country."

The assistant postmaster who received this message forwarded it to Secretary of State Stimson, who dismissed any thought of intervening, even diplomatically. Too many Latin Americans "seem to think that the United States exists in order to intervene in their behalf with the operation of the government in their own country of which they disapprove. If we complied with all of these requests, our hands would be full indeed and, however much these factions might like it, we should make ourselves extremely unpopular with every country in Latin America."[47]

Meanwhile, the same Cuban opposition leader who had requested Ambassador Guggenheim's assistance in 1930 returned to the embassy in 1932 to insist again that "the United States should settle the chaotic conditions in Cuba." Now the argument was that "the United States would have to intervene in the affairs of Cuba anyway, and that it were far better that it did so before blood had been spilled and a state of complete chaos reached." Guggenheim once again rejected the idea, but suggested to Secretary of State Stimson that he might have a talk with the Machado's ambassador in Washington.

Stimson's snippy reply: "You are in fact recommending a radical departure from the attitude of 'strict impartiality. . . . Cuba is an independent and sovereign nation. In the interest of self-government it should, therefore, endeavor to solve its own problems." He certainly would not call in the Cuban ambassador, and "you will refrain from taking any attitude or position with respect to Cuban internal political questions."[48]

And that is where the Hoover administration left it, with Secretary Stimson telling an incoming Roosevelt adviser that "he did not regard the Cuban situation of sufficient importance . . . to give it much attention."[49]

THE LAP INTO which Cuba policy dropped was that of Sumner Welles, one of the fresh voices from the early 1920s, now back in the State Department and listed in its *Register* as assistant secretary of state "charged with Latin American questions and such other duties as may be assigned to him by the Secretary of State"—this at a time when there was only one assistant secretary, with only a single undersecretary between Welles and Secretary of State Cordell Hull.[50] He and his principal associate, Laurence Duggan, were going to be responsible for U.S. policy toward Latin America for a full decade, from 1933 to 1943. Within the State Department, they often were something of a Bad Cop / Good Cop duo.

Unlike his behavior as a junior officer, the Welles of the 1930s appears to have become something of a menacing character. One of his deputies now noted his "condescending manner and his occasional frosty formality"; one of his predecessors complained that "he suffered somewhat from an unbending personality," and FDR's private secretary noted his "cold and somewhat forbidding exterior." "Welles was not an easy man to know," wrote a future secretary state, Dean Acheson; "his manner was formal to the point of stiffness. His voice, pitched much lower than would seem natural, though it had been so since he was a boy, lent a suggestion of pomposity." "If he ever smiles, it has not been in my presence," wrote Secretary of the Interior Harold Ickes, a key Roosevelt adviser; "he conducts himself with portentous gravity and as if he were charged with all the responsibilities of Atlas. Just to look at him one can tell that the world would dissolve into its component parts if only a portion of the weighty secrets of state that he carries about with him were divulged." These critics agreed with FDR's private secretary—Welles "possessed a clear and forceful mind"—but few who worked with him seemed to have enjoyed doing so.[51]

Welles's major asset was his relationship with the president. While less affluent, his wealthy New York family ran in the same social circles as the Roosevelts, and at the age of twelve Welles had held Eleanor's bridal train as she walked down the aisle to marry a fifth cousin, Franklin.

Welles had left the Diplomatic Service in 1922, just shy of his thirtieth birthday and at a time when his first marriage was falling apart. Almost immediately Secretary Hughes had asked him to accept a presidential appointment as a special representative to the Dominican Republic, where he negotiated the Marines' withdrawal, and that had been followed by a brief assignment to mediate among rival factions in Honduras. Then in 1925, two weeks after his remarriage to a prominent and extremely wealthy Washington divorcee, his career hit a brick wall. Asked by the State Department to approve the appointment of five citizens, one of them Welles, to an international pool of experts regarding Central America, President Coolidge wrote across State's letter: "All O.K. except Sumner Welles. If he is in the govt service, let him be dismissed at once."[52]

The next few years were consumed with constructing the new couple's country mansion in Maryland, with writing a useful two-volume study of the Dominican Republic, and with reestablishing relations with Franklin Roosevelt, elected governor of New York in 1928 and obvious presidential timber.[53] White House logs indicate he had four hundred appointments with FDR between 1933 and 1943, astounding access for the occupant of a sub-cabinet position.

Welles's principal deputy was Good Cop Laurence Duggan, "a man who united a powerful and honest intellect with great personal charm," Welles said at his memorial service, while a close outside observer considered Duggan "one of the most faithful and capable public servants the country has ever had." A deputy found him to be "a human being of great personal charm"—"as attractive a human being as it was my privilege to know"—but if he had a weakness it was being "a sucker for the underdog [who] worried constantly about the downtrodden masses." "I myself had scant patience with the 'downtrodden.' Many of them, I believed, were the way they were mainly because, in terms of human potential, they represented inferior raw material." In contrast, Duggan "suffered from ultraliberal impulses."[54]

Duggan did not circulate in Welles's social firmament. His left-leaning mother was the director of the Negro Welfare League of White Plains, New York, and his father was a mere professor, a member of the faculty at the City University of New York and the founding director of the Institute of International Education.[55] The two saw to it that their son received an elite-level education—Phillips Exeter (1923) and Harvard (1927), after which he entered the Foreign Service and was given the title Divisional Assistant in the Latin America division. Duggan's career-making moment came shortly after Welles returned as assistant secretary in 1933, at a time when the divisional chief was ill, and by mid-1936 he was listed in the State Department *Register* as Chief of the Division of Latin American Affairs—this at the age of thirty-one and after only six years in the Foreign Service. He would hold this position until 1944.

Although he never lived anywhere in Latin America and never learned more than rudimentary Spanish, Duggan compensated for his inexperience with a strong Good Neighbor commitment. In the final essay of his life he criticized Washington's "missionary zeal to make over the world in our own image"—a zeal that had led the United States "to inflict on others the humiliations which we have been spared."[56]

WITH A COMPLETELY new cast of characters and with a train wreck waiting to happen in Cuba, in mid-April 1933, a month after FDR's inauguration, the president allowed Welles to take a leave from his position as assistant secretary and appointed him ambassador to Cuba. In language almost certainly drafted by Welles himself, Secretary Hull instructed Welles to act as a hands-on proconsul, arranging "a definite, detailed, and binding understanding between the present Cuban Government and the responsible leaders of the factions opposed to it, which will lead to a truce in the present dangerous political agitation to continue until such time as national elections can be held in Cuba and the responsible officials of a new constitutional government can be elected under reasonable guaranties of popular suffrage without fraud, without intimidation, and without violence." Good Neighbor Roosevelt was sending Welles to do what Hoover's Guggenheim had been told not to do—improve Cuban politics.[57]

Meeting first with Machado's foreign minister, Orestes Ferrara, Welles announced that he "was disposed in every possible way to facilitate, behind the scenes, conciliation," and was pleased to report that Ferrara, speaking for President Machado, would "be only too glad to hear our views at any time and to adopt our suggestions." Taking advantage of that entrée, Welles reported, "I told him that at an appropriate occasion, I intended to offer some observations to the President regarding both the Constitution and the Electoral Code."[58] To do so he recruited Columbia University's Howard McBain to identify the reforms needed for a fair election, and by early August a report was on Welles's desk. He considered it "admirable in every way and if carried out will eliminate a very material percentage of fraud and of motives for corruption."[59]

Meanwhile, Welles had set out to bring all sides together. "I formally declared mediation proceedings commenced this morning," he informed Secretary Hull, and it did not take him long to conclude that "there is absolutely no hope of a return to normal conditions in Cuba as long as

President Machado remains in office." Machado departed a few days later. "As soon as I learned your opinions," Machado wrote FDR from Canada, "I acceded to the request to resign." Roosevelt replied that Welles had simply brought Machado "a proposal adopted by the groups in opposition to Your Excellency's Government [and] it was put forward by Mr. Welles on behalf of these groups."[60]

Welles approved of the Cubans who had taken over, telling Washington that he had an "intimate personal friendship with [Carlos Manuel de] Céspedes," the new provisional president, and "I am now daily being requested for decisions on all matters affecting the Government of Cuba." But other Cubans were demanding the keys to the presidential palace, and in less than a week Welles reported that "a general process of disintegration is going on." A few days later the Cuban army's noncommissioned officers rebelled and, Welles reported, "the Céspedes Cabinet resigned and President Céspedes left the Palace to go to his own home," replaced by a group "composed of the most extreme radicals in Cuba," and "a sergeant named Batista had been installed as Chief of Staff."[61]

Insisting that the Céspedes government be restored, Welles telephoned Secretary Hull to request "a temporary landing of possibly a thousand men [to] lend its assistance in the maintenance of public order." In a follow-up dispatch he assured Secretary Hull that "the landing of such assistance would most decidedly be construed as well within the limits of the policy of the 'good neighbor.'"[62]

No doubt aware of the effect that yet another armed Caribbean intervention would have upon his upcoming trip to the inter-American conference at Montevideo, a skeptical Hull hand-carried Welles's request to FDR and, he later recalled, "strongly expressed to him my opinion that we could not and should not think of intervening in Cuba even to a limited extent." After gaining the president's agreement, Hull went back to his office and cabled Welles: "The President has decided to send you the following message: armed intervention would be regarded as a breach of neutrality, as favoring one faction out of many, as attempting to set up a government which would be regarded by the whole world, and especially throughout Latin America, as a creation and creature of the American Government."[63]

Welles responded with an analogy: the Marines "should be construed as just as much of a friendly act as the facilitating of a loan. In the one case we would lend the Cubans police and in the other money, neither of which they possess." Clearly upset by this pushback, Hull cabled all U.S. envoys in Latin America, including Welles, that "there is not the slightest intention of intervening or interfering in Cuba's domestic affairs."[64]

Welles then set out to acquaint Washington with the shortcomings of Cuba's new provisional government led by Ramón Grau San Martín. "He is utterly impractical" and supported only "by students, by a few university professors, by the small group called ABC radicals which is chiefly composed of boys from 16 to 20 years of age." After meeting with leaders of the student directorate ("about 4 are girls"), "the general impression I gained was one of complete immaturity, of a failure to grasp even a rudimentary sense of the grave dangers which the Republic confronts and a feeling of almost impermeable self-satisfaction." Worse yet, "the Communist wave is spreading with the utmost rapidity and facility throughout the country." There was only one bright spot: "I have concluded an interview with Batista," the leader of the Sergeants' Revolt that overthrew Céspedes, and "his attitude throughout the conversation was extremely reasonable."[65]

While unwilling to entertain Welles's request for troops, FDR and Hull accepted his recommendation that the United States refuse to recognize Grau's government, and as historian Jules Benjamin discovered, "all forms of economic aid ceased and were replaced by a program of economic denial."[66] With that, and with the Navy surrounding the island with thirty warships, the question became how long any unrecognized Cuban government could hang on.

The answer was four months. Grau was replaced in early 1934 by leaders entirely beholden to Fulgencio Batista, whose presence would serve as the leitmotif of Cuban politics for the next quarter-century. Welles's justification, offered a decade later: "The United States would have been derelict in its obligations to the Cuban people themselves had it given official support to a de facto regime which, in its considered judgment, was not approved by the great majority of the Cuban people."[67] While Welles insisted that his approach "completely allayed the suspicions and antagonisms of its American neighbors," he apologized to FDR, pointedly through Secretary Hull: "You know how sincerely I believe in the policy of non-intervention in Cuba," he told the president; "I likewise am convinced that the Cubans can never govern themselves until they are forced to realize that they must assume their own responsibilities."[68]

After that mea culpa a chastened Welles became FDR's nonintervention enforcer among State's officials who disapproved of the new policy. Apparently there were more than a few, at least enough for Laurence Duggan to divide them into two classes: those who were indifferent to the new policy and those who were inhibited by anything new. "Indifferent were those fond of the 'society' of the upper crust. They did not attribute importance to the nascent middle class, the 'uncultured' workers and the tattered peons. Inhibited was a larger group whose receptivity to new ideas and whose originality and resourcefulness had been blunted by the stamp of the Foreign Service, [where] plodding along the path of those who have gone before has been the surest and usually the quickest road to success."[69]

THE PRINCIPAL DEPRESSION-ERA issues were economic, of course, but economic problems always have political repercussions, and they were the immediate test of the hands-off policy, particularly in Central America, where the bottom had fallen out of the markets for sugar, coffee, hardwood, and even bananas.

In Guatemala "a practical state of general moratorium exists," reported a U.S. chargé in 1930; "nearly everybody owes everybody else and nobody pays." A Wall Street loan was "the only thing which would pull the country out of its present bad financial condition." The Hoover-era response had been crystal clear: the United States was not going to serve as an intermediary. Guatemala should "initiate direct negotiations with responsible banking institutions."[70]

Nor had the Hoover administration intervened when President Jorge Ubico entered office via a one-candidate election in 1930, and this hands-off policy continued into the Roosevelt years. In 1935 the U.S. minister to Guatemala, Matthew Hanna, reported that Ubico had decided to remain in office despite a constitutional prohibition on reelection—Guatemala's foreign minister had insisted that Ubico "could not disregard the spontaneous and universal demand made by all classes of the Guatemalan people." When Hanna asked Washington if he should register disapproval, he was ordered to express "no attitude, either of sympathy or lack of sympathy." Ubico held a "consultation" three weeks later, where citizens stood in line in order to express their preference to Ubico's fellow military officers—99.9 percent (843,168) of Guatemalan voters thought he should continue in office; 0.1 percent (1,227) thought he should not.[71]

Also attempting to keep the uplifting spirit alive was the U.S. minister to Nicaragua, Arthur Bliss Lane, who reported in 1934 that "from being present at interviews last night between [President Juan] Sacasa and [Guardia commander Anastasio] Somoza I gather that the former has little control over the latter."[72] In 1931 an inexperienced Laurence Duggan, barely into his second year at the State Department and having never set foot in Central America, had already decided this had been inevitable. "A non-partisan constabulary is impossible in Nicaragua. Not only is it contrary to Latin American political-historical development, but Nicaragua is handicapped by a special circumstance, namely, the vitriolic animosity of the two parties, which is as bitter today as it was two hundred years ago. Therefore it is difficult to understand why hope was ever entertained that a non-political military force could be established."

But the Marines had only recently been withdrawn and Nicaragua was still considered something of a special obligation, so here in 1934 Sumner Welles authorized Minister Lane to express his views on internal quarrels if they would help to avoid bloodshed, but to do so quietly and as a personal statement.[73]

President Sacasa wanted more—a public statement in support of the constitutional processes that had brought him to power—and to that end he dispatched his brother to Washington. Lunching with a lower-level official, Federico Sacasa insisted that the administration's "silence at this time might also be interpreted as a kind of intervention, that is, as acquiescence in whatever might be done." When that elicited no response and the meal was completed, the disappointed envoy stood up to leave. "As we parted Dr. Sacasa said that he regretted that I hesitated to give him advice, I said that there was no hesitation at all on my part; that I was determined not to give him advice." Back in Managua, Minister Lane once more declined President Sacasa's request to issue a statement of support for constitutional processes, which both Sacasa brothers referred to as "advice." Lane's response: "We do not 'advise' Great Britain as to how its elections or political matters should be held. Why should we so 'advise' Nicaragua?"[74]

Then brother Federico Sacasa, still in Washington, went up the ladder to Sumner Welles, who had a note-taker: "Dr. Sacasa stated that he was confident that the Nicaraguan Government could look for the friendly moral assistance of the US Government. Mr. Welles said that he was not quite sure just what Dr. Sacasa meant . . . but any question of interference by the United

States in the domestic internal problems of Nicaragua was out of the question and utterly impossible."[75]

At this point the Roosevelt administration sent a new minister to Managua, the onetime ultra-uplifter Boaz Long, who had served as chief of State's Division of Latin America during the Woodrow Wilson years. In those days he had advocated "extending our influences over these less favored people . . . and making them good citizens of a democracy."[76] A Democrat, Long had sat out the Republican 1920s, but now in 1936 he arrived in Nicaragua with Welles's instructions "not only to decline comment or advice, but scrupulously to avoid giving ground for belief that this Government is taking any part in Nicaragua's domestic affairs."

Long began as instructed, but started to waver as the political ground continued to shift in Somoza's favor. Soon he asked for permission to say something that might be helpful to President Sacasa, and was immediately pulled back into line, told to make no statement "or in any other manner endeavor to influence events in Nicaragua."[77] And so the Roosevelt administration, true to its nonintervention commitment, stood aside and watched the cookies crumble: President Sacasa was forced out a few months later, Anastasio Somoza won a subsequent election supervised by his National Guard, and a three-decade family dictatorship began.

Meanwhile, in neighboring El Salvador the U.S. minister requested permission to express disapproval of an uncommonly brutal president's plan to remain in office indefinitely. No doubt aware of the hands-off instructions to his colleagues in Guatemala and Nicaragua, Minister Francis Corrigan offered the innovative argument that Central America had a special exemption to the Good Neighbor policy: the 1923 General Treaty of Peace and Amity denied recognition to unconstitutional Central American governments. Corrigan pointed out that the treaty had been negotiated in Washington at U.S. insistence, and that the United States, while not a signatory, had made a public commitment to follow the treaty's stipulation. Given this commitment, Corrigan requested permission to voice opposition to an unconstitutional election. "Failure of a Mission to use its influence constructively may become a sin of omission with consequences fully as grievous as the former sins of commission. It would be useful to know the Department's point of view as to possible steps that might be taken."[78]

Welles assigned the task of drafting a response to assistant division chief Willard Beaulac, the same official who had given Federico Sacasa the blank stare over lunch. He began by pointing out "the action of Guatemala in 'suspending' the constitutional obstacles to President Ubico's continuance in office lay it open to the charge that it has violated Article V of the 1923 treaty,"* that "General Somoza, Commander of the Nicaraguan National Guard, has expressed his determination to succeed Dr. Sacasa as President of Nicaragua despite the circumstance that he is apparently prohibited by the Nicaraguan constitution from becoming a candidate," and that "President Carías of Honduras is openly planning to extend his term of office in contravention of the Constitution." Given this situation in three of the five Central American countries and now a pending fourth, El Salvador, Beaulac's view was that time had overtaken the 1923 treaty: "We are no longer warranted in invoking the Treaty as a reason for denying recognition [and] to do so would be arbitrary and capricious and would constitute 'meddling' of a flagrant kind."[79]

Welles then used Beaulac's argument to prepare a policy statement, the gist of which was that however much any U.S. official may personally oppose a dictatorship, it was impossible to be both a Good Neighbor and meddlesome. This statement was sent to every U.S. envoy in Latin America over the signature of Secretary Hull and written in the first person to emphasize that this was more than just another cable from Washington: "I desire to make it clear that the Department expects its diplomatic representatives in Central America to conduct themselves in their relations with the Government to which they are accredited, and with the people of the countries, in exactly the same manner they would if they were accredited to one of the large republics of South America or with any non-American power; that is to say, they should abstain from offering advice on any domestic question, and if requested to give such advice they should decline to do so."

Even this did not give pause to Minister Corrigan, a recent political appointee. Since Washington had decided it was no longer a question of complying with a 1923 treaty, Corrigan wrote that the unconstitutional re-election of a brutal dictator "brings up the question of whether there is not a moral responsibility implicit in the interpretation of the 'Good Neighbor' policy."

---

*Article V required the signatories "to maintain in their respective Constitutions the principle of non-reelection to the office of President and Vice-President," and those whose constitutions lacked such a stipulation were obligated "to introduce a constitutional reform to this effect."

Welles responded, pointedly "for the Secretary of State": "Avoid expressing opinions or giving suggestions with reference to internal policies."[80]

THE DOWNSIDE OF any nonintervention policy is exactly what Minister Corrigan mentioned: the moral consequences of turning a blind eye to repression.

As the war clouds gathered during the 1930s, some officials began referring to Latin America as the nation's "soft underbelly" and arguing that U.S. security required leaders who could maintain order and smoke out subversives, even if it required embracing acknowledged despots, as illustrated by one each from Cuba, the Dominican Republic, and Nicaragua.

The first such leader from Cuba was not Fulgencio Batista but president-elect Miguel Mariano Gómez, although everyone knew who was running the country—in 1938 the U.S. ambassador explained the island's political pecking order with one sentence: "Colonel Batista has had conferences recently with leaders of the parties in Congress, with the result that a better understanding between the Executive and Congress has been reached."[81]

U.S. Army chief of staff Malin Craig had invited Colonel Batista to Washington five days earlier. The Cuban leader had never traveled abroad, and General Craig clearly wanted Batista's first overseas venture to include a warm welcome, beginning with an offer to fly him from Miami. Batista preferred the train, so the Army provided two private cars, and both General Craig and Undersecretary Welles were waiting to greet him at Union Station. Then Craig took the Cuban leader up Pennsylvania Avenue in an open limousine— highly unusual for a visiting military officer. Later that day he went to the White House for a long talk with FDR.

Writing from Havana, Ambassador J. Butler Wright reported that the mere announcement of this visit had "enormously strengthened" Batista. "His prestige has greatly increased, and the whole country considers the visit as of immense importance to Cuba." When the Cuban chieftain returned home, his arrival was celebrated with a four-hour parade, during which Batista, although not Cuba's president, viewed the event from the balcony of the presidential palace. The embassy reported that he then gave a speech "stressing the benefits, spiritual and real, already derived, and to be derived, from his visit."[82]

Four years later, in 1942, with Batista now president and providing substantial support for the Allied war effort, Sumner Welles convinced FDR to roll out the red carpet: "Since the overthrow of Batista might plunge the Island during this critical period into chaos, it is essential, if he is to remain in office, that his visit to Washington not be a failure."[83] FDR therefore was driven to the Army's Bolling Field, across the Potomac from Reagan National Airport, to welcome Batista as he and his wife stepped off their plane. They drove to the White House, had tea with the First Lady, and then were shown to their guest room, where they rested before attending a dinner with forty-three guests. After that the two leaders retired to FDR's study, where they talked for nearly three hours, until 12:45 A.M.

As for Nicaragua, never before or since has a Latin American leader been welcomed more grandly than Anastasio Somoza. In 1939 the Nicaraguan strongman found both the President and First Lady waiting to greet him and his wife at Union Station. "The question involved is how long should the President be made to stand," wrote one of the White House staffers responsible for choreographing the welcome.[84] Given the need to play both national anthems and to offer the press a photo opportunity, the answer was close to half an hour, something the polio-stricken FDR normally would not have been asked to do. But he was asked to do it and he did. After that the two leaders rode slowly—at walking speed—up Pennsylvania Avenue to the White House in an open limousine, part of an elaborate military parade witnessed by thousands of government employees who had been authorized to leave their jobs so they could line the route from 11 A.M. until 1 P.M. After a formal White House luncheon, the Roosevelts drove the Somozas to Mount Vernon, where the Nicaraguan leader placed a wreath on Washington's grave. On the way back they stopped at Arlington Cemetery so that Somoza could place a second wreath on the Tomb of the Unknowns.

Strangely, there was no dinner, no one-on-one in FDR's study, and no overnight stay in the White House—only a very brief White House meeting the next morning, which must have been social rather than substantive because it included both leaders' spouses and the Somozas' daughter.

The contrast between an exceptionally elaborate welcome and the rest of Somoza's visit was explained by Edwin "Pa" Watson, the Army general upon whose arm the President leaned while standing. In a memo to the White House press secretary, Watson began: "The Committee in charge of arrangements for the reception of the President of Nicaragua, which will be a rehearsal for the King and Queen of England, ..."[85] A rehearsal. Who would have guessed? Somoza and his wife arrived on May 5; King George VI and

Queen Elizabeth were coming on June 8. The Union Station photographs of the two events are basically identical, with General Watson's uniform the only significant difference—the Army had switched to summer whites on June 1. For the king and queen there was the same parade as for the Somozas (with another two-hour break for government employees), another White House lunch, and another drive around Washington. From that point forward the two itineraries differed dramatically, with infinitely more attention given to the British monarchs.

Like Batista, Somoza returned home to tout his welcome as evidence of Washington's support, which in both cases had become a statement of power. Batista signaled his success with a four-hour parade; Somoza's triumphant return included issuance of a postage stamp picturing his address to the House of Representatives.

Exit Somoza, enter Rafael Trujillo, technically not the Dominican Republic's chief of state, but, as in Cuba, everyone knew who was running the country. U.S. minister Henry Norweb reported from Santo Domingo that President Jacinto Peynado "professed complete ignorance as to the nature of the conversation between Secretary Hull, General Trujillo and Mr. Pastoriza," the Dominican minister in Washington.[86] This conversation was about how to abrogate the 1924 treaty giving the U.S. government the right to appoint the country's general receiver of customs until foreign bondholders had been paid. Trujillo met with FDR only briefly, for tea, and then again in the Oval Office for about eight minutes when he stopped in Washington on his way home from Europe. An agreement on the collection of customs receipts was reached at lower levels, and the Dominican receivership, begun in 1904, finally ended in 1941, when the bondholders had been paid in full.

After returning home, Trujillo would spend the next two decades bathing in the Narcissus pool, renaming more or less everything, from the country's capital (Ciudad Trujillo) to the Caribbean's highest mountain (Pico Trujillo). But for now the Dominican Republic had a stable, accommodating government. As a 1940s-era ambassador would recall, "the Trujillo formula was pragmatic and simple: do not quarrel with the United States." In response, the Roosevelt administration did nothing to bother Trujillo.[87]

"How nice it would be if the president of the United States, faithful to his democratic and pacific principles, would in the name of suffering people condemn more explicitly the creole autocrats who consider Mr. Roosevelt his 'great and good friend.'" That was the commentary of Víctor Raúl Haya de la Torre, a rising star in Peruvian politics with a growing following among Latin Americans.[88] In the eyes of these critics, nonintervention was a form of intervention when it implicitly blessed the status quo.

FDR probably would have responded that most neighbors are not perfect and had to be taken for better and for worse. That Good Neighbor commitment, so different from the Progressive-era belief that the United States should help turn bad neighbors into good neighbors, rested alongside the gathering war clouds in Europe. Batista's Cuba, Somoza's Nicaragua, and Trujillo's Dominican Republic were soon going to be outposts protecting the Panama Canal and shipments of raw materials from the rest of Latin America, especially petroleum from Venezuela and bauxite (aluminum) from the Guianas. Taken together, the Good Neighbor commitment and World War II mandated that there be no effort to improve Latin American politics.

Economic uplifting was an entirely different matter.

CHAPTER 6

Breaking New Ground

Uplifting Institutions

I hereby direct you, as Coordinator of Inter-American Affairs, to formulate and execute a program to aid and improve the health, safety and general welfare of the peoples of Mexico, Central and South America and the outlying islands including the West Indies.

—President Roosevelt to Nelson Rockefeller, March 1942

NEVER UNDERESTIMATE THE impact of the Great Depression and World War II on today's effort to improve the lives of Latin Americans.

Beginning with the 1929 stock market crash, U.S. consumers cut back on everything imported from Latin America, watering down their coffee, treating sugar as a luxury, and foregoing purchases of durables, many containing raw materials from Latin America. With far fewer customers, Latin American producers slashed production and furloughed workers, while tax revenues dropped to the point that many of the region's governments were unable to meet their payrolls, let alone service their debts—by 1939 a full $1.2 billion of $1.6 billion of the dollar bonds issued or guaranteed by Latin American governments were in default. Refinancing? After an 89 percent collapse of the Dow-Jones Industrial Average, Wall Street was not going to come to the rescue.

In his final annual message President Hoover repeated what he had been saying all along: "Economic depression can not be cured by legislative action or executive pronouncement." Instead, he urged each citizen "to assist his neighbors who may be less fortunate," insisting until his last day in office that "the best contribution of government lies in encouragement of this voluntary cooperation."[1] Although vague during the campaign, FDR's plans were unambiguous on the basic point: no more waiting for the private sector to pull the economy out of the ditch.

The voters thought this over and then handed the Democrats 483 of 532 electoral votes. Washington's tow truck was on its way.

PRIME AMONG THE New Deal initiatives that helped both U.S. and Latin American citizens was the creation of the government-owned Export-Import Bank (Eximbank) to stimulate U.S. exports, which had fallen by a devastating 70 percent between 1929 and 1932. It provided foreign purchasers with low-cost financing of goods made in the United States. "The Bank's objective in authorizing loans, guarantees, insurance, and credits shall be to contribute to maintaining or increasing employment of United States workers."

That sentence in the original 1934 legislation has never been changed, but it was not on anyone's mind in February 1934 when the Export-Import Bank's first loan went to shore up Cuba's new provisional government led by Carlos Mendieta. In January Colonel Fulgencio Batista had handed him the presidency (but not power) after overthrowing the government of Ramón Grau San Martín, the leader Sumner Welles had opposed. Now, as a U.S. embassy officer recalled in his memoir, "there was no denying the sincerity of Washington's efforts to assist Cuba once recognition had been extended to an acceptable successor."[2] And Cuba could certainly use some assistance. Sugar was selling far below the cost of production, bottoming out at a half-cent per pound ($.0058), about one-fifth of pre-crash prices, and the volume of Cuban sugar exports had dropped from 5.8 million to 2.2 million tons. As a result, Cuba's imports from the United States had plummeted by almost 90 percent.

Pleased by Grau's departure, the Roosevelt administration had recognized the Mendieta government almost immediately, and within a week the U.S. Surplus Relief Corporation had extended Cuba a $2 million credit to buy U.S. food (which was helpful to U.S. farmers). Then a few days later Sumner Welles's telephone rang. It was Treasury Secretary Henry Morgenthau Jr. who "called me up by instruction of the President to advise me that he had just discussed with the President a plan for providing immediate financial relief to the Cuban Government through a silver purchase operation." The plan was for the Federal Reserve to loan Cuba's fragile government the money needed to purchase fifty thousand ounces of U.S. silver (helpful to Western miners) at the current price of about 45 cents per ounce. When the Philadelphia mint had converted the ingots into Cuban pesos, their face value would be about 64 cents an ounce, yielding the fragile Mendieta government an estimated seigniorage profit of $11 million.[3]

There ensued some tweaking of Morgenthau's plan, as the administration sidelined the Federal Reserve and created instead "The Second Export-Import Bank of Washington, D.C.," exclusively for Cuba.[4] Wholly owned by the U.S. government, the Bank had the authority to make loans backed ultimately by the U.S. Treasury, and in this case the loan agreement was a simple letter of credit stating that the Mendieta government had $4.0 million from the new bank to purchase U.S. silver. Cuba took that letter of credit to U.S. silver dealers and exchanged it for bullion valued at $3.8 million. Once it had been minted, the Mendieta government used some of the coins to repay the Bank at the standard 1:1 dollar/peso exchange rate. The rest was sent to Cuba. The result: 3.8 million dollar bills were in the pockets of Rocky Mountain silver producers and Cuba had $11 million (minus the $3.8 million) silver pesos to pay the back salaries of government employees, tamping down disaffection and stimulating the island's struggling economy. The tow truck worked like magic.*

Another loan of $4.4 million, for identical purposes, came later in 1934, and by that time the Eximbank's executive committee had decided to finance trade with any country. But in its first two years (1934–1935) more than $13 million of the Bank's total lending of $14 million went to Cuba, all for silver purchases.[5]

That stimulus was not quite enough. Visiting Havana in 1935, Laurence Duggan reported that Cubans "are disappointed and disillusioned with the Mendieta government [and] the question on many lips is how long Batista will continue to support Mendieta in the face of mounting opposition." The U.S. ambassador had already reported that "no Government, this or any other, could last a day, if opposed by Batista."[6]

Duggan's "How long?" question was quickly answered: ten months. More silver loans supported Batista's next pick, José Agripino Barnet (six months),

---

*The Eximbank had the money on its books but none of the dollar bills that U.S. silver miners demanded so they could pay for food at the grocery store, so the trail of the letter of credit eventually led to the U.S. Treasury, which printed the money. That was the magic.

and his next, Miguel Mariano Gómez (seven months), and his next, Fed-
erico Laredo Brú (four years). By 1941, when Batista himself was president,
Cuba had received $27.3 million—one-third of all Eximbank loans to Latin
America—and a candid State Department analyst wrote that the silver loans
were "not so much of a monetary measure as a credit to assist the Cuban
Government."[7]

A QUITE DIFFERENT use of the Eximbank was to resolve the conflict over
Mexico's 1938 nationalization of U.S. oil companies, with side agreements
aimed at assisting Mexico.

Determined not to allow the question of compensation to degenerate into
a dogfight reminiscent of the 1920s, the administration explored almost every
avenue except the solution proposed by California senator William McAdoo,
who argued that "Lower California is an integral part of California and it
ought to be under our flag." His idea was "to pay Mexico enough money for
Lower California and for the rectification of the Arizona-Mexico line so as
to bring the mouth of the Colorado River under our sovereignty, to enable
Mexico to satisfy all the claims for the valuable American properties she has
thus far taken." McAdoo suggested $150 million as a fair purchase price.

"I am grateful to you for giving me the benefit of your views," Sumner
Welles replied for the administration, fully aware that the very last thing
twentieth-century Mexicans would do is sell even a square inch of their land,
least of all to the United States. "The resentment of the Mexican people following such a proposal might be so great as to jeopardize the prospects of
reaching any satisfactory solution."[8] But the United States did not want to
abandon the principle of compensation, so the two governments spent nearly
four years negotiating a complex settlement, the gist of which was that the
Mexican government agreed to pay the oil companies $24 million, much of
which would come from the U.S. government.[9]

By this time the rules governing Eximbank loans had changed. Cuba aside,
in its early years the Bank primarily had provided short-term loans for purchases of U.S. agricultural products, mostly cotton, and longer-term loans
for U.S. heavy equipment, mostly locomotives and rolling stock. But then
at a 1940 meeting with foreign ministers in Havana, hastily called in the
wake of Germany's conquest of France, Secretary of State Cordell Hull
promised to help Latin American governments finance their unwanted surpluses, primarily sugar and coffee, which several governments had purchased

from local producers as a last resort, generally printing the currency to do so.

A bill to expand the Eximbank's authority was already winding its way through Congress, and after the 1940 Havana meeting FDR asked Congress to allow the Bank to "be of greater assistance to our neighbors south of the Rio Grande, including financing the handling and orderly marketing of some part of their surpluses."

This request was slipped into an existing debate, ongoing to our day, which challenged the Bank's existence as an infringement upon territory belonging to the private sector—Wall Street. "Our distinguished Republican from Ohio a few moments ago put his finger on one of the Ethiopians in the wood-pile," began a second Republican representative as he entered the debate. "I want Uncle Sam to stay home and stop playing Santa Claus to non-Americans. Keep out of foreign entanglements and foreign wars. Charity begins at home. I sincerely hope this House will defeat this indefensible, camouflaged, un-American legislative monstrosity," the Export-Import Bank.[10]

Facing a hundred-seat Democratic majority, House Republicans could not mount much of a challenge. The new law increased the Bank's lending authority from $200 million to $700 million, of which $500 million was reserved for Latin America. It also allowed the Bank "to assist in the development of the resources, the stabilization of the economies, and the orderly marketing of the products of the countries of the Western Hemisphere." As a State Department economist noted, with this sentence "the whole orientation of the enterprise changed."[11] Basically, the Export-Import Bank began making loans whose collateral was more or less worthless—Latin America's agricultural surpluses.

This $500 million increase in 1940 also became a crucial element of the $24 million settlement coaxed out of Mexico. One of that settlement's side agreements provided for the United States to purchase Mexican government highway construction bonds with dollars, ostensibly so that Mexico could use the dollars to purchase road-building equipment made in the United States, although most of the proceeds from the bonds were understood to be used for the wages of Mexican road builders. These workers' wages would be paid in pesos, of course; the Mexican government kept the dollars for other uses, such as paying the oil companies. Also, the U.S. Treasury (not the Eximbank) agreed to purchase silver from the Mexican government, and to purchase in addition an unspecified amount of Mexican pesos, paying for them with U.S. dollars—not because the Treasury had any need for the silver or the pesos, but because Mexico needed $24 million. In case that was not enough, a final agreement committed the Eximbank to be "disposed to consider sympathetically other requests for credits for developments in Mexico."

A *New York Times* editorial pointed out the obvious—the Roosevelt administration was "furnishing Mexico with the funds to pay for the property it has expropriated." But the editors conceded that the arrangement "terminates a troublesome controversy with a neighboring country at a time when it is of vital importance to maintain and strengthen friendly relations."[12] The agreement was signed eighteen days before Pearl Harbor.

Much the same agreement was reached with Bolivia, which had steadfastly refused to compensate Standard Oil for the 1937 seizure of its facilities. No settlement had been reached by January 1942, a few weeks after Pearl Harbor, when the hemisphere's foreign ministers gathered for an emergency meeting in Rio de Janeiro. Washington's goal was to enlist all of Latin America in the Allied cause; Bolivia wanted to see what the United States had to offer in exchange for its enlistment.

So Sumner Welles and Bolivia's foreign minister sat down in a side room at Rio and hammered out an agreement. First, Bolivia would pay Standard Oil $1.5 million for the property it had confiscated. Then the two countries would immediately create "a corporation to carry out a program of economic cooperation between the United States and Bolivia and the extension of credits to that corporation by the Export-Import Bank."* An initial $15.5 million Eximbank loan was "for agricultural, mining and other industries and for transportation." "There is no real economic justification for this credit," reported the U.S. embassy, but it "would assure Standard Oil settlement since the credit should not be opened until after payment is made."[13]

In subsequent negotiations Bolivia was promised another round of Eximbank credits of up to $15 million, plus an additional $2.1 million from the U.S. government's Rubber Reserve Corporation and $1 million for health and sanitation projects from a new Coordinator of Inter-American Affairs, bringing the total to $33.6 million. There also was a commitment to "stabilize" Bolivia's currency with the infusion of dollars from the U.S.

---

* "Economic cooperation" was the Good Neighbor term for "foreign aid" or today's "development assistance."

Treasury, which simply purchased an unspecified amount of Bolivian currency by transferring a dollar equivalent into Bolivia's account with the Federal Reserve Bank of New York.[14] In return, Bolivia compensated Standard Oil, severed relations with the Axis, and gave the United States preferential wartime access to its tin, lead, zinc, tungsten, and rubber.

The Bank had already risen to yet another special Latin American challenge in 1938, when France closed its ports to Haitian coffee until Haiti resumed payment on bonds held by French investors. Here, only four years after the Marines' departure, Haiti was being pushed to the edge of complete collapse, and the Eximbank stepped in to finance labor-intensive public works projects. Although a U.S. construction company would be the prime contractor and all foreign materials would be purchased in the United States and transported to Haiti on U.S. flag carriers, those benefits were entirely incidental.[15]

And Haiti was not the only country whose roads were improved by Eximbank loans; in Depression-era Latin America the most frequent type of Eximbank loan was for building sections of the Pan-American Highway, a decades-old dream now coming true with Bank loans to fourteen Latin American governments.[16] As in Haiti, the U.S. private sector was potentially a beneficiary: each low-interest, long-term highway loan, all to shaky borrowers, specified that foreign equipment purchases had to be made from U.S. manufacturers. But the roads typically were being built by laborers using shovels, picks, and wheelbarrows. There was little need for overseas purchases.

While the primary purpose of these loans to Latin American governments was for something other than creating jobs in the United States, there was some of that as well. Announcing a $20 million loan to Brazil for the construction of a steel mill, the State Department emphasized that the money "is to be spent in the United States, through contracts with from 250 to 300 different manufacturers and suppliers." Less directly, the loan "will also tend to improve the general standard of living in the country and thereby increase the market for products from the United States."[17]

This effort to boost U.S. overseas sales was especially evident in the Bank's so-called "unfreezing loans," the first of which provided Brazil's central bank with dollars so that it could pay U.S. exporters for goods sold to Brazil's importers. Typically these sales had been negotiated in Brazilian currency, which was generally worthless to U.S. exporters—they needed the Brazilian government to rescind (unfreeze) its ban on converting local currency into dollars, and the government would not do so because it wanted to select how Brazil's limited supply of dollars would be used. So the Eximbank loaned Brazil the dollars. Unfreezing loans were also authorized for Colombia, Costa Rica, Nicaragua, Paraguay, and Peru.

Given such obvious assistance to U.S. economic interests, it is possible to argue that most Eximbank loans created jobs in the United States, but the documents left behind in the archives suggest a more important foreign policy interest in helping Latin Americans cope with the Depression. In Cuba the initial U.S. interest was political—to sustain a fragile government that had overthrown a government of which Washington disapproved. Later, as war clouds gathered in Europe, security became the primordial U.S. interest. As Sumner Welles would point out in 1944, "operations of the bank have been highly effective in counteracting Germany's efforts to exercise financial and commercial control over the national economies of many of the other American republics."[18]

It is difficult to overstate the significance of all this: Hans Morgenthau realists had created the first permanent institution that could be used to improve Latin Americans.

THEN THERE WAS a second New Deal innovation, the Reciprocal Trade Agreements Act.

Fully aware of the damage done by the 1930 Smoot-Hawley tariff increases, in 1934 Congress granted FDR permission to negotiate *reciprocal* tariff reductions and then to implement them without first obtaining congressional approval. "The stated purpose of this proposal is the expansion of foreign markets for the products of the United States," the bill's floor manager told his Senate colleagues. "It means freight for our railroads and ships. It means traffic for our ports. It means increased business in all activities which serve trade. All these propositions together mean increased employment, increased business, and a return of industrial and agricultural stability"—in other words, the promotion of U.S. interests.[19]

While that mandated purpose was never ignored, the first reciprocal agreement was, once again, to help Cuba. The idea was to support the new Mendieta government by lowering U.S. tariffs on Cuban goods, particularly sugar and cigar tobacco.[20] Cuba was promptly followed by others—next came an agreement with Brazil, followed by agreements with eleven more

Latin American countries by late 1941, when the United States entered the war. As Congress required, each agreement was reciprocal, designed to boost U.S. exports and to reduce U.S. barriers to imports.

Then World War II changed everything, as the United States lined up with the other fighting nations to buy almost anything Latin Americans had to sell. The U.S. Commodity Credit Corporation contracted to purchase all or most of Central America's bananas, Uruguay's wool, Argentina's wheat and corn, Cuba's sugar, and Nicaragua's, Haiti's, and Peru's cotton. Similarly, the U.S. Metal Reserve Company contracted to purchase the entire production of copper from Bolivia, Chile, and Mexico, manganese from Brazil and Cuba, antimony from Mexico and Peru, zinc from Mexico, and chromium from Chile. Some countries helped more than others, and some with greater enthusiasm than others, but active cooperation rose to a level unknown in the history of inter-American relations, before or after.[21]

It is impossible to exaggerate the long-term significance of the wartime purchase agreements, the Export-Import Bank Act, the Reciprocal Trade Agreements Act, and the 1934 Sugar Act, which guaranteed Latin American producers a significant slice of the U.S. sugar market. These initiatives encouraged Latin American governments to look toward Washington—not only for help with the current economic downturn, but also with their longer-term dreams of having smooth highways, clean water, and dial telephones.

Initially the Eximbank was crucial. It opened a previously locked door to the U.S. Treasury, behind which was the magic machine that manufactured as many dollars as Washington wanted now that the country was off the gold standard. Until 1934 every U.S. loan to every Latin American government had come from Wall Street. Now a U.S. government bank was offering to finance a steel mill for Brazil, a highway for Chile, and a program of economic cooperation for Bolivia, all at cut-rate prices and often, tacitly, with no hard-currency repayment expected.[22] Then came the reciprocal tariff agreements, which were even more significant in the long run. They made U.S. consumers more accessible to Latin American producers. After that, the wartime purchases taught Latin Americans that bargaining with Washington was not the same as bargaining with Wall Street—the U.S. government had a different incentive structure, a give-and-take not necessarily negotiated with a concern for the bottom line.

Lured by these attractive New Deal innovations, the Latin American camel now had its nose under the Washington tent, and it clearly liked what was inside. So did the U.S. private sector, which gained a competitive edge with low-cost government financing and lower barriers to entry into Latin American markets. The result: no administration has ever matched FDR's for its impact on U.S.–Latin American economic relations. Washington was not where the goods and services were located, but it was becoming a site of decisions about their distribution.

ALONGSIDE THESE ECONOMIC innovations was a major effort to expand the influence of U.S. culture among Latin Americans, which many considered (and some still consider) a form of uplifting.

This effort was best chronicled by the softhearted Samuel Guy Inman, a self-described "writer and teacher of inter-American relations" but also a Disciples of Christ minister who had spent ten years as a missionary in northern Mexico, both before and during the Mexican Revolution.[23] After that decade Inman had helped create the private Committee on Cooperation in Latin America, which coordinated the mission work of Protestant denominations. Although he was based in New York, his duties as the Committee's executive secretary led him to travel widely in Latin America, including attendance at the 1923 (Santiago) and 1928 (Havana) inter-American conferences. Inman simultaneously pursued a writing career, beginning with the 1919 publication of *Intervention in Mexico,* which was highly critical of U.S. policy, and he also moonlighted as an adjunct instructor at Colombia University, offering what was probably the nation's first course on inter-American relations.

The optimistic tone of his books written during the Good Neighbor years suggests he had been seduced by the Roosevelt administration, and the seduction probably began in late 1933, when Inman was aboard the steamship *American Legion* as it sailed from New York on one of its regularly scheduled trips along the east coast of South America. Among the other passengers booked to Montevideo were the members of the U.S. delegation to the Seventh International Conference of American States, led by Secretary of State Cordell Hull. Also aboard were two of the Cubans representing the Grau San Martín government. Because the United States did not recognize Cuba's government, Secretary Hull felt he could not acknowledge the Cubans' existence during the eighteen-day voyage, and that posed a problem for his physical fitness. Inman stepped in: "I was able to see that Mr. Hull and the unrecognized Cuban delegations [delegates?] took their constitutional on deck at different times."

That was Inman's entrée, as was his fluency in Spanish and his experience at the 1923 and 1928 conferences—only one of the delegates accompanying Secretary Hull in 1933 had attended either. "I am glad you are along on this trip," Inman recalled Hull as saying, "for you seem to be one of few who have been to these conferences. I know little about them or these countries, but I want to learn." So, Hull continued, "you come to see me every morning and we will go over these problems together."[24] Who among us would not have been seduced?

Three years later, the same *American Legion* carried Hull and the U.S. delegation to the Inter-American Conference for the Maintenance of Peace at Buenos Aires. (FDR traveled on a Navy cruiser.) This time Inman was "an official adviser on cultural relations, the first ever appointed by the United States to an international conference," he wrote. "During meetings aboard ship on the trip south, the [State] Department presented to its delegation a proposed treaty providing for the exchange of students," which was "enlarged by the delegation to include an exchange professor," a splendid addition. During these shipboard discussions a decision was made to "designate or create an appropriate agency or appoint a special officer" to implement the exchanges.[25]

Inman spent much of his time in Buenos Aires attending sessions of the working group on cultural relations, which agreed with the U.S. recommendation that each country create an agency or designate an individual to supervise exchanges. This seed was carried back to Washington and planted in the State Department garden, where it was carefully tended by Laurence Duggan, whose father had devoted his career to the exchange programs of the private Institute of International Education, based in New York and funded primarily by the Carnegie Endowment for International Peace. Soon a seedling appeared: State's Division of Cultural Relations, whose principal task was to develop educational exchanges with Latin American countries. In time this would become today's Fulbright fellowship program, administratively outsourced to the Institute of International Education, an arrangement that continues to this day.[26]

This new division was positioned alongside another newcomer, an Interdepartmental Committee on Co-operation with the American Republics, chaired by Sumner Welles and designed to improve Latin Americans' technical skills via advisory relationships—such as the U.S. Bureau of Mines providing experts to advise equivalent Latin American bureaucracies. Congress authorized the Committee to carry out what would soon come to be called "technical assistance," but its initial appropriation was almost nothing— $95,000—and neither the Committee nor State's new Division of Cultural Relations had accomplished much before 1940, when Nelson Rockefeller stepped onto the Washington stage and stole the uplifting show.

GRANDSON OF THE Rockefeller, in 1937 the twenty-nine-year-old Nelson had recently returned from a three-month trip to Latin America, the primary purpose of which had been to become familiar with the family's Standard Oil holdings. But the trip's principal effect was to solidify Rockefeller's altruistic commitment to Latin America's economic and social development. His initial attempt to convince the Roosevelt administration to launch such an effort did not get beyond presidential adviser Harry Hopkins, but in early 1939 Hopkins arranged for him to meet with FDR for the purpose of requesting a brief radio message celebrating New York's Museum of Modern Art, a principal philanthropic interest of the Rockefeller family. The radio message would be part of the ceremony inaugurating MOMA's new building on West 53rd Street.

It was fifteen months until the two men met again, in mid-1940, with Europe now at war and Rockefeller armed with a plan to challenge Axis influence in Latin America—to protect U.S. security interests. Not coincidentally, it was a month after Secretary Hull had met with Latin America's foreign ministers in Havana, where he had promised not simply to help finance Latin America's agricultural surpluses, as mentioned above, but also to consider "methods for improving the standard of living of the peoples of the Americas."[27] The White House aide responsible for alerting Rockefeller to his opportunity, Harry Hopkins, guided Rockefeller into the Oval Office and the rest is history: an "Office for Coordination of Commercial and Cultural Relations between the American Republics," with an initial budget of $3,425,00 from the president's emergency fund, and with Rockefeller as its director.[28]

Some follow-through on Hull's Havana commitment would have occurred anyway, but the success of this Office cannot be explained without reference to the evidence that FDR enjoyed Rockefeller's company. Although they were a generation apart, they came from the same New York social elite, they were both progressives with a strong commitment to assisting the poor, and they both had positive, outgoing personalities. Over the next few years they would occasionally get together for private lunches, small family dinners, movies at the White House, and on one occasion they drove together to Shangri-La, the presidential retreat known today as Camp David. The message was clear: give this Republican upstart a long leash.

Meanwhile, Rockefeller set to work building his Office, the first formal U.S. foreign aid program, and for that reason he probably qualifies as the second-most influential citizen in the history of U.S. policy toward Latin America. (Theodore Roosevelt will always be first, and Fidel Castro would move Rockefeller into third if noncitizens were included.) U.S. aid had occurred earlier with occasional contributions to relief efforts after natural disasters and with infrastructure projects during the Progressive-era protectorates, but Rockefeller's Office was the first formal aid institution explicitly aimed at improving Latin Americans.[29]

In September 1940, six weeks after Hull's Havana commitment and three weeks after FDR's executive order, the State Department produced a report aimed at coaxing funds out of Congress. It justified Rockefeller's Office as meeting compelling national security concerns, warning that "the United States has the choice between abandoning everything south of the Rio Grande to Germany or of taking drastic steps to protect its interests."[30] Those interests were largely related to the access of raw materials, and many of those—such as rubber in the Amazon jungle—were located in unhealthy regions.

Congress agreed, and in the middle of World War II a member of the House of Representatives summarized what he thought Rockefeller's Office was supposed to be doing: "cooperate with the governments of other American republics to help solve critical health and economical problems that impede the war effort." That sentence prefaced a question: "Would you say everything we have done there has something directly to do with the war effort?" "Absolutely" was Rockefeller's one-word response. The official history of the Office emphasized that "the agency operated as a part of the war machine."[31]

ROCKEFELLER HAD MORE than that in mind. He carved out two areas for wartime attention, the first of which had already been accepted as a mechanism of soft power: propaganda. It consisted of a vast panoply of anti-Axis activities, which were gently criticized by a skeptical Laurence Duggan as a "campaign to convince the Latin American peoples we were not the mercenary materialists that our enemies called us, that we thought their painting, music, literature exciting, enchanting." In Duggan's opinion, this effort to reprogram the grandchildren of Rubén Darío and José Enrique Rodó was bound to be a failure. "Only the French can effectively mix propaganda and culture; and they do it in small doses, served with infinite casualness and grace."[32]

From a twenty-first-century perspective there is good reason to look askance at many of the initiatives designed to show how much the United States appreciated Latin American culture. Rockefeller turned down one suggestion for concerts in the United States featuring Latin American composers ("there is not enough good Latin American symphonic material to sustain a series"), but he was proud of a "Yale Glee Club concert in March at the Pan American Union at which 10 or 12 Latin American songs were sung." Rockefeller also organized U.S. tours by the Chilean national ski team and the Uruguayan national soccer team, and at one point wrote about a plan to enter a group of Argentine gauchos in U.S. rodeo shows.[33] The idea was not so much to educate U.S. citizens as it was to convince Chileans, Uruguayans, and Argentines that the United States respected their achievements.

That said, the primary propaganda activities presented U.S. culture to Latin Americans, many of whom were learning about the United States from motion pictures. In this area, "one of our first concerns has been to correct some of the unconscious practices which have made motion pictures a source of trouble to our public relations." For example, the film "Down Argentine Way" was detrimental to U.S.-Argentine relations because "the second most prominent Argentine character in it was a gigolo [and] the only Argentine character heard speaking any Spanish spoke with an obvious Mexican accent." Worse yet, "the whole plot revolved around a crooked race at the famous Buenos Aires Jockey Club—an institution of which Argentinians are very proud."

Films distributed in Latin America were carefully vetted thereafter. One report noted that "when Paramount recently produced its picture, 'The World in Flames,' the Division induced them to inject into the South American prints of this film, reference to South American heroes Bolivar and San Martin." Rockefeller also reported that "because of South American objections to [playboy] Clark Gable in the role of Simon Bolivar, Louis B. Mayer has placed Robert Taylor in the part instead."[34]

The film effort was merely the tip of the propaganda iceberg. There were dozens of additional activities, especially to subsidize friendly Latin American media but also to produce war-focused publications such as a beware-of-subversion magazine, *En Guardia*. Rockefeller appears to have given his associates a green light to try everything they could think of trying, except the Argentine gauchos.[35]

But his primary interest was not in propaganda but in development projects—in uplifting. "Nelson Rockefeller came in for lunch," Adolf Berle told his diary in mid-1941. "He has the South American division of propaganda but he thinks propaganda by itself is nothing. It ought to go along with a solid constructive program."[36]

Then in December came Pearl Harbor, and it produced not only the opportunity Rockefeller wanted but also no doubt more than he could ever have dreamed of obtaining. On March 13, 1942, three months after Pearl Harbor, he and FDR had a private lunch; on March 15 they had Sunday lunch with their spouses; on March 24 Roosevelt upgraded Rockefeller to first class from a middle seat in Row 43:

> I hereby direct you, as Coordinator of Inter-American Affairs, to formulate and execute a program to aid and improve the health, safety and general welfare of the peoples of Mexico, Central and South America and the outlying islands including the West Indies. The duties and responsibilities in this connection will be to carry out measures for the control and prevention of disease, sanitation, sewage disposal, housing, improvement of food and water supplies, building of roads, highways, transportation facilities and public works, nutrition, general medical treatment and the education and training deemed necessary to achieve these objectives, together with such additional measures as you may deem necessary or advisable to protect the health, safety and general welfare of the inhabitants.[37]

Here was a green light for improving more or less everything, and it sent Rockefeller into overdrive. Seven days after receiving FDR's letter, his office created an Institute of Inter-American Affairs, a nonprofit Delaware corporation funded by the U.S. government but free from bureaucratic roadblocks that might pop up while implementing a form of government assistance that had never been attempted except with the modest *servicios* during the 1915–1934 takeover of Haiti. Now Rockefeller's Institute set out to create a set of these cooperative development programs in each Latin American country—a Servicio Cooperativo Interamericano de Salud Pública, for example, housed in each country's Ministry of Public Health, with the director of each *servicio* a U.S. expert.[38] Soon the *New Yorker* featured Rockefeller in one of its "Profiles," referring to him as "Best Neighbor," and in it he identified his goal: "to produce a better life for the people under the democratic system."[39]

Along with enlarging his mandate, FDR had also upgraded Rockefeller bureaucratically. Originally appointed as "Coordinator of Commercial and Cultural Relations," now he had become the far more imposing "Coordinator of Inter-American Affairs." Prior to this, there had been the usual bureaucratic bumping as Rockefeller staked out his turf, but he used little of his new authority to displace others; rather, he packed an empty space with a staff that eventually peaked at over fourteen hundred. The official history of the Office gently pointed out that "the great enthusiasm of the men making up the Coordinator's Office, coupled with a lack of formality and a failure to observe customary procedures, proved to be a slightly disturbing influence in the rather sedate atmosphere of the State Department."[40]

Certainly Rockefeller tried to be cooperative. At one point he approached Sumner Welles about jointly creating "country commissions" that would propose a set of development projects. Initially one country would be selected for a feasibility study "by specialists of the various United States Government departments and agencies," and then the projects considered feasible would be implemented by the agency best suited to do so, not necessarily by Rockefeller's Office.

Rockefeller was also unfailingly cordial, as in 1941, when for Christmas he gave Welles a picture by one of his favorite painters, the Brazilian Cândido Portinari, accompanied by an unctuous post–Pearl Harbor note: "Your unfaltering serenity and courage in these critical days have been a source of inspiration to all of us." But the note's salutation was "Dear Mr. Welles," and Welles's thank-you note began with "Dear Mr. Rockefeller," hardly what one would expect from two men who had been working together for over a year.[41] This tone was undoubtedly set by Welles, who clearly preferred formality to collegiality; in contrast, Duggan and Rockefeller exchanged "Dear Larry" and "Dear Nelson" letters.

Yet Duggan did not hesitate to complain when the newcomer entered an unauthorized area. "We frankly have something of a problem with Mr. Rockefeller," Duggan told Welles in late 1942. "He sent Christmas greetings to all the presidents whom he knows personally. Owing to a mix-up the message intended for the President of Brazil went to [Chilean] President Ríos. It conveyed 'Sincere best wishes for your great country which is carrying forward its war effort in so magnificent a fashion under your brilliant directions.'" At this point Chile was doing nothing of the kind—it had not even severed relations with Germany, and some of its leaders clearly favored the Axis. "I wonder, therefore, whether sometime you [Welles] would suggest to Mr. Rockefeller that in the interests of good Government administration he confine his correspondence with Chiefs of State to strictly personal matters."[42]

One fast-rising Foreign Service officer, Ellis Briggs, did not complain about turf invasions; rather, he complained that Rockefeller's "program of adventurous diplomacy demonstrated the folly of good works unleavened by experience. It likewise proclaimed the difficulty inherent in persuading developing societies to abandon their untidy habits in favor of Kleenex, antiperspirants, and bingo on Saturday evenings." None of this ever rose to the level of bureaucratic warfare, however, and the official history of Rockefeller's Office probably came close to describing what actually existed: "reasonably effective cooperation, especially as long as Sumner Welles, and particularly Laurence Duggan, remained with the Department."[43]

But by 1943 Sumner Welles's State Department career was coming to an end, and he would take Duggan down with him.

IT IS NOT possible to understand the fate of the Good Neighbor policy and, more important, the evolution of what was to come—early Cold War policy—without first discussing what was about to happen: State's Division of American Republics Affairs would be without leadership for sixteen months, and soon there would be another vacancy for two full years. Those vacancies left State's Latin Americanists unable to access the highest decision-making levels at a time when uplifting other parts of the world was becoming a feature of U.S. foreign policy.

The problem was the relationship between Undersecretary Welles and Secretary Hull. Projecting an image of exceptional self-confidence, Welles was one of those people for whom doubt is an irritant, to be brushed away as if it were lint on his lapel. Hull was invariably doubtful, always cautious. "The way Secretary Hull leads the Department it would never decide anything," Welles complained to Vice President Henry Wallace, while Assistant Secretary Breckinridge Long told his diary, "Welles thinks so fast and moves so rapidly that he gets way out in front and leaves no trace of the positions he has taken or the commitments he has made. . . . He acts independently and forgets to tell the Secretary. At least that is what Cordell said. It worries him, because he likes Welles."

That was written shortly after Long had joined the administration. A year later he again noted that "they are of entirely different types—Welles daring, thorough, quick thinking, clear headed—but possibly a little on the too daring side, [whereas] Hull, on the other hand, is wary, scrupulous in exploring all the ground around, slow to come to conclusion"—"very, very awfully slow at decision."[44] Now that Long was more familiar with the terrain, he did not mention anything about Hull liking Welles.

After their 1933 disagreement over sending troops to Cuba, there was only one major policy conflict related to Latin America. It arose when Welles represented the United States at a January 1942 Rio conference, called immediately after Pearl Harbor to secure united Latin American support for the Allies. With Chile and especially Argentina reluctant to make a commitment, Welles felt obliged to accept a compromise recommendation that all the participants sever relations with the Axis; Hull had expected a requirement. When Welles telephoned to report the outcome, Hull recalled, "I then spoke to him more sharply than I had ever spoken to anyone in the Department. I said I considered this a change in our policy, made without consulting me."[45]

"This has been a bad week," wrote assistant secretary Adolf Berle, who (along with FDR and Duggan) had listened in on the Hull-Welles telephone call. Neither Duggan nor FDR left behind their impressions, but Berle's recall closely resembles Hull's memoir: "The Secretary was a thoroughly angry man. . . . It was a violent conversation [and] it is obvious that now there is a breach between the Secretary and Sumner which will never be healed." "Along past midnight, Duggan and I left to get a stiff drink," and after the drink had gone home to tell his diary what had happened. Hull was "spiritually torn to pieces. . . . The Rio incident did raise a square question as to who is the real Secretary of State."[46] Soon Hull was telling Breckinridge Long that "he could no longer trust Welles—he was laying plans for himself, was making speeches without approval."

This was compounded by a closely related problem: Welles regularly by-passed Hull and went straight to the Oval Office. Breckinridge Long recalled that once, when he was chatting with FDR's appointments secretary, "to my surprise he entered in his quite outspoken way on the criticism of Welles for trying to 'take over' Hull's functions; said he was continually trying to confer with the President." And Long now saw for himself that Hull "resents Welles' constant contact with the President—which are over his mental objection, though he has never spoken of it, he said, except to his wife and to me." On yet another occasion Hull told Long that "he felt he was working somewhat in the dark and was being short-circuited—and resented it." Postmaster General James Farley also could see that "Hull resents the relationship between Welles and the President." "I am certain he sees Welles more frequently than Hull, and that [Welles] is more influential, in particular as far as the running of the Department is concerned."[47]

That may have simply reflected the fact that Welles was quick and Hull was not, and for FDR "a moment of boredom was a desperate ordeal"—or so said one of the president's close friends. "His mind was sure to range ahead of any slow speaker." As a result, Roosevelt "often preferred to consider foreign relations with Walton Moore, counselor of the State Department, or Sumner Welles or others who came to the point quickly, instead of with Cordell Hull, who had a rare quality of wisdom but was given to building up his case fact by fact and reason by reason." That probably helps explain why Welles's name would appear on FDR's White House appointment calendar so often. Hull's name appears more frequently—561 times versus 400—but he had fifteen more months in office and was, after all, the secretary of state.[48]

"Sumner is really preserving a direct line of power through the White House," wrote Adolf Berle; "the Secretary will be satisfied with nothing less than cutting that off."[49]

Added to this was the issue of Welles's alleged homosexuality at a time when that was an instant disqualification for public service, to say nothing about criminal prosecution. "There is a lot of talk about Welles's departure being on account of difference in opinion about policy," wrote Breckinridge Long, but "that is not the case. The trouble was purely and simply that Welles was accused of a highly immoral bit of conduct." The conduct allegedly occurred on a train in September 1940, when an allegedly drunk Welles had allegedly propositioned one or more Pullman porters.

"Hull talked to me at great length on many occasions," Long continued, "expressing his anxiety that the public would get the story, that there would be an explosion and not only the reputations of the Department would be involved but, worse, the President himself be besmirched because of the conduct of one of his closest intimates and associates." Welles's replacement as undersecretary, Edward Stettinius, recalled that in his first transition meeting with Hull, the secretary "discussed very, very privately Sumner Welles's situation and the whole personal situation—certain things he had given [leaked] to the press and his relations with the press and a very personal private situation."[50]

FDR had been forced to confront the alleged train incident shortly after it occurred, when William Bullitt, his former ambassador to the Soviet Union and to France, and Welles's most intense rival, wrote as if he had lectured the president: "He [FDR] was thinking of asking Americans to die in a crusade for all that was decent in human life. He could not have among the leaders of a crusade a criminal like Welles. I added that . . . I wanted to do all I could to accelerate our preparation for war but that under no circumstances would I take any position in the Department of State or in the Foreign Service until he should have dismissed Welles."

Roosevelt's reaction? "At this point the President pressed the button under his desk and summoned General Watson. I rose and remarked that I would expect to hear from him the end of the week and took my leave. The President, when General Watson entered the room, said: 'Pa, I don't feel well. Please cancel all my appointments for the rest of the day. I want to go over to the House.'" A year later Vice President Henry Wallace wrote in this diary: "The President somehow got started talking about Bill Bullitt. He said Bill Bullitt was perfectly terrible. I asked him why. He said because of that awful story he spread all over town about Sumner Welles. He said Bill ought to go to hell for that."[51]

Given their differing temperaments, what seems remarkable today is that Hull and Welles managed to work together for an entire decade. Had the potential for a scandal not arisen, Hull probably would have found another reason to force Welles out. Hull himself insisted that Welles's discharge was only because of their conflict over authority and initiative. The certainty is that in mid-1943, three years after the alleged episode, Welles met alone with the president to offer his resignation, and then, Hull recalled,

"Welles came to my office immediately and indicated his belief that the President had acted at my instance. . . . I have not talked with him since." Within a week Welles had cleaned out his desk and left the State Department, never to return. A White House press release announced his resignation "in view of his wife's health," accompanied by FDR's expression of "deep and sincere regret."[52]

For Welles it was all downhill until his death in 1961. His son saw the serious deterioration accelerate after his wife Mathilde died in 1949: "His remaining years were marked by loneliness, illness and suicidal dissipation."

"The world will soon march by the little tragedy and it will be smothered in the dust of rapidly succeeding events," Breckinridge Long wrote in his diary.[53] So it was, but not before Hull erased any trace of his undersecretary's influence, notably Laurence Duggan. This eliminated the only other person who might have effectively represented Latin America at the highest level of foreign policy making.

In early 1944, five months after Welles's ouster, Secretary of War Henry Stimson and Secretary of the Navy Frank Knox went to Hull's office for their normal weekly meeting. "Hull started out by telling us of an interview he had had yesterday, I believe, with the President on the subject of Sumner Welles." Hull had shown FDR evidence that a resentful Welles, in retirement, was still leaking confidential information to columnist Drew Pearson, and convinced the president that Welles was not simply an outcast but an adversary whose access to sensitive information needed to be stopped. "Consequently this morning Hull was feeling quite chipper. He told us that he was having a housecleaning of the State Department and was getting rid of the men that he thought were not loyal to himself. This was necessary because Welles had been building up quite a machine of his own."[54]

Duggan offered his resignation seven months later. He soon took over from his father the directorship of the Institute of International Education, but in 1948, at the age of forty-three, he fell to his death from the Institute's sixteenth-floor offices in New York City, perhaps a suicide. He left a wife and four children, but no note.[55]

Once Welles had been pushed out in mid-1943, the position of principal Latin Americanist was left vacant for over a year, allowing State's "internationalists" to suppress the "regionalists" and especially the Latin Americanists, who now had no high-ranking voice at a special moment—a unique

moment—when more or less everything was up for grabs, including crucial
questions about whom to uplift and how.

THEN IN DECEMBER 1944, sixteen months after Welles's departure and two
months before a meeting with Latin America's foreign ministers in Mexico
City, an assistant secretary was needed. So FDR pulled Nelson Rockefeller
out of his coordinator's office and asked him to fill Welles's position as the
administration's principal voice for Latin America policy. A bureaucratic
reshuffling had occurred during the interregnum, and Rockefeller had the
distinction of becoming the first formal "Assistant Secretary of State for
American Republic Affairs."[56] Selected because of the goodwill he had created with his wartime uplifting, Rockefeller could help Washington gain
Latin American support before the upcoming San Francisco conference to
create the United Nations.

ROCKEFELLER HAD TWO problems to confront before Washington's Good
Neighbors could hand off the baton to the next generation of Latin Americanists, soon to be called the Cold Warriors, and the first of the two would
not have been resolved as it was, had Sumner Welles still been in the saddle.
Here is where the Good Neighbor policy began to die.

This first problem came out of the blue in early 1945, when FDR wrote the
presidents of six of the ten South American countries, all of which had already severed relations with the Axis, to inform them that "it is being increasingly urged that invitations to the coming United Nations Conference
on world security organization should be limited to those nations which are
signatories of the United Nations Declaration." That was a polite way of
saying that if these six wanted to participate in the San Francisco conference to organize the United Nations, they now had to sign the 1942 United
Nations Declaration, which was a declaration of belligerency (from the Latin
bellum gerere, to wage war).[57]

The war was all but over. Italy had already been conquered, Germany
would surrender in four months and Japan in seven. A declaration of bel-
ligerency by six South American countries would be meaningless—except
that the Great Powers had now given it meaning by agreeing that belligerency was the price of admission to the San Francisco conference. The reason
Washington wanted the six to pay it was simple: at the moment, Stalin was
insisting upon membership for each of the sixteen constituent Soviet repub-

lics, all belligerents. The Roosevelt administration wanted all twenty Latin American countries at its side.

Five of the South American six quickly caved in; Chile did not. Its response to FDR's letter was an *aide-mémoire* indicating that it did not appreciate the letter's wording, which classified Chile as an "associated nation." Chileans told Ambassador Claude Bowers that the term "smacks of Versailles and is outmoded"—an indicator that Chileans had not forgotten their disrespectful treatment by the major powers at the 1919 conference ending World War I.

The *aide-mémoire* also pointed out that Chile had severed relations with the Axis two years earlier, in January 1943 (albeit a year later than the United States had wished), and Chile's foreign minister reminded Ambassador Bowers that his country "is giving her full economic resources against the Tripartite Pact and she has long been giving her full possible military resources by patrolling and protecting 2,000 miles of Pacific coast with her naval vessels that are under orders to fire on any Axis vessel or submarine found in these waters."[58]

Then came several more days of back-and-forth, all of which underscored the fact that Chile did not want to do what the United States wanted it to do. We have no opinion polls to consult, but Chileans were probably not too different from what a U.S. embassy official in La Paz had reported about Bolivians: "They have no real convictions one way or the other. They are not pro-Nazi or pro-Argentine. Neither are they pro–United Nations [Allies] in the abstract. They are first pro-themselves and second pro-Bolivia from a narrow and immediate economic point of view."[59] Chileans pointed out that the United States had waited more than two years to enter the war, and that it did so only after being attacked at Pearl Harbor. Thousands of miles away from the fighting, Chile had never been attacked. This was not Chile's war.

President Juan Antonio Ríos also reminded Ambassador Bowers that Chile was only four weeks away from parliamentary elections, and a declaration of war would not be popular among a substantial number of voters, perhaps a majority. "We are fully alive to the delicacy of this matter," replied Secretary of State Edward Stettinius, Cordell Hull's successor, advising President Ríos to sell the declaration to his voters by saying that Chile had been at war all along—that is, by "softpedaling the declaration of a pre-existing state of belligerency as only a formality."[60]

Seeing no alternative, Chile agreed to "recognize the fact of existing bel-ligerency," but President Ríos's letter with those words was not quite sufficient. To be absolutely clear, FDR's State Department then instructed Ambassador Bowers to inform Ríos "that it would be necessary that Chile address to the Department a private note saying that this action is 'equivalent to war.'" President Ríos did as demanded, writing FDR that "the Government and people of Chile are in full accord with Your Excellency's views, and I have the honor and pleasure of making this known in my reply."[61]

This never would have happened had Sumner Welles been in charge. Per-haps with the help of Rockefeller and Duggan, he would have quietly coaxed the letters out of all six governments. Perhaps the issue would have simply disappeared—in the end, Stalin agreed to reduce his demand from sixteen to two.

THE ONE NONBELLIGERENT FDR had not even bothered to write, lost-cause Argentina, was responsible for triggering the second problem with Latin Americans in the waning days of the Good Neighbor policy. It occurred at the pre–San Francisco meeting with Latin Americans at Chapultepec, the old imperial castle in the heart of Mexico City, which began on February 21, 1945, seven days after Chile capitulated.

Several months earlier, in October, Argentina had asked the governing board of the Pan American Union to convene a meeting of foreign ministers so that it could refute Argentina's "presumed non-compliance with its com-mitments" regarding the war. The request had gone to the chair of the Pan American Union's board of governors, Secretary of State Cordell Hull, who had been dealing with obstreperous Argentine governments since the 1933 Montevideo conference. Wide and deep had grown the hole into which Secretary Hull would have liked to deposit Argentina's leaders, and he was not alone in Washington, where you could count Argentina's friends on ten fingers, all of them belonging to Argentina's ambassador. FDR had recently ordered his undersecretary of state to "make a face to the Argentineans once a week. You have to treat them like children."[62]

That was the atmosphere in which Secretary Hull received Argentina's request for a meeting of the governing board of the Pan American Union. Ill, exhausted, and five weeks from retirement, Hull had not been interested in holding a conference with Latin Americans, but Mexico's foreign minister had recently expressed an interest in a meeting to address issues related to the transition from war to peace, especially the widespread concern that the war's end would be followed by an abrupt drop in demand for Latin America's raw materials. On the U.S. side, a meeting would provide an opportunity to solidify a unified front at the upcoming United Nations conference in San Francisco. So Washington agreed to meet and convinced Mexico (which appears to have needed little convincing) to invite only the belligerent governments, which excluded Argentina.[63]

The agenda proposed by Mexico included the discussion of how to handle Argentina's October request for a meeting to clear its name. A handful of leaders, including most of the reluctant six, especially an embittered Chile, took over from there, making it clear that the United States had to choose between inviting Argentina to join everyone else at San Francisco, on the one hand, or losing much of Latin America's support at San Francisco, on the other. As a compromise, the final act at Chapultepec lobbed the ball onto Argentina's court: it could participate in the United Nations conference, but only if it declared war. It did so on March 27, forty-two days before Germany surrendered and twenty-nine days before the San Francisco conference was called to order.

Other than deciding how to handle Argentina, Washington seems to have had only solidarity to pursue at Chapultepec—just a friendly meeting, with the U.S. delegates authorized to say, vaguely, that the United States was willing to cooperate on economic issues. The newsworthy item: Washington would indicate the importance it attached to Latin American affairs by sending its new secretary of state. As it happened, Edward Stettinius flew to Mexico directly from the all-important Big Three meeting at Yalta, with only a refueling stop in Brazil, and seemed content to do little more than follow his aides' instructions—one member of the U.S. delegation wrote in his diary about Stettinius's "cheerful ignorance."[64]

That placed the laboring oar in the hands of Assistant Secretary Rockefeller, and it did not help that he had brought along Dana Munro as his special adviser. Out of the Foreign Service since 1932 and now a history professor, here in 1945 Munro was still writing 1920s-style memos, including this period piece: "We have special responsibilities in the Caribbean region and special reasons for an active policy designed to help the countries there in achieving stability and social progress."[65]

The most observant U.S. delegate appeared to be Adolf Berle, a brash member of FDR's brain trust who had recently been named ambassador to

Brazil. His conversations at Chapultepec led him to conclude that most Latin American delegates were fearful that the United Nations, dominated by the major powers, would dictate to the region, just as FDR had recently dictated to the six nonbelligerents. And Berle found Washington's closest Latin American ally, Brazil, to be particularly concerned about future meddling by the warlike Europeans. Uruguayans agreed: they "think that the British would throw them to the Argentines. The rest of South America simply thinks we don't know what we are doing—and I must say I think they are right."[66] Sumner Welles was missed.

PRESIDENT ROOSEVELT DIED in April 1945, four months after forcing six good neighbors to declare war against their own wishes, and two months after the Chapultepec meeting. In June, a week after the San Francisco conference, President Harry Truman pushed out the secretary of state, Edward Stettinius, FDR's choice, in favor of James Byrnes, his choice. Byrnes dismissed Assistant Secretary Rockefeller six weeks later, and Rockefeller's uplifting base, the Office of Inter-American Affairs, was abolished a few months after that.[67]

The problem with that: Latin Americans were now asking to be uplifted.

CHAPTER 7

To Improve or Not to Improve?

The Cold War Question

> The single problem which most affects our relations with Latin America is their desire for capital from the United States for economic development.
>
> —*Briefing Material for the Secretary*, January 4, 1950

THE CENTRAL QUESTION during the Depression had been whether the United States could be a good neighbor, and the answer had been yes. The central question during World War II had been whether Latin Americans were going to be good neighbors, and the answer had been yes. Then communism filled the space left vacant by the defeated Axis.

However much they may have disliked his domestic witch hunt, a large proportion of the U.S. public and its leaders agreed with the flamboyant Senator Joseph McCarthy, who warned that "today we are engaged in a final, all-out battle between communistic atheism and Christianity. The modern champions of communism have selected this as the time. And, ladies and gentlemen, the chips are down—they are truly down."[1] Now Washington's central question about Latin Americans was this: On which side of the table were they going to place their chips?

The answer here in the early 1950s depended upon which of the 150 million Latin Americans you might ask. Most were leading lives that made the question irrelevant. As Aldous Huxley pointed out, a major function of the brain is to shut out irrelevancies, "leaving only that very small and special selection which is likely to be practically useful."[2] He would not have expected Latin Americans to pay attention to a senator from Wisconsin. They had other rows to hoe, other questions to ask, many about the distribution of chips within their own countries.

Most of the ensuing confusion regarding those chips would reflect the fact that the Cold War was largely undeclared, with the rival Soviet Union and Red China often supporting proxy forces whose behavior was almost always open to more than one interpretation. From whom did the members of these "liberation movements" want to liberate themselves? From colonial masters? From corrupt dictators? From poverty? From fickle global markets? Looking back on his 1950s presidency, President Dwight Eisenhower wrote that "it was difficult to differentiate positively between Communist influence and uncontrolled and politically rebellious groups."[3]

FOR U.S.–LATIN AMERICAN relations, the Cold War was neatly divided into two parts: the early years, from the end of World War II until 1959, and then the three-decade period after 1959, the year Cuba's revolutionary government began moving its chips to the Soviet side of the table. High-level U.S. officials gave little attention to Latin Americans in the earlier part; Washington had pressing concerns elsewhere, and most Latin American governments behaved more or less as the early Cold War Truman and Eisenhower administrations (1945–1961) wanted them to behave. They, too, were anticommunists. "We have received a consistent support of Latin America on virtually all of the important issues in the United Nations," reported a fast-rising State Department Latin Americanist in 1952. "Their twenty votes constitute an important force in the present system of world debate and are generally applied in support of the West."[4]

So the little attention given Latin America by senior officials often seemed to be offhand, such as in early 1950, when the minutes of a staff meeting have Secretary of State Dean Acheson saying "that he wanted to know more about the situation in South America. He said he was rather vague on this particular point. He wanted to know whether they were richer or poorer, going Communist, Fascist, or what? He said he would like to be carefully briefed on this entire area."[5]

Someone must have told him that State's Latin Americanists had just finished drafting such a report, and a copy was delivered to the Secretary's office the next day: "The first problem vis-à-vis Latin America which had to be dealt with was the feeling on the part of the Latin Americans that since the end of the war the U.S. had become preoccupied in other parts of the world and had lost interest in hemispheric affairs." Fortunately, the report continued, this issue of neglect had been put to rest by Secretary Acheson's recent speech to the Pan American Society in New York—"the most complete restatement of Latin American policy in many years."[6]

It had been nothing of the kind; Acheson had nearly put himself to sleep with sentences like this: "If I have said nothing new tonight, it may well be because, in a family of nations as in families of individuals we should expect nothing more sensational than growth." The briefing paper acknowledged that the speech had "attracted relatively little attention domestically," but "it was hailed throughout Latin America as constituting in itself a reversal of what they had feared was our attitude of neglect."[7]

The rest of the briefing paper provided a quick sail across placid waters—nothing demanding immediate attention, although "the single problem which most affects our relations with Latin America is their desire for capital from the United States for economic development. There is a tendency to measure the extent of our interest in their welfare according to the extent to which we advance public funds for economic development." Latin Americans were asking for assistance.

While this briefing paper was definitely carried upstairs to Acheson's office, there is no evidence he read it, and the best bet is that he did not. "The problems of Latin America bored Dean Acheson," wrote a foreign service officer who worked closely with him; another concluded that "he didn't give a damn about Latin America."[8] The secretary's 798-page memoir barely mentioned the region, and the little attention it received was dismissive: "In that area of special American worry, the Good Neighborhood, there was plenty to worry about. Here Hispano-Indian culture—or lack of it—had been piling up its problems for centuries. An explosive population, stagnant economy, archaic society, primitive politics, massive ignorance, illiteracy, and poverty—all had contributed generously to the creation of many local crises." Not one of these problems appears to have required more than cursory attention, and certainly not sustained interest. Referring to his 1951 meeting with Latin American foreign ministers, Acheson wrote that "experts in these matters judged it a success, though little if anything concrete happened as a result of it. However, pent-up resentments were released, thus reducing emotional pressures."[9]

That probably says everything that needs to be said about the thinking of the man who sat at or near the top of the U.S. foreign policy apparatus during most of the Truman administration, as undersecretary from 1945 to 1947 and as secretary of state from 1949 to 1953. His successor during the Eisenhower years was John Foster Dulles, one of whose ambassadors wrote, "Mr. Dulles was so preoccupied with other areas of the world that perhaps he did not recognize the tremendous importance of the Latin American area, and events there were swept under the rug."[10]

Taking this cue from the Department's senior officers, State's principal Latin Americanist, Edward Miller, closed a 1950 meeting of the Inter-American Economic and Social Council with the observation that it had been "not one of the most spectacular, [but] in the nature of things, great decisions are not always to be expected." You never can tell when something important might come up, however, so, he added, "our delegation is in favor of holding a get-together of this nature every year."[11]

WERE THEY HERE today to explain their neglect, these early Cold War leaders would begin by pointing out that the United States now stood as the most powerful nation in history, the only major country whose infrastructure had not been severely damaged by the war. Except for Pearl Harbor, it had not even been touched. At war's end the United States accounted for perhaps half of the world's industrial production, and U.S. farms were so productive that Washington would soon be giving food away to a hungry world, driven in part by Adam Smith altruism (it was the right thing to do) and in part by Hans Morgenthau realism (it was important to keep surpluses from depressing domestic prices). As a result of its superpower status, every major problem was being dropped on Washington's doorstep. With one major exception, discussed below, none was coming from Latin America, and in that one case—Guatemala—it would be almost effortless for the United States to show what would happen when push came to shove in the Western Hemisphere.

But there was one back-burner problem identified in the 1950 briefing paper given to Secretary Acheson: "the impact of a new social consciousness on a society which until recently had been comparatively static for centuries." This consciousness was triggering "an excessively rapid trend towards the adjustment of social rights which could not but result in a greater degree of political instability."[12] Because it might affect the placement of Latin

America's chips, this problem would dominate Washington's debates about Latin America during these early Cold War years. Except for Guatemala, the debates were always at lower levels, and they always focused on one question: Does the United States need to step in and do something about this trend toward the adjustment of social rights—a redistribution of wealth and power from the few who had both to the many who had neither?

IT WAS NOT a question addressed during Washington's first postwar encounter with Latin America, which occurred at the San Francisco conference creating the United Nations.

The conference convened on April 25, 1945, seven weeks after the Chapultepec conference had given Argentina a path to participation, and twelve days before Germany surrendered. Having declared war thirty days earlier, Argentina was in attendance, but its military government was still considered fascist-friendly by both the United States and the Soviet Union, so there was no assurance that it would receive the votes needed for membership. Latin Americans held the largest single block of votes, however, and they were rallying behind Argentina's admission.

And tightly tied to the Argentine question was a second membership issue: At their recent Yalta meeting, Churchill and FDR had agreed to Stalin's demand that the UN admit the Ukraine and Byelorussia, both widely considered part of the Soviet Union rather than independent states. Like Argentina, those two might not have the needed votes. Then at one meeting of the U.S. delegation, Assistant Secretary of State Nelson Rockefeller pointed out the link between the two, warning that if the Soviet Union insisted on admitting its two allies, "he could not be held responsible for delivering the [Latin American] vote if nothing was done on the Argentinian question."

At a follow-up meeting Senator Tom Connally, a U.S. delegate and chair of the all-important Committee on Foreign Relations, asked why the United States was so opposed to Argentina's membership. "Sentimentally we oppose it," replied Secretary of State Edward Stettinius; "we just cannot let Argentina come in at the last minute." That was a poor answer. Foreign policy is not about sentiment; it is about protecting and promoting interests, and John Foster Dulles, then one of the delegation's advisers, argued that the United States had an interest in promoting Argentina's membership, however repugnant that might be. "If the Conference votes down the proposal [to admit the two Soviet republics], there is every reason to expect a blow-up. The Russians would accuse us of having sent Nelson Rockefeller around to tell the Latin American governments to vote against the proposal."[13]

Secretary Stettinius conceded, and former Secretary Cordell Hull, now writing his memoir, blasted Argentina's charter membership as "the most colossal injury done to the Pan American movement in all its history."[14]

THAT DID NOT resolve what came to be known as "the Argentine question": What should be done with a Latin American country whose government had refused to support the Allies during World War II? No high-level official had time for this question, but the way it played out at lower levels had a major impact upon the extent to which Latin Americans' concerns about the adjustment of social rights would receive a hearing in early Cold War Washington.

The Argentine question was going to be addressed at a time when the United States was (1) closing Rockefeller's wartime office responsible for improving Latin Americans and (2) emerging as the uplifter-of-last-resort for much of the rest of the world. The standard explanation for neglect of Latin Americans is that events elsewhere were far more important and immediate, but the longer anyone looks at the documents left behind in the archives (or, more important, the dearth of documents about Latin America that reached senior officials), the more obvious it becomes that the officials responsible for adding considerations about Latin America to early Cold War policy debates dropped the ball. The question of Latin Americans' adjustment of social rights was never added to these debates.

Recall Sumner Welles's resignation in September 1943, after a full decade of service as the principal Latin Americanist in Washington. His power was extraordinary, unequaled before or since. He could walk into the Oval Office whenever he wanted, and that goes a long way to explaining why FDR, who was every bit as busy as his two successors, Truman and Eisenhower, had found time for Latin Americans. Those four hundred FDR-Welles meetings were not to chat about the weather; most were to talk about Latin America.

But Welles was forced out, and Secretary of State Cordell Hull refused to appoint a replacement as State's principal Latin Americanist; instead, he went after Welles's colleagues. For more than a year—sixteen months—there was no high-level official representing U.S. interests in Latin America during discussions about postwar policy. It was only after Hull retired in late 1944 that a new secretary of state, Edward Stettinius, realized he would need some help at the upcoming conferences at Chapultepec and San Francisco. Nelson

Rockefeller was chosen, not because he had any clout in Washington, but because he had spent the past few years handing out foreign aid to Latin Americans. If anyone could convince them to do what Washington wanted, it would be Rockefeller.

He did his job well, but in August 1945, immediately after San Francisco, this agreeable, unpretentious Republican was dismissed and replaced by a disagreeable, pretentious Democrat, Spruille Braden, who had never served in Washington and was viewed by Undersecretary Dean Acheson as "a bull of a man physically and with the temperament and tactics of one, dealing with objects of his prejudices with blind charges, preceded by pawing up a good deal of dust."[15] Senior officials were not inclined to invite Braden to their meetings.

Braden would serve for two crucial years, from mid-1945 to mid-1947. During that time these senior officials were involved in setting up the postwar structure of international relations, while he was involved in an unimportant dispute with one of his own ambassadors. It was about the Argentine question—a policy disagreement that turned into a heated alpha-male contest with the U.S. ambassador to Argentina, George Messersmith. For two crucial years Braden and Messersmith arm-wrestled over entirely insignificant Argentina while the rest of Washington was getting organized for the Cold War. At the important meetings no one was warning about Latin America's "excessively rapid trend towards the adjustment of social rights."

SPRUILLE BRADEN WAS heir to what little the Depression had not snatched from his family's mining fortune. While working for the Braden Copper Company's El Teniente complex in Chile, he had married a Chilean and become fluent in Spanish, which served primarily to increase the number of people he could offend without a translator. But this would surface later; in the 1930s Braden had needed a job and the private sector was not hiring, so he asked influential friends to see if FDR might be willing to appoint him ambassador to Chile. The Santiago embassy went to a career officer, but as a consolation (and probably to look him over) he was invited to serve as a delegate to the 1933 Montevideo conference—the important one where Cordell Hull made the commitment to nonintervention.[16] His Spanish was useful and his demeanor apparently passed diplomatic muster, for he was then invited to participate in two other delegations, and they opened the door to appointments as ambassador to Colombia and then Cuba, where he spent most of World War II.

At war's end he was transferred to Argentina, where he was already convinced that the military government dominated by Colonel Juan Perón was fascist. As it happened, Argentina was about to have an election, with Perón the hands-down favorite because his working-class backers, the *descamisados,* were the largest segment of the electorate. They were focused on the adjustment of social rights. Focused instead upon yesterday's problem, fascism, Ambassador Braden decided to do whatever he could to stop Perón's juggernaut, giving one partisan speech after another and leaving everyone surprised that the government did not declare him persona non grata. Then in October 1945, before Argentina's election, Braden had been brought back from Buenos Aires to serve as Rockefeller's replacement.

A few months earlier, in April, Harry Truman had inherited the presidency and confessed in his diary to being unprepared: "I knew the President had a great many meetings with Churchill and Stalin," but "I was not familiar with any of these things." As vice-president-elect and as vice president he had talked with FDR only four times, never alone.[17] Now Truman was president, and because none of his administration's immediate problems involved Latin America, he had not simply left Latin America in the backseat; he moved it into the trunk.

Braden's assignment was to preside quietly over relations with the whole of Latin America, but he continued from Washington his campaign against Argentina's government, focusing upon its upcoming election. Two weeks before the voting, the State Department released its inflammatory Blue Book accusing Perón of being a fascist: "The totalitarian machine in Argentina is a partnership of German Nazi interests with a powerful coalition of active Argentine totalitarian elements."[18] Publication of this pamphlet had been opposed by Braden's successor as ambassador in Argentina, George Messersmith, who had been ambassador to Mexico at the time of the Chapultepec conference in early 1945. Argentina had not been invited, but it had an embassy in Mexico City and its ambassador had indicated that Argentina was ready to cooperate with the United States. The message cabled by Messersmith to FDR was that "the Argentines seem prepared to desert the Axis and join the good neighbors."[19]

During his rise through the Foreign Service ranks, Messersmith had developed some shortcomings of his own. First, he became presumptuous. "To tell me how to run the govt" is what President Truman jotted on his daily appointment sheet after Messersmith had come to the Oval Office for a courtesy call before leaving for Argentina.[20] Messersmith told everyone how to do everything and, equally unsurprising, few enjoyed working with him. "There were two kinds of Foreign Service officers," wrote Ellis Briggs, who served under Messersmith in Mexico: "those who had always heard that Ambassador Messersmith was difficult, but had not served with him; and those who had served with him, and were sure of it." The curator of the Messersmith Papers at the University of Delaware commented delicately, "One's first impression . . . is that he is somewhat pompous and pedantic, but occasionally his warmth shows through." Atop that was his world-class verbosity: Messersmith dictated what are unquestionably the longest memos in the history of U.S. foreign policy. "When he wrote a dispatch there was no such thing as one page or one hundred pages," Briggs continued; "it just went on, and on, and on."[21]

Now Messersmith's dispatches from Buenos Aires were urging Washington to accept Perón's electoral victory and seek to normalize relations. Braden insisted otherwise, using the most pejorative word in 1940s English: "Appeasement will be fatal and we must rigidly stand by our principles; . . . if we appease now and allow situation to drift, we will either be faced for a long time to come with a Fascist anti-U.S.A. Government under German tutelage and or [sic] eventually revolution in Argentina in which case supply of foodstuffs from this country might cease."[22]

Meanwhile, someone (probably Braden) was leaking unkind material about Messersmith, and so, presumptuously, Messersmith decided to complain directly to President Truman. "There is no doubt that he is talking to newspaper men in a way that he should not. . . . It is a matter of deep regret to me that I have to write you about this aspect of our problem, but it is a situation which has not been raised by me. It has been raised entirely by Spruille Braden, who simply is thoroughly unhappy because he sees a solution in sight."[23] Six weeks later, an Associated Press story, obviously based upon information from a State Department insider, charged Messersmith with criticizing Braden "to many Congressmen, and even to some of Mr. Spruille Braden's subordinates. Some of the letters were 15,000 words long, and as a matter of fact, one ran to 65,000."[24]

PULLING UP ALONGSIDE this bickering was an entire convoy of woes, highlighted in early 1946 by George Kennan's "containment" telegram from Moscow, which was followed twelve days later by Churchill's "Iron Curtain" speech in Missouri.

With the wartime allies now separating into hostile camps, President Truman's advisers made an urgent case that the United States had little choice but to assist anticommunist forces threatened by Moscow-leaning rivals. The president's announcement of what came to be known as the Truman Doctrine (March 1947) was implemented immediately with aid to allies in Greece and Turkey. With the State Department laser-focused upon Soviet moves in Europe, a new secretary of state, five-star general George Marshall, cabled Messersmith: "Your resignation has been accepted."[25]

No resignation had been offered. "I am frankly unable to understand the reasons for this precipitate acceptance of 'my resignation,'" Messersmith replied, but "if the President so desired I would be ready, in accord with the conversations which I have had with him and his indications to me, to accept another suitable post in the field." The morning of this reply found the secretary of state at Harvard University, unveiling one of the major initiatives in the history of U.S. foreign policy, the Marshall Plan. Clearly determined not to spend another minute on minor annoyances, Marshall returned to Washington and immediately fired Braden.[26] Then to ensure that Latin America not escape again, the trunk into which President Truman had placed Latin America was now secured with a tamper-proof bureaucratic padlock: no assistant secretary for Latin America was appointed for the next two years.

That made it impossible for State's leaderless Latin Americanists to present their ideas to senior officials. An assistant secretary was finally appointed in mid-1949, and after eighteen months of trying was finally able to schedule a presentation about inter-American relations to Marshall's Policy Planning staff. One of his advisers wrote that the high point of the meeting "was when almost the entire staff rushed to the window to see some fire engines."[27]

WITH BRADEN GONE, reasonably cordial relations were soon reestablished with Argentina, which tacitly agreed to annoy the United States no further, at least this time around. That cleared the way for a security conference that had been called for in 1945 at Chapultepec.[28] This 1947 conference would produce the Inter-American Treaty of Reciprocal Assistance, the first such collective defense agreement in U.S. history, and it was sufficiently important for President Truman to travel to Rio de Janeiro to address the closing ceremony.

At a predeparture press conference a reporter had asked if the administration was "taking any notice of the clamor on the part of Western Hemisphere nations for a Marshall plan," which had been announced for Europe two months before the Rio meeting. With no assistant secretary to coach him, Truman demonstrated that even an accomplished pianist can hit an off key, replying, "There has always been a Marshall plan in effect for the Western Hemisphere. The foreign policy of the United States in that direction has been set for one hundred years, known as the Monroe Doctrine."[29]

Then it was off to Rio, where Truman assured the delegates, "We in Washington are not oblivious to the needs of increased economic collaboration." He promised that these needs "will be approached by us with the utmost good faith and with increased vigor in the coming period," and vaguely committed the United States to "useful forms of economic collaboration with our friends." The details would ironed out at an economic conference to be held at an unspecified date.[30]

It turned out that what U.S. observers considered an unremarkable speech to a security conference was considered by Latin Americans as notable for its economic promise. For the next decade—a full ten years—there would be two entirely different mental frameworks contesting for primacy in early Cold War Washington. Both were focused on controlling what Secretary Acheson's 1950 briefing paper had referred to as Latin Americans' "excessively rapid trend towards the adjustment of social rights."

The framework selected initially by the United States emphasized improving the ability of Latin American governments to maintain internal security—to control this excessively rapid trend. The framework preferred by Latin Americans emphasized improving the region's economies, which, they argued, would improve the lives of the poor and slowly reverse this trend. This is where State's Latin Americanists would normally have been expected to insert Latin Americans' view into policy discussions. It was where strong leadership of State's Latin America bureau was sorely missed.

WASHINGTON'S INTERNAL SECURITY framework required the improvement of Latin America's military forces, an endeavor based entirely on the U.S. interest in containing the spread of communism.

During the Progressive era and the 1920s, the United States had created and trained constabularies and the like in the Caribbean and Central America. In every case the purpose of these forces was to maintain domestic tranquility. After World War I this assistance had spread southward, as a few South American governments began looking for replacements for the trainers who had been provided by Germany, now defeated. In 1920 Congress granted the Navy's request "to detail officers of the United States naval service to assist the Governments of the Republics of South America in naval matters," and Peru contracted almost immediately for four officers to reorganize the Peruvian navy. That was followed by Brazil, which hired nine officers to teach at Brazil's Naval War College. A 1926 law authorized the Army to send advisors as well.[31]

Latin American governments paid for this assistance, but most had been unable to shoulder the expense during the Depression. In mid-1939, just before Germany's attack on Poland, there were only eight U.S. military missions, with a total of twenty-four officers, in all of Latin America. But U.S. embassies were reporting on the Latin American military's admiration of Hitler's achievements on the battlefield, and of his revival of the German economy, and Washington's response was to assign at least one military attaché to every embassy—in mid-1939 there had been only six in all of Latin America.[32]

These quasi-diplomats "attached" to the embassy were not quite salesmen, but they began facilitating arms purchases by governments whose European sources were no longer available, and the arrival of military hardware frequently led to military advisers. The U.S. embassy in Buenos Aires reported as early as 1938, "There have been recently delivered here a number of American military planes [and] it offers us an opportunity to supply technical assistance to the Argentine Army which thus far has been given along general military lines by German officers."[33] The major spurt in the number of advisers occurred after the fall of France in 1940, when Congress authorized FDR "to assist the governments of American Republics to increase their military and naval establishments."[34] That included hardware at low or no cost, especially after 1941 when Congress passed the Lend-Lease Act.

Soon after the war a member of Congress asked Secretary of State Marshall, "If we sell arms, does that mean we will follow the sale of arms with military missions to South American countries?" His terse reply: "I assume so."[35] Always referred to as a "mission," the job of these advisers was quite different from that of the attachés. Working side by side with their hosts, they taught the purchasers how to use and maintain their new hardware. In these early years most advisers were placed on leave from the U.S. armed forces and inducted into their hosts' military. A U.S. Navy captain served as chief of the Peruvian Navy's General Staff during World War II, and the

U.S. admiral in charge of the U.S. Navy mission to Brazil was also a rear admiral in the Brazilian navy. At one point ten other U.S. officers were concurrently Brazilian officers.[36] These were close ties.

Except regarding Brazil, little of this wartime aid was motivated by an expectation that Latin Americans would fight alongside Allied troops. "They have never served a useful purpose" was the assessment of a Navy admiral during a 1943 discussion about the recently established Inter-American Defense Board. When State's Sumner Welles pointed out that Latin America's cooperation was helpful in other, nonmilitary ways, Admiral Frederick Horne replied that finding a way to occupy the Board's time was a problem for the State Department, not his Navy. "We feel the same way," added Army General Joseph McNarney, but softening the tone: "The War Department would be very happy for suggestions as to how it could be used so that the Board could be kept busy." Not wanting to quarrel, Admiral Horne agreed to be accommodating. "I am willing to give them anything we can with the understanding that we don't have to pay any attention to them."

Nothing could be more revealing than the need to guard the airfields being constructed in Cuba so that U.S. aircraft could scan the Caribbean for submarines. The Army suggested using U.S. troops, but Welles insisted, no doubt correctly, that "the Cuban reaction to any proposal of this character would not be worse—couldn't be worse. . . . It would be regarded as an offense to their national pride and dignity." An Army colonel mentioned the availability of Spanish-speaking soldiers ("We have been under considerable pressure to find some useful purpose for Puerto Rican troops"), and General McNarney added, "We have a large number of negro units which we could send to Cuba, but I am sure that would be more unsatisfactory than Puerto Ricans." The obvious choice—Cuban soldiers—was also the last choice. "We might as well put up a barbed wire fence."[37]

SETTING FIGHTING CAPABILITIES aside, the effect of World War II had been twofold.

First, it led to the withdrawal of European missions, leaving the United States as the only reliable source of both hardware and expertise. At war's end the Army had seventeen missions in thirteen Latin American countries—486 soldiers—and an admiral informed Congress, "We have naval missions in all of the countries that have navies, and they all have representatives in Washington." Another admiral reported that the naval academies of Brazil, Colombia, Ecuador, Peru, and Venezuela had adopted the textbooks and the curriculum used at the U.S. Naval Academy.[38] During the war 2,652 Latin American soldiers had been trained in U.S. facilities, an activity that was institutionalized immediately after the war when the U.S. Army opened its School of the Americas in the Panama Canal Zone.

Second, the war led President Truman to request that Congress approve his proposed Inter-American Military Cooperation Act of 1946. The proposal was a product of quiet meetings that had begun in 1943, when representatives of the Department of War and the Department of the Navy began to plan postwar policies. Their key agreement was that the next war, whenever it came, would not come slowly, as had World War II: "In the future, neither geography nor allies will render a nation immune from sudden and paralyzing attack."[39] So if Washington were to allow another powerful adversary to do what Imperial Germany and then Nazi Germany had done before the two world wars—infiltrate the Latin American military—the United States might lose the entire region before a war even began.

So the Army-Navy planners recommended that the United States promote "the standardization by the American Republics upon United States equipment and training doctrine to the exclusion of foreign materiel and military influence." A few months later the secretary of war told the secretary of state that "the presence of Military Missions is an essential part of the machinery required to reorient the military thought of Latin America from European influence to the democratic lines of our military doctrine."[40]

Given all else going on at the time, it is hardly surprising that it took a couple of years for a concrete proposal to wend its way to the Oval Office, but in mid-1945, soon after Germany surrendered, the Navy, Army, and State Departments warned a new president, Harry Truman, about the same danger faced in the prewar days, when "important elements in the armed forces of the American republics had been indoctrinated in the alien ideals espoused by aggressor nations, and had been imbued with an admiration for the warmaking methods of these nations." They asked for permission to "act forthwith to obtain the agreement of the other American republics to the adoption by them of United States military doctrine, United States military methods and procedures, and the United States standards of military equipment. Such agreement would envisage the dispatch by the United States of military missions to the other American republics to indoctrinate and train their armed forces."[41]

That became the gist of President Truman's proposed Inter-American Military Cooperation Act, but domestic politics were working against his administration. The 1946 off-year election would hand Republicans both houses of Congress, their first majorities in nearly two decades, and they were already focusing their deficit-sensitive eyes on cost-cutting. Still others simply saw no reason for military aid. Surely no European country was in any condition to challenge the United States in Latin America.

There also was opposition within the State Department, which questioned the wisdom of arming dictatorships. Former vice president Henry Wallace told his diary that Assistant Secretary Spruille Braden "is very much against our furnishing arms to all the Latin American countries," that Braden "says that with a bill of this sort in effect, middle-class liberalism would have no chance in Latin America." One of Braden's deputies, Ellis Briggs, was also a vigorous opponent. At his most recent post, as ambassador to the Dominican Republic, he had argued that "Trujillo's dictatorship represents the negation of many of the principles to which the United States subscribes." The effect of improving this or any dictator's army "might primarily be to give greater security to the dictator in question, permitting him to add to the chains whereby the citizens of that country are already shackled. This does not appear to me to be an objective to which our Government would wish to lend itself."[42]

President Truman's proposal failed to gain congressional approval three times in a row—in 1946, 1947, and 1948.[43]

The most important opponent turned out to be Undersecretary of State Dean Acheson, who endorsed the thinking of his midlevel colleagues. He told the secretary of war and the secretary of the Navy that "encouragement of expenditures on arms by the Latin American countries runs directly counter to our basic economic and political policies which aim to encourage an improvement in the living standards and economic welfare in those countries." Whether dictatorship or democracy, "the economic handicaps imposed by the proposed arms program would perpetuate and aggravate conditions of economic and political instability which already constitute a serious security problem for this Government in Latin America."[44]

Secretary of War Patterson's response: "The question we face in Latin America is not 'Shall they have arms?' The basic question which is the vital crux of the whole subject is 'Shall they have United States or foreign arms?'" Then Navy Secretary James Forrestal threw down the trump card: "It would seem that we are playing into the hands of the communists if by our own decision we disable ourselves from the tender of military assistance."[45]

The stalemate was resolved a month later at a meeting of the three secretaries—State, War, and Navy—chaired by Secretary of State Marshall, who understood that if he and his two fellow cabinet members could not agree, then the next step was to request a decision by a president who had already made his decision by signing off on the initial aid proposal. A note-taker at the meeting wrote that Acheson obediently fell on his sword: "Mr. Acheson said that he had over-ruled objections within his department against the Bill and that the State Department would now support it." A month later Marshall told the House committee considering the proposed legislation, "We should do everything within our power in a reasonable manner to unify the entire Western Hemisphere, so far as we can, in our own thinking and in our arrangements, for our own security, for our own well-being."[46]

Then Secretary Marshall, first and foremost a military officer (he answered his State Department telephone with "General Marshall speaking"), shipped Ellis Briggs off to exile in Uruguay, fired Spruille Braden, and accepted with honest appreciation Acheson's planned resignation. All three personnel moves occurred in the course of six days, and State's leaderless Bureau of American Republics Affairs got the message: a memo five months later noted that "generally ARA has, in recent months, taken a position of 'no political objection' to any arms sales to Latin America."[47]

NOW THE COLD War climate went from very bad to much worse. Czecho-slovakia slipped behind the Iron Curtain in early 1948, and a few months later the Soviets cut off land access to West Berlin, while the pro-Western government of Greece fought for its life against forces aligned with Moscow. Then the Chinese Nationalists suffered major losses soon after Truman's 1948 election victory, and within a year the U.S. side in that conflict had retreated to Taiwan.

The Truman administration's principal reaction was to take the lead in creating the North Atlantic Treaty Organization. On the same day he signed the NATO ratification in mid-1949, Truman asked Congress to authorize $1.4 billion in military assistance. The measure breezed through Congress, largely because it stipulated that all of the money would go to European al-lies, but the door to improving the Latin American military was cracked open by a line in the law permitting "procurement assistance" for Latin American governments seeking arms from U.S. manufacturers.[48]

Then in mid-1950 U.S. forces entered the war in Korea, and one effect of the heightened anxiety was for Washington to begin paying for the arms Latin Americans had recently gained help in procuring: $38 million in grant aid in 1951 and $51 million in 1952. In 1952 Ecuador became the first to negotiate a bilateral military assistance agreement (one was now needed to obtain arms and training), followed by Peru two days later and then by ten more Latin American countries over the next six years. Eventually U.S. training missions were established in every Latin American country except Mexico. Some had one (an Air Force mission in Uruguay) and several had three (Army, Navy, and Air Force), including Fulgencio Batista's Cuba and Rafael Trujillo's Dominican Republic.[49]

At the same time, the Good Neighbor policy of feting Latin America's military leaders continued, especially after 1942 when Congress created a new honor, the Legion of Merit. Eligible for this honor were foreign military officials who "shall have distinguished themselves by exceptionally meritorious conduct in the performance of outstanding services."[50]

Awarding the Legion of Merit became an especially sensitive topic during the early Cold War years, when the Truman and especially the Eisenhower administrations at times appeared insensitive to violations of human rights. Decorating Cuban military officers "is damaging to our standing with the Cuban people," complained the U.S. ambassador in 1953, a year after Fulgencio Batista's coup d'état. "The Cuban tends to read great significance into any action on the part of the United States. He will find in the exchange of decorations virtually open approval by the United States of Batista and his regime."[51]

Also criticized was a 1954 award to Venezuelan dictator Marcos Pérez Jiménez, a thank-you for hosting the OAS Meeting of Consultation that authorized Washington's effort to overthrow Guatemala's democratic government. "No Latin-American doubts the integrity and decency of President Eisenhower," wrote a critic, "but men are asking themselves what the merit of Pérez Jiménez consisted of. Might it have been to kill without pity and to torture with refinement?" A 1959 report from the House of Representatives gently noted that "the accordance of special honors to certain heads of state has, in some instances, created an impression that the United States is indifferent to the sufferings of oppressed peoples."[52]

Anticipating this concern, the administration's initial request to Congress, in 1946, had promised that assistance would "be guided by a determination to guard against placing weapons of war in the hands of any groups who may use them to oppose the peaceful and democratic principles."[53] But in 1957, when Cuban rebels were intensifying their attack upon the Batista dictatorship, a former Mutual Security Agency official was commissioned to examine military aid to Central America and the Caribbean, and he submitted a report that ignored the issue of aiding dictators.[54] In 1958, Batista's final year, the number of U.S. military advisors in Cuba doubled from fourteen to twenty-eight.

MEANWHILE, MOST OF Latin America's leaders preferred the United States to focus on improving the region's economic performance, but the 1957 report on Central America and the Caribbean indicated that "there are no loan activities for economic development purposes under the foreign assistance program in this area." After his 1947 commitment at Rio for "increased economic collaboration [that] will be approached by us with the utmost good faith and with increased vigor," President Truman had returned to Washington and a more pressing set of problems.

This was quite different from 1940, when Secretary Hull had met with the region's foreign ministers in Havana, immediately after the fall of France and the Netherlands, both of which had colonial outposts in the Caribbean and the Guianas. The United States achieved its goal at Havana: a declaration that any Western Hemisphere colonies of nations overrun by the Axis "shall be placed temporarily under the provisional administration of the American Republics." And Latin Americans achieved their goals: promises to help disposing of agricultural surpluses and to address "methods for improving the standard of living of the peoples of the Americas."[55] Then Hull, unlike President Truman in 1947, had returned to Washington and within sixteen days an executive order had created Rockefeller's Office for the Coordination of Commercial and Cultural Relations between the American Republics, the nation's first foreign aid bureaucracy, exclusively for Latin America.[56]

Next came the emergency meeting at Rio in early 1942, immediately after Pearl Harbor, and the U.S. delegation led by Sumner Welles had agreed "to request the Governing Board of the Pan American Union to convoke an Inter-American Technical Economic Conference charged with the study of present and post-war economic problems."[57]

Wartime demand for everything Latin America had to sell made this meeting less urgent, but when victory (and an anticipated reduction in demand for raw materials) seemed only a matter of time, the conference was scheduled for September 1944. When that month arrived, the State Department's Latin Americanists had no leadership and the administration was immersed in the all-important Dumbarton Oaks Conference to draft the UN Charter, which was in session from August 21 to October 7. And it also was impractical to hold an inter-American conference without Argentina, whose military government the United States was refusing to recognize, so the meeting promised at Rio in 1942 had still not been held when the Chapultepec conference was called to order in early 1945.

Now Latin American leaders were even more worried about a decline in demand for their countries' exports, and some were also worried as they watched Juan Perón mobilize Argentina's urban proletariat into a formidable political force. "What does America expect of this Conference?" asked Mexico's foreign minister at Chapultepec's initial plenary session. "The first thing it expects is practical resolutions, resolutions that relieve the misery, the helplessness of a great section of our masses." Democratic governments "must offer assurance of work, fair salaries, decent homes for the people; it must build schools, hospitals, gardens, but above all, and this is what characterizes democracy, it must guarantee economic security."[58]

Two conference committees then set to work on economic issues, one focusing on moderating the effect of a drop in demand for Latin America's raw materials, and the second discussing several different topics, including continuation of the assistance Rockefeller's Office had been providing. The United States agreed to taper off its raw materials purchases (pent-up postwar demand for consumer durables largely handled that problem), but the U.S. delegation was unprepared to talk about specifics in the second committee. Senior officials had been focused on Yalta and the upcoming San Francisco conference, not Latin America, and so the administration simply agreed to convene the "Inter-American Technical Economic Conference" that Sumner Welles had promised at Rio in 1942. Unlike that vague wartime agreement, when security was the understandable focus, here at Chapultepec Latin Americans insisted upon a precise commitment: the economic conference was to convene in five months, on June 15, 1945.[59]

But then FDR had died in April and Washington had so many more important balls in the air, including the San Francisco conference, which did not end until late June. That was after the surrender of Germany and only a few weeks before the first atomic bomb was dropped on Japan. With everyone struggling to keep their heads above water, especially a new secretary of state, James Byrnes, the June conference was postponed until November, but the position of assistant secretary of state had been vacant from mid-August, when Rockefeller was dismissed, until October 29, when Spruille Braden took the oath of office. November came and went, as did all of 1946.

Then came President Truman's 1947 Rio promise to explore "useful forms of economic collaboration," which could logically be a focus of the 1948 conference of foreign ministers at Bogotá. Who better to lead this discussion than Mr. Foreign Aid himself, Secretary of State George Marshall? Braden had been fired, so there was no assistant secretary to help craft Marshall's speech, and when his turn came he talked about the "staggering and inescapable responsibilities" that the United States had assumed elsewhere. "We must face reality," he insisted, and this reality was that Latin America, a tangent to the curve of postwar policy, would receive little more from the United States than increased Export-Import Bank loans. A member of the U.S. delegation recalled, "You could see people literally going down like a pricked balloon when he made that speech."[60]

SECRETARY MARSHALL WAS correct to note that the United States now had staggering responsibilities elsewhere, but a larger roadblock was that few U.S. officials understood why postwar Latin Americans thought the United States should help with their development. This is where an effective interpretive voice in the State Department was sorely needed; under normal circumstances a senior official would have explained why Latin Americans were not simply disappointed but offended at Bogotá.

Any such explanation would have begun with the Good Neighbor policy, which had turned Latin Americans' eyes toward Washington. FDR's generation had taught Latin Americans that Washington was where important uplifting decisions were made, and that the United States could be uncommonly generous when security interests were in play. Witness the deals struck with Mexico in 1941 and Bolivia in 1942.

Then, this explanation would have continued, after Pearl Harbor the United States needed Latin America's assistance. Alcohol was needed to manufacture tires, for example, and Cuba stepped up to the plate, selling the United States all of its sugar at low prices. A U.S. envoy reported that "in a remarkably short time we had an agreement to buy Cuban sugar at 3.25 cents a pound (this was later increased to 3.50 cents). If Batista had insisted on holding out and demanding all the traffic would bear, he could have had several times that amount." Cubans would have pointed out that this envoy got the numbers wrong—the price was 2.65 cents per pound—but the broader point was this: Latin Americans had sold low.[61]

Cuba was typical of Latin America, and at war's end nearly every leader in the region could have written what President José Figueres wrote about Costa Rica: "During World War II the coffee market was fixed by the Office of Price Administration at a level that turned out to be one half of the market price when controls were released. This meant that the coffee producing countries contributed to the war effort, during three or four years, fifty percent of the gross value of their main crop." And, Figueres continued, "when the war was finished, the coffee countries had accumulated large surpluses of dollars in the United States, not because they could afford any savings, but because American industry could not ship many goods under the circumstances."[62]

Uruguay was a good example. During the war years it sold meat, wool, and hides to the Allies, and because the Allies had little or nothing to sell in exchange, Uruguay accumulated a $24 million trade surplus with the United States and a $22 million surplus with Great Britain, its principal trading partner. Some of those earnings were used to pay for imports from Argentina and Brazil, but most were simply sitting in Uruguay's account at the Federal Reserve Bank of New York, waiting to be spent when goods became available. Then when wartime price controls were eliminated in the United States, pent-up domestic and worldwide demand raised the prices of the manufactured goods Uruguay typically imported.[63] After selling low in support of the Allied cause, Latin Americans now had to buy high.

Of course, the United States could reply that it had paid in blood to protect not only themselves but all of Latin America, and could add that U.S. consumers were also affected by postwar inflation, sitting on waiting lists to spend their war bonds. What was beyond debate is that many Latin Americans, having sold in a controlled market, now saw no alternative but to buy in a free market, where demand was high, where supply was still limited, and where inflation was devouring their accumulated surpluses.

Regardless of who deserved what from whom, this was the context as Latin Americans had listened in March 1947, six months before his Rio speech, when President Truman announced his Doctrine aimed initially at Greece and Turkey. It was an open-ended commitment to aid any country threatened by communism. Three months later they had listened when Secretary of State Marshall unveiled the U.S. plan to rebuild Europe, then traveled to Bogotá to tell Latin Americans about Washington's "staggering and inescapable responsibilities" elsewhere.

What many Latin Americans heard was that the United States had plenty of money but simply did not feel it was possible to give any to the Latin Americans who, as Costa Rica's Figueres believed, had given so much to the war effort. Aside from Eximbank loans and technical assistance, all that Latin Americans could extract from Secretary Marshall at Bogotá in 1948 was an agreement to hold the economic conference first promised at Rio in 1942.

Then Marshall had returned home to more important matters, and his subordinates were soon backing away from the conference. A new assistant secretary was finally named, and in 1950 he told a gathering of Latin American officials that "the huge, complicated problem of economic development does not lend itself to solution through the mere holding of conferences." He was worried because "there has been some tendency to attribute many of the economic ills of the hemisphere to the delay in holding that Conference [and] there has been a tendency also to blame the United States because the Conference has not yet been held." So, for the record, he added, "I would like to make my Government's position perfectly clear. We would be delighted to attend any conference, anywhere, anytime, provided only that we knew what we were going to talk about once we got there."[64]

In a recent speech to a U.S. audience, this assistant secretary, Edward Miller, had complained that Marshall Plan aid to Europe and Rockefeller's wartime aid to Latin America had created what he called "an obsession," and not simply in Latin America. "It has become dogma in some circles that the United States is under a continuing obligation to help other nations." It was his view that "we are under no such obligation," but he added, "We are especially concerned with improving material standards of living in the Americas."[65] While Miller did not elaborate on what he meant, the papers he left behind in the Truman Library and the National Archives suggest he never quite decided how he felt about providing Latin America with development assistance.

The promised conference was not held during the Truman years, 1945–1953.

IN APRIL 1952, a few months before the U.S. nominating conventions, a change of government occurred in Bolivia—some called it a revolution, and it clearly demonstrated the political clout of that country's organized miners, a surprisingly militant proletariat. That made some worry about the placement of Bolivia's chips, and during the presidential campaign the Republican candidate, Dwight Eisenhower, made a campaign promise to give more attention to Latin America.

True to this promise, in early 1953, a month after his inauguration, President Eisenhower told Secretary of State Dulles that he was thinking of sending his brother on a fact-finding trip to Latin America. Dulles approved: "That was a very good way of doing things—in South America that was the way they should be done. The Secretary said that you have to pat them a little bit and make them think you are fond of them."[66] Following a whirlwind trip around South America, in late 1953 Milton Eisenhower, then president of Pennsylvania State University, handed his brother a report underlining Latin Americans' growing impatience: "They want greater production and higher standards of living, and they want them *now*." The not-so-subtle warning was that "economic cooperation is without question the key to better relations between the United States and the nations to the South."

Not yet ready to accept this advice, in his State of the Union address two months later the president told Congress that "military assistance must be continued. Technical assistance must be maintained. Economic assistance can be reduced."[67]

That was the end of Round 1 of what was slowly developing into a tug-of-war between the Eisenhower State Department and the administration's cost cutters. "The Treasury Department would always object to whatever it was we wanted," recalled C. Douglas Dillon, undersecretary of state for economic affairs; they "were always fighting this rear guard action against anything that might cost anything."[68]

One reason State lost Round 1 was the personal influence of Treasury Secretary George Humphrey, a Cleveland iron ore executive whose attachment to unfettered markets was nothing short of a fetish, and who was fully aware that Milton Eisenhower's term "economic cooperation" meant foreign aid.

Early on, Humphrey had persuaded President Eisenhower to appoint Clarence Randall, a midwestern steel executive, to chair a Commission on Foreign Economic Policy. Noting that "underdeveloped areas are claiming a right to economic aid from the United States," the Randall Commission had insisted that "we recognize no such right."[69] That arrived in the Oval Office in January 1954, two months after Milton Eisenhower's report.

The second reason was the Eisenhower administration's belief that it had a different way to handle Latin Americans' rising expectations. Two months after the Randall Commission report, Secretary of State Dulles, legendary for not wanting to waste time, was spending fourteen days at an inter-American conference in Caracas, where he obtained a vague green light to overthrow the government of Guatemala. As President Eisenhower would write in his memoir, the Caracas resolution "formed a charter for the anti-Communist counterattack that followed."[70]

THE PROBLEM OF communism was supplemented by a concern that some Latin Americans were not accepting U.S. leadership. In late 1952, as Bolivia's radical reformers had started nationalizing U.S. property, the State Department's Thomas Mann had written, "We should make it clear, by our acts rather than words, that cooperation begets cooperation; that the United States is capable of reaction when unfairly attacked; and, above all, that their own self-interest is best served by cooperating with us. In doing so, our purpose should be to arrest the development of irresponsibility and extreme nationalism and their belief in their immunity from the exercise of United States power."[71]

The Guatemala problem fit this thinking. It could be traced back a decade, to 1944, when a military coup had overthrown the dictatorship of General Jorge Ubico. After ushering him off to a comfortable New Orleans exile, the coup leaders turned the government over to civilians who proceeded to enact a series of major reforms, one of which expropriated over a quarter-million acres owned by the United Fruit Company. The idea was to redistribute this land to impoverished peasants. The expropriation occurred in 1953, when John Cabot was assistant secretary of state for Latin America and when the president of United Fruit was his brother, Thomas Dudley Cabot.

The Guatemalan reforms occurred during the McCarthy years, and Washington, with or without United Fruit, had no difficulty spotting signs of communism in Guatemala, especially the rising strength of the working class. One sign was the policy of giving workers the right to form unions; another was the policy of allowing citizens to form political parties, something General Ubico had considered inappropriate. That included a worrisome Workers' Party. As in Argentina and Bolivia, the proletariat appeared to be seizing control.

These reforms were open to multiple interpretations. A minority in Washington thought the goal was to improve the lives of Guatemala's downtrodden poor. A majority perceived the dark hand of communist subversives, and they believed it was better to be safe than sorry. State's Thomas C. Mann argued that "non-intervention does not mean that the United States must sit by with crossed hands if a clearly communist regime should establish itself in the hemisphere."[72]

That became the administration's Guatemala policy. For its implementation the Eisenhower administration turned to disaffected military officers, one of whom, Colonel Carlos Castillo Armas, had been cashiered for an earlier rebellion and was eager to participate in another. With Washington's assistance, in 1954 these disaffected military leaders overthrew the regime, halted the reforms, returned United Fruit's land, and over the next four decades killed somewhere around two hundred thousand communists, communist sympathizers, and, overwhelmingly, innocent bystanders.[73] This staggering disaster—the all-but-complete extermination of village after village, largely of indigenous peoples—was not to be equaled elsewhere in Cold War Latin America.

Returning to Washington soon after the coup, U.S. ambassador John Peurifoy misled Congress: "My role in Guatemala prior to the revolution was strictly that of a diplomatic observer." The CIA eventually declassified 5,120 documents—fourteen thousand pages—many of which showed exactly the opposite, but this declassification would occur a half-century later; when he lied about U.S. involvement, Ambassador Peurifoy had no fear of contradiction.[74]

The overthrow of Guatemala's radical reformers was followed by the first major Cold War foreign aid program for a Latin American country, with the Eisenhower administration instantly providing the new Castillo Armas government with $6.4 million, half of which was for vague "general purposes," plus a new military assistance program. This was 100 percent from the realist side of the altruism / realism continuum.

Three years later the 1957 report commissioned by the U.S. Senate indicated that "the present program of economic assistance in Central America and the Caribbean area is confined to a program of defense support in Guatemala," and in this case "defense support" was a euphemism for a gift of cash.[75] Another "thank you" was a visit by Vice President Richard Nixon in 1955, four months after an election in which Castillo Armas's opponent received 0.08 percent of the vote.

The black sheep was back in the fold, now breaking all existing records for subservience to the United States. "Tell me what you want me to do and I will do it," Castillo Armas told Vice President Nixon. President Eisenhower wrote that Castillo Armas "was a farseeing and able statesman [who] enjoyed the devotion of his people."[76] He was assassinated in 1957.

BY THIS TIME State Department officials were arguing that it was time to provide Latin Americans with some uplifting. The 1954 Act of Caracas had expressed "the determination of the American States to take the necessary measures to protect their political independence against the intervention of international communism." It had been the product of Committee I, which addressed juridical-political matters. To obtain the necessary support in this committee, Secretary Dulles had attended a meeting of Committee II, on general economic matters, where he acknowledged, "Many of you feel that some adjustments of United States economic policies would be mutually beneficial. You may be right. Certainly, these are matters which we are prepared to consider openmindedly." Then he added, "We seek economic welfare because, here in the Americas, we believe that all human beings, without regard to race, religion or class, should have the opportunity to develop in body, mind, and spirit. That can only happen in a healthy society. Therefore, we seek it as something which is a good in itself, not merely as a defensive mechanism against communism."

So the United States could hardly object to Committee II's resolution to convene a meeting of ministers of finance at Rio de Janeiro "in the fourth quarter of this year, 1954." The Rio meeting "will facilitate the Economic Conference of the Organization of American States in the city of Buenos Aires," as promised by Sumner Welles at Rio in 1942.[77]

Five months after the Eisenhower administration had engineered the Guatemala coup, the first of these two economic conferences convened at Quitandinha, a resort in the highlands not far from Rio de Janeiro. Speaking to New York's Pan American Society, a new assistant secretary of state, Henry Holland, provided a preview of what the United States hoped to accomplish: "We shall try to be consistent with those sound principles which experience has demonstrated to be the basis of strong economies. One of these is the principle that governments should invade the field of business only when absolutely necessary and then, if possible, only on a temporary basis." Holland acknowledged "the growing determination among men everywhere somehow to achieve better living standards," but said that the responsibility rested with Latin Americans, not the United States. "We can, however, hasten the process somewhat by our own helpful policies."

Concretely, the Eisenhower administration intended to offer again in 1954 exactly what Secretary Marshall had offered six years earlier in Bogotá: an increase in Eximbank lending plus the continuation of Point 4 technical assistance, discussed shortly. Assistant Secretary Holland added that the United States would not consider helping Latin Americans to stabilize the volatile prices of their principal export commodities, a central concern at the time, nor was the administration willing to support the creation of an inter-American development bank, another Latin American initiative, because it would either compete with private lending or duplicate lending from the Export-Import Bank, which by now was restricted to funding the purchase of U.S. products. In other words, Holland concluded, the administration's proposals would "include no dramatic, startling new element that will create a theatrical impact at Rio. I am grateful for that."[78]

Because this was a conference to address economic issues, the delegations were led by each nation's minister of finance, which for the United States meant Treasury Secretary George Humphrey. "He is utterly convinced that a soft policy and a policy of winning Latin America by spending money on them is not the way to go about it," reported the White House staffer sent to feel out Humphrey's views; "he believed the way to control Latin America is by a tough hard-hitting policy which would envisage, if necessary, the use of force."[79]

True to this position, Humphrey told his fellow ministers that "two basic principles should underlie all our thinking. The first is our belief that the road which will lead most surely and most directly to the goals which we seek is that of the vigorous free enterprise system. . . . The other is our belief that we as governments should reduce to a minimum the scope and the duration of our own intervention in the fields of commerce and industry."

And so, he insisted, "our greatest opportunity and our greatest responsibility lies in creating in our several countries those conditions which will give maximum access to the great reserves of private-investment capital that are available throughout the world."[80]

Shortly after the Rio conference, Secretary Humphrey told a meeting of the National Security Council, including President Eisenhower, that the United States should "make it clear that we are quite willing to support dictatorships of the right if their polices are pro-American." At a subsequent NSC meeting Humphrey added that "wherever a dictator was replaced, Communists gained. In his opinion, the U.S. should back strong men in Latin American governments."[81] Until 1958, that was the Eisenhower administration's policy toward Latin America.

THE RIO MEETING was primarily to prepare for the Buenos Aires meeting, which occurred in late 1957. A few months earlier President Eisenhower had written Humphrey a polite personal note asking him to be a bit more flexible: "The spirit of nationalism, coupled with a deep hunger for some betterment in physical conditions and living standards, creates a critical situation."[82]

Perhaps nudged by this evidence that soft-power uplifters were capturing the president's thinking, or perhaps simply tired of four long years in Washington, Humphrey resigned only three weeks before the Buenos Aires conference began, and was replaced by Robert Anderson, a Texas oilman. According to C. Douglas Dillon, then deputy undersecretary of state for economic affairs, Anderson held free-market views similar to those of Humphrey, but "he wanted to deal with Latin Americans and make them happier."[83]

The State Department's lower-level officials had not yet seen this happy side of Treasury's new chieftain, and so they stayed on the track laid out by Secretary Humphrey, informing Secretary Dulles that "the Buenos Aires Conference is, in essence, a continuation of a long-standing effort by the Latin American countries to obtain from the United States special economic concessions which we are not prepared to grant."[84]

Once in Buenos Aires, Secretary Anderson stayed on that track as well. His speech at the opening session threw cold water on what had become Latin Americans' central request: the creation of an inter-American bank to provide soft loans for development purposes. Anderson's position: "We believe that the adequacy of capital to meet the needs of sound development is not a question of additional institutions but the fuller utilization of those in being."

Then he flew back to Washington, leaving State's Dillon in charge of the U.S. delegation during a meeting that continued for three weeks. "I found that a good many of the things that they had to complain of at that time seemed to have a good deal of justice on their side," Dillon later recalled, "so I got very interested in this, and came back [to Washington], and from then on tried to move things in that direction." In 1960 Dillon, his position now bumped up from deputy undersecretary to undersecretary, would be the principal U.S. official who cooperated with Latin Americans to create a new institution, the Inter-American Development Bank, and also the official who convinced President Eisenhower to pressure Congress to appropriate $500 million for the lion's share of the Bank's initial capital.[85] This 1960 concession to Latin America was a significant victory for those who had long opposed Secretary Humphrey's positions, and a victory made infinitely easier by Cuba's revolutionaries, victorious in 1959 and now understood to be moving their chips to Moscow's side of the table.

BUT WE ARE getting ahead of ourselves. That victory would occur in 1960; in 1957, still at Buenos Aries, Latin Americans were told their needs would be addressed by Point 4 technical assistance. This would become the principal form of development assistance to Latin America in the twenty-first century, especially in the area of governance.

While President Truman's Point 4 brought this type of uplifting assistance to the forefront of U.S. foreign policy, the technical assistance ball had started rolling during the Progressive era, with its money and democracy doctors, and with its use of the U.S. Army's Corps of Engineers and related development institutions, particularly in public health. Then in 1938 the Roosevelt administration had created an Interdepartmental Committee on Scientific and Cultural Cooperation, which sent U.S. government employees to provide one-on-one advice to foreign governments. It was short-lived, in part because of the war and in part because Rockefeller's *servicios* were soon providing this same type of assistance.[86]

Then came Point 4. As Secretary of State Acheson said in presenting it to Congress in 1950, "The bill now before you establishes economic development of the underdeveloped areas for the first time as a national policy. Its purpose is to encourage the exchange of technical skills and promote the flow of private investment capital where these skills and capital can help to raise standards of living, create new wealth, increase productivity, and expand purchasing power."[87]

This required an administrative unit, and unlike both the Interdepartmental Committee and Rockefeller's Office, created by executive orders and subject to reversal with a stroke of any president' pen, a new Technical Cooperation Administration was created in 1950 to implement an activity mandated by law. Until it was repealed, the TCA was in business.[88]

Soon its deputy director wrote, "In this year of 1953, more than two thousand Americans, from such towns as Keokuk, Elko and Bennington, are helping people to fight against suffering and want in places like Tegucigalpa." All two thousand were employees of the Technical Cooperation Administration, and all were portrayed as motivated by "the satisfaction of doing a job that needs doing, of trying to build a better world, little by little." An assistant secretary of state added a security concern, signaling the altruist / realist condominium of motivation that continues to this day: "It was in the U.S. interests, especially in facing the communist threat, that poor people find ways to improve their lives under non-communist social systems. It was useful for the poor and illiterate to learn that Americans wanted this to happen badly enough to live under harsh conditions to help them."[89]

Whatever their motivation, many of the two thousand did perform their tasks under harsh conditions. Such was the case of two TCA agricultural specialists who in 1954 were assigned to help modernize farming in rural Chile. The TCA office in Santiago requested hardship pay because there was "a complete lack of public entertainment," which included no playground for the two families' children except the ones found at two social clubs, and "it is doubtful if American personnel will be invited to join these clubs." And this site (Chillán) was in the center of a notorious earthquake area, so housing was of reinforced concrete, which meant that it was "very cold and hard to heat. Interiors and ceilings are usually spotted with areas of mold during the winter and clothes mildew. People generally suffer from colds all winter." Schools were "completely inadequate," "there is no refrigeration," and even in this agricultural area there was "a definite milk shortage at all times." And what little there was had to be boiled before using, while fruits and vegetables had to be dipped in chlorinated water. In addition to all that, the two TCA families had to cope with "a large amount of drunkenness and stealing," and with the unpleasant fact that "people spit everywhere." The one bright spot: "It is isolated from the world and one does not worry so much about international problems."[90]

Living 250 miles to the north, in Santiago, were several TCA employees enjoying a less-spartan existence. One of them was field officer Albion Patterson, who in 1953 had been transferred from Paraguay to Chile, where the U.S. embassy had diagnosed an outbreak of "structuralism," a fast-metastasizing strain of malignant economic thinking.[91]

As the name suggests, 1950s structuralism focused on the basic architecture—the structure—of the global economy, with a special interest in the different roles being played by wealthy and not-so-wealthy countries. As one of the latter, Chile's principal role in the international economy was to export copper and other minerals, the mining of which was largely controlled by corporations based in the United States. Structuralists understood that the prices of raw materials moved up and down, sometimes to Chile's advantage, but on balance, they argued, Chile was like most of Latin America: locked into an unfavorable long-term trading relationship characterized by an increasing gap between the rising prices of manufactured goods they imported, on the one hand, when compared to the prices received for the raw materials and foodstuffs they exported, on the other.

The structuralists' solution was government policies to improve these terms of trade, using mechanisms such as government-subsidized import substitution industrialization and public ownership of major export industries, so that more of the profits remained at home to finance start-ups. That was what Mexico had been doing with its petroleum since 1938, and that is what other Latin American countries should do now. "We have no desire for our countries to be the producers of raw materials at low wages," wrote Costa Rica's José Figueres, also in 1953. "We object to such arrangements as tend to refine our crude sugar in the industrial countries, make the furniture from our timber, manufacture the tires from our rubber, lay the rope from our fiber, smelt the metals from our ores." As for foreign investment, "we refuse to surrender to foreign companies the control of our public services, which we deem a major part of our economic sovereignty."[92]

Albion Patterson's assignment was to excise this malignant thinking before it became Chile's economic orthodoxy and killed the economy. He did so by introducing Julio Chaná, dean of the faculty of economics at the Catholic University of Chile, to Theodore Shultz, an economist at the University of Chicago, an institution whose Department of Economics advocated the polar opposite of structuralism. As its best-known faculty member explained, "Chicago stands for belief in the efficacy of the free market as a means of organizing resources [and] for skepticism about government intervention into economic affairs."[93]

Chaperoned at a discreet distance by Albion Patterson, Chile's Catholic University and the University of Chicago's Department of Economics were soon locked into an intimate relationship: Chicago faculty would teach at the Catholic University, and Católica students would pursue their doctoral studies at Chicago. Then they would return to Chile, and in time become the "Chicago Boys," ready to convert Chicago's ideas into Chile's economic orthodoxy at an opportune moment, which came in the 1970s.

The TCA and its two successor bureaucracies paid for the startup, beginning in the mid-1950s with an initial grant to the University of Chicago of $350,000—over $3 million in 2018 dollars. By 1958 there were four University of Chicago faculty serving in Santiago as contractors of the TCA's successor bureaucracies.[94]

This Chile project was only the beginning of a region-wide effort to move Latin America's universities away from left-leaning ideas, and similar programs soon became a standard part of the U.S. technical assistance program. In 1962 State's Bureau of Intelligence and Research, pinned to the realist extreme of the altruism / realism continuum, argued that "careful distribution of aid to education can weaken the universities and faculties which are politically oriented to the left by building up universities and faculties which, because of their own participation in the Alliance [for Progress], will tend to support it." Then "as these graduates grow into their work of construction and leadership, they will swell the ranks of the moderate, centrist minded groups on the political stage."[95]

TECHNICAL ASSISTANCE HAD its twentieth-century heyday during what appeared to be a relatively quiet decade in the history of Washington's effort to improve Latin Americans, but the appearance was deceptive. Seeking congressional approval for President Truman's Point 4 initiative in 1950, Secretary Acheson had warned that "increasingly numbers of these people no longer accept poverty as an inevitable fact of life. They are becoming aware of the gap between their living standards and those in the more highly developed countries. They are looking for a way out of their misery. They are not concerned with abstract ideas of democracy or communism. They are interested in practical solutions to their problems in terms of food, shelter, and a decent livelihood. When the Communists offer quick and easy remedies for all their ills, they make a strong appeal to these people."[96]

Three years later, just before he accompanied Milton Eisenhower on his fact-finding tour, Assistant Secretary of State John Cabot sounded like Paul Revere: "Social reform is coming. . . . The people to the south of us are aflame with determination to improve their material lot, [and] there is nothing more dangerous from the point of view of long-range American policy than to let Communists, with their phoney slogans, seize the leadership of social reform."[97] Few senior officials paid attention when Cabot sounded that alarm in 1953, but he convinced Milton Eisenhower, who probably needed little convincing.

The one-two punch of realists such as those who worked in State's Bureau of Intelligence and Research and of altruists such as Milton Eisenhower was slowly convincing others to consider uplifting Latin Americans when Vice President Richard Nixon ran into a shower of spit during his 1958 goodwill trip to South America. That had triggered another mission to Latin America by the president's brother, whose second report was released in early 1959, only days after Fidel Castro's rebels marched into Havana. It was not much different from his 1953 report urging greater assistance, except for "Now I must add a note of urgency." At almost the same time, Congress's nonpartisan Legislative Reference Service noted that "the easy assumption that economic aid to the less-developed areas undercuts communism seems to have gained currency."[98]

It had taken more than a decade to wring that sentence out of Washington—and, not coincidentally, it was written six months after Fidel Castro had led a group of revolutionaries down from Cuba's mountains, ousted a Washington-friendly dictator, sent the Pentagon's military advisers home, announced an agrarian reform that would seize the property of U.S. investors, and appeared to be moving its chips to the Soviet side of the table. Hand in hand, the altruists and the realists were ready to turn an enormously important corner.

CHAPTER 8

Cuba Determines the Answer

The major issue is the fight against communism,
but to them, those who live to the south of us,
the fighting is against poverty and disease and illiteracy and
ignorance.

—Senator John F. Kennedy, September 1960

IF SOMEONE WERE to ask you to identify the most important single day in the history of United States policy toward Latin America, a good answer would be January 1, 1959. Cuba's Fulgencio Batista had fled to the Dominican Republic shortly after midnight, leaving power in the hands of rebels headquartered on the eastern end of the country, near Santiago. They moved into the city later that day, and its Parque Céspedes became the site of the first speech by Cuba's new leader. Fidel Castro promised that "this time, fortunately for Cuba, the revolution will truly achieve power. It won't be as in 1895, when the Americans came at the last hour and took over the country."[1]

Five hundred miles to the west, in Havana, some U.S. embassy personnel did not understand the allusion, but those who did explained: Late in the nineteenth century, after years of waging an increasingly effective war for independence from Spain, Cubans had seen U.S. soldiers arrive to administer the coup de grâce on an enfeebled Spain. Then the United States took over the country. Obviously, that had not been forgotten.

The Eisenhower administration's first move was to close the barn door, refusing to allow Batista to spend his golden years at his home in Daytona

Beach and replacing amateur ambassador Earl Smith with a professional. "Wonder of wonders!" cheered the embassy's youngest Foreign Service officer. "An ambassador who could speak Spanish and had some idea of how to run an embassy and conduct relations with another government."[2]

Most of Washington was soon disturbed by the summary justice handed *batistianos,* by the brusque demand that U.S. military advisers be removed ("No law requires us to keep those who were teaching our soldiers to kill Cubans"), by the legalization of the Communist Party, and by the decision to delay elections. But "democracy is my ideal," Castro told a *Meet the Press* audience when he visited Washington four months after his Parque Céspedes speech. "I am not Communist. I am not agreed with communism. There is no doubt for me between democracy and communism."[3]

"I was reassured," said a leading senator, as did an equally relieved member of the House: "I was neutral and suspicious before, but today I was very favorably impressed. I think we should help him."[4]

Without requesting or accepting help with anything, Castro then returned to Cuba and announced an agrarian reform that basically confiscated the land of U.S. investors. Far more upsetting was the February 1960 visit to Havana by Soviet deputy premier Anastas Mikoyan, who struck an oil-for-sugar trade agreement. After that, President Eisenhower recalled, "there was no longer any doubt in the administration that 'something would have to be done.'" In March he authorized the CIA to prepare for a repeat of what had been done to Guatemala in 1954—"covert contingency planning to accomplish the fall of the Castro government," as Secretary Dulles referred to it.[5] Meanwhile, South Dakota senator Karl Mundt voiced Washington's disappointment: "We who in living memory rescued the island from medieval bondage; we who have given order, vitality, technical wisdom and wealth are now being damned for our civilizing and cooperative virtues!"[6] Six full decades of nearly continuous uplifting, and not an ounce of gratitude.

The senator's views had been published in mid-1960, just before the presidential nominating conventions and in the country's most popular magazine, *Reader's Digest.* The Cuban revolution was hitting closer to home than anything from Latin America ever had, largely because of another revolution, this one in communications technology. For the first time television was bringing a major Latin American event into the public's living rooms. These filtered glimpses convinced nearly everyone that Cubans were serious about reforming more or less everything, including their relations with the

United States. Viewers who enjoyed watching "Leave It to Beaver" and "Father Knows Best" were finding it especially difficult to stomach the televised snippets of Cuba's bearded leader, whose style was captured in an early report from the U.S. embassy:

> Castro in his standard uniform of rumpled fatigues, radiating health and boundless energy, hunched over the table as he talks, waving arms and hands, with the eternal cigar always at hand. Words pour from him like a ceaseless torrent. He appears literally capable of talking forever, on any subject under the sun. He is a dynamic, forceful speaker, with that rare quality of fixing and swaying his audience regardless of the contents of his words. His language was careless and informal. He spoke with tremendous vitality and rapidity. At one point he was timed at over three hundred words per minute. He was somewhat incoherent.[7]

That and much more could be seen on the nightly news by the voters in Peoria, many of whom were still coming to terms with Elvis Presley, whose suggestive movements had been setting a poor example for their adolescent children. Most parents were confident that school counselors and religious leaders could handle the threat posed by rock and roll, but voters looked to their elected officials to understand the world's hot spots and know what to do about them.

And those leaders were now especially attentive to voters as an election approached. By mid-1960, the leaders of both political parties were convinced that Cuba was a problem, and what to do about it became the central foreign policy issue of that year's presidential campaign. After the scheduled four debates, the first ever televised, Republican Richard Nixon challenged Democrat John Kennedy to a fifth to focus exclusively on Cuba. Having made his point (that those who lost Cuba should be ushered out), JFK declined.

The Eisenhower administration expired before the CIA's preparations were complete, so in early 1961, one day before leaving office, the president (a five-star general) warned his successor (a lieutenant, junior grade) that "we cannot let the present government there go on."[8] John Fitzgerald Kennedy took this handoff and ran into a brick wall three months later at the Bay of Pigs. "They should have been ashamed to be engaged in this battle of Goliath against David," chided Fidel Castro before a wildly cheering audience, "and to lose it besides." But there was no joking during his speech a few months later, when he announced, "I am a Marxist-Leninist and will be a Marxist-Leninist until the last day of my life."[9]

THE EFFECT OF the Cuban revolution on Washington's policy toward the rest of Latin America was to blow open the uplifting floodgates. In 1958, ten months before the rebels' victory, the Department of State, the Department of Defense, and the International Cooperation Administration (the immediate predecessor of today's Agency for International Development) had issued a soothing assessment that "economic development in Latin America is for the most part being maintained at a satisfactory rate." President Kennedy's view in 1961, eight weeks after his inauguration: "Latin America is seething with discontent and unrest. We must act to relieve large-scale distress immediately."[10]

What ensued was night-and-day different from Progressive-era uplifting. Like 1900s Progressives, 1960s Cold Warriors were still being guided by the belief that responsible Latin Americans would welcome Washington's assistance in their improvement. But Progressive implementation of a policy based on this belief had been rudimentary: send the Marines to establish order, provide money doctors to draw up financial plans, broker Wall Street loans to pay off accumulated debts, designate customs collectors to ensure the loans' repayment, and create constabularies so the Marines could come home. That was easier said than done, but the model was simplicity itself.

Cold War uplifting was far more complex now because Latin America was more complex. For one thing, it included everything south to Antarctica, not simply the Caribbean basin. And the threats to U.S. interests were far more numerous. As their principal security concern, Progressives had worried about a violation of the Monroe Doctrine by European debt collectors. Cold Warriors had two concerns. One was about the "awakening" of the region's downtrodden poor—and, as a consequence, that excessively rapid trend toward the adjustment of social rights. The other was about the expansion of communism. Then in mid-1959, six months after Cuba's rebels seized power, the Library of Congress's respected Legislative Reference Service put one and two together: "The setting is dominated by two broad developments: a 'revolution of rising expectations,' as it has been called, on the part of a billion and [a] half people in Asia, Africa and Latin America; and the persistent efforts of the Sino-Soviet bloc to capitalize on this unrest in

its relentless drive to submerge the West." Now, a month after Cuba announced its agrarian reform, that sentence captured an almost-perfect consensus: communism flows from poverty.[11]

THIS ARTICLE OF faith had all the trappings of a religion. Its priests were
social scientists and its seminaries were the nation's universities, where novices were trained to believe that salvation from communism lay in "development" or "modernization." Many of these novices would eventually create
competing sects, some highly critical of Cold War U.S. policy, but not yet.
This pioneering generation of development specialists had the pulpit to themselves, united in a belief that came close to holy writ: the United States of
America, a benevolent force in international relations, is responsible for protecting the Free World from communist advances. That required a crusade
to develop the underdeveloped, beginning in Latin America.

"It was the theological aspect of foreign aid that depressed me," commented President Kennedy's undersecretary of state, George Ball.

Among the most prominent early members of this priesthood were two
MIT social scientists, Max Millikan and Walt Rostow, both of whom were
frequently asked for advice by Cold War Washington, but they were not the
only ones. "It was the golden age for development theorists," George Ball
continued, and "some university faculties were almost denuded as professors left their tranquil campuses to instruct the natives in the dank far reaches
of the world." It would have been more accurate to say that the professors
were sending their students to these dank corners; "swarming into Washington" was Ball's corrected observation about the professors. "The prospect
of leading the Third World into the twentieth century offered almost
unlimited scope for experimentation not only to economists but also to so-
ciologists, psychologists, city planners, agronomists, political scientists and
experts in chicken diseases."[12] Uplifters all.

By far the most influential link between academia and Washington was
the one involving Millikan and Rostow. Early on, in 1954, they had offered
the CIA this advice: "Where men's energies can be turned constructively and
with some prospect of success to the problems of expanding standards of
living in a democratic framework we believe the attractions of totalitarian
forms of government will be much reduced."[13] This was a policy-relevant version of that article of faith already being accepted in academia, but Rostow
and Millikan also hoped for its adoption by the nation's leaders. Unfortu-

nately, they "have not yet understood completely our responsibility for economic and ideological leadership."[14]

In defense of the nation's leaders, it was 1954, just as the United States was putting an end to Guatemala's left-leaning experiment in expanding standards of living. As a result, some unconverted officials wondered whether Washington's economic and ideological leadership was essential in out-of-the-way areas like Latin America. Better the Big Stick—employed covertly now that FDR had signed away the right to send in the Marines. Moreover, during President Eisenhower's first term any leadership would have had to involve Treasury Secretary George Humphrey, and he was deeply worried about how much this leadership would cost. He certainly would have agreed with a young Representative John Kennedy, who had told his House colleagues that Latin America was "not in the line of the Soviet advance."[15]

But JFK had said that in 1951, ancient history by Washington's fast-paced standards. Now those academics who had spent most of the 1950s proselytizing on behalf of U.S. assistance to "develop" Latin America had the Cuban revolution as a perfect example of what happens when policymakers fail to heed their warnings. The lesson learned, by late 1960 the leaders of both parties, altruists and realists alike, agreed that an appropriate policy was to help Latin Americans meet their rising expectations in order to avoid more Cubas.

FOR TWO DECADES the United States had been plugging away with inexpensive technical assistance, and the Cuban revolution was living proof that more was needed, much more. Yet Washington's only experience with a large-scale aid project, the Marshall Plan, had been to help industrial economies get back on their feet after World War II. There the foundation already existed, particularly in human capital, so it had been relatively easy to rebuild something that had already been built. In this sense, the Marshall Plan was simple disaster relief. Now there was agreement to attack an infinitely more complex problem—helping "underdeveloped" peoples build modern economies that satisfied citizens' rising expectations. How do you build that?

The model Walt Rostow advanced in his 1960 book, *The Stages of Economic Growth,* emphasized that economic development occurs in five steps: 1. traditional society→ 2. preconditions for take-off→ 3. take-off→ 4. drive for maturity→ 5. high mass consumption. This perfectly timed volume went through a dozen printings in its first four years.

Rostow used less than one of the slim book's 167 pages to explain how the ball begins to roll during Stage 1, where it had rested since time immemorial: "All that lies behind the break-up of the Middle Ages is relevant to the preconditions for take-off in Western Europe," Rostow wrote. "The more general case in modern history, however, saw the stage of preconditions arise not endogenously, but from some external intrusion by more advanced societies. These invasions—literal or figurative—shocked the traditional society and began or hastened its undoing."[16]

After this external intrusion but still during the traditional stage, "the idea spreads not merely that economic progress is possible, but that economic progress is a necessary condition for some other purpose, judged to be good: be it national dignity, private profit, the general welfare, or a better life for the children." Specifically,

> education, for some at least, broadens and changes to suit the needs of modern economic activity. New types of enterprising men come forward—in the private economy, in government, or both—willing to mobilize savings and to take risks in pursuit of profit or modernization. Banks and other institutions for mobilizing capital appear. Investment increases, notably in transport, communications, and in raw materials in which other nations may have an economic interest. The scope of commerce, internal and external, widens. And here and there, modern manufacturing enterprise appears, using the new methods. But all this activity proceeds at a limited pace within an economy and a society still mainly characterized by traditional low-productivity methods.

As this continues, the economy gradually moves from Stage 1 to Stage 2, when the pace quickens. "The new class of entrepreneurs expands; and it directs the enlarging flows of investment in the private sector. The economy exploits hitherto unused natural resources and methods of production. New techniques spread in agriculture as well as industry, as agriculture is commercialized, and increasing numbers of farmers are prepared to accept the new methods and the deep changes they bring to ways of life." Stage 3, takeoff, would be quite brief: "In a decade or two both the basic structure of the economy and the social and political structure of the society are transformed in such a way that a steady rate of growth [Stage 4] can be, thereafter, regularly sustained [Stage 5]."[17]

Economists were not impressed. "There are on every page bold assertions, immense claims, sweeping insights, unsubstantiated by analysis or documentation." That was from an unfriendly assessment in the *American Economic Review,* which added that "the author darts like a dragon fly over the dazzling expanse." Another academic reviewer criticized not simply Rostow's five steps ("boundary lines of specious precision") but also "his choice to ignore virtually the whole body of statistical information about growth that has been assembled in the last decades." Then the reviewer asked, "How much violence is it permissible to do to history in order to dramatize it?"[18]

Perhaps the most trenchant early criticism came from John Coatsworth, a precocious graduate student focused on Latin America's economic history who would become one of his generation's most distinguished Latin Americanists. Coatsworth zeroed in on Rostow's assumption that traditional (Stage 1) societies "have virtually no modern history of their own" and were waiting quietly for what Rostow called "some external intrusion by more advanced societies." Quite the contrary, Coatsworth argued: "Underdeveloped societies were not simply standing still while the western nations developed. They were underdeveloping, under western tutelage, and acquiring many of those characteristically backward institutions which now present themselves as historic obstacles to economic growth. Western colonialism, and economic penetration in general, first destroyed indigenous industry and imposed enclave economies upon developing societies throughout the third world."[19]

Coatsworth and his skeptical cohort of graduate students were not Rostow's targeted audience, of course; he was writing for policymakers, and it would take a decade for them to catch up—to realize that this budding academic got it right: their emperor had no clothes. In the interim, Rostow rode a wave of popularity, lauded by reviews in the daily press. His book "permits a mass of detailed facts and information to be handled simply by our limited minds," wrote the reviewer for the *New York Times,* and it provides "a powerful new framework of ideas which can be used to improve our understanding both of the past and the present, as well as of the alternatives the future holds"—"a shaft of lighting through the murky mass of events which is the stuff of history. This is an impressive achievement." The *Washington Post* classified Rostow's book as "a tour-de-force."[20]

Although Rostow contributed to the 1960s consensus that the poor would have rising expectations once they had been shocked out of their slumber, his two principal contributions were, first, to identify a point in the modernization process—takeoff—where the United States could zero in with its assistance, and, second, to assure the budget-conscious that a permanent commitment was unnecessary—he emphasized that a substantial push to takeoff would not "open the United States to an endless, open-ended, world-wide claim on its resources."[21]

This was especially true of Latin America, where Rostow had concluded that the region's larger economies had already reached the "preconditions" stage, so takeoff could be accomplished in a decade if the United States would simply bump-up its assistance. "Launching a country into self-sustaining growth is a little like getting an airplane off the ground. There is a critical ground speed which must be passed before the craft can become airborne; to taxi up and down the runway at lower speeds [i.e., Point 4 technical assistance] is a waste of gasoline."[22] U.S. funds and U.S. pilots were needed to get the economy into the air; then the United States could bail out and Latin Americans could take control.

ROSTOW'S FIVE-STEP PROCESS seemed perfectly logical to so many in Washington, probably because he drew his examples from the already-industrialized capitalist countries. Indeed, his steps were exactly what Rostow's readers had studied in their required undergraduate course on Western Civilization—in the two syllabus sections that came after "The Middle Ages," usually listed as "The Renaissance" and "The Industrial Revolution." You can look back at the early 1960s and almost see the nation's leaders smack their foreheads: Of course that is how development works; how stupid of me not to have remembered.

Undersecretary of State George Ball was one of the few Washingtonians who dismissed Rostow as "an articulate amateur tactician,"[23] even if he had to admit that the professor's pedigree was exceptional. After doing only half a year in each of the first three years of grammar school and excelling in his other years of grammar school and high school, he had entered Yale at the age of fifteen, won a Rhodes Scholarship to Oxford, returned to Yale and earned his doctorate in economics at the age of twenty-four. But he had an Achilles' heel, unrecognized at first: he knew next to nothing about the countries of the nonindustrialized world. In 1960, when Rostow published his *Stages of Economic Growth,* he probably had never set foot in Latin America or in any other "underdeveloped" region.

And he was not the only one; indeed, inexperience was common among the founding generation of modernization specialists. But they knew their Western Civilization. Rostow's particular specialty was the British economy, which he knew the way Vince Lombardi knew football. When a development problem arose in, say, poverty-stricken northeast Brazil, he could expound at length about how the British had resolved the exact same problem in 1838 by building the London-Birmingham railroad, or in 1846 by the repeal of the Corn laws, or in 1867 by the Second Reform Act, or in 1880 by the creation of the National Eisteddfod Association. Brazilians should do the same, and he told them so during a 1964 visit to Rio. "The task in the northeast is to move into take-off in a situation where most of the preconditions now exist. The analogies of southern Italy and the TVA circa 1933 are strong and relevant."[24]

In short, Rostow conceived of Latin Americans as Anglo-Saxons, but lagging two or three centuries behind. And he had Washington's ear. After JFK's election, Rostow became McGeorge Bundy's deputy national security adviser, eager to put his "stages" argument to work. Seeing a major aid program being prepared for Latin America, he suggested that JFK pursue a more ambitious "Economic Development Decade." His idea was that they could push "more than 80% of Latin America and well over half of the other underdeveloped portions of the Free World" into takeoff "if we work hard for a decade."[25]

The Bay of Pigs invasion occurred six weeks after Rostow wrote that memo, and the fiasco triggered a personal turning point. "We have, initially, not done terribly well," Rostow told Defense Secretary Robert McNamara, but "there is one area where success against Communist techniques is conceivable and where success is desperately required in the Free World interest. That area is Viet-Nam." That was another place Rostow had not yet seen with his own eyes.

WHEN TWENTY-FIRST-CENTURY READERS pick up a book by Rostow or by most other first-generation modernization specialists, they enter into an especially good example of Clifford Geertz's imaginative universes. Because their thinking was rarely the product of direct and detailed observation of the people whom the United States intended to uplift, they imagined how rational individuals like themselves would behave as they were steered onto the runway and given the fuel to take off. Adam Smith knew this thinking was perfectly natural. "As we have no immediate experience of what other men feel, we can form no idea of the manner in which they are affected, but by conceiving what we ourselves should feel in the like situation."[26] And so it was that these Cold Warriors imagined a simple universe: a simple adversary (communism), a simple problem (rising expectations), and a simple solution (takeoff), which should not take long (a decade or so). That thinking would now produce the Alliance for Progress.

PROPONENTS OF DEVELOPMENT assistance had been nudging the Eisenhower administration since 1953, when Milton Eisenhower took his first fact-finding tour. It appears that by 1957 the president was convinced when he asked Treasury Secretary George Humphrey to stop opposing foreign aid proposals. Next year came Vice President Nixon's ill-fated trip to South America, followed by intensified pressure from Latin American leaders.

Only days after the Nixon attack, Brazilian president Juscelino Kubitschek wrote to President Eisenhower. "The hour has come for us to undertake jointly a thorough review of the policy of mutual understanding on this Hemisphere." Richard Goodwin, the Kennedy aide who would draft JFK's 1961 speech introducing the Alliance for Progress, dismissed Kubitschek and his proposed "Operation Pan America" as nothing more than "an earlier proposal for hemispheric development," but he could not have been more mistaken. This Brazilian initiative was the Alliance for Progress three years before the Alliance for Progress.

President Eisenhower replied to the Brazilian leader immediately. "Our two governments should consult together as soon as possible," he wrote, and as an indicator of his interest he asked Assistant Secretary Rubottom to hand-carry his letter to Rio de Janeiro. While there, Rubottom also was to arrange for a visit by Secretary Dulles.[27]

Although the executive branch roadblock to assisting Latin America had been removed with the departure of Treasury Secretary Humphrey, economic aid was still unpopular in Congress. Two months before Kubitschek's letter, the House Committee on Foreign Affairs had published a list of every conceivable criticism of the day's modest foreign aid program, ninety-six questions in all, and asked the administration to respond to each. The committee's bias could be deduced from the tone of the questions, the first of which was to ask for a response to the assertion "Nowhere is corruption in

Government more apparent than in what we call foreign aid." (Response: "Unsupported by fact.") Number 22 was "Have we financed public baths for Egyptian camel drivers?" (Answer: Yes, but not for the exclusive use by camel drivers.) Number 59 was "Have we furnished ice boxes to Eskimos?" (Answer: No.)[28]

That was in March 1958. Then in mid-July, six weeks after Kubitschek's letter, the President's brother had returned from his second fact-finding trip and weighed in on the side of those who were encouraging an expanded effort to improve Latin Americans.[29] Secretary Dulles landed in Rio three days later, where he and President Kubitschek "emphasized that the first step was to agree on the major aspects of an economic program."

The two also agreed that Brazil would circulate an *aide-mémoire* to the other Latin American governments, the first sentence of which indicated its purpose: to provide "a clearer definition of the objectives of Operation Pan America." That would require "a high-level meeting among the republics of the Hemisphere" to prepare a "dynamic and progressive program for the struggle against underdevelopment." On his flight home, Dulles wrote to thank Kubitschek for his initiative: "I hope that 'Pan-American Operation' will concentrate primarily upon the injecting into this hemisphere . . . increased determination to evolve peacefully but vigorously in a way which will improve the lot of all men."[30]

Fidel Castro's rebels threw out Batista five months later. Six weeks after that the National Security Council issued a new "Statement of U.S. Policy toward Latin America" warning that "its peoples' aspirations for higher living standards, more industrialization and popularly-based governments are rising more rapidly than they are being satisfied."[31]

IT WAS NOW an easy coast to Washington's appropriation of Operation Pan America. It gathered momentum when President Eisenhower visited Brazil in early 1960, where he and President Kubitschek issued a call to action: "The belief that the aspiration of the peoples of the Americas to an ever-improving way of life, moral and material, presents one of the great challenges and opportunities of our time. This challenge should be met by joining together, ever more closely and harmoniously, the efforts of all countries within the inter-American community in order that, through coordinated action, there may be an intensification of measures capable of combating underdevelopment in the vast area of the American continents."[32]

Then in September 1960 the Organization of American States produced the "Act of Bogotá," subtitled "Measures for Social Improvement and Economic Development within the Framework of Operation Pan America." The signatories, including the United States, agreed that "within the framework of Operation Pan America, the economic development of Latin America requires prompt action of exceptional breadth in the field of international cooperation."[33] A week earlier Congress had authorized $500 million to promote Latin American development, and in the same legislation made a commitment that would have been unthinkable only two years earlier, before the Cuban revolution: "to give careful and sympathetic consideration to programs which the President may develop for the purpose of promoting these policies."[34]

JFK'S VERSION OF Operation Pan America, the Alliance for Progress, began to emerge during the 1960 campaign for the White House, when he asked an aide to approach FDR brain truster Adolf Berle. "He hoped I would try to work out the outline of a Latin America policy," Berle wrote in his diary; "this has not been a region to which Kennedy has given much thought." The idea was to have a discussion with the candidate at some unspecified moment, but no meeting was held, perhaps because the candidate needed no advice to see the political value of continuously condemning Republicans for losing Cuba; beyond that, JFK's campaign featured dire predictions that all of Latin America was on the verge of going communist, with promises aplenty but few specifics.

After the election another Kennedy aide asked Berle if he would lead a small task force to prepare a report for the president-elect on "Latin American affairs."[35] Berle would be assisted by two professors (Robert Alexander of Rutgers and Arthur Whitaker of the University of Pennsylvania), two well-respected Puerto Rican politicians (Arturo Morales Carrión and Teodoro Moscoso, who had led the island's "Operation Bootstrap"), and Lincoln Gordon, who is difficult to categorize. A well-connected Harvard graduate with a doctorate from Oxford, earned while he was a Rhodes scholar, for the past two decades Gordon had been moving around from government office to government office, interspersed with teaching at Harvard's business school, first as an adjunct (1946–1950) and then as a professor of international economic relations (1955–1961). He had not visited Latin America until 1959, a year before he joined Berle's task force.

The final task force member was Kennedy speechwriter Richard Goodwin, fresh out of Harvard Law and a Supreme Court clerkship with Felix Frankfurter. He admitted that his Latin America experience consisted of "one orgiastic night" in a house of prostitution just over the Mexican border. When compared to the other members of Berle's group, Goodwin recognized that his "qualifications were much slimmer—a layman's interest in the area, preparation of the candidate's speeches, a short Berlitz course in Spanish."[36]

Using the skills acquired as an assistant secretary of state and as an ambassador to Brazil during the Good Neighbor years, Berle produced a report without much assistance. "The task force assignment was not a heavy one," Lincoln Gordon recalled. "We were to meet on a few occasions in New York for an afternoon and then arrange a two or three-day meeting to wind up."[37]

The report combined the development focus of Operation Pan America with Cold War realism. "Full-scale Latin American 'cold' war is underway," was the first sentence of the executive summary (titled "The Guts of It" in Berle's crusty style), followed by an equally worrisome second: "A bloody guerrilla phase active in Cuba threatens to spread to all other Caribbean countries." Privately Berle worried that "eight governments may go the way of Cuba in the next six months unless something is done."[38] Similar thoughts were interlaced with a set of recommended economic development projects—projects that would have been impossible to consider before the Cuban revolution: breaking up large estates and distributing parcels to peasants was especially popular, as were dramatically expanded government services in education, housing, and public health. All became standard uplifting fare in the Kennedy years.

A rival report also surfaced. Perhaps because no one from Rostow's MIT had been included in Berle's task force, its CIA-funded Center for International Studies organized a one-day preinaugural conference to prepare a second advisory document for the new administration, this one unrequested. Of the twenty-six participants, one was Kennedy adviser Angier Biddle Duke, heir to two very large family fortunes and recognized as being close to the Kennedys. (He would become JFK's chief of protocol.) Twelve were corporate leaders (United Fruit, Ford, Whirlpool, and so on) and eleven were academics—four from MIT, including Walt Rostow, whose fingerprints could be found on every one of the document's twelve pages: "Development of self-sustaining economies is the target. In many Latin American countries this is feasible within a decade."

As in the Berle report, a first-page sentence asserted that "demands for radical, speedy solutions to social and economic inequities are urgent," followed by a warning that "Mr. Castro is not a cause, but a symptom. He is a symptom of legitimate demands for long overdue reforms which have been either ineptly met or ignored by many regimes in Latin America and have failed to evoke adequate support from United States policy makers."[39]

The reforms proposed by both advisory panels came at exactly the time Hans Morgenthau was completing his seminal article, *A Political Theory of Foreign Aid,* published in 1962. He would place foreign aid alongside diplomacy, military action, and propaganda. "They are all weapons." Certainly there was a dose of altruism, but enlarging and improving the weapon called "foreign aid" is what the Alliance for Progress was about.

WITH EVERYONE ON board, President Kennedy signed off on the takeoff of Latin Americans. It began with JFK's inaugural address, which contained an Adam Smith promise. "To those peoples in the tents and villages of half the globe struggling to break the bonds of mass misery, we pledge our best efforts to help them help themselves, for whatever period is required." He mentioned a special interest in an "alliance for progress" (no capitals) with Latin America.

Two months later, the Marine Corps band struck up "Hail to the Chief" as the president grandly entered the East Room and walked to a podium with Richard Goodwin's speech in his hand. Once Latin America's ambassadors and their spouses had been invited to sit down, JFK announced that the United States was prepared to launch "a vast cooperative effort, unparalleled in magnitude and nobility of purpose, to satisfy the basic needs of the American people." If Latin Americans would join the United States in this Alliance for Progress (now capitalized), then within a decade "the living standards of every American family will be on the rise, basic education will be available to all, hunger will be a forgotten experience, the need for massive outside help will have passed, [and] most nations will have entered into a period of self-sustaining growth."[40] The Alliance would show the world what the United States could do when it set its mind to improving Latin Americans.

Soon Treasury Secretary Douglas Dillon (Eisenhower's former undersecretary of state for economic affairs) met with his Latin American counterparts at Punta del Este, and together they crafted a Charter of the Alliance for Progress with no help from Cuba, whose delegation was led by the president of Cuba's Central Bank, Che Guevara. Everyone else seemed pleased by Washington's commitment, and a cable to Washington indicated that Secretary Dillon's presentation was "received by [a] large audience with prolonged applause."[41]

The next step was to build an army of altruists to wage this war on underdevelopment, 99 percent of whose generals were Morgenthau realists. The new administration took the existing International Cooperation Administration (ICA), including its lending arm, the Development Loan Fund, and merged them into a cleverly named Agency for International Development—AID or, as the Agency now prefers, USAID. The administration also created the Peace Corps, and it convinced Congress to appropriate already-authorized funds for the new (1960) Inter-American Development Bank and the World Bank's new (also 1960) International Development Association. Although it had begun two decades earlier with Nelson Rockefeller's Office for Coordination of Commercial and Cultural Relations between the American Republics, this *institutionalization* of foreign aid would be the Cold War era's principal contribution to today's twenty-first-century uplifting.

UPLIFTING TWO HUNDRED million Latin Americans was going to involve more than creating institutions; someone had to run them, and that explains much of the rocky start. AID's new leaders were working overtime with ICA holdovers to manage an expanded range of development projects being implemented by an expanded staff stationed in an expanded array of countries, each of which was supposed to prepare a national development plan. Programming of this magnitude would not be accomplished overnight, especially given that none of the proposed recipients had experience in planning for their takeoff. Nor did such skills lie with the in-country U.S. personnel inherited from the ICA; until now they had been focused on modest technical assistance projects.

These start-up problems were compounded by a confusing management structure. JFK had asked the brusque Adolf Berle to direct a new Inter-Departmental Task Force on the Americas, where he rubbed like forty-grit sandpaper against the officer in charge of State Department management, Undersecretary Chester Bowles, who thought no task force was needed. He was especially annoyed that "the thoughtless assignment of Adolf Berle as special assistant to everyone in general made it impossible to undertake the urgently needed reorganization of the Bureau of Inter-American Affairs."[42] Reporting on an early meeting of the Operations Coordinating Board (OCB), an NSC staffer told McGeorge Bundy that Berle "explained that his group would be concerned only with policies and programs, but would not get into 'operational' matters. The [OCB] Chairman noted, however, that mostly 'operational' matters were discussed at the 3½ hour informal meeting."[43]

Also heavily involved was another key Kennedy aide, special counsel Arthur Schlesinger Jr., a historian by trade who years earlier (in 1946) had written a prescient article about Latin America's "ground swell of inarticulate mass dissatisfaction"—about the poor "held down past all endurance and now approaching a state of revolt."[44] Then for the next fifteen years Schlesinger's focus had been elsewhere, but the Cuban revolution rekindled his interest. Once in the White House, it took him only six months to conclude that the problem was not the turf-grabbing Adolf Berles but the Foreign Service Officers, who "form a sullen knot of resistance to fresh approaches. Their attitudes are entrenched, their minds are set, and they regard new approaches and ideas with automatic skepticism. They are predominantly out of sympathy with the *Alianza*."[45]

And then there was the rambunctious Richard Goodwin. "I am deeply involved in the day-to-day conduct of Latin American affairs," he told JFK nine months after the inauguration. "This involvement is inevitable as long as I am acting as an agent of yours in your effort to reenergize a long-dormant and ineffective area of our policy." Like Schlesinger, he did not like what he had seen so far: "Nothing is more discouraging than to compare the caliber of people who were drafted into the Marshall Plan effort with those who now run our Latin American Aid program."[46]

The feeling was mutual. One CIA officer who got in Goodwin's way considered him "a sleazy little self-seeker," an FSO wrote him off as "the *enfant terrible*," and an assistant secretary of state dismissed his warmed-over thinking as "full of New Deal ideas for which he was an energetic salesman." Arthur Schlesinger later commented that Goodwin "was certainly driving and often impatient; those who he overrode called him arrogant. But he was a man of uncommon intelligence, perception and charm." (Schlesinger was not as generous a few years later, when he characterized Goodwin as "a great idea man and a very entertaining man, that's all.") "The consensus," wrote a dissertation writer who interviewed many of Goodwin's associates, "was that Goodwin was very bright but totally lacking in experience and with extremely bad judgment." If by "truth" he meant "wisdom," McGeorge Bundy probably captured the man best: "Goodwin doesn't have a whole lot of truth in him but he's bright as hell."[47]

The problem went far beyond personalities. "The ablest and most articulate people in the Administration have had almost no prior knowledge of foreign affairs," Undersecretary Chester Bowles complained to his diary. "You have Lyndon Johnson, Dick Goodwin, Bob Kennedy, and Arthur Schlesinger with almost no experience in foreign affairs—indeed, who have hardly traveled out of this country—suddenly in a position of discovering the importance of world affairs."[48]

Rather than fight off these philistines beating at the State Department's door, the new assistant secretary of state for inter-American affairs, Thomas C. Mann, decided to get out of town. Now a well-regarded senior professional with multiple postings to Latin America, Mann had held his position for only a few months but had been serving as assistant secretary for economic affairs since 1957 and therefore was due for an overseas assignment. Then he learned about the upcoming Bay of Pigs invasion by Cuban exiles. Two weeks before it occurred Mann approached Undersecretary Bowles, who handled State's personnel assignments, and told him that he "had no desire to play a major role in the Latin American debacle which was about to occur."[49]

Unlike Chester Bowles, one of only two central figures who repeatedly warned that the invasion would violate the most basic Good Neighbor principle of nonintervention (Senator William Fulbright was the other), Mann simply believed it would be a failure. He doubted the CIA's claim that Cubans would rise up against the Castro government once the invasion began, and argued instead that "we would, I believe, be far better off to do whatever has to be done in an open way and in accordance with the American tradition"—an apparent reference to the Big Stick takeovers of the Progressive era.[50]

Three days later, McGeorge Bundy told JFK that "here, in sharp form, are the issues on Cuba. Bissell [the CIA deputy director responsible for preparing the invasion] and Mann are the real antagonists at the staff level." But then two weeks before the invasion, when JFK went around the table asking for a go or no-go vote, the meeting's minutes indicate that "Mann expressed general approval."[51] Mann's appointment as ambassador to Mexico was announced two weeks later, on the second day of the three-day Bay of Pigs fiasco.

That left the Latin America bureau without competent leadership immediately after one of the most egregious failures in the history of U.S. foreign
policy. No prominent outsider could be convinced to take the job. After two
months Arthur Schlesinger warned JFK that the position needed to be filled
quickly, and the next day a reporter asked the president to comment on "a
multiplicity of advisers in the White House duplicating and sometimes over-
ruling people in the State Department." JFK's weak response: "I was sorry
that we did not secure a replacement for Mr. Mann more quickly," but "I
did talk to almost eight people [and] in every case we were not successful."[52]

The search then turned inside, and Robert Woodward was selected. A
career official with prior postings in nine Latin American countries, including
three as ambassador, he was "a nice Foreign Service Officer, but lacking in
stature and depth"—so wrote Undersecretary Bowles in his diary.[53] Unmen-
tioned was the fact that Woodward had the misfortune of being assistant
secretary when the White House shipped Richard Goodwin off to Foggy
Bottom to serve as Woodward's deputy.

Goodwin believed he had been sent to prod State's career officials, so prod
he did. "There is a tremendous amount of mediocrity in high places," he reported to JFK. Later he recalled that "the course had been set, but the
sailors were still holding meetings on the beach. It was my job to get them
on board, order them into the riggings, leave the tranquil harbor of indeci-
sion behind. I would go to the State Department, not to find a warm spot
in the belly of the beast, but to kick the huge, somnolent, indifferent mon-
ster in the ass."[54] Now here he was, surrounded by devout FSOs, cursing in
their temple.

Four months after Goodwin informed JFK of State's mediocrity, and only
eight months into Woodward's tenure, Undersecretary of State George Ball
(Chester Bowles's replacement) pulled another senior FSO, Edwin Martin,
out of a meeting. "The President and Secretary wanted me to take over ARA
as soon as possible as they needed a firmer hand on Dick Goodwin." Woodward's oral history matches Martin's account: Undersecretary Ball "told me
quite frankly that he thought that Ed Martin would be able to work out a
better coordination of the work with my deputy than I could; that I wasn't
firm enough with him."[55]

Martin was not anxious to take on the job. "I spoke no Spanish and had
never served in the area," he protested, but "this got me nowhere so I said
OK." He quickly solved the Goodwin problem by ignoring his existence,

holding important meetings that the *enfant terrible* learned about only after they had been held. So Goodwin stopped coming to the office. "I left. Not formally, of course, but without resigning or even asking permission. . . . Fuck them all, I thought; they could fire me if they wanted, but I wasn't going to let them cut off my balls . . . I am sure they didn't miss me."[56]

Even though Martin was an accomplished manager, his appointment came at the cost of placing State's Latin America bureau in the hands of someone who was both inexperienced regarding Latin America and "a little too fussy and detail minded," as National Security Adviser McGeorge Bundy described him.[57] He became assistant secretary just as the Alliance for Progress had passed through its setup period, and now the takeoff clock was ticking. After a trip to spackle over the cracks created by the Bay of Pigs tremor, UN ambassador Adlai Stevenson had recently reported that Latin America's leaders were eager for visible progress "in the months ahead."[58]

AT HOME, THE stylish Kennedy administration enjoyed an extended honeymoon—perhaps because the Democrats held a 263–174 majority in the House and a 65–35 margin in the Senate—and Secretary of State Dean Rusk extended it further by sprinkling a few examples of successful Alliance projects into his speeches.[59] But there always seemed to be too few examples, so Edwin Martin was obliged to spend much of his time explaining why takeoff was going to take longer than expected.

Most of his fifty-nine formal speeches over a two-year tenure were some version of the explanation he gave a Pasadena audience in 1962: First, he informed them about Latin America's rising expectations: "All these people, recently greatly helped by vast numbers of cheap transistor radios, have been learning more and more about what life means to other, more privileged peoples, and demanding more instead of less." Then came his description of the wide gap between rising expectations and mediocre achievements, a gap that could be closed only if Latin Americans were to adopt "new ways of doing things." "Most important is an approach to life which seeks practical or compromise solutions of conflicting interests rather than the ultimate theoretical right or wrong."

Fortunately, "there are many in Latin America who have these qualifications and they are leading their countries into the future," but changes of this magnitude were going to take time, primarily, as Martin would write in retirement, because they were Hispanics. "Their origin unfortunately brought them mostly handicaps" and their "sense of personal responsibility to perform well was weak. . . . In such a culture, corruption was a normal and accepted part of everyday life whether it took the form of taking home money that wasn't yours, or not doing the job you were being paid for, or not paying the debts or taxes you owed."[60]

This use of Hispanic culture as an explanation for lackluster results was hardly limited to the recently initiated. The broadly experienced Thomas Mann would soon argue that Latin America's political problems were based upon "structural weakness of a cultural kind"—"too much demagogy, too much thought by politicians of a short-term personal advantage and not enough thought about what is good for the country in the long run, too much thought about 'after me, the deluge.' The only important thing is to get elected to office and to stay in office, and who cares about these long-term problems?" In contrast, Mann continued, "we do have an enlightened capitalist system in this country, people with a sense of responsibility and patriotism," while "the capitalist in Latin America is a different breed [with] different standards of morality, different standards of conduct."[61]

Edwin Martin and Thomas Mann were two peas in the New Frontier pod, both emphasizing the inferior raw material with which the Alliance was forced to work.

IF SUCCESS IS to be measured by the altruistic goals set out in the Charter signed in 1961 at Punta del Este, the Alliance failed. Taken as a single unit, those goals were to transform Latin American societies, primarily by improving their economic performance. That required redistributing resources, farmland in particular, to people who would use it to pull themselves up by their bootstraps. It also required modernizing infrastructure and creating social welfare programs, everything from highways and hydroelectric power to health clinics and schools, all of which would facilitate economic development.

Some of that occurred, but not enough to satisfy critics, who were soon writing books with titles such as *The Alliance That Lost Its Way*. These volumes offered many reasons for the failure, but the reason heard most frequently in Washington was that Latin Americans failed to change their "thinking and habits and moral standards," to use the explanation Thomas Mann gave to the Senate. Despite Washington's best effort, Mann told JFK's successor, Lyndon Johnson, that Latin Americans failed to learn how "to subordinate their personal ambition for teamwork and to move towards discipline, responsibility, simple Christian charity, respect for law, and dedication to the right values."[62]

That said, few noticed that the realists' goal was achieved: no more Latin American governments moved their chips to the Soviet side of the table, and that was not its only achievement. It also produced a set of uplifting institutions that Washington's Hans Morgenthaus now considered essential to the promotion of U.S. interests. So when the Alliance petered out—it was never formally abandoned—these institutions remained and serve as the foundation of today's twenty-first-century uplifting industry.

CHAPTER 9

Losing Panache, Entrenching Institutions

> It is time that we committed ourselves as a nation
> —in both the public and private sectors—
> to assisting democratic development.
>
> —President Ronald Reagan, 1982

THE TRANSITION FROM JFK-era hyper-uplifting to today's low-intensity uplifting began about the time Vice President Lyndon Johnson moved into the White House. Walt Rostow somehow convinced himself that "Johnson, from his first days of responsibility, gave special attention to Latin American development," but he was the only one who thought so. JFK's assistant secretary of state for Latin America complained that the Alliance "continued in name but its political spirit was dead," and a senior AID administrator wrote that "a more dramatic shift in tone and style of U.S. Alliance leadership would have been difficult to imagine."[1]

Tone and style are always open to debate, but the dollar data are clear. Economic aid to improve Latin America peaked at $888 million in 1966, LBJ's second budget year. Then it declined through the Johnson administration's remaining three budgets and continued downward during the eight Nixon-Ford years, bottoming out in the final Ford budget at $190 million, a drop of 79 percent from 1966 to 1977—or more: the $888 million in 1966 would have had to grow to $1.7 billion in 1977 simply to keep up with inflation. After that, the turmoil in Central America would require the United States to pay more attention to Latin Americans' improvement, but budget increases would be highly skewed toward a few of the region's smaller but least-stable countries.

If the Alliance did not die in 1963 with JFK, surely it did in 1965 with LBJ's invasion of the Dominican Republic, the first obvious-to-absolutely-everyone violation of the 1930s Good Neighbor commitment to noninter-vention. After that came articles with titles such as "Spiritless Alliance" and "Alliance without Progress." In 1968, when LBJ's final assistant secretary of state tried to convince Congress that "after 6 years of the Alliance for Progress, I think we can say with real confidence that the course of the hemisphere is set in the right direction," a skeptical House member bluntly disagreed: "I think we are still in sight of where we started."[2]

And what about Cuba, the match that lit the Alliance fire? Ten days after JFK's assassination, assistant secretary Edwin Martin updated Secretary of State Dean Rusk on Operation Mongoose, the effort to terrorize Cubans into submission: "Exerting maximum pressure by all means available to the U.S. Government, short of military force, to bring about a degree of disor-ganization, uncertainty and discontent in Cuba which will predispose ele-ments in the military and other power centers of the regime to bring about the overthrow of the Castro / Communist group."[3] That updating occurred on the same day LBJ called Senator William Fulbright to get his advice. Don't do anything impetuous, Fulbright began, but barely got that out of his mouth before being interrupted: "I'm not getting into any Bay of Pigs deal," President Johnson said; "no, I'm just asking you what we ought to do to pinch their nuts more than we're doing."[4]

And so it was. As would his successors for the next half-century, LBJ de-liberately made life painful for everyday Cubans, even if he gave them little attention. McGeorge Bundy advised LBJ two months after his conversation with Senator Fulbright, "The chances are very good that we will still be living with Castro some time from now [and] we might just as well get used to the idea. At the same time, we should probably continue our present nasty course."[5]

This is what the CIA's Desmond FitzGerald probably meant in 1964 when he confided to a colleague that "unfortunately, the new President isn't as gung-ho on fighting Castro as Kennedy was," and this is also what the CIA's Ray Cline meant when he recalled, "I don't think there was a big change in policy, but after Jack's death the spirit was just a little different." Over in the State Department, meanwhile, the Coordinator for Cuban Affairs re-called that "during the Kennedy period, I used to get a call from McGeorge Bundy or one of his assistants every day about something, about some problem that they saw or didn't understand or something like that." Then "under Johnson, the calls dropped down to probably once a week, and then maybe once every two weeks or once a month by '65, when I got out." Nod-ding in agreement was the officer in charge of the State Department's Cuba office in Miami: "After Kennedy's assassination, late 1963 on, the whole Cuban issue was off front and center as Johnson increasingly became involved in Vietnam."[6]

Take "Cuba" out of that paragraph, insert "Latin America," and you have U.S. policy during the Johnson administration, from late 1963 to early 1969. Almost everyone could see that the new president had other ideas about how to spend his time and political capital—a stunning domestic agenda that reached into every home in the country: Medicare for the elderly, Medicaid for the needy, Head Start for the young, integration for the segregated, voting rights for the disenfranchised, and, for everyone, unleaded gasoline, ciga-rette warning labels, mandatory seat belts, highway beautification, National Public Radio, and two institutions to challenge the mind and nourish the soul: the National Endowment for the Humanities and the National En-dowment for the Arts.

IF NO ONE was surprised when LBJ did not mention Latin America in his final State of the Union address, neither was anyone surprised a few days later when Richard Nixon failed to mention Latin America in his inaugural address. Assessing his first year in office, in 1970 President Nixon told his three principal White House staffers, "Our greatest weakness was in spreading my time too thin—not emphasizing priorities enough." Beginning immediately, he said, "all I want brought to my attention are the following items," all five of which were focused on East–West relations. "I do not want to see any papers on any of the other countries," including "all of the coun-tries of the Western Hemisphere with the exception of Cuba."[7] After having held out hope for a decade, in 1973 the Organization of American States dis-banded its committee to help implement the Alliance.

And so only two of President Nixon's fourteen trips abroad were to Latin America; both were to Mexico and for only as long as courtesy required—a few hours in Ciudad Acuña to dedicate a dam along the border, and an overnight stay in the sleepy resort town of Puerto Vallarta (no repeat of Caracas), where he and President Adolfo Díaz Ordaz put the final touches on a border agreement. While filling the last two and a half years of Nixon's second term, Gerald Ford took a single trip Latin America: arriving midmorning in Nogales on the Mexican border, laying a wreath at the monument to Benito Juárez, then helicoptering fifty miles inland with President Luis Echeverría to lay a second wreath at the tomb of Padre Eusebio Kino. Back to Arizona for lunch.

Of course, no one was speaking any longer about assisting Latin Americans' takeoffs into sustainable development. "We wanted to encourage in every appropriate way that our friends to the south learn to stand on their own two feet—*to become mature,*" wrote one well-placed Foreign Service officer. "We would not let their problems become our responsibility. Slowly over time, just as with a young adult leaving home for the first time, we felt confident that the initial pain and the feeling that 'you don't love me anymore' would eventually be replaced by the gratifying sense of independence, freedom, and the respect and dignity one achieved as a mature person."[8]

BUT THE AGENCY for International Development had inherited from its predecessors a fairly large but inexpensive program of Point 4 technical assistance, and to that the Alliance had initially spent most of its sharply increased uplifting budget on high-visibility infrastructure projects—dams, highways, and the like. At the same time, entire regions (such as northeast Brazil) and entire countries (Colombia) became development "showcases," funded not project by project, but by large "program grants" for a bundle of development projects—schools, health centers, housing, and so on.

AID was not yet the whipping boy it would eventually become, but critics soon began to complain about the modest payoff from both the infrastructure projects and the omnibus program grants. Both were said to have improved the lifestyle of middle-class bureaucrats in the capital city, with little trickle-down into the impoverished countryside and urban slums. One corrective was suggested by an LBJ adviser, who argued in his memoir that "the problem is not 'underdeveloped nations' or 'underdeveloped economies,' but rather underdeveloped people. What the people of Latin America need is not fine public buildings, nor highways and dams alone, but better health, more food, broader opportunities, a more equitable distribution of income, and, above all, better education."[9]

So the idea took hold that the "think-big" Alliance approach should be replaced by less-ambitious, narrowly targeted activities aimed directly at improving the daily lives of the poor. In its 1973 New Directions legislation, Congress required AID to focus on what it called "basic human needs."[10] Meanwhile, Congress had stipulated that "emphasis shall be placed on assuring maximum participation of the people in the developing countries, through the encouragement of democratic private and local government institutions."[11] This was Title IX, a 1966 amendment to the 1961 Foreign Assistance Act. It required AID to focus on political improvement.

"Maximum participation" and "basic human needs" were only the beginning. After JFK, each new Cold War Congress and administration—LBJ, Nixon, Ford, Carter, Reagan, and Bush—added new development activities, most of which supplemented rather than replaced whatever existed at the moment.

Some of these new responsibilities would severely damage AID's reputation; most were related to the pacification of Vietnam. AID's personnel doubled to seventeen thousand during that war, and Agency employees became involved in almost every aspect of a profoundly unpopular war. One of its responsibilities was to help neutralize the fifth column of agitators in South Vietnam—the subversives, not the combatants. JFK ordered AID to "give considerably greater emphasis to police assistance programs in appropriate less developed countries," and to do so, "AID should envisage very substantial increases in the global level of the FY1963 program, with further increases in subsequent years."[12]

The ink had barely dried on President Kennedy's signature before AID had created an Office of Public Safety (OPS), had located an unused trolley car barn in Georgetown for its new International Police Academy, and had stationed "public safety" advisers in every Latin American country except Cuba. In 1965 LBJ's principal Latin Americanist, assistant secretary Thomas Mann, told Congress that the OPS was active "above all in helping them build up their files. What they really need, the best defense against this [communist subversion], is an FBI, an efficient national police force in each country."[13]

This immediately spilled over into Latin America. By 1966, 10 percent of all AID officials in the region were public safety officers, with the largest program in Brazil, where twenty-three OPS advisers were teaching the police of a military dictatorship how to maintain internal security; meanwhile,

AID's Washington academy was training 647 higher-ranking Brazilian police officials, many of them on loan from the military services.[14]

So Congress began holding hearings with titles such as *Torture and Oppression in Brazil,* often linking abuses by Brazil's security services to U.S. government assistance, as in *United States Policies and Programs in Brazil.*[15] It was not long before this opposition broadened from Brazil to include much of Latin America, especially Anastasio Somoza's Nicaragua, where opposition to a three-decade dictatorship was growing. In the late 1960s, AID (not the Pentagon) was training thirty-nine officers of Somoza's Guardia Nacional, twenty-seven of them at the International Police Academy.[16]

This effort to improve Latin America's police might have continued indefinitely had not its principal public safety focus been on Vietnam, where the national police force grew from 10,000 in 1964 to 120,000 in 1973. During those years the war's opponents convinced Congress that AID's Office of Public Safety was funding torture. Especially important were revelations about the "Tiger Cages" on Con Son Island, with some of the most incriminating evidence provided by AID itself. A 1964 memo by the Agency's public safety director in Vietnam explained that "in Con Son II, some of the hardcore communists keep preaching the 'party' line, so these 'Reds' are sent to the tiger cages in Con Son I where they are isolated from all others for months at a time. This confinement . . . may include immobilization—the prisoner is bolted to the floor." Then in 1973 an Air Force doctor described the result for Congress:

> Each man has spent months or years without interruption in leg shackles while subsisting on a diet of three handfuls of milled white rice and three swallows of water per day. This combination of prolonged immobilization and starvation has to my knowledge never occurred before on such a scale. A computer review of 1200 medical journals and a personal search through medical literature on the health of POW's produced no descriptions similar to the above. Their paralysis together with the causative conditions are unique in the history of modern warfare, and the U.S. bears a heavy burden of complicity.[17]

In late 1973 Congress halted police training overseas, in 1974 it prohibited training in the United States, and in 1975 the International Police Academy was converted into a training school for the Customs Service.[18] By that time AID had lost its credibility among a generation of altruists.

Then in 1976, a year after the U.S. withdrawal from Vietnam, voters elected Jimmy Carter, who mollified many with his focus on the protection of human rights, perhaps the most altruistic uplifting activity in the history of U.S.–Latin American relations—with no payoff other than the pleasure of seeing a reduction in torture and other forms of cruel and inhuman treatment, from "disappearance" to prolonged detention without trial. Pushing for action was a new institution, the State Department's Bureau of Human Rights and Humanitarian Affairs (today's Bureau of Democracy, Human Rights and Labor), and both State and AID had designated human rights officers in every Latin American embassy and mission.

But in 1981 the early Reagan administration decided to shift its uplifting back to Latin America's economic improvement, with an emphasis upon the privatization of state-operated enterprises. Its Private Enterprise Initiative and its subregional Caribbean Basin Initiative sought to encourage "increased reliance on private enterprise, individual initiative and entrepreneurship, the encouragement of competition, and reliance on market forces." AID created a Bureau for Private Enterprise, and told Congress that it had shifted "from a predominantly public sector, or government-to-government, focus to one that emphasized market forces and active private indigenous productive sectors." A congressional assessment at the end of the Reagan years noted that the Initiative "has brought the problems of private enterprise in the developing world into the mainstream of the U.S. foreign aid program."[19]

Uninterested (and often opposed) to this private-sector approach to Latin Americans' economic improvement, and adamantly opposed to the Reagan administration's unrelated policies in war-torn Central America, most of the altruists whom the Carter human rights policy had brought back into the uplifting fold departed once again.

After Ronald Reagan came the final Cold War president, George H. W. Bush. Inaugurated in January 1989, he waited until September to go before a nationwide television audience: "Good evening. This is the first time since taking the oath of office that I felt an issue was so important, so threatening, that it warranted talking directly with you, the American people. All of us agree that the gravest domestic threat facing our nation today is drugs." Then he unveiled his National Drug Control Strategy, which placed blame on everyone involved in the production, transport, and consumption of illicit drugs, but singled out for attention Latin America's Andean nations, with a new Andean Initiative. Not once did President Bush say the word "communism."[20] The Cold War was over in Latin America.

Elsewhere it took a little longer, although by the time of President Bush's speech the Hungarians had already opened their border to Austria and Solidarity had already won a stunning electoral victory in Poland. Then the Berlin Wall came down two months after the president spoke, followed in weeks by Czechoslovakia's Velvet Revolution. When the Soviet Union dissolved in late 1991, the Cold War was over everywhere.

President Bush's Latin America policy went beyond the drug war—his administration will also be remembered for negotiating the NAFTA agreement and for its unremitting hostility toward Cuba, culminating in the 1992 Cuban Democracy Act. When asked in late 1991 if he had any intention of engaging Fidel Castro now that the Soviet Union had disappeared, he said it would be futile. "What's the point of my talking to him? All I'd tell him is what I'm telling you, to give the people the freedom that they want. And then you'll see the United States do exactly what we should: Go down and lift those people up."[21]

POST-JFK COLD WAR policy also included a renewed emphasis upon improving the Latin America military, an effort openly designed to protect U.S. interests, particularly U.S. security.

The raw numbers are what anyone would expect: total military aid to Latin America during the Cold War was $4.1 billion, of which 85 percent ($3.5 billion) was provided after the beginning of the Cuban revolution, which was, of course, a longer period. That region-wide total masks a focus on countries where subversion seemed particularly worrisome, such as Nicaragua. In the fifteen pre-Castro Cold War years, military aid to Nicaragua totaled $1.6 million, about $100,000 per year. Then in the fifteen years from 1962 to 1977 it jumped to a total of $30.5 million, about $2 million per year.

At first, in the 1960s, the change most in tune with the times was a new effort to encourage Latin America's militaries to uplift the poor—Washington called it "civic action." Although he did not originate the idea, Walt Rostow was responsible for introducing the Kennedy administration to the concept. Two weeks before JFK's inauguration, Rostow told incoming Secretary of State Dean Rusk that "there is one particular aspect of our programs in the under-developed areas which bears in a quite specific way on the deterrence of guerrilla warfare; and that is the role of the local military in the economic development process."

Rostow said the same thing to JFK, who in turn said this at the White House kickoff of the Alliance for Progress: "The new generation of military leaders has shown an increasing awareness that armies can not only defend their countries—they can, as we have learned through our own Corps of Engineers, they can help to build them." A few weeks later Rostow sent JFK a copy of a lecture by General Edward Lansdale (referring to him as "your favorite current author") who "underlines the strictly military reasons why the local armies should be encouraged by us to engage in economic development."[22]

Jumping at this opportunity to participate in the Alliance, the Joint Chiefs of Staff soon sent JFK a memo calling for a "Latin American Civilian Conservation Corps," which would be under the supervision of each country's armed forces. In Bolivia, for example, "these labor battalions could, in addition to getting the unemployed out of the mining towns and cities [could also] help resolve the serious problem of the excess mineworkers who so frequently rise up in opposition to the government." Meanwhile, Latin America's air forces could engage in "agricultural spraying, aero-medical services, search and rescue."[23] The State Department agreed: in Latin America's least-developed countries—here Paraguay—the military "can perform functions in this primitive, frontier society with which domestic civilian elements are unable to cope." State saw this as a two-goal effort: the U.S. military aid programs "are designed to support economic and social development and to promote democratic ideals and concepts in the Paraguayan armed forces."[24]

"Civic action" gave Latin America's military forces an improved reputation in 1960s Washington, where, Vietnam aside, it now was common to talk favorably about "the modernizing military." When UN ambassador Adlai Stevenson was sent by JFK to South America on a post–Bay of Pigs attempt to smooth relations, he returned to report that "the leaders of the armies of most of the nations I visited have acquired a deeper consciousness of the importance of democratic institutions. In several cases the army is proving democracy's strongest bulwark and most constructive promoter."[25] Nelson Rockefeller said the same thing after his 1969 Latin American study trip for the Nixon administration: "The pressures of these military groups to take over, in my judgment, are not the ambitions of men as they were in the past to have the old style dictatorship. It is more trying to create a framework with which social programs can be achieved."[26]

To the extent that Latin American military officers balked at becoming uplifters, the challenge to U.S. military advisers was to use training and hardware as leverage to encourage exactly what JFK's assistant secretary, Edwin Martin, was encouraging Latin American civilians to do—to replace their undesirable values with desirable values.

This value swap had been one of the goals of U.S. military assistance since the Progressive era, and now, here in the 1960s, the Pentagon's principal response to critics was "when they come to our schools both here and in the Panama Canal Zone, there is a lot of the U.S. way of life that rubs off." This occurred because "the average Latin American officer often looks to them [their U.S. instructors] for advice and guidance in many military matters that cannot strictly be categorized as technical." And when cuts in military aid were proposed for human rights reasons in the Carter 1970s, the Pentagon continued to insist that "by giving young South and Central American leaders and their families an opportunity to experience the U.S. way of life on a first-hand, and many times extended basis, our concept of democracy and human rights has been transferred at a very modest cost."[27]

THAT SAID, THE core assignment of the Latin American military was unchanged: maintain internal security. In 1962, three years into the Cuban revolution and one year after Fidel Castro had announced he had become a Marxist-Leninist, the Department of Defense repeated to the Senate what it had been saying since the mid-1940s: "the principal threat faced in Latin America is Communist subversion and indirect attack." In 1969 the Joint Chiefs reported that "the Armed Forces of Latin America have been and will continue to be, at least for the short term, the strongest obstacle to any communist seizure of power."[28]

Everyone in Washington would have liked to see in the Latin American military a commitment to both development and security, but U.S. officials understood that a choice often had to be made. Driven by the fear of another Cuba, the United States threw its full support behind anticommunist dictators who were hunting those they identified as subversives.[29] Two such cases would trigger a momentous shift in Washington's efforts to improve

Latin Americans: a shift from economic to political uplifting that continues to this day.

IN BRAZIL A 1964 military coup was central to the 1966 effort to add to the Foreign Assistance Act a democracy-promotion requirement—Title IX.

The data surrounding U.S. involvement in the coup have been pored over by two generations of scholars, every one of whom agrees on this: after Attorney General Robert Kennedy's late-1963 meeting with Brazil's left-leaning president, João Goulart, the U.S. government considered a coup desirable.[30] Also unquestionable is the Johnson administration's pleasure with the outcome. "I hope you are as happy about Brazil as I am," State's Thomas Mann said to LBJ immediately after the coup. "I am," the president responded, and the next day he told reporters, "This has been a good week for this hemisphere." A few days later Ambassador Lincoln Gordon reported from Rio de Janeiro that "while we do not seek to justify extra-legal processes adopted by revolutionary leaders to carry out 'Operation Clean-Up,' a substantial purge was clearly in order."[31]

Pleased to be sure, but how involved? No one has found a smoking gun indicating direct U.S. participation, and given the amount of searching that has occurred, it probably does not exist. Yet many critics argued at the time that Brazil's generals never would have acted without decades of grooming by the United States.

This grooming began in 1917 with the arrival of a U.S. naval mission, but it became especially prominent during and immediately after World War II, when a Brazilian division had fought alongside U.S. forces in Italy. At this time the two countries created a Joint Brazilian United States Military Commission (JBUSMC), a coordinating mechanism that continued until the late 1970s. During this Cold War period the chief of the U.S. delegation reported, "The chairman and the head quarters staff of the U.S. delegation, JBUSMC, are co-located with the Brazilian delegation in a Brazilian Government building in Rio de Janeiro. The Army, Navy and Air Force sections of JBUSMC are physically located in their respective Brazilian ministry buildings. This provides daily contact with Brazilian counterparts at all levels from action officer to Cabinet minister. The atmosphere has been and is today [1971] one of friendly cooperation and mutual respect in dealing with whatever matters may arise."[32]

The single most important human link between the two countries' militaries, on the one hand, and the 1964 military coup, on the other, was Colonel Vernon Walters. "I was the only American in the middle of 19,000 Brazilians in Italy for a year and a half," Walters wrote of the World War II campaign, and after the war he had served in Brazil as a military attaché.[33] As Washington became increasingly concerned about the leftward tilt in Brazilian politics, in late 1962 Walters was pulled from a European assignment and returned to Brazil. "On my arrival in Rio, I was met, to my surprise, by some thirteen general officers who had served in Italy with me." Walters called it "a typically warm Brazilian gesture of friendship," but readers arriving at any Brazilian airport will be disappointed if they expect to find even one general to greet them. Indeed, Walters's reception may have been the only time in the history of the world where a colonel walked off an airplane to find thirteen generals waiting to welcome his arrival.[34]

That greeting was followed the next day by Walters's meeting with U.S. ambassador Lincoln Gordon, who gave him his marching orders: "First, I want to know what is going on in the Armed Forces; second, I want to be able in some measure to influence it through you; and third, most of all, I never want to be surprised."

And so Walters set to work. In his 1978 memoir, written in an extremely defensive tone after several accusatory studies had been published, Walters repeatedly emphasized that his every encounter with Brazilian officers "was very formal, except when I was alone with old friends who would pour out their worry at seeing their country drifting toward becoming what so many called 'another Cuba.'" He listened and then reported but, he insisted, never voiced his own views nor those of the United States government.

That was even true when meeting with the officer with whom he had been closest in Italy:

> General Castelo Branco was commanding the Fourth Army in Recife in northern Brazil. Once or twice he came to Rio and I had lunch or dinner with his wife and him. She was a very close friend of my mother's [who had followed Walters to his posting] and they enjoyed speaking French together. Castelo Branco had always spoken with pride of the professionalism of the Brazilian Armed Forces and of his unwillingness to take part in any revolutions. When we would meet we would speak of the world, the United States, Vietnam, Europe, the Soviet Union or China. Rarely did we speak of internal Brazilian affairs and he spoke of them only with great circumspection.

Then when Castelo Branco became army chief of staff and was brought back to Rio, "I saw him frequently but almost never did our talks touch on current

Brazilian affairs. He had always expressed the belief that Brazilians could and would solve their own problems." After the military takeover, he wrote, "I saw President Castelo Branco from time to time. We spoke of the world, of NATO, or Europe and Asia. We did not discuss Brazilian politics. Had I attempted to do this, he would have told me that it was none of my business."[35]

Perhaps Walters protested too much, but he stood by every word until the day he died. Was he telling the truth? Until some sleuth uncovers incriminating documents, let us take him at his word, which was that he did not encourage the coup. That does not mean we should accept what U.S. ambassador Lincoln Gordon told Congress: "The movement which overthrew President Goulart was a purely, 100 percent—not 99.44—but 100 percent purely Brazilian movement. Neither the American Embassy nor I personally played any part in the process whatsoever."[36]

In the case of Brazil and elsewhere, this question of Washington's influence upon the Latin American military hinges upon the maddeningly vague concept of the *mentality* that accompanied a half-century of providing military hardware and training, and of embedding U.S. officers in Brazil's armed forces. Searching through the Brazilian and U.S. archives for a document showing Walters holding a smoking gun is not the same as sinking analytical teeth into reports such as one in 1947, where the U.S. Navy informed Congress that the Brazilian Navy had "adopted as nearly as possible, the curriculum of the United States Naval Academy." That meant more than learning how to sail U.S.-surplus warships, but no one can pinpoint how much more.[37] In 1969 the Pentagon claimed that

> the US military assistance program has had an impact on every aspect of the Brazilian military, and US influence has been predominant in the training and development of all branches of the services. Brazil reorganized its Army along US lines. Budgeting, planning, accounting, and materiel inventory systems as well as logistics procedures reflect US influence. Training in the US and the Canal Zone for over 5,600 officers and enlisted men up through FY 1968 has raised the professional competence and technical capabilities to a higher level, in addition to exposing these students to American ideas and doctrine. This orientation has greatly contributed to the pro-US inclination of some military leaders, and to the increasing stress placed on counterinsurgency.[38]

So when a careful scholar such as Carlos Poggio Teixeira writes that "the Brazilian generals needed no indoctrination," he concedes that the indoctrination occurred, then notes that "attributing which part of the difficulties [the coup] was the direct result of US policies and which part lies within domestic factors and other international conditions is a challenging endeavor." Teixeira would agree with Gaddis Smith, who pointed out that "there are times when it is unnecessary to spell out c-o-u-p," but neither he nor anyone else can be sure 1964 Brazil was one of those times.[39]

In any event, democratic Brazil became a military dictatorship for the next two decades. Soon came the U.S. assistance, beginning with a visit by Walt Rostow, who was deeply impressed. "We could not conceive of a government in Brazil more mature, more level-headed about relations with the U.S., and in its attitude towards private enterprise." Rostow assessed the coup leader, General Humberto Castelo Branco, as "a remarkable Latin American chief of state."[40]

ON THE OTHER hand, there are almost too many smoking guns to count in Cold War Chile, whose politics had long featured democratic participation by both a Socialist and a Communist Party, which Washington should not have confused with the communist parties of the Soviet bloc, but did. With their observation heavily influenced by the Cuban revolution, the officials who would advise President Nixon had grown apprehensive as Chilean politics moved to the left during the Kennedy and Johnson administrations, culminating in the 1970 election of Socialist Salvador Allende, whose Popular Unity coalition included the Communist Party.[41]

The question of the Chilean military's attitude toward elected authorities was raised in 1969, during President Nixon's first year in office, when the Joint Chiefs of Staff reported that "the Chilean military, a strong, professional institution, is one of the few Latin American Armed Forces that has a long and deeply ingrained tradition of non-involvement in politics." However, "in a situation where the threat to continued order, or to the continuation of orderly political processes were to arise, the military could be expected to intervene." That said, "their tradition would make them very reluctant to overthrow any constitutionally elected government, even if it were of Marxist ideology." In other words, anything could happen.

If there was one certainty it was that Washington's aim to exclude European providers had been as successful with Chile's military as it had been with Brazil's. In 1969 the Joint Chiefs also reported that "the Chilean Armed Forces have maintained close relations with their US counterparts since World War II, strengthened through the US military assistance program."

The two countries' military assistance agreement "has been instrumental in increasing US influence over the three services."[42]

Allende's election a year later triggered a test of that influence. National security adviser Henry Kissinger reportedly told President Nixon, "I don't see why we need to stand by and watch a country go Communist due to the irresponsibility of its own people." The president agreed.[43]

First came a preinauguration effort to trigger a military coup. The plan for the period between Allende's October election and his November inauguration was for the Chilean military to overthrow the lame-duck government of Christian Democrat Eduardo Frei, who was popular but prohibited from consecutive terms. Having seized power, the military junta would immediately hold a new election in which the ousted Frei, now technically not seeking a consecutive term, would defeat Allende's coalition, which in the recent election had barely eked out a plurality.

There was a glitch: President Frei would almost certainly not agree to participate in this charade unless the country were on the verge of collapse. So CIA headquarters instructed its Santiago station, "It is our task to create such a climate climaxing with a solid pretext that will force the military and the President to take some action in the desired direction."[44]

A subsequent Senate investigation noted that the CIA had inadequate contacts within the Chilean military; "however, a U.S. military attaché in Santiago knew the Chilean military very well due to his broad personal contacts." The attaché was ordered "to work closely with the CIA chief, or in his absence, his deputy, in contacting and advising the principal military figures who might play a decisive role in any move which might, eventually, deny the presidency to Allende." And so this attaché "informed both an Army General . . . and an Air Force General of the pro-coup U.S. policy." Two days later he "approached members of the War Academy in Santiago who in turn asked him to provide light weapons."

Although it cost the life of the Chilean army's uncooperative chief of staff, who preferred to support his country's Constitution, this plan for a preemptive coup came to naught, and Allende was inaugurated. Meanwhile, the effort to engineer the economy's collapse was under way—"make the economy scream" had been President Nixon's instruction to CIA director Richard Helms. One obvious tool was to halt the purchase of Chilean raw materials, especially copper. Another was to cut economic assistance, which had averaged $55 million per year in 1963–1970; it dropped to an average of

$1.1 million for the three Allende years.[45] Rather than reduce or discontinue social welfare programs, the Allende government generally chose to print the money to keep them operating. Along with a host of additional factors, the aid cutoff contributed to near-runaway inflation and shortages of basic foodstuffs. With the economy screaming and citizens protesting, in 1973 the military stepped in.

Then came the leaks about Washington's contribution to the coup. Everyone knew of the U.S. hostility, but few had imagined what congressional committees eventually uncovered—ream after ream of documents and day after day of sworn testimony that chronicled the destruction of a democratic government and the creation of an uncommonly brutal military dictatorship, and U.S. complicity in both.

Tanya Harmer concluded that "the international history of Allende's overthrow is a far more complex story than a simple case of 'who did it?'" Her careful study concluded that "a confluence of different local and international actors driven apart in a battle between socialism and capitalism determined what happened." "U.S. funding for opposition groups and their media outlets in Chile bolstered the challenge they were able to pose to Allende's presidency. The CIA's propaganda and black operations campaigns fueled doubts concerning the UP's [Allende's coalition] democratic credentials and the far Left's relationship with Allende. And the Nixon administration's credit freezes, together with private companies' lawsuits against Santiago, forced the Allende government into a defensive scramble for economic support." That said, "the United States did not manipulate or force its Chilean contacts to do anything that they did not want to do"— "there is enough responsibility for what happened in Chile to be spread around."[46]

Forced from office by the unrelated Watergate scandal, President Nixon left Gerald Ford to justify U.S. actions, many of which could never have been taken without the ties between the two countries' militaries. These actions were "in the best interest of the people of Chile and, certainly, in our own best interests," President Ford insisted. "I am not going to pass judgment on whether it is permitted or authorized under international law. It is a recognized fact that historically, as well as presently, such actions are taken in the best interests of the countries involved."[47]

Just like Walt Rostow had flown down to Rio in 1964, now Secretary of State Henry Kissinger flew down to Santiago and told General Augusto

Pinochet, "You did a great service to the West in overthrowing Allende. . . . We are sympathetic to what you are trying to do here. . . . We want to help."[48]

IF ONE FEATURE of the Brazilian and Chilean military coups is not debated, it is that the Rostow-Kissinger enthusiasm for the ensuing dictatorships did not go unchallenged, and here is where the U.S. effort to promote democracy acquired new energy.

First came the "Brazil" effect. Called before the Senate in 1965 to explain the quick expansion of economic assistance to Brazil's generals and the administration's use of foreign aid to support other dictators, AID administrator David Bell explained that "it is obviously not our purpose or intent to assist the head of a state who is repressive. On the other hand, we are working in a lot of countries where the governments are controlled by people who have shortcomings." Similarly, Thomas Mann, State's principal Latin Americanist (the one who said "I hope you are as happy about Brazil as I am") used a commencement address three months after the coup to argue that "we cannot put ourselves in the doctrinaire straightjacket of automatic application of sanctions to every unconstitutional regime which arises in this hemisphere." That argument convinced Senator Stuart Symington, who commented, "In all probability the only permanent governments could either be Communist governments, like Castro, or military governments a la Trujillo, which we hope would be better. But there is no chance of developing the true democratic form of government, at least as it is conceived of and executed in the United States."[49] Should you be commissioned to select the most contemptuous comment ever made about Latin Americans by a member of Congress, that would be worthy of your consideration.

Meanwhile, in 1966 President Johnson lay claim to the high ground. "In the Latin American countries we are on the side of those who want constitutional governments," he told a university audience. "We are not on the side of those who say that dictatorships are necessary for efficient economic development or as a bulwark against Communism."[50]

Most Cold War presidents made similar comments, but in the mid-1960s, with Vietnam becoming a true calamity, the purpose of LBJ's speech was to counter the many members of Congress who had concluded that the always-fragile balance between idealism and realism had been lost. Representative Donald Fraser, the most prominent congressional proponent of an activist policy to protect human rights abroad, argued for "a basic reorientation of our thinking." "The problem of the developing nations has been described largely in economic terms, [but] there is increasing evidence that the major shortcoming in the developing nations lies in their political and social structures. Until we address ourselves to this reality, little progress will be made."[51]

Three weeks after LBJ's speech, Congress added Title IX to the Foreign Assistance Act. It stipulated that the United States should use its foreign aid programs to encourage "democratic private and local government institutions."[52] Up to this time, most foreign aid officials had thought of themselves as economic and not political uplifters, and Title IX therefore triggered a period of internal debate, at the end of which AID officials decided never to send another funding request to Congress without saying at least a few words about their active interest in promoting democracy. They never have.

TITLE IX SLIPPED easily into a stream of thinking that stretches back to the mid-nineteenth century. Recall the 1840s, when U.S. envoys were instructed to point out "the example of our own country where all controversies are decided at the ballot box." But they were to do nothing more: Secretary of State James Buchanan followed that sentence with "We recognize the right of all nations to create and re-form their political institutions according to their own will and pleasure. We do not go behind the existing Government to involve ourselves in the question of legitimacy."[53] That had been U.S. policy since Thomas Jefferson announced it in 1793, and that had been the central point of John Quincy Adams's Independence Day address in 1821, given at a time when some advocated sending U.S. aid to Latin Americans who were fighting for their independence.[54]

This hands-off policy was occasionally ignored in the second half of the nineteenth century. In 1866 the Grant administration refused to recognize the government of Peru because, as Secretary of State William Seward explained to his minister in Lima, "the policy of the United States is settled upon the principle that revolutions in republican states ought not be accepted until the people had adopted them by organic law." (Minister Alvin Hovey replied that if the United States insisted on a democratic government, it would "be a far distant day before our country is represented at all in Peru.") A decade later, the Rutherford Hayes administration also refused to recognize the Mexican government of Porfirio Díaz "until it shall be assured that his election is approved by the Mexican people."[55]

This legitimacy test became the norm for Washington's relations with Caribbean-area governments during the Progressive era. In 1907 the Roosevelt administration and in 1923 the post-Progressive Harding administration agreed not to recognize any unelected Central American government. Sandwiched in between was Woodrow Wilson's 1913 announcement that cooperation with any Latin American government "is possible only when supported at every turn by the orderly processes of just government based upon law, not upon arbitrary or irregular force"—hence his refusal to recognize the Mexican government of Victoriano Huerta and his decision to seek Huerta's overthrow. This was when President Wilson is alleged to have said that his policy was to teach Latin Americans to elect good leaders.

As with Secretary of State Buchanan in the 1840s, during the Woodrow Wilson years the State Department's principal legal officer warned that "we cannot become the censors of the morals or conduct of other nations and make our approval or disapproval of their methods the test of our recognition of the governments without intervening in their affairs." Ignoring this advice, President Wilson instructed the officials in charge of the Dominican Republic to focus upon both political and economic uplifting: "to improve the laws and economic condition of the country."[56]

Then came the 1920s and early 1930s, when Washington struggled to withdraw from its protectorates but first felt responsible for creating governments chosen in free and fair elections. These democratic transitions were difficult to orchestrate—"We oversimplified the problem," admitted the State Department's Dana Munro—but the Harding, Coolidge, and Hoover administrations managed to transfer power to nominally democratic governments. When those were quickly overthrown, their new military dictators were recognized, and a disinterest in democracy promotion became a hallmark of the ensuing Good Neighbor policy. Both Herbert Hoover and FDR dealt with governments as they were, not as the United States would wish them to be. "We have reestablished the sensible practice of our forefathers," wrote Hoover's secretary of state, Henry Stimson.[57]

This no-political-uplifting policy has been praised ever since for its commitment to nonintervention but criticized for its friendship with dictators. The Good Neighbor officials who thought of themselves as more altruistic than realistic, such as Laurence Duggan, simply hoped that "the consolidation of democracy will parallel the tempo of industrialization, agrarian reform, and education." Without that, "our gestures of moral support for democracy, unless they are supplemented by down-to-earth measures to increase production, will suffer the usual fate of sterile preachments divorced from action."[58]

The tight Good Neighbor rein on democracy-promoting field officers was relaxed a bit during and immediately after World War II, only to be abruptly yanked to a stop early in the Cold War, beginning a long decade of befriending an entire stable of thoroughbred anticommunists, not half of whom were democrats. Anticommunism aside, most Cold War U.S. leaders appear to have shared Duggan's Good Neighbor belief that economic development produced political development. That probably helps explain why the 1961 Charter of the Alliance for Progress focused on Latin Americans' economic improvement and gave only a passing nod to democracy promotion—nothing more than that the promised economic reforms should be "carried out in accordance with democratic principles," with "equal opportunities for all, in democratic societies."

Not everyone agreed that such a mild statement was sufficient. "We should give every dictator a sense of impermanence," Arthur Schlesinger urged President Kennedy, and "make it absolutely clear that we regard dictatorship and the suppression of popular rights as ultimately incompatible with the principles of the hemisphere." But a U.S. ambassador offered Robert Kennedy a contrary argument: the armed forces "represent one of the very few stabilizing influences in this time of turbulent change. . . . In almost every Latin American country, the armed forces literally stand between the communists and the Palace."

Given the absence of a consensus, the Kennedy administration pushed to reverse a 1962 coup in Peru, gaining a promise of prompt elections, and in 1963 it halted both military and economic aid after coups in the Dominican Republic and Honduras. But relatively little attention was given to military takeovers in Argentina and Ecuador, and JFK-era officials learned to live with coups and their resulting dictators. In the end, wrote another JFK aide, Theodore Sorensen, "the military often represented more competence in administration and more sympathy with the U.S. than any other group in the country. To halt work on the Alliance in every nation not ruled by a genuine democracy would have paralyzed the whole program."[59]

That left JFK's Peace Corps, consisting primarily of well-scrubbed recent college graduates, to serve as the administration's only consistent promoters of democracy. Volunteers in community development were "teaching democracy on a community level [by] encouraging the people to work together—a new idea for most of them." Meanwhile, volunteers working to create cooperatives were not simply assisting with economic development; "the people participating in these co-ops are also being exposed to democratic procedures, many of them for the first time." When asked to select which volunteers provided "the best possible working lesson in democracy," Peace Corps publicists chose those assigned to youth groups, who were "opening new horizons for these young people and giving them new insights into how communities can work together to solve common problems."[60]

AFTER CONGRESS ADDED Title IX to the Foreign Assistance Act in 1966, during the Johnson administration, AID created a "Division on Title IX" in its Office of Program and Policy Coordination, and assembled a Title IX Advisory Committee composed of five social scientists who were said to be knowledgeable about how to promote democracy. There were no new activities yet, but Agency officials slowly began to produce memos indicating that they were ready to get ready to think about what those activities might be: "Title IX requires AID not only to consider new types of activities, but to view the developmental process in different and much broader terms than before: it will not do simply to relabel and multiply on-going AID activities consistent with Title IX's objectives. It is evident that the successful, long-run implementation of this provision requires a serious and extensive analytical effort on the part of the Agency into aspects of the developmental process to which inadequate attention has hitherto been given."[61] This serious and extensive analytical effort continued for the remaining eighteen months of the Johnson administration. In the meantime, State's Thomas Mann insisted that "there is no basis under international law for equating recognition with United States approval of the internal political policies and practices of another government."[62]

If LBJ's successor, Richard Nixon, was interested in promoting democracy, he hid it better than he hid most of his secrets. When a U.S. investor in the Dominican Republic complained about the State Department's hostile attitude toward that country's dictator, Nixon replied: "Let me be clear about [unintelligible] my position. I have no patience with those who are against the Dominican Republic. That is the attitude of the State Department, it's not mine. They're against it because they consider it a dictatorship. I don't give a damn what it is. I'm for them." On another occasion he told the chair of the Joint Chiefs of Staff and the Secretary of Defense, "When you look at Latin America, [unintelligible] not a very encouraging place to see, is it? Except those countries that got dictators in it and successful dictators, they're in a hell of a mess."[63]

There was never any doubt about Jimmy Carter, who entered office in 1977 after a campaign in which he criticized the Nixon-Ford policy of undermining democracy and supporting dictatorships. When President Ford claimed in a presidential debate that the United States did not support repression in South Korea, Carter fired back: "Mr. Ford didn't comment on the prisons in Chile," where "his administration overthrew an elected government and helped to establish a military dictatorship."

But President Carter entered office at a time when the promotion of democracy had to take a back seat to an immediate focus upon the widespread abuses that characterized a set of uncommonly depraved military dictatorships, particularly in the Southern Cone (Argentina, Chile, and Uruguay) and Central America (especially Somoza's Nicaragua). While this focus on more abhorrent human rights violations (and on a set of unrelated misfortunes) left President Carter little time for direct democracy promotion, during his administration it was common to hear altruistic politicians proposing to assist Latin Americans overthrow dictators. Few disagreed with one of the most altruistic members of the House, Tom Harkin, who told a Washington audience that "we always hear it said, 'Well, we don't want to interfere in those countries. We don't want to go in there and mess in their internal affairs.' I don't see why not? We are going to influence Latin America. We will influence every country there. Are we going to stop supporting these dictators down there who violate human rights with some sense of security? Or will be forcefully, once and for all, say 'No, we won't put up with it'?"[64] Theodore Roosevelt never said it better.

That position was an open invitation to the realists who gained access to power during the administration of Jimmy Carter's successor, Ronald Reagan. With both mainstream Washington and U.S. public opinion intensely divided over what to do about the turmoil in Central America, the Reagan administration seized upon the unifying idea of promoting democracy.

This was marketed as a method of attacking communism, a national security interest. Outlining "a plan and a hope for the long term—the march of freedom and democracy which will leave Marxism-Leninism on the ashheap of history," in 1982 President Reagan told the British Parliament, "It is time that we committed ourselves as a nation—in both the public and private sectors—to assisting democratic development." This idea became a law eighteen months later, when President Reagan signed the National Endowment for Democracy Act, authorizing funding of a new institution "to encourage free and democratic institutions throughout the world."[65] Created near the end of the Cold War, the National Endowment for Democracy would become a central institution for today's effort to improve Latin American governance.

SO HERE WE were, at the end of a long Cold War featuring varying amounts of attention to and neglect of Latin America. Except for the Cubans, Latin Americans had kept their chips on the U.S. side of the table.

Those who downplay U.S. influence and emphasize instead the independent behavior of Latin Americans can argue that the region's leaders would have kept their chips where they were without Washington's assistance. Perhaps, but the fact is that the United States was assisting, particularly with military and police assistance in the prominent cases where chip-moving seemed likely: Cuba and Guatemala in the 1950s, Brazil (and almost everywhere else) in the 1960s, Chile in the 1970s, and Central America in the 1980s. While no one would deny Latin Americans a large measure of agency, Hans Morgenthau surely got it right: "Military aid is bound to have an impact upon the distribution of political power within the receiving country."[66]

One thing is certain: motivated by a consuming desire to contain the spread of communism, a string of Washington administrations, equally Republican and Democrat, cemented into place a set of permanent institutions designed to improve Latin Americans. Some of these institutions provided economic assistance to help Latin Americans satisfy their rising expectations, and some provided help in maintaining order. Every one of these institutions was created not by Adam Smith altruists but by Hans Morgenthau realists seeking to protect U.S. security interests and, of far lesser importance, U.S. economic interests.

When the Cold War era began, Latin Americans were asking for assistance with their economic development, but in the late 1940s and 1950s the United States found itself saddled with unprecedented responsibilities, and the improvement of Latin Americans was not considered one of them. Then came the Cuban revolution, and Latin America's takeoff into self-sustaining economic growth became a true obsession. After a few years Washington's eyes turned to Southeast Asia, but the uplifting needle never dropped to zero in Latin America, even if the second half of the 1960s and most of the 1970s were characterized by a lull. Then in 1979 Nicaragua's Sandinistas ended the Somoza dynasty, and nine days later the Sandinista leadership was in Havana, standing alongside Fidel Castro on the reviewing stand for Cuba's 26th of July celebration. Fearful that another chip was moving to the Soviet Union's side of the table, the United States spent the final decade of the Cold War destroying Nicaragua's new government and ensuring with economic and military assistance that the rest of Central America stayed on Washington's side.

And so with a combination of hard and soft power the United States won the Cold War in Latin America. Given Latin Americans' own interests, Washington probably would have won without trying, but no one can be certain. Beyond doubt, however, is that the final decades of the Cold War saw a rebirth of the Progressive belief in Latin Americans' need for political improvement. Although it was difficult to see at the time, the creation of the National Endowment for Democracy in 1983, late in the Cold War, was the best indicator that today's era of good governance was getting underway.

CHAPTER 10

The Evolution from Economic to Political Improvement

Our mission is to nourish and defend freedom and democracy.

—State of the Union Address
Cold War President Ronald Reagan, 1985

We understand our special calling: This great republic will lead the cause of freedom.

—State of the Union Address
Post–Cold War President George W. Bush, 2004

IF YOU HAD been among the many thousand government employees and contractors assigned to win the Cold War in Latin America, you might now be wondering how long you were going to be paid to do what no longer needed to be done. For the moment your team of altruists was still suited up, but the managing realists were disoriented. After four decades of continuous competition, the archrival communists had simply walked off the field, which was no longer marked for a two-sided contest. It was not marked for anything. Now what game was Team USA supposed to be playing, and against how many of whom?

The answer was many different games based upon many different interests. In 2008, almost two decades after the Cold War victory, the Agency for International Development was sponsoring four uplifting teams in Latin America: the Peace and Security team, with $208 million to fight terrorism, organized crime, and the smuggling of drugs and people; the Investing in People team, with $390 million for the now-standard work in education, health care, and sanitation, plus several new activities such as "preparation for potential natural disasters"; the Economic Growth team, with $206 million to help Latin America's poor obtain "productive assets," to explore "possibilities for alternative fuels," to encourage governments to be more market-friendly, and to reduce corruption; and finally AID's rising star, the Governance team, with $158 million "to create competitive and inclusive political systems" and, as inevitable as gravity, "to oppose tyranny in Cuba."[1]

Although this $962 million for all of Latin America was far less than what AID was spending in two trouble spots—Iraq ($2.5 billion) and Afghanistan ($1.8 billion)—the next year promised to go over the billion-dollar mark. The chair of the House subcommittee handling foreign assistance told delighted AID officials in early 2009, two weeks after Democrat Barack Obama moved into the White House, "No Member of this Subcommittee would disagree with me that we need to significantly increase foreign aid to our neighbors in Latin America and the Caribbean."[2]

While there were some new activities, from helping Latin Americans fight terrorism to teaching them how to use alternative fuels, most post–Cold War uplifting activities had existed during the Cold War.[3] That said, the post–Cold War era saw the culmination of three major changes in the way U.S. officials thought about Latin America. These changes began during the Cold War and have been routinized during our post–Cold War era. They all involve uplifting.

THE FIRST WAS a dramatically increased focus on improving Latin American institutions. The original Cold War framework, drawn from the academic literature on development, had been that the United States would help Latin Americans change the way they *thought,* which would change the way they *behaved.* Then this new behavior would lead to "development." Recall JFK's assistant secretary of state, Edwin Martin, who spoke of helping Latin Americans adopt "scientific or rational habits of thought, as opposed to the traditional or emotional approach to problems." This, he continued, would encourage Latin Americans to adopt "new ways of doing things"—new behavior.

Soon it became obvious that no one knew how to help Latin Americans take that first step—to change the way they thought, although more or less everyone agreed that economic growth was central to the process. So, given an urgent need to meet the communist challenge alongside Latin Americans' rising expectations, it had seemed logical to focus on economic development. The United States would show Latin Americans developed ways of doing things—new ways to behave—and rational habits of thought would eventually appear. Note the transposition: new thinking→ new behavior was out; new behavior→ new thinking was in.

But as JFK's Treasury secretary recalled, in the 1960s "we had (in hindsight) too great confidence that economic growth by itself would be sufficient."[4] Eventually, nearly all U.S. officials concluded that Latin Americans should be accepted as they are, thinking as they thought. The U.S. role would be to teach them how properly functioning institutions could constrain their undesirable ways of doing things—basically, the same thinking that had led Progressive-era uplifters to create constabularies, but much more sophisticated. Here is what AID was doing to improve Latin America's political institutions in 2005, fifteen years after the Cold War ended:

> USAID's governance programs promote accountability and transparency in national and local-level government institutions, strengthen civil society organizations to advocate for citizens' rights, and increase the capacity of national and local governments to manage resources and provide services. Anticorruption programs, such as establishment of transparent management and recordkeeping systems or auditing agencies, improve citizen oversight and build local capacity to address weak governance, entrenched political institutions, and poor public sector management. USAID investments since 1990 have led to adoption of national-level integrated financial management systems by all USAID presence countries in LAC [Latin America and the Caribbean], bringing transparency to national budgets for the first time. At the local level, technical assistance and training for municipal leaders improves coverage of basic public services and infrastructure, transparent financial administration, and public participation in decision making.[5]

Every one of these activities was designed to constrain undesirable behavior—what Assistant Secretary Edwin Martin would have characterized in the 1960s as the Latin American way of doing things. Twenty-first-century Washington now considers such paragraphs completely normal—business as usual. There is no evidence that post–Cold War leaders understand they have embarked upon an uplifting effort that is almost infinitely more ambitious than anything ever attempted. Verb by verb, it simply happened.

THE SECOND MAJOR change was an unprecedented increase in the number of implementing organizations. In 1991, just as the Soviet Union was taking its last gasp, the Congressional Research Service had warned that "U.S. foreign assistance is overburdened with goals and expectations that either reflect international conditions that no longer pertain, or cannot be met, or are so numerous as to be contradictory."[6] In 2008 Oxfam America reported that the basic U.S. foreign aid law contained 247 directives, specified thirty-three different goals, and required attention to seventy-five priority areas. Twelve of the fifteen cabinet-level departments plus eighty-five independent agencies and offices were providing overseas development assistance.[7]

Congress mandated nearly all of this, as it slowly became addicted to expanding the scope of the 1961 Foreign Assistance Act. By 2016 it had grown to 280 pages, up from its original 41.[8] One simple section, §502B, prohibiting military aid to repressive governments, fit onto one page when added to the Act in 1974—three brief paragraphs with 229 words. In 2018, §502B was ten times longer, 2,883 words.

In twenty-first-century Washington there are so many different uplifting activities lodged in so many institutional nooks and crannies that no one would hazard a guess about their size. This uplifting industry is so big that no one knows how big it is. And those 247 directives are not simply suggestions; they are the law, many assigning mega-responsibilities such as Title IX, which requires that "emphasis shall be placed on assuring maximum participation of the people in the developing countries, through the encouragement of democratic private and local government institutions."

Yet over the decades AID has seen its number of direct-hire personnel (a term covering several types of government employees) bob up and down but mostly down. It started high—8,600 in 1962—when AID inherited the personnel of the International Cooperation Administration, most of whom were involved in small-scale technical assistance projects. Then it rose to over 17,000 during the Vietnam War, when AID's development projects were focused on southeast Asians. After that the number dropped to about 6,000 in 1980, to 4,700 in 1988, to 3,400 in 1992, immediately after the Cold War ended, and bottomed out at about 2,000 just before the terrorist attacks in 2001. It then rose to 4,200 in 2012—most working in Iraq and Afghanistan—before dipping to exactly 3,146 at the beginning of 2015.[9]

That was a drop of 25 percent since 1988, the year before the fall of the Berlin Wall, and it occurred at time when AID's responsibilities were growing dramatically, especially its governance work in the countries of the former Soviet Union and, after 9/11, in Afghanistan and the Middle East.

More responsibilities, fewer people. Outside contractors filled the gap.

OUTSOURCING IS THE third change, but not entirely new—it stretches back to the early Progressive era, when university professors would take a leave from their teaching to serve as money and democracy doctors. Outsourcing was also a small part of the Good Neighbor policy, as when the Institute of International Education in New York was contracted to implement cultural exchanges. But the major expansion began after World War II, when Point 4 technical assistance projects often required highly specialized expertise available only at the nation's universities. The 1950s-era Technical Cooperation Administration and its successor, the International Cooperation Administration, did not have a staff that could help Chileans select an economic policy more in line with U.S. interests, so the ICA hired the economics department of the University of Chicago.[10]

Then in the 1960s AID's worldwide responsibilities required significantly increased outsourcing, and at a time when the private sector was thought to provide better results. At an early contract-signing ceremony with the National Rural Electric Cooperative Association in 1962, AID's first administrator, Fowler Hamilton, insisted that "what these gentlemen and ladies are going to take down to Latin America in their heads is going to be a lot more important than what Government bureaucrats carry in their pockets."[11]

Over the ensuing half-century, outsourcing slowly became the government's standard way of conducting its uplifting business. By 2015 AID's own offices were being run by 1,432 "Institutional Support Contractors," which were semipermanent contractors doing administrative work, not implementing the Agency's development projects. Of these, 657 were staffing AID's Bureau for Management, primarily working on information technology, and another 202 were staffing AID's Bureau for Democracy, Conflict and Humanitarian Assistance—six employees of Catapult Technology operated the Bureau's computer help desk, for example, and one more maintained the Bureau's website.[12]

Few students of today's foreign assistance programs think of these staffing contractors when they think of outsourcing. That word is reserved for contractors who respond to the government's continuous stream of requests for proposals to design, implement, and evaluate specific development projects.

Congress has encouraged their use, presumably after concluding that private contractors would be less expensive or would be able to provide higher-quality services, or both. In 2002 Congress went so far as to cap AID's operating budget, from which the Agency's direct-hire personnel were paid, but not the programming budget, from which contractors were paid. Then it added to the tasks it required AID to perform.

Entirely typical of this outsourcing is the group of public health professors who established the International Fertility Research Program at the University of North Carolina at Chapel Hill. In the 1960s AID had little expertise in family planning, which was needed in order to defuse what was then known as Latin America's "population bomb." So the Agency hired these UNC professors to figure out how to convince Third World peoples to produce fewer children, and then to implement their findings. As the contracts grew in number and size and frequency, in 1971 the professors cut out the university, which was skimming off much of the overhead, and created a nonprofit corporation, Family Health International, rebranded in 2010 as FHI and again in 2014 as FHI 360. By that time it was AID's fifth-largest contractor (AID refers to them as "vendors"), with total revenue of $589 million, 78 percent coming from AID and another 4 percent from the State Department.[13] In 2016 it had more than four thousand employees, a third more than AID itself.

In twenty-first-century Washington, then, the few thousand government-employed uplifters are supplemented by many tens of thousands of contractors—Chemonics, AID's third-largest contractor, had thirty-five hundred employees in 2017; Creative Associates International, the twenty-seventh-largest, had a thousand employees, and many of these top vendors regularly contract with subvendors to do the actual work. Together these government employees and nongovernmental contractors compose today's uplifting industry.

Although no systematic research has been conducted, most of these thousands appear to be altruists in their professional outlook, but in their personal outlook they have interests to protect.[14] Like the rest of us, they need to make their car payments and buy the groceries. Unlike government employees, who have their own set of career and organizational incentives, today's army of contractors cannot survive without contracts. The novices or the less ambitious contractors simply submit bids in response to an agency's requests for proposals; the major players, frequently led by retired AID officials, help government uplifters develop ideas for new projects. In 2018, FHI 360's chief executive officer was a retired member of the Foreign Service, where he had spent his entire career at AID, rising to become senior deputy assistant administrator in the Africa Bureau, AID's largest, before taking on the daunting role of AID's mission director in Afghanistan, a strong indicator of his stature within the Agency and, ipso facto, of his value to FHI. A list of the senior executives of major outsourcing contractors would be a Who's Who of retired AID officials.

Many observers consider this outsourcing lamentable, and some publish articles with titles such as "Is the U.S. Government Outsourcing Its Brain?"[15] Even the assiduously neutral Congressional Research Service seemed worried in 2009 about the "steep decline in personnel, expertise, and capabilities within USAID in recent years, and the reliance on outsourcing." In that same year Thomas Carothers, the highly respected vice president for studies at the Carnegie Endowment for International Peace, observed that "for most projects, the USAID mission brings in a U.S. organization to design the project. The mission then hires another U.S. organization to implement the project. At the end of the project, it hires yet another U.S. organization to evaluate the project." The result: "a hollowed-out organization more preoccupied with administration and management than the substance of development work." "A check-writing agency" is how another researcher dismissed twenty-first-century AID—"little more than a contract clearinghouse."[16]

It is for others to determine whether outsourcing is a good idea; let us treat it as a fact of life and recognize that most twenty-first century observers, especially those from Latin America, see little difference between "government" and "nongovernment" when discussing Washington's uplifting industry. Some of the components of this industry use an Internet address that ends in .gov; others' addresses end in .edu, .com, or .org. Think of those who use .gov and those who do not as two halves of a zipper, with the outsourced half of the zipper best understood as supply generated by demand. Over the years—the decades—Congress and the executive branch have kept demanding more uplifting by government agencies whose personnel grew slowly, if at all. AID actually shrank. The only alternative to ignoring the ever-expanding demands for more of almost everything was to seek outside help—to issue a request for proposals to design, implement, and evaluate whatever new activity is required by the next new directive. Suppliers began to appear out of nowhere.

THOSE, THEN, ARE the three changes that occurred late in the Cold War era and the early post–Cold War era. The first was a belief, resuscitated from the Progressive era, that the United States should focus its uplifting of Latin Americans upon improving institutions that constrain undesirable behavior and encourage desirable behavior—yesterday's belief in the importance of constabularies, today's belief in the importance of good governance writ large. Second was a dramatically enlarged set of uplifting responsibilities, many related to good governance. Third was an ever-increasing reliance upon nongovernmental contractors.

The best example of how all three changes occurred together is the National Endowment for Democracy, the NED, always pronounced as a single word, not as three letters.

IN 1983, FAIRLY late in the Cold War but at a time when Central Americans were believed to be moving their chips to the Soviet side of the table, Congress passed and President Reagan signed a law authorizing government funding of the NED, which, the law pointed out, "is not an agency of the United States Government." It had been incorporated as a private nonprofit organization four days earlier. Its purpose: to improve how other peoples govern themselves.

The idea of an institution to focus on promoting democracy in Latin America had been around at least since the early 1960s.[17] Among the early promoters was Yale professor Charles Lindblom, best known for a well-received article, "The Science of 'Muddling Through,'" published three months after Cuba's revolutionaries had begun to demonstrate their unwillingness to slow down and muddle through anything. Lindblom, who had no professional interest in Cuba or anywhere else in Latin America, wrote that "democracies change their policies almost entirely through incremental adjustments. Policy does not move in leaps and bounds, [and] a wise policymaker consequently expected that his policies will achieve only part of what he hopes, and at the same time will produce unanticipated consequences he would have preferred to avoid. If he proceeds through a *succession* of incremental changes, he avoids serious lasting mistakes."[18]

Lindblom's article was published in a journal aimed at academics, but his well-presented argument in favor of gradual reform reached a considerably broader audience. That led to speaking engagements, some in Latin America, from which he returned in 1962 with a modest proposal: "We might explore the problem of developing appropriate political skills in Latin America," he suggested. "Our politicians, whose brains and morals are not a whit superior to those of politicians in Latin America, have learned a set of skills that Latin American politicians have yet to learn." His idea: "a large number of training institutes for young would-be politicians."[19]

The same idea popped up in Congress three years later, after the U.S. invasion of the Dominican Republic, when Senator William Fulbright, chair of the powerful Committee on Foreign Relations, said he was thinking about drafting a bill "to give technical assistance to the Dominicans as to how to run a democratic system." That appears to have been little more than an off-hand comment, and there the matter rested for two years, until early 1967, when left-leaning *Ramparts* magazine took out full-page ads in the *New York Times* and the *Washington Post* to announce that its next issue would feature a startling exposé: more than a decade of covert CIA funding of the international activities of the National Student Association (NSA). A preview on the front page of the *Times* outlined fifteen years of fully approved CIA funding accepted by fully aware student leaders.[20]

The CIA officer in charge of this program, Cord Meyer, subsequently explained that the funding was intended to counter "the growing Communist ability to organize and orchestrate vast international meetings of youth and students from around the world." Once the NSA was receiving CIA funding, the Soviets "found the American student community much better organized to challenge their control over these events."

But in the late 1960s, with university students leading the opposition to the war in Vietnam, a junior NSA staffer stumbled across the evidence and decided to leak it. Any reader of the *Ramparts* story would have agreed with Cord Meyer: this evidence cast the CIA-NSA relationship "in the worst possible light and accused the Agency of having seduced, bribed, and manipulated a generation of American college students for its nefarious purposes." Then once the story broke, Meyer continued, "the Soviets predictably jumped on the bandwagon and excoriated the imperialistic subversion of innocent youth by the monstrous CIA." Even worse: "the non-Communist left in the United States was almost as harsh in its denunciation." So were noncommunist centrists, including a team of *Los Angeles Times* reporters who dug up a list of twenty-one foundations and family trusts that funded the NSA. Eighteen of the twenty-one "have no apparent reason for being except as CIA fronts."[21]

Given this publicity, President Johnson had to do something, and he chose to appoint a small committee to investigate the *Ramparts* accusations: Undersecretary of State Nicholas Katzenbach, CIA director Richard Helms, and HEW secretary John Gardner, because the NSA was a student organization. This, the Katzenbach Committee, uncovered more detailed documents, all of which confirmed what the mainstream press had been uncovering ever since *Ramparts* broke the story: the NSA was only one among a host of domestic organizations receiving CIA funding. At the top of the list was the AFL-CIO, whose Latin American arm, the American Institute of Free Labor Development (AIFLD), would soon be exposed as little more than a CIA subsidiary.[22]

After ordering an end to the covert funding, President Johnson accepted the committee's recommendation that an alternative be created—a "public-private mechanism to provide public funds openly for overseas activities of organizations which are adjudged deserving, in the national interest, of public support."[23] Seizing this opportunity was Dante Fascell, a member of the House of Representatives with a career-long commitment to outsourcing, who proposed the creation and then the overt government support of an Institute of International Affairs.

It was an idea whose time had not come in those Vietnam-focused days, and it took a full decade for a similar proposal to resurface during the more-congenial Carter human rights years, when Fascell joined with Representative Donald Fraser, the principal human rights activist in the House, to sponsor legislation creating the same type of organization, now to be called the Institute of Human Rights and Freedom—private but openly funded by the U.S. government.[24] It, too, was greeted with indifference.

THEN AN APPARENTLY unrelated idea came out of nowhere. In 1977 a private citizen, George Agree, had written a document titled "Proposal for a Pilot Study of International Cooperation between Democratic Political Parties" and given it to Republican congressman William Steiger. Steiger had passed it to William Brock, chair of the Republican National Committee, who shared it with the chair of the Democratic National Committee, Charles Manatt.[25]

George Agree died in 2001 at the age of eighty, and initial researchers have found him a difficult man to nail down. After service in World War II, he held a variety of Washington-based positions—as a lobbyist for the American League for a Free Palestine (free from Britain), as the director of the National Committee for an Effective Congress (founded by Eleanor Roosevelt), and briefly as director of the Republican Legislative Research Association. After that he continued to move from job to job in Washington, including one as a Republican party fundraiser.

From 1976 to 1979, the time of the "Pilot Study" proposal, Agree called himself a "consultant, campaign finance reform," about which his papers reveal little except this: He wrote on letterhead indicating he was also the director of a project titled "Transnational Interactions of Political Parties," which, the complex letterhead continued, was "A Freedom House Study." At the time, Freedom House was noted for its annual ranking of nations as "free," "partially free," or "not free," and in the late 1970s it was still reviled by left-leaning critics for its 1965 endorsement of the Johnson administration's escalation of the war in Vietnam.[26]

Agree's "Pilot Study" proposal, now being considered by the Republican and Democratic national committee chairs, was for these two political parties "to establish structured on-going relations with counterparts elsewhere in the democratic world." It pointed out that the parties of other Western democracies had international departments, but earlier efforts to create them in the United States had foundered on the question of who would pay for their operation. West Germany's political parties had answered this question by turning to the public coffer. For two decades these government-funded *stiftungen,* each aligned with one of Germany's political parties, had been providing both technical assistance and cash to ideological counterparts abroad. The Social Democrats' Friedrich Ebert Foundation and the Christian Democrats' Konrad Adenauer Foundation had been especially active in Latin America.[27]

The two party chairs encouraged Agree to flesh out his "Pilot Study," both of them emphasizing that Agree would "arrange for the funding."[28] More than a year of meetings ensued, at the end of which, in October 1979, the two parties announced the creation of a nonpartisan American Political Foundation (APF), the president of which would be George Agree. The vague initial goal was to promote "foreign understanding of American politics" and "American understanding of foreign politics." Activities "will be implemented as resources become available."[29]

At this point the Agree papers at the Library of Congress introduce Michael Samuels, a former Peace Corps volunteer in Africa and a midcareer Republican who, after serving in various positions in the Nixon / Ford / Kissinger foreign policy apparatus, had been the Ford administration's ambassador to Sierra Leone. With the Democrats back in control of the executive branch in the late 1970s, Samuels was back in the private sector as executive director for Third World studies at the conservative Center for Strategic and International Studies, then a part of Georgetown University. In early 1980 Samuels wrote Agree that he was passing along a new proposal for "a more comprehensive feasibility study of the concept of a quasi-governmental, American political development foundation." The letter suggests that he and Agree had been discussing the issue, and that the letter was Samuels's idea of what the two of them had decided.

It proposed to do something quite different from Agree's initial proposal to promote "understanding." Samuels wrote that "the U.S. has insufficient foreign policy machinery for promoting the development of democratic-pluralist forces abroad, despite the national security need for such a capability." He envisioned a focus on turmoil in Third World governments, singling out the recent revolution in Nicaragua, where "Sandinista guerrillas, strongly influenced by Marxist-Leninist doctrines, succeeded the Somoza system, and maintenance of conditions favorable to U.S. interests are severely endangered."[30] The Samuels proposal was to create an institution reminiscent of the Lindblom-Fulbright-Fascell idea: an uplifting school teaching others how to be democrats. And as for funding, now national security would serve as a justification for government assistance.

Agree replied that he was uncomfortable pursuing government money— he wanted the two parties to pay.[31]

There the matter sat at a low simmer for over a year, until mid-1982, with Republican Ronald Reagan now in the White House. That was when the two party chairs, Republican William Brock and Democrat Charles Manatt, wrote President Reagan: "The United States is involved in many areas of international assistance but has a very meager capability when it comes to support for democratic forces in other countries." Fortunately, they continued, the Agree-Samuels American Political Foundation was preparing to conduct a study about how to create that capability, and hoped for the President's support.[32]

It could not have been a coincidence that President Reagan was to address the British Parliament four days later, and that his speech would be about the Cold War competition with communism. Obviously, some political midwife, still unidentified, had alerted Brock and Manatt to an opportunity, and in those four days the White House speechwriters incorporated the Brock-Manatt letter into the President's address.

As researcher Robert Pee indicated, President Reagan's Westminster Speech was "first and foremost an anti-Soviet address that portrayed the Cold War not as a geopolitical conflict, but as an ideological conflict that pitted freedom and democracy against communist totalitarianism."[33] In this speech President Reagan said his goal in promoting democracy was to "leave Marxism-Leninism on the ashheap of history," and to that end the "leaders of the national Republican and Democratic Party organizations are initiating a study with the bipartisan American political foundation to determine how the United States can best contribute as a nation to the global campaign for democracy."[34]

"Initiating a study" was not quite accurate. "Still trying to find the money to initiate a study" would have been better, but President Reagan's speech unlocked the public purse. AID provided $150,000 to cover half the cost of a "Democracy Program Feasibility Study," with the other half to come from private sources. When fundraising continued to be unsuccessful, even with this presidential endorsement, the White House reached into its "Unanticipated Needs Account" and pulled out the second $150,000.[35]

The study was conducted by a half-dozen individuals led by George Agree and Michael Samuels, who had moved to the U.S. Chamber of Commerce as "Vice President, International."[36] Also involved were representatives of the two parties and the AFL-CIO, representing labor. The initial idea was for Republicans and Democrats to replicate the West German party foundations, but now two more "core grantees" were added: labor (the AFL-CIO) and management (the U.S. Chamber of Commerce). The four would be linked through a new central institution.

THE DETAILS OF that institution had not yet been specified when a competitor appeared. In early 1983, six months after President Reagan's Parliament speech and only a few weeks after the American Political Foundation had received its $300,000, President Reagan authorized a completely separate initiative promoted by his close friend Charles Wick, who was serving as director of the U.S. Information Agency, the USIA. The goal of this rival initiative was to strengthen "the various aspects of public diplomacy of the United States Government relative to national security."

Evidence is lacking, but it is fair to presume that USIA personnel, having listened to the president's speech, were concerned that a private-sector rival was preparing to invade their public-sector turf, and decided to take action. The equally turf-conscious State Department would also have been worried; so would AID, which so far had cornered the democracy-promotion market with its Title IX responsibility. Hence the USIA's request for the presidential directive. It created four interagency committees, one of which was to focus on how to counter "aggressive political action moves undertaken by the Soviet Union" by promoting "the growth of democratic political institutions and practices."[37]

Aware of the APF's headstart, these four interagency committees quickly produced a laundry list of proposed activities, and within a month Secretary of State George Shultz was presenting "Project Democracy" to the House subcommittee through which any authorization would have to pass.* Because Dante Fascell was the subcommittee chair, and because he had favored funding a nongovernmental organization since the 1960s, Secretary Shultz had to explain how Project Democracy fit with the APF's current feasibility study. "The program we are proposing today is compatible with the direction of this study," Shultz reassured Fascell; "both will become part of a larger, broader effort."

As Secretary Shultz was failing to convince the subcommittee to endorse Project Democracy, Agree and his colleagues at the American Political Foundation were rushing to cobble together an interim feasibility study that a subsequent GAO evaluation strongly criticized—"Issues which the APF intended the study to examine were not addressed."[38] No matter; the interim report had just enough substance to be palatable. Specifically, it proposed creating three new organizations: a National Republican Institute for International Affairs, a National Democratic Institute for International Affairs, and a Center for International Private Enterprise led by Chamber of Commerce vice president Michael Samuels. These three new organizations would be joined by the Free Trade Union Institute, created in 1978 by a consolidation

---

*This USIA-State "Project Democracy" was unrelated to Oliver North's "Project Democracy" that produced the Iran-Contra scandal.

of the AFL-CIO's regional "institutes," but largely inactive since the end of CIA funding.[39]

This dream coalition then called in the lawyers to incorporate their umbrella organization, the National Endowment for Democracy, with Dante Fascell as its first board chair. Four days later Congress handed President Reagan a bill he immediately signed into law. Its first sentence: "Congress finds that there has been established in the District of Columbia a private, nonprofit corporation known as the National Endowment for Democracy." The law authorized the executive branch to provide the NED with money. Six days later a second law appropriated $18 million to fund the NED's initial activities, and the nation's first government-funded institution to focus exclusively on democracy promotion was in business.[40]

UNLIKE THE NATIONAL Endowment for the Arts or the National Endowment for the Humanities, both of whose Internet addresses end with ".gov," the NED is a ".org" and has always downplayed its dependence upon the U.S. government—witness its 2014 annual report, which acknowledged the generous support of thirty-seven disparate organizations, from Google and Microsoft to the Embassy of Lithuania, and of twenty-one individuals, including former secretaries of state Henry Kissinger and Condoleezza Rice. Not a word was said about government funding, but the auditor's report indicated that of total revenue of $155,791,056, the sum of $153,360,180 (98.4 percent) came from the U.S. government; in 2015 it was 98.9 percent, and in 2016 it was 99.1 percent—basically unchanged since the NED's creation in 1983.[41] Nevertheless, NED's long-serving president has invariably insisted that the NED is "autonomous, independent, self-generating, over which no one, not even Congress nor the administration, has veto power."[42]

In practice, the NED has been independent from Congress. That was decided in 1993, when Democrat Bill Clinton had moved into 1600 Pennsylvania Avenue and when left wing Democrats had been alienated by the NED's recent activities in Nicaragua (see Chapter 11). In addition, the 1992 election had produced 110 rookies in the House, and few were persuaded of the need for an organization openly sold as a mechanism to fight communism. Others were simply opposed to the lack of congressional oversight during the NED's first decade. That group included Bernie Sanders, then a member of the House, who complained to his colleagues that the NED "is a private organization which funnels most of its budget to private groups and agencies that are accountable to no one." The result was a 243–181 vote to stop funding.[43]

As the battle moved to the Senate, the Clinton White House stepped in to argue that "the NED has been a dynamic and cost-effective organization that has contributed greatly to the American foreign policy objectives." Mainstream Democrats lined up to sing its praises, from Senator John Kerry, who insisted that the NED was "one of the best investments in democracy building," to Senator Fritz Hollings, who claimed that the NED "is, by crackey, doing a job for democracy."[44]

One of the NED's conservative opponents pointed out, correctly, that "we have laws on the books that make it illegal to have foreigners fund our campaigns," and another equally conservative senator captured the long-simmering resentment among his like-minded colleagues, who were tired of being brushed aside as know-nothings. "If you do not agree with the democracy-speak or the international-speak or the trade-speak here in Washington, DC, then you are an isolationist. What about building democracy in this country?"[45]

With both the Republicans and Democrats funding their institutes exclusively with NED money, and with the AFL-CIO and Chamber of Commerce doing the same with their centers, the deck was stacked against these challengers. Republican and Democratic leaders, labor and management executives—"this is the toughest target I have ever seen," lamented one NED opponent. "This is one that has not only Ronald Reagan lobbying for it but everybody but Herbert Hoover [dead since 1964], and he may well have written a letter on behalf of NED. We have had columnists in every leading newspaper—Democrat, Republican, Conservative, Liberal, Independent—write glowing letters on behalf of the endowment. What is more, many of our distinguished Members have had an opportunity to travel with NED." The NED's officers "are not stupid. They know how to keep the money flowing. Just put all these folks on the board."

After a few more senators voiced their opposition to the defunding, the amendment's principal sponsor threw in the towel: "I have made a horrible mistake, obviously. I never realized until this afternoon and this evening that democracy in the entire world hinges on $35 million for the National Endowment for Democracy." A few minutes later the Senate voted 74 to 23 to continue funding the NED. The opponents consisted of twenty conservative Republican opponents joined by only three of the fifty-seven Democrats. The majority agreed with the NED's board chair, William Brock, who warned that even a small budget cut would be damaging "when you are trying to do what we are trying to do, which is to build institutions so that people can have a choice between political parties, between a free press, and alternative methods of delivery of communications."

Then the House reversed itself, 259 to 172, and thereafter the NED has had no trouble surviving mild congressional oversight and even attempts at closure.[46] Advocates appear to have convinced would-be critics that the NED is successfully promoting both democracy and U.S. interests in areas where government programs would be impossible, making outsourcing essential. As the NED's two bureaucratic competitors told Congress during the 1993 defunding attempt, "AID and USIA are also engaged in helping build democracy . . . but the NED and its four recipient institutes . . . have repeatedly demonstrated that they can respond quickly to crises and to opportunities."[47]

An example came after the 2003 invasion of Iraq, when President Bush used his next State of the Union Address to ask Congress to double the NED's funding so that it could "focus its new work on the development of free elections and free markets, free press and free labor unions in the Middle East. And above all, we will finish the historic work of democracy in Afghanistan and Iraq, so those nations can light the way for others and help transform a troubled part of the world." The next NED appropriation was for $60 million, up from $40 million, then $74 million in 2006 and 2007 and $99 million in 2008. By 2018 it was $170 million.[48]

THE QUESTION OF the NED's independence from the executive branch is far more complex than the question of its independence from Congress. Since 1985 the NED's authorizing legislation has stipulated that the Endowment "shall consult with the Department of State on any overseas program . . . prior to the commencement of the activities," and the NED said it was pleased to do so: consultation helps "to insure that the Endowment's activities are broadly in accord with U.S. foreign policy objectives, although as noted in the Endowment's statement of Principles and Objectives, as a private nongovernmental organization NED sets its own policies and makes its own decisions."[49]

In 1983, when Congress provided the NED's initial $18 million, it did so as an earmark in the appropriation for the U.S. Information Agency. The rationale was that the USIA was responsible for public diplomacy, and the NED was initially considered part of that effort. Prior to handing over the $18 million, the USIA asked the NED to sign an outsourcing contract simply stipulating how the money would be used. In response, the NED's board chair (who was also chair of the Republican Party) sent a friendly "Dear Charlie" letter to the USIA director and fellow Republican, Charles Wick. Please call off your lawyers, he wrote, emphasizing that "the National Endowment Board and its charter were structured to be independent of any government agency."[50] Wick handed over the $18 million, no questions asked.

The USIA was absorbed into the State Department in 1999, and since then State's Bureau of Administration has cut the NED's check in the amount specified each year by a congressional earmark. As standard procedure, the Bureau appointed a grant officer for direct supervision; in the NED's case, it initially was an official of the Bureau of Democracy, Human Rights, and Labor (DRL). Only in 2015 did State's Office of Inspector General look into that arrangement and conclude that the State Department had abrogated its oversight responsibilities. DRL incorrectly "believed the NED Act limited their oversight requirements," wrote the Inspector General, but it was a mistaken belief. Citing the specific clause in the law mandating oversight, the Inspector General insisted "the Department must audit NED's financial transactions for each fiscal year," and that included "monitoring and evaluation of performance" of each NED grant.[51]

Everyone agrees that the NED has always been careful not to bite the hand that feeds it. The NED's deputy to the president explained in 2016, "We listen to them; we communicate a lot. They know they don't have a veto, but you don't want to tick them off; you don't want to be dismissive." She added that consultation also occurs with the relevant U.S. embassies, which frequently identify in-country organizations worthy of the NED's support, and she insisted that Congress was being consulted almost continuously, with any query from a congressional office answered immediately.[52]

MEANWHILE, CONTROL OF the Endowment has rested in the hands of the NED's board of directors. The initial members were selected by representatives of the four core grantees and the small group associated with the American Political Foundation, plus representatives of the Democratic and Republican National Committees. Ever since, the board has simply chosen members as it sees fit, as private-sector organizations do.[53] Presumably all board members are uplifters, comfortable with intervening in the internal affairs of countries that the board and its staff consider insufficiently democratic.

In 1983, at the time of the NED's creation, congressional conservatives such as Senator Jesse Helms had feared that the NED board of directors would be dominated by liberals, especially organized labor, which in his view "has gone around the world already on taxpayers' money promoting Socialist reorganization of economic systems, and leaving disaster in their wake, [so] I would object to giving more funding to the AFL-CIO to prepare the way for communism around the world."[54] Quite the contrary, concluded a surprisingly critical 1993 study by the conservative Cato Institute. The "NED invariably winds up playing favorites. . . . The Republican party, business (represented by the Chamber of Commerce group), and organized labor all generally adopt a conservative stance when it comes to foreign policy. That leaves only the National Democratic Institute to represent more liberal views."[55]

It must be strongly emphasized that "liberal" or "Democrat" does not mean "altruist," nor does "conservative" or "Republican" mean "realist." From the beginning, when President Reagan told the British Parliament that his goal was to use democracy promotion as a weapon to combat communism, the overwhelming number of Democratic board members have been hardcore realists such as Zbigniew Brzezinski, President Carter's National Security Advisor, and Madeleine Albright, President Clinton's hawkish secretary of state. Typically, Republican board members have also been realists, and while there is no focused research on this topic, careful observation suggests that every board member believes that what is good for the protection of U.S. interests is also in the best interests of the country whose governance is being targeted for improvement by the NED.

If there is one topic about which there is absolutely no doubt, it is that the NED's board and choice of activities and target countries have strongly reflected the thinking of the NED's first and only president, Carl Gershman, age seventy-five in 2018. At the time he was hired by the board of directors in 1984, Gershman was a senior aide to President Reagan's representative to the United Nations, neoconservative icon Jeane Kirkpatrick. Immediately before that he had been at Freedom House as a "senior fellow," a title that in Washington frequently identifies an individual in a holding pattern while looking for a better opportunity. While at Freedom House,

Gershman prepared a critique of Kirkpatrick's predecessor as UN ambassador, Andrew Young, a Carter appointee, attacking his "inability to see any distinction between authoritarian and totalitarian societies." Specifically, Gershman took issue with Ambassador Young's statement that the Cuban troops in Angola were a stabilizing force. Young's comment was an indicator of his "lack of commitment to political freedom, and his ability to turn a blind eye to oppression"—he was "an advocate of U.S. acquiescence in a new system of tyranny."

Published in mid-1978 in *Commentary,* the leading neoconservative magazine, Gershman's article preceded by more than a year Jeane Kirkpatrick's signature contribution to neoconservative thinking: the view that communist totalitarians maintain an unassailable grip on power, unlike noncommunist authoritarians. As Gershman argued, Andrew Young's error was to ignore the recent lessons of Greece, Spain, and Portugal: "He did not seem to understand that right-wing regimes in these countries could be replaced as quickly and as smoothly as they were precisely because they were not totalitarian." Seventeen months later, Kirkpatrick again appropriated that distinction to criticize the Carter administration's opposition to Nicaragua's Anastasio Somoza, a mere authoritarian: *"It brought down the Somoza regime,"* she wrote, underscoring every word; Carter officials *"acted* repeatedly and at critical junctures to weaken the government of Anastasio Somoza." In 1979 this led to Somoza's replacement by the Sandinistas, whom neoconservatives classified as totalitarians.[56]

The collapse of communism made this authoritarian / totalitarian thinking irrelevant in Washington, and by that time the fire-and-brimstone Gershman had acquired the smooth Teflon coating that has always characterized successful midlevel members of the Washington apparat. Over an exceptionally long tenure, he built the NED into an uplifting institution based upon the strong Washington consensus that it was in the interests of the United States to help other countries improve their governance.

WHILE THE TWENTY-FIRST century NED is a central part of Washington's democracy promotion, it holds no monopoly. As a close observer reported in 1996, a half-dozen years into the post–Cold War era, promoting democracy had become "a minor growth industry populated by people from nongovernmental organizations, consulting firms, think tanks, universities, and the U.S. government itself, who careen around the world helping to draft constitutions, observe elections, reform judiciaries, strengthen parliaments, build civil societies, empower local governments, and train journalists."[57]

Among the NED's allies is the Agency for International Development, which since 1966 has been required by Title IX to encourage "democratic private and local government institutions." After four years of effort, in 1970 the Agency official responsible for implementation complained that this directive was "an almost classic example of Congressional initiative thrust upon an unprepared and resistant Executive." Now, here in the Nixon years, dictatorships were not being discouraged and the Agency's personnel were still thinking of themselves as focused on economic rather than political development. "There lingers in AID a large contingent of people unreceptive to the new approach," the implementing officer continued, and Congress had left too much wiggle room. "The legislation is itself ambiguous, its objective liable to diverse interpretations, [and] its impact thus far in changing the programing priorities of the Agency for International Development has been practically nil."[58]

That changed during the 1980s, when President Reagan made democracy promotion a particularly prominent part of his policy in warring Central America. By 1993, when peace had come to Central America and the Cold War had ended, the GAO used a round number of $900 million as the cost of that year's democracy promotion. Of that, a quarter ($214 million) was focused on Latin America, but both numbers were only informed guesses. "There is no central U.S. government-wide democracy program, no overall statement of U.S. policy regarding U.S. objectives and strategy for democratic development, no specific and common definition of what constitutes a democracy program, and no specificity regarding the roles of the foreign affairs and defense agencies in promoting democratic processes." By 2017 the cost of democracy promotion had risen to $2.3 billion.[59]

Meanwhile, the Clinton administration created an "Interagency Working Group on Democracy and Human Rights," and the State Department's Bureau of Human Rights and Humanitarian Affairs was renamed today's Bureau of Democracy, Human Rights, and Labor. The Working Group never established much of a presence, but democracy promotion continued to grow for the next decade. The Bush State Department upped the ante in 2006 by creating an Office of Foreign Assistance Resources (often referred to as "the F bureau"), and it promptly created an uncommonly elaborate Foreign Assistance Framework, one of whose "strategic objectives" was *Governing*

Justly and Democratically. It had four sub-objectives which, taken together, called for increased attention to every one of the pathologies that make good governance difficult, with a focus on weak and malfunctioning institutions.[60]

By that time an observer unfamiliar with Washington's uplifting momentum might have assumed that any such strategic objective was not meant to apply to Latin America, where in 2006 nearly every government was in the hands of elected officials. But Washington's uplifters, displaying an impressive agility, had quietly bounded across an enormous intellectual chasm, from the promotion of democratic transitions, generally defined by the finite task of ending a dictatorship, to the improvement of democracy, a never-ending task.

This leap could have been anticipated since 1992, when AID felt it needed a definition of democracy and outsourced the job to a contractor. It opened the door to an expansive set of activities: "To be democratic, a society requires a high degree of personal and political freedoms, the institutional basis to conduct free and fair elections, an openness to competition for political power, and the ability of elected officials to obtain meaningful political power."[61] Or, as President Obama told a Chilean audience in 2011, "the work of perfecting our democracies, of course, is never truly done."[62] Two years later, the once-reluctant Agency for International Development reported that it was "integrating democracy programming throughout our core development work, focusing on strengthening and promoting human rights, accountable and transparent governance, and an independent and politically active civil society across all our work. At the same time, we remain committed to fundamental democratic empowerment activities, including supporting free and fair elections, up-to-date technology for new and traditional media, as well as the rule of law."[63]

So here, two decades into the twenty-first century, post–Cold War Washington had adopted the century-old Progressive-era belief that the improvement of Latin Americans should be heavily focused on improving their governance. But unlike Progressives, who had at their disposal nothing but the Marines and a small handful of democracy doctors, the twenty-first-century U.S. government now has permanent uplifting institutions to promote good governance.

CHAPTER 11

Promoting Good Governance

America will not impose our own style of government on the
unwilling. Our goal instead is to help others find their own voice,
attain their own freedom, and make their own way.

—President George W. Bush Inaugural Address, 2005

NICARAGUA IS AN instructive place to begin any examination of how Cold
War uplifting blended into post–Cold War uplifting.

In 1981, eleven days after his inauguration but ten years before the Soviet
Union ceased to exist, President Ronald Reagan signed a secret "finding" that
set in motion perhaps the most public secret effort in the history of U.S. foreign policy. It was to "support and conduct [redacted] paramilitary operations
against the Cuban presence in Nicaragua and the Cuban-Sandinista support
infrastructure in Nicaragua."[1] The goal was to oust the *cachorros* (puppies)
of Sandino, as the Sandinistas liked to refer to themselves. They appeared
to be moving Nicaragua's chips to the Soviet side of the table.

The National Endowment for Democracy joined this effort as soon as it
opened its doors in late 1983, working through the AFL-CIO's Free Trade
Union Institute, the only one of its four "core grantees" that was up and
running. The NED's first annual report indicates that the Institute received
an unspecified amount "to encourage a cultural atmosphere conducive to
the growth of democratic unionism." According to the scholar-activist who
knew as well as anyone what the United States was doing on the ground in

Nicaragua, that meant NED funding "kept the right-wing CUS [Confederación de Unificación Sindical] labor federation alive through training and travel programs for its leaders and social-welfare services for its members."[2]

Fiscal 1985, which began when the Endowment was not yet a year old, saw a major increase in the NED's activities in Nicaragua, continuing support for opposition labor groups and new support for the principal opposition newspaper, *La Prensa,* at a time when the Sandinistas' control over foreign exchange was making publication difficult. Specifically, the NED filtered a $100,000 grant for *La Prensa* to purchase paper and ink through a U.S.-based organization, the Friends of the Democratic Center in Central America, or PRODEMCA. Another $200,000 NED grant to PRODEMCA was to create "a private nonpartisan center devoted to the study and discussion of democratic ideals."[3]

The grants grew as the NED's three other core grantees began to function:

1986: $298,560
1987: $454,757
1988: $807,248

and then, once the date of a presidential election had been announced,

1989: $3,600,000
1990: $7,576,535[4]

During these years the CIA and the Pentagon were arming and assisting Nicaragua's paramilitary contras—counterrevolutionaries—who were waging a guerrilla war. For one among dozens of revelations, the *Los Angeles Times* reported that the mining of Nicaragua's harbors "was a U.S.-run operation from start to finish. The mines themselves were slipped into three Nicaraguan harbors—Corinto, Puerto Sandino and El Bluff—by South American commandos. The commandos, who were brought in aboard a CIA-run 'mother ship,' slipped into the ports in agency-supplied speedboats, and U.S.-piloted attack helicopters supplied air cover."[5]

To complement this war effort, the U.S. embassy focused on consolidating the Sandinistas' splintered civilian opposition into what emerged as the United Nicaraguan Opposition (Unidad Nicaragüense Opositora, or UNO,

Spanish for "one"). A member of Oliver North's sub-rosa group within the Reagan White House—the group that would produce the Iran-Contra scandal—wrote in a confidential memo that UNO was "a creation of the USG [United States Government] to garner support from Congress," a majority of whose members were opposed to supporting guerrilla groups but willing to assist the Sandinistas' nonviolent civilian opposition. "When it [UNO] was founded a year ago, the hope was it would become a viable organization. In fact, almost anything it has accomplished is because the hand of the USG has been there directing and manipulating."[6]

That was written in 1986. Then in mid-1989, with an election scheduled for 1990, UNO needed a campaign infrastructure, beginning with a central office—a secretariat. The Republicans' Central America field officer reported to her superiors in Washington: "UNO General Secretariat: In Carl [Gershman]'s mind, this program is ready to go. NDI and NRI have been asked to reprogram current funds in order to provide $100,000.00 each to set up the UNO office and get it going for two months. Then the Institutes would be expected to keep the secretariat going for four more months at $50,000 per month. In Carl's proposal to the NED Board he is prepared to ask for $400,000 for the Institutes to run this program."

President Gershman, she continued, had asked UNO officials "to send him the number of a bank account in Miami as soon as possible in order to receive the $200,000 in start up costs," and not to bother with a proposal: "Now that he has had time to think this through, he does not know who would be able to sign a grant agreement or even if one is necessary."

A second topic in the same memo focused on a NED-funded television blitz supporting UNO candidates: "We need to find out from Carl if Carl is planning on putting us in charge [of] this program or if NED wants it." This required a bit of turf maintenance—the Republican field officer was less worried about the NED taking direct control than she was about the rival Democrats taking over: "NDI may go to Managua at the end of August with some of their consultants. I have told our folks that I may drop by also."[7]

The suspicion of this Republican field officer, Janine Perfit, was well-founded. In 1987 the president of the NED's Democrats, Brian Atwood, a realist who did his best to dress in altruistic clothing, and who would soon become the AID chieftain, told researcher William Robinson, "We have set out to unify the opposition and orient its anti-Sandinista activities." Atwood's director of Latin America programs, Martin Edwin Andersen, carried this on his curriculum vitae: "December 1987 to May 1990: Led political training mission to Managua, Nicaragua, which assisted in the formation of a united and ultimately successful democratic opposition front against the Sandinista regime."[8]

During 1990, the year of Nicaragua's election, the NED gave $6,254,753 to the two U.S. party institutes to pass along to UNO and to two additional UNO-related organizations. This dwarfed anything else the NED was doing worldwide, and required special funding from the Agency for International Development. AID was in the process of handing out $32 million to the Sandinistas' opposition between 1986 and 1990. Of that amount, $11 million was outsourced to the NED.[9]

Always unmarked, now the funding trail became impossible to follow. Take the Friends of the Democratic Center in Central America—PRODEMCA—founded in 1981 at the very beginning of the Reagan years, probably at the initiative, and certainly with the encouragement, of President Reagan's national security adviser, Richard Allen. In 1985 and 1986 PRODEMCA received $251,500 from the NED. Then it stepped over an important line by using much of that money to take out full-page ads in several newspapers, including the *New York Times:* "We Support Military Assistance to the Nicaraguans Fighting for Democracy" was the headline, followed by the signatures of sixty-four conservatives—from Harvard's Samuel Huntington, who had recently served on the Reagan administration's National Security Council staff, to the Cuban American National Foundation's Jorge Mas Canosa, to the Carter administration's hawkish national security adviser, Zbigniew Brzezinski.[10]

The law authorizing the NED's funding for 1986 and 1987 prohibited the support of partisan organizations, and here in 1986 nothing could have been more partisan either in the United States or in Nicaragua than siding with the contras: they were opposed by most Democrats in the United States and by every Sandinista in Nicaragua.[11] So when the newspaper ad led to complaints that the Reagan administration was using the NED to influence U.S. public opinion, PRODEMCA was quietly folded into Freedom House, which at the time was something of a neoconservative safe house. It continued to receive NED funding, but the trail to PRODEMCA was lost.

Then there was UNO, which could not have been more partisan—it was a political party with its name beside candidates' names on the ballot. The

NED worked around this by funding new organizations with nonpartisan names such as an Institute for Electoral Promotion and Training, created on the same day Congress provided a special appropriation for technical assistance with Nicaragua's election.[12] Its board of directors was composed exclusively of UNO leaders. To this day no outside researcher has learned how this Institute spent the NED's money; it appears to have vanished into one of those Miami bank accounts. Another NED grantee was the International Democrat Union, an organization of conservative political parties with headquarters in Norway. The NED sent the money to Oslo, which sent it back across the Atlantic to Nicaragua's Conservative Party, the keystone of the UNO coalition. This was money laundering, pure and simple, and even one of the NED's most ardent supporters agreed that the Endowment's work in Nicaragua "strained the bounds of nonpartisanship."[13]

Meanwhile, opposition to supporting guerrilla warfare grew in Washington, especially among nongovernmental organizations related to mainstream religious denominations, including important groups within the Catholic Church. They lobbied successfully for a string of congressional initiatives to restrict and condition U.S. aid. Most focused on direct funding of the contras, and the Reagan administration's efforts to evade these restrictions led to the Iran-Contra scandal. Strong congressional criticism also focused on the U.S. involvement in Nicaragua's 1990 election. "We are into this election process [for] $1 billion," complained one left-leaning member of the House; "we funded the Contras, we have destroyed their economy, we have taken Mrs. Chamorro, and we buy her newsprint, we pay for her newspaper to run, we make sure that she has access to newsprint, we funded her entire operation." As that suggests, the United States had found another Adolfo Díaz—that is, a Nicaraguan willing to be cooperative. Her name was Violeta Chamorro, and now, continued the same member of Congress, "we are going to provide her the very best election that America can buy."[14]

Having lived through nearly a decade of guerrilla warfare and of truly extraordinary economic disarray, much of it unquestionably and intentionally caused by the United States, Nicaragua's exhausted voters gave Chamorro their support. As Marine Smedley Butler had commented in the 1920s, "our candidates always win."[15]

And just as the Marines stayed after Nicaragua's 1928 U.S.-supervised election, Washington's post–Cold War involvement was not over. "The Endowment was honored and privileged to be able to have played a role in assisting the democratic processes," a triumphant Gershman told Congress, but "if they are to remain on a democratic course, they will need significant assistance, including private sector [i.e., NED] support for the development of democratic political institutions and processes."[16]

That is exactly what General Frank McCoy had said after supervising Nicaragua's 1928 election: "The election itself, however important as an example of fair and peaceful settlement of Nicaraguan issues, is but one detail of the country's general problem. The preservation of order, the development of communications, especially between the east and west coasts, the elimination of widespread corruption in the government, the improvement of health conditions and the extension and modernization of schools, are all matters of prime importance."[17] The Marines had stayed until 1933.

And so here, a half-century later, the NED stayed in Nicaragua, joined by AID, which had withdrawn its mission and stopped all assistance to the Sandinista government during the Reagan years. The Agency returned as soon as Violeta Chamorro became president, and within a month the U.S. Congress had passed a $300 million "Dire Emergency" appropriation, which, as the GAO reported, "played a critical role in keeping the new government afloat." Most ($178 million) was simply a transfer of cash to pay for imports, especially petroleum. A smaller part was "for a preliminary analysis of Nicaragua's 1987 [Sandinista] Constitution, identifying governmental and political weaknesses that impede social and economic programs and prevent full economic development." A third part was to provide eight hundred Nicaraguan leaders with "specific training and an understanding of the workings of a free enterprise economy in a democratic society."[18]

So now, just as the Soviet Union was disintegrating, a policy designed during the Reagan administration to protect U.S. security interests was being completely transformed by the succeeding Bush administration. The initial goal had been to destroy "the Cuban-Sandinista support structure"; now the principal goal was to improve Nicaraguan politics.

THIS IS EXACTLY what had happened during the Progressive era. The 1898 Spanish-American War was about ousting the Spanish, but Cuba's improvement became the new goal once that initial mission was accomplished. By 1912 the Taft administration had accepted responsibility "to take such steps as may be appropriate and necessary to undo and redress any wrongs which the Cuban people may have suffered at the hands of the Cuban government."

So what at first had been the Cubans versus the Spanish was transformed in a blink to become the responsible Cubans versus the irresponsible Cubans. As in Cuba, so in Nicaragua, where a late-1920s envoy pointed out that "we have been the scrupulous protector of their independence, not only against Europe but sometimes even against themselves."[19] Those last three words, "even against themselves," heralded the creation of a belief that continues to guide twenty-first-century efforts to promote good governance around the world.

This belief was broadly shared by 1997, now well into the post–Cold War era, when the Clinton administration told Congress that "progress to continue to deepen Nicaragua's democracy and free market is of paramount importance to the United States." This statement was so uncontroversial that Congress did not bother to discuss AID's Clinton-era plan to improve Nicaragua's governance:

> Civil society institutions must take hold and provide an outlet for people to express their interests. Local authorities must exercise more power relative to national government. The legislature must mature and demonstrate that it is a professional body capable of making legislative compromises that overcome partisan interests for the benefit of society as a whole. The judicial system must be modernized and reformed to achieve credibility in the eyes of the public as a fair arbiter of criminal and civil disputes. The military and police must scrupulously avoid appearances of partisanship, demonstrate a commitment to punish human rights abusers among their ranks, and take strides to modernize. The civil bureaucracy must slim further, and become more efficient and accountable to the public at large.

Civil society, local government, legislature, judiciary, military and police, civil bureaucracy—here at the turn into the twenty-first century the United States seemed determined to help improve more or less everything related to how Nicaraguans govern themselves.[20] Only Enoch Crowder in 1920s Cuba had embarked upon a more ambitious uplifting agenda.

A decade later, in 2007, the Sandinistas returned to power, fairly elected, and by 2016 AID was worried about "irregularities and allegations of fraud during the past three national and local elections and the January 2014 constitutional reforms—which consolidated the power of President Daniel Ortega and further undermined democratic governance checks and balances. The space for civil society and the media to participate in public debate is rapidly closing."[21] The United States needed to step in and protect Nicaraguans from their government. For 2017 the Obama administration asked Congress for $14.5 million, of which 70 percent was targeted to improve Nicaragua's "Democracy, Human Rights, and Governance."[22]

The NED also ramped up its assistance. By 2013 it was supporting fourteen different Nicaraguan groups, all at odds with the Sandinista government. Typical was a $156,790 grant to the Network of Nicaraguan Businesswomen (REN—Red de Empresarias de Nicaragua), whose executive director, Marina Stadthagen, had been an official of the previous non-Sandinista government. The grant was intended to improve "the advocacy skills of women entrepreneurs." The grant-receiving organizations' names kept shifting, but another grant for women entrepreneurs in the same amount came in 2014, along with a grant to an unidentified Nicaraguan organization for "women as political actors." In 2015 the NED made a second grant for the same purpose to, again, an unidentified organization, and in 2015 the NED gave $154,639 to one of its core grantees, the Center for International Private Enterprise (CIPE) for a project called "Raising the Voice of Women Entrepreneurs" in Nicaragua. CIPE did not say to whom it regranted the money, but it was heavily involved in supporting Ms. Stadthagen.[23]

All this was now completely normal, uplifting as usual. The uplifting industry was prepared to continue indefinitely its effort to improve the way Nicaraguans govern themselves, an effort that had begun more than a century earlier, in 1911, when the Marines landed.

CHILE WAS THE site of the second major effort to promote democracy in the final years of the Cold War. For years the United States had been involved in Chilean electoral politics, spending $3 million to influence the 1964 presidential election, for example, and a larger but unspecified amount to influence the 1970 election, after which a major effort had been made to see that the winner of that contest, Socialist Salvador Allende, was removed from office.[24] That removal had occurred in 1973, during the presidency of Richard Nixon, who justified his administration's policy: "As long as the Communists supply external funds to support political parties, factions, or individuals in other countries, I believe that the United States can and should do the same."[25]

General Augusto Pinochet's 1973 coup had been applauded by the Washington neoconservatives who reached power with the 1980 election of Ronald Reagan, and they immediately began to remove the sanctions that had been imposed for human rights reasons during the preceding Carter years. Less than a month after the president's inauguration, Secretary of State Alexander Haig informed the White House that he was ready to reverse the Carter-era prohibition on both Eximbank lending and military aid; after that, he noted, "we will have a full inter-agency review in about one month to decide on further adjustment."[26]

Flying to Chile a few months later, the Reagan administration's ambassador to the United Nations, neoconservative Jeane Kirkpatrick, met with General Pinochet and then told reporters, "I had a very pleasant conversation with the President . . . he seemed to me to be a very serious man, very honorable and very pleasant."[27] The message she conveyed was "that the Reagan administration intends to treat Chile and other friendly Latin American states as full partners in our effort to reassert Western interests and values." So reported Ambassador George Landau to Washington, who added that "Kirkpatrick's visit was extremely valuable in accelerating the return to cooperative relations"; General Pinochet "was particularly gratified that Ambassador Kirkpatrick had not come with the intention of offering advice to the military on internal Chilean affairs." His conclusion: "The legacy of suspicion about U S intentions and doubt about U S leadership has been largely swept away."[28] That was one month before Amnesty International issued an update on Chile's dictatorship: "Torture still appears to be a systematic part of official policy."[29]

President Reagan's reversal of the Carter policy aroused Washington's liberals, who disliked the Pinochet government at least as much as Washington's conservatives disliked the Sandinistas. These liberals were already challenging the hostile policy toward Nicaragua, and as a conservative academic noted, "the fact that the Reagan administration began to push hard for democracy in Nicaragua and not in Chile allowed critics of its Nicaragua policy to accuse it of hypocrisy."[30]

Then in 1982, barely a year into the eight Reagan years, most of Latin America entered what came to be known as "the lost decade," a severe economic downturn that triggered street protests in Chile—pot-banging *cacerolazos* vigorously repressed with tear gas and the water cannons Chileans half-humorously call *guanacos* (both spit).* In 1983 an emboldened set of mainstream opposition groups united in an Alianza Democrática to demand free elections, and the State Department's Bureau of Inter-American Affairs began to worry about the viability of a military government whose strength among civilians rested upon a healthy economy. In late 1984 the Bureau's chief informed Deputy Secretary Kenneth Dam, "We would be satisfied if Pinochet would simply do what he said he would do when he overthrew Allende, that is, return Chile to democratic government." Any such change would run the risk of a leftist victory, so "the key to protecting long-term U.S. interests is strengthening the disorganized moderates, specifically, weaning them away from the radical left."[31]

As the downturn continued, in 1985 a larger group of twenty-one Chilean parties and party factions united to demand an orderly transition to democracy. Prompted again by his Latin America bureau, Secretary of State George Shultz informed President Reagan that "there is a growing tension between our national interest in an orderly and peaceful process and Pinochet's apparent desire to hang on indefinitely." Soon the administration's new assistant secretary for Latin America, neoconservative Elliott Abrams, his reputation not yet sullied by the Iran-Contra scandal, was telling Congress that "U.S. Government policy toward Chile is straightforward and unequivocal: We support a transition to democracy."[32]

This policy change required a new ambassador. In 1982, before the street demonstrations, George Landau had been replaced by a political appointee, the reliably conservative James Theberge, best known for his publications warning about Soviet advances in Latin America.[33] In 1985, with Chile increasingly unstable, Theberge was replaced by a professional diplomat, Harry Barnes, who was instructed to implement the administration's new policy and was clearly pleased to do so.

This shift in ambassadors occurred at a time when Chileans were already scheduled to go to the polls. Five years earlier, in 1980, with the economy strong and the opposition terrorized, General Pinochet's military government had gained voter approval to replace Chile's 1925 Constitution, and

---

*Along with llamas, alpacas, and vicuñas, guanacos are members of the camel family native to South America. Camels spit regurgitated food when annoyed—like water cannons, an unmistakable sign that you should back off.

that had required a set of transitional measures. One stipulated that a plebiscite be held in 1988, after eight more years of dictatorship, when voters would determine, yes or no, if a candidate chosen by military leaders should remain in power for another eight years.[34]

In the run-up to this plebiscite, Ambassador Barnes and his embassy made it clear that the United States supported a return to democracy. And as he was encouraging the "No" vote in Chile, in Washington the administration was making its new policy clear by abstaining on multilateral development bank loans to Chile and supporting UN resolutions critical of the dictatorship's human rights violations. An irritated General Pinochet eventually complained that the ambassador "did nothing except spread political propaganda against the government in order to destroy it." That is why he declined to offer Barnes a farewell interview when he left Chile. "To that man I say neither adiós nor hasta luego."[35]

IN LATE 1987, less than a year before Chile's plebiscite, progressive senator Tom Harkin had steered through Congress a special $1 million appropriation for the National Endowment for Democracy to promote a democratic transition in Chile.

The NED had been involved in Chile since 1984, when, as in Nicaragua, it was ready to act only on the labor front through its Free Trade Union Institute (FTUI). It reported that "FTUI assistance to the Central Democrática de Trabajadores (CDT) has helped it become the principal voice of free trade unions." It was nothing of the kind, but the FTUI considered the CDT moderate when compared to the rest of Chile's labor movement, and after deducting its expenses gave the CDT what was left of $450,000 from the NED.[36]

Soon the Endowment's three other core grantees were functioning, and in fiscal year 1988, which ended a month before Chile's October voting, the NED was supporting the "No" vote with $1,620,909. Fifty-seven percent ($929,765) was given to one of the NED's core grantees, the National Democratic Institute. The Republicans' Institute received one-ninth as much—$105,144.

By this time fourteen opposition parties had united in a Concertación de los Partidos por el No, and they convinced 56 percent of the voters to vote no on the proposition that the military should continue in office. As required by the transitional provisions of the 1980 Constitution, an election was held in late 1989, and in 1990 the Concertación's moderate Christian Democrat, Patricio Aylwin, became Chile's first freely elected president in seventeen years. As in Nicaragua, so in Chile: voters produced the outcome Washington had paid to promote.

But unlike Nicaragua, where it is absolutely certain that U.S. aid in its many forms was instrumental in producing the electoral overthrow of the Sandinistas, no one will ever be able to pinpoint the effect, if any, of the U.S. effort to improve Chile, where the United States spent a roughly estimated $12 million between the Reagan administration's 1984 policy change and Patricio Alywin's inauguration.[37] That was a tiny fraction of what was spent in Nicaragua, and Washington's influence had always been far weaker in Latin America's Southern Cone, but it is difficult to conclude that the $12 million had no impact whatever.

Before the plebiscite, NED president Carl Gershman had told reporters that the uplifting would continue. "Our objective in Chile is not in the short term, but in the long term. We hope to be able to contribute for a long time, because democracy is a permanent, long term process."[38] But unlike Nicaragua, by 1995 the NED had decided that Chileans no longer needed the Endowment's assistance.

THE NICARAGUA ELECTION had pleased the Republicans; the Chile election had pleased the Democrats. Together, the two contests went a long way toward establishing the NED's credibility. Here, at exactly the moment when the Cold War was ending and a new era was beginning, an untested institution had thrown itself into both of the major "democracy" battles that dominated U.S. policy toward Latin America during the 1980s and early 1990s, during the turn into the post–Cold War era. Now the Endowment could claim to have contributed to the success of U.S. policy in both countries.

Chile was especially important. Because the NED had been a Reagan Republican idea, its principal challenge had been to gain support among Democrats—to broaden and solidify the original support from centrist Democrats led by Dante Fascell. One left-of-center Democrat was Senator Tom Harkin, who had sponsored the NED's special appropriation for Chile. Another was Representative Ted Weiss, who had visited Chile with Carl Gershman in 1987. Back in Washington, he told a congressional committee that "the work that the National Endowment did last year in regard to the site in Chile was truly outstanding, and had, I think, a very significant effect on the fairness of that election, and the outcome of that election." "A very gracious comment," replied the NED's board chair, "and I thank you very much,

Congressman."[39] As in the House, so in the Senate, where a progressive Christopher Dodd argued in 1993 for continuing NED funding. "We have more democracies today in this hemisphere than have ever existed, [but] if we do not make a sustained effort to try to support them and shore them up, I fear in a number of cases we will lose them."[40]

And so the NED sailed into the post–Cold War era with the uplifting wind to its back. In 2016 it was promoting democracy with 237 grants in fourteen Latin American countries.[41] Forty-five of the 237 were to promote good governance in Cuba.

REGARDLESS OF HOW one assesses the successes and the shortcomings of the Cuban revolution, surely we can all agree that any government led by the same two brothers for over half a century without a competitive election is not a democracy.

And we can also agree that bolstering Cuban democracy has not always been Washington's priority. One of the low-priority moments occurred in 1952, when a military coup returned Fulgencio Batista to power. It occurred at one of the darkest moments of the Cold War, when U.S. troops were fighting in Korea, when Senator McCarthy was riding high, when containing the spread of communism had become a true obsession in Washington, and when first-graders were having duck-and-cover drills in grammar schools. Batista knew exactly how to endear himself: he cut off relations with the Soviet Union, and with the CIA's close guidance he created Cuba's Bureau for the Repression of Communism, an intelligence organization that served several purposes, most notably the repression of Batista's rivals. In 1955 Vice President Richard Nixon publically toasted the dictator, noting what he shared in common with Abraham Lincoln.[42]

But Batista was clearly unpopular with a large proportion of Cuba's citizens, and his government was overthrown in 1959. The country's new leaders called themselves revolutionaries, and one of their revolutionary ideas was to be less willing to accommodate Washington's interests. The United States complained about more or less everything the new government did, including its refusal to hold competitive elections, but Washington's primordial concern was that the Castro government was moving its chips to the Soviet side of the table. With varying degrees of intensity, U.S. policy from 1960 to 1990 was to make Cubans move their chips back to the U.S. side.

First came the 1961 Bay of Pigs invasion, when President Kennedy stepped on a rake, followed by the activities collectively known as Operation Mongoose, a combination of state and state-sponsored terrorism. The Soviet placement of missiles in Cuba could be interpreted as a reaction to Washington's menacing behavior, prompting some U.S. leaders began to worry that more of the same might trigger a nuclear war. Soon national security adviser McGeorge Bundy was advising against the use of force, but said, "We should probably continue our present nasty course; among other things, it makes life a little tougher for Castro and raises slightly the poor odds that he will come apart and be overthrown."[43]

"Our present nasty course" was a reference to the economic embargo designed to strangle the Cuban economy. That had begun in mid-1960 with the withdrawal of Cuba's sugar quota, and soon Vice President Richard Nixon was telling campaign audiences, "We are cutting off the significant items that the Cuban regime needs in order to survive [and] we will quarantine this regime so that the people of Cuba themselves will take care of Mr. Castro."[44] With varying levels of intensity and with a few notable exceptions, an entire generation of Washington leaders, Republican and Democrat, said the same thing.

But the Cuban people had not overthrown their government by the end of the Cold War, when a new justification for the embargo was needed. So ten months after the Soviet Union's disappearance, a Democratic Congress passed and a Republican President Bush signed the 1992 Cuban Democracy Act. Becoming law at exactly the time Cubans were struggling with the loss of Soviet subsidies, this new legislation tightened the economic screws in a variety of ways, from prohibiting the overseas subsidiaries of U.S. firms from having any dealings with Cuba, to prohibiting any ship entering a Cuban port from entering a U.S. port for the next 180 days. And the law stipulated that the president could end the embargo only after the Cuban government had held free elections supervised by international observers, allowed opposition parties to organize and campaign with full access to all media, and shown respect for civil liberties and human rights. "Castro will not survive," promised the first President Bush.[45]

After four years the 1992 law had not produced the desired transition to democracy, so in 1996 a Republican Congress passed and a Democratic President Clinton signed the Cuban Liberty and Democratic Solidarity Act, always known as the Helms-Burton Act. It strengthened the embargo but also authorized the president to support "democratic and human rights groups in Cuba." "Our first grant to fund NGO work in Cuba will be awarded to Freedom House to promote peaceful change and protect human rights," announced President Clinton.[46]

When these two post–Cold War laws failed to topple the Cuban government, in 2003 the second President Bush created a Commission for Assistance to a Free Cuba. Its 423-page report was explicit about the goal: "to bring about an expeditious end to the Castro dictatorship," and the first of the report's six chapters was titled "Hastening Cuba's Transition."[47] It contained sixty-two steps that the United States was already taking or preparing to take. They can be divided into two categories. One was old (more tightening of the embargo) and the other was new (helping Cubans unite in opposition to their government).

The new was built upon the long-standing belief that Cubans were disgruntled and, if given the opportunity, would rise up against their government. But first they needed to be directly in touch with one another, with their connection unmediated by the government; then they could begin to organize and coordinate their activities. Note that Cubans already had a civil society—all societies do—but it was the wrong kind of civil society. The United States would help Cubans replace the wrong kind with the right kind.

To achieve this aim during the George W. Bush administration (2001–2009), the United States supported a fairly large set of anti-Castro Cuban American organizations, such as the Miami-area's Democracy Support Group (Grupo de Apoyo a la Democracia) led by Francisco ("Frank") Hernández Trujillo, who in 2005 commented, "We see the Cuban government as a piece of furniture that has been eaten away by termites, [and] we are the termites." AID supported the Grupo for over a decade, and assistance continued even after a 2006 GAO audit reported that Hernández Trujillo "could not justify some purchases made with USAID funds, including a gas chainsaw, computer gaming equipment and software (including Nintendo Gameboys and Sony PlayStations), a mountain bike, leather coats, cashmere sweaters, crab meat, and Godiva chocolates." Hernández Trujillo insisted that the items were purchased "to show the people in Cuba what they could attain if they were not under that system."[48]

In 2009 the Obama administration inherited a raft of similar efforts to promote democracy in Cuba that, not coincidentally, also supported the

Cuban American community in the United States, most based in electorally crucial Florida.[49] That included continued funding of Frank Hernández's Grupo de Apoyo. It received three AID grants in 2015 totaling $806,660 to improve "the rule of law and human rights" in Cuba, the details of which, so far, are denied to the public.

The Obama administration also supported the Center for a Free Cuba, created in 1997 by Frank Calzon, a longtime anti-Castro lobbyist in Washington. AID had provided Calzon's Center with several "building civil society" grants during the George W. Bush administration, but then a former employee, Felipe Sixto, was arrested for stealing $579,274 from the organization, more than $400,000 of it AID money.[50] He was sentenced to thirty months in prison and AID cut off the Center. Not so the NED, which had begun supporting Calzon's Center with a small grant ($17,000) in 1998 and then continued every year thereafter except 2006. Obama-era funding included a $102,000 NED grant in 2014 to "promote democratic values among Cuban youth through a week-long training program in Europe." A $107,000 NED grant in 2016 continued a 2015 grant vaguely described as an effort to "provide activists with resources that will permit them to carry out their work in a more effective manner."[51]

Another such grantee was the Foundation for Human Rights in Cuba, a spin-off of the Cuban American National Foundation (CANF), which had been a Washington powerhouse in the final two decades of the twentieth century but then declined after the 1997 death of its founder, Jorge Mas Canosa. CANF was the first Cuba-related organization funded by the NED—$60,000 in the NED's first year—and it was the NED's only Cuban-focused grantee for the next four years. Then the NED also began funding the CANF-related Coalition for Human Rights in Cuba, with $110,000 in 1986. Annual funding continuing into the post–Cold War 1990s, but "CANF was doing too much domestic advocacy," recalled one NED official, so the Coalition was renamed the Foundation for Human Rights in Cuba, and the NED started funding it and stopped funding CANF.[52]

The Foundation's principal Obama-era activity was "Connect Cuba," designed to "continue growing the underground network 'Internet without Internet' in Cuba, providing civil society with the resources they need, including flash drives, computers, smart phones, and other technologies to share open, uncensored information with each other, and the world." It is not certain that any such network existed, and most of the activities for which the Foundation took credit appear to have been organized and conducted by others, such as the "Hey Cuba Hackathon," an activity featured on the Foundation's Obama-era website but was conducted by an entirely separate organization, ¡Apretaste! ("Tighten!" or "Squeeze!"), which thanked the Foundation for "funding our prizes and accommodations, and adding valuable guidance."[53] The unresearched impression is that the Foundation for Human Rights in Cuba was serving as a distributor, doling out small sums to Cuban American organizations that had received CANF's seal of approval. In 2015 AID provided the Foundation with $565,002.

As for the NED, it made 187 Cuba grants totaling $20,120,115 during the Obama years.[54] Among the recipients was the Miami-based Evangelical Christian Humanitarian Outreach for Cuba ($230,074 in 2014–2016), which conducted short-term visits to Cuba by fundamentalist Protestants. Jesus "has empowered us with authority," wrote its president, Teo Babun Jr., "[and] we must activate this empowerment by visiting our Brothers and Sisters in Cuba."[55] Another NED grantee was the Cuban Soul Foundation, which received $255,000 in 2014–2016 "to empower independent artists to produce and perform their work in uncensored community venues." The largest slice of the NED's Cuba pie, $1,950,000 in 2014–2016, went to the Directorio Democrático Cubano—another Miami-based distributor that spread the NED's money to organizations such as Radio República, one of whose regular programs was "A La Luz de la Verdad" (In the Light of the Truth). To discuss President Obama's March 2016 visit to Havana, it hosted a Miami roundtable titled "The Failure of Normalization of Relations with Cuba."

When the Obama archives are opened to researchers, they probably will confirm what most observers have suspected—that these inherited programs supporting Cuban Americans were funded because prominent Democratic members of Congress and campaign contributors insisted they be funded, and also because Democrats never want a repeat of 2000, when they lost the White House by 537 Florida votes.

There also was something new. In 2008 candidate Barack Obama told a Cuban American audience that his goal would continue to be a transition to democracy, but added, "It's time for a new strategy." After quickly adding, "I will maintain the embargo," he promised to "immediately allow unlimited family travel and remittances to the island. . . . It's time to let Cuban American money make their families less dependent upon the Castro regime."[56]

President Obama followed through with this narrow campaign promise, while liberal Democrats argued that he was taking too long to do more. His defenders pointed out that Cuba was a mere mote in Washington's eye alongside a sandstorm of more important issues, ranging from an economic meltdown to the struggle for universal health care to the wars in the Middle East and Afghanistan.

Although the relevant documents have not yet been made public, it appears that what came next was determined by Latin Americans. Citing Cuba's exclusion, the presidents of Ecuador and Nicaragua had refused to attend the 2012 Summit of the Americas in Cartagena, and other Latin American leaders had quietly made it clear at the Cartagena gathering that public opinion in their countries would make it impossible for them to participate in the 2015 Summit in Panama unless Cuba's president also attended.

And so a handful of White House officials began to negotiate with the Cuban government, and in late 2014 President Obama announced, "Today, America chooses to cut loose the shackles of the past. . . . It does not serve America's interests to try to push Cuba toward collapse." Then in his State of the Union message a month later he announced, "We are ending a policy that was long past its expiration date. When what you're doing doesn't work for fifty years, it's time to try something new." To the extent permitted by the 1996 Helms-Burton Act, the embargo was being abandoned.[57]

Barack Obama and Raúl Castro met in Panama a few months later and agreed to embark upon a new beginning. The two countries' embassies were reopened in July 2015, and in March 2016 President Obama visited Cuba, where he told Cubans, "I have come here to bury the last remnant of the Cold War in the Americas." At the same time, he could not resist pointing out a few areas where Cubans might improve: "It should be easier to open a business here in Cuba. A worker should be able to get a job directly with companies who invest here in Cuba. Two currencies shouldn't separate the type of salaries that Cubans can earn. The Internet should be available across the island, so that Cubans can connect to the wider world [and] we want our engagement to help lift up the Cubans who are of African descent."[58]

How similar this was to 1906, when Secretary of War William Howard Taft addressed a Cuban audience. "Perhaps you will pardon me if I invite your attention, as an educated and intelligent audience, to some of the difficulties of your people." Among those difficulties was that "the young

Cubans who are coming forward into life are not sufficiently infused with the mercantile spirit. . . . What you need here among the Cubans is a desire to make money."[59] So here it was again, 110 years later. Washington always seems to know what Cubans need and never seems to be shy about saying so.

NOR HAS WASHINGTON ever been reluctant to help Cubans meet those needs. A month after President Obama's visit, President Castro informed the Communist Party Congress that the United States was trying to hasten Cuba's transition. "We are not naive nor do we ignore the aspirations of powerful external forces that are committed to what they call the 'empowerment' of non-state forms of management, in order to create agents of change in the hope of putting an end to the Revolution and socialism in Cuba by other means."[60] He was referring to Washington's effort to improve Cuba's civil society, and here there was no doubt. All anyone had to do was visit AID's website to see that the Agency had spent about $155 million of its good governance budget to promote democracy in Cuba during the Obama years. And the Obama-era NED was also heavily involved, funding forty-five "grantees" in 2016 with $5,837,329, most coming from State's Bureau of Democracy, Human Rights, and Labor, not from the NED's congressional earmark.

For fiscal year 2016, which began a few weeks after the embassies were reopened, AID announced that "U.S. assistance will support civil society initiatives that promote democracy, a market-based economy, human rights, and fundamental freedoms, particularly freedom of expression and association. Programs will provide humanitarian assistance to victims of political repression and their families, strengthen independent Cuban civil society, support the Cuban people's desire to freely determine their future and reduce their dependence on the Cuban state, and promote the flow of uncensored information to, from, and within the island."[61]

IT IS NOT clear how much of this money was funneled to the Cuban American community and how much was for something new. In his 2016 Presidential Policy Directive guiding U.S.-Cuban normalization, President Obama insisted, "We will pursue democracy programming that is transparent," but then his administration turned around and conducted a series of covert programs to improve Cuba's civil society with technology.[62] Social media had become a hot topic in Obama-era Washington, and now the central thrust of U.S. policy was to engineer the needed changes in Cuba's civil society by enabling Cubans to communicate with one another without being observed by their government.

One such project began late in the second Bush administration, when AID signed a contract with DAI Global (formerly Development Alternatives, Inc.), one of the largest of the "beltway bandits." With overall contracts totaling $272 million in a typical Obama-era year, 2015, DAI was Number 8 on AID's list of Top 40 Vendors.[63] This particular contract was for DAI to begin building the electronic structure essential for social media, a task it subcontracted with JBDC (Joint Business Development Center), a small company that consisted of Alan and Judy Gross. They knew how to provide Internet connectivity in locations where there was none, and how to avoid prying eyes. Alan Gross explained, "My projects through JBDC focused primarily on facilitating the use of information and communications technology ('ICT') to aid citizens in other countries with limited access to ICT. Over this period [the ten years before his arrest by Cuban authorities], I set up and managed approximately 150 fixed-earth stations to increase Internet access. To do this work, I usually would purchase the required components and assemble what I call a 'teleo in a bag.' These kits would contain 'BGANS,' which are commercially-available modems that permit connectivity from anywhere in the world by accessing satellites."[64]

Gross took the first of his five DAI-contracted trips to Cuba in early 2009, soon after the inauguration of President Obama. Each was with Jewish groups participating in "people to people" exchanges with Cuba's small Jewish community. Without their knowledge of his purpose, Gross spread his electronic equipment among the luggage of each group's participants. In his fourth trip he carried twelve iPods, eleven smartphones, three computers, six external drives, three satellite modems, three routers, three controllers, eighteen wireless access points, thirteen memory sticks, three VoIP phones, and a bundle of networking switches. His return report to DAI: "Wireless networks established in three communities; about 325 users."

On his fifth trip he was arrested while carrying a chip that would keep the location of satellite phone transmissions from being located within 250 miles. Although Gross insisted that he purchased his equipment from commercial suppliers, others said this particular chip was available only through U.S. intelligence agencies and the Department of Defense.

Charged under a law that prohibits "acts against Cuba's independence and territorial integrity," Gross told the court that he was "deeply sorry for being a trusting fool. I was duped. I was used." Finding that excuse unconvincing, as would anyone with access to Gross's self-incriminating post-trip reports to DAI, the Cuban court sentenced him to fifteen years in prison. Meanwhile, Judy Gross sued DAI and AID for failing to adequately prepare and supervise her husband. She and DAI eventually reached a confidential settlement at the same time DAI was seeking $7 million from AID for "unanticipated costs" incurred while implementing the contract.[65] Soon after Gross's release in December 2014, AID settled with him for $3.2 million.

As Alan Gross sat in his jail cell, AID was launching another effort to improve Cuba's civil society, this one to construct a Cuban Twitter, code-named ZunZuneo after the Caribbean hummingbird that darts from spot to spot and is so small—perhaps the world's smallest bird—that often the only sign of its presence is the "zun zun" sound of its wings, beating eighty times a second. A ZunZuneo would be a gathering of this species, as Woodstock was a gathering of hippies. Cuba's ZunZuneo would be electronic, virtual.

The principal ZunZuneo contractor was Creative Associates International, one of AID's midsize vendors—Number 27 in 2014, with $114 million in contracts. For Creative, the $15.5 million 2008 AID contract was a big one, but it was making plans to grow with the help of two senior vice presidents, one of whom formerly was AID's assistant administrator in charge of the Agency's Africa Bureau, and the other formerly was director of AID's Iraq Infrastructure Reconstruction Program from 2001 to 2003—they were AID's best and brightest, each with decades of experience in contracting.

Like DAI, Creative also lacked in-house expertise, so it subcontracted primarily with Denver-based Mobile Accord, which received ten subcontracts to implement ZunZuneo. Two additional subcontracting grants went to NiteMedia, a Nicaraguan business focusing on mass email messaging. NiteMedia was operated by a relative of Creative Associates' operations manager.[66]

While more ambitious than the DAI-Alan Gross effort, the guiding idea was exactly the same: build a site for civil society to gather electronically. ZunZuneo would not bypass the Cuban government's server, however; rather, it would appear to be harmless chatter among Cubans. As AID subsequently explained, the contractors "initially sent news, sports scores, weather, and trivia. After which, the grantee [Creative Associates / Mobile Accord] did not direct content because users were generating it on their own." Eventually ZunZuneo funded text messaging, e-mail newsletters (via NiteMedia), a Facebook page, a Twitter account, and a website. Despite President Obama's promise of transparency, ZunZuneo was a covert operation. Once news of its existence had been leaked to reporters, AID would claim it had about sixty-eight thousand users but, strangely, would not explain why the project was quietly shut down in 2012.[67]

With no explanation, some concluded that AID had decided not to risk another Alan Gross brouhaha, but the Associated Press team that broke the ZunZuneo story had its own explanation: "The operation had run into an unsolvable problem." It was handing AID's money over to the Cuban government. Creative Associates' subcontractor, Mobile Accord, had created a shell company in the Cayman Islands, MovilChat, which paid for the messages but had neither employees nor a physical existence. (Mobile Accord paid Cayman Management Ltd to transfer funds to Cuba using MovilChat's name.) The recipient of these transfers was Cubacel, the state-run monopoly that owned the infrastructure through which ZunZuneo messages traveled and that billed MovilChat for its use. So, the Associated Press continued, "tens of thousands of dollars in text messaging fees were thereby channeled to Cuba's communist telecommunications monopoly routed through a secret bank account and front companies. It was not a situation that it could either afford or justify—and if exposed it would be embarrassing, or worse."[68]

Although it was terminated in 2012, ZunZuneo's existence was not public knowledge until 2014, when the Associated Press journalists revealed most of the above information. AID's public relations office responded four days later with "Eight Facts about ZunZuneo," a press release and blog post that broke new ground in misrepresentation: "The [Associated Press] article suggested that USAID spent years on a 'covert' program to gather personal information to be used for political purposes to 'foment' 'smart mobs' and start a 'Cuban spring' to overthrow the Cuban government. It makes for an interesting read, but it's not true. USAID's work in Cuba is not unlike what we and other donors do around the world to connect people who have been cut off from the outside world by repressive or authoritarian governments. USAID's democracy and governance work focuses on strengthening civil society, governance, and promoting human rights." A *Washington Post* editorial applauded this effort, calling it nothing more than "an updating of the

United States' admirable past efforts to pierce the Iron Curtain, and a rather innovative one at that."[69] Two years later, Russia made exactly the same innovative effort to influence the 2016 U.S. election.

By this time AID had hired another high-tech contractor—the Washington-based New America Foundation, later simply New America. A blue chip by any measure, it was funded by the likes of Bill and Melinda Gates and overseen by a board of directors chaired by Google chieftain Eric Schmidt, who by mid-2017 had provided New America with $21 million in family and corporate money. Also on the board was the son of philanthropist George Soros, whose Open Society Foundation funded progressive causes. For its president and CEO, New America hired Anne-Marie Slaughter, a pedigree-perfect law professor (Chicago, Harvard) and dean (Princeton's Woodrow Wilson School). She had been director of policy planning in Hillary Clinton's State Department, a post she gave up in order to spend more time with her family and to write "Why Women Still Can't Have It All," said to be the most-read online article in the history of the *Atlantic Monthly*.[70] Like Secretary Clinton, Slaughter and New America were classified as ever-so-slightly to the left of center.

Heavily tech-oriented and fluent in tech-speak (one conference room was called "The Eric Schmidt Ideas Lab"), New America billed itself as "committed to renewing American politics, prosperity, and purpose in the Digital Age." Within New America was a Soros-funded Open Technology Institute (OTI), which "supports free expression and open technologies at home and around the world, and is committed to supporting engaged, self-sufficient communities by promoting safe and affordable access to connectivity." New America's OTI had broad interests, with a staff producing articles with titles such as "Casting an Internet Lifeline to Low-Income Americans," and the New America website explained that "OTI works at the intersection of technology and policy to ensure that every community has equitable access to digital technology and its benefits."[71] The Institute's founding director, Sascha Meinrath, told the *New York Times* that a major OTI goal, not specific to Cuba, was "to build a separate infrastructure where the technology is nearly impossible to shut down, to control, to surveil. . . . This disempowers central authorities from infringing on people's fundamental right to communicate."[72]

"Commotion" was the suggestive name given to the infrastructure's software, which would permit the operation of wireless communications networks that bypass government networks. It was developed with grants from the State Department's Bureau of Democracy, Human Rights, and Labor and also from AID, which provided a $4.3 million three-year contract in 2012. The AID money came from its Cuba budget. "OTI does not deploy Commotion," said the Institute, insisting that instead it "supports the work of communities by providing trainings, tools and resources to community partners to decide how they want to engage and how they want to use our tools."[73] Two of these "community partners" were the Obama State Department and AID, both of which wanted to use OTI's tools to improve Cuba's governance.

The only person left out of the loop was the director of New America's U.S.-Cuba Policy Initiative, Anya Landau French, a knowledgeable Cuba specialist who was part of the Washington community urging the normalization of relations. She found out about AID's $4.3 million contract purely by accident and was not happy about it.[74] "I'm not involved in any USAID grants—and I frankly don't want to be," she said; "I think I'm pretty clearly on record in my belief that USAID's programs in Cuba have largely failed in their objectives and are in fact often counterproductive to anyone associated with them."[75] She voiced her opposition to New America's president at the time, Steve Coll, arguing that the AID-OTI relationship would run counter to New America's position on Cuba, but Coll took the money and Landau French resigned.

At about the same time, New America's next president, Anne-Marie Slaughter, brought in one of her staff members from the Hillary Clinton State Department, Emily Parker, who initially was referred to as New America's Cuba specialist. Writing that she had "spent a great deal of time" with Havana's dissident bloggers, Parker appeared to know little about the island except what she had learned from those she interviewed for her 2014 book, *Now I Know Who My Comrades Are: Voices from the Internet Underground,* which also covered Russia and China. "Why Cuba Needs the Internet" was one of Parker's online articles. A list of her publications provided an idea of the scope of her interests, from "Why Don't We Care About Syria?" (*Slate*) to "The Burden of Being Japanese" (*Wall Street Journal*).[76] Parker was not the type of policy advocate who buries herself in a specialized subject. But like both Secretary of War Taft in 1906 and President Obama in 2016, here was the employee of an AID contractor, New America, once again pointing out what Cuba needs. In this case it was the Internet: "Connectivity will be the real force for change in Cuba," Parker argued.[77]

Cuba always seems to need a force for change, a push along to wherever Washington believes it should be going. What was new since the Taft days? The existence of today's uplifting industry, one major part of which is a twenty-first-century army of contractors. The outsourcing of Latin Americans' improvement began early in the twentieth century with an occasional money doctor, and moved on in the 1960s to skill-specific contractors and eventually to an entire industry composed of general-purpose uplifters like FHI 360, DAI, Creative Associates, and New America. Exactly like the Progressive-era university professors who contracted as democracy doctors, they are for hire.

"Can't repeat the past?" asked Jay Gatsby. "Why of course you can."[78]

Conclusion

Whose Best Interests?

If I knew for a certainty that a man was coming to my house with the conscious design of doing me good, I should run for my life.

—Henry David Thoreau, *Walden,* 1854

OVER THE COURSE of a century, the improvement of other peoples has become a part of the nation's culture. It is now a habit, something the United States does automatically, mechanically, year after year, and something nearly everyone in Washington expects to keep doing. Relentless low-intensity up-lifting is now the norm.

That leaves us with two concluding questions. What caused the United States to move from no uplifting late in the nineteenth century to funding the largest uplifting industry in human history? And what might that tell us about the future?

THERE ARE TWO polar theories about the cause. One was offered by Adam Smith, who believed it is a part of human nature to take an interest in assisting others who are less fortunate, with the payoff being simply the pleasure of seeing their improvement. And so as the United States became rich and powerful, and as its citizens noticed that many others remained poor and weak, human nature nudged Washington to establish "protectorates" and to send money and democracy doctors. After more than a century of nearly continuous practice, Washington's Adam Smiths could write ten-verb paragraphs to describe their effort to improve Hondurans.

At the opposite pole sits Hans Morgenthau, the stern voice of realism. Realists focus on the exercise of power, and over the course of the twentieth century they became increasingly interested in the exercise of soft power. Like Morgenthau a half-century ago, today's realists argue that assisting with the improvement of other peoples is a useful way to protect and promote a nation's interests. FDR's generation called this tool "economic cooperation." For the Cold War generation it was "foreign aid." "Development assistance" has been popular in post–Cold War Washington. Whatever its label, it is self-interested, but not necessarily to be frowned upon. Unlike the altruists, those who wield this soft power consider any improvement of the recipient a gratifying but incidental by-product. The idea is to pursue U.S. interests, and, again, there is nothing inherently wrong about that. But it is selfish.

Eleven chapters of observation have demonstrated that absolutely pure Adam Smiths and equally pure Hans Morgenthaus are few and far between. Like most of us, most policymakers are some combination of the two, both altruistic and selfish. The question, then, is: *How much* of each theory explains the U.S. effort to improve other peoples?

Because altruism is the obligatory idiom of U.S. policy toward Latin America, it is not helpful to ask senior policymakers for an answer. As JFK promised in his inaugural address, "we pledge our best efforts to help them help themselves, for whatever period is required—not because the communists may be doing it, not because we seek their votes, but because it is right." You could almost hear the altruists' hearts flutter, but an Everest-high mountain of research by several generations of competent scholars has revealed the overwhelmingly dominant motivation of the Kennedy administration's uplifting: a national security interest in containing the spread of communism.

More recently, a notable feature of the Introduction-opening paragraph about Honduras is the absence of any reference to drug trafficking and its associated violence, one of those difficult-to-resolve problems that has partially replaced communism in the twenty-first century. In the five years from FY1994 through FY1998 (which eliminates Cold War anticommunism as a causal factor), Hondurans received an average of about $26 million per year in all types of U.S. assistance, economic and military.[1] Then Honduras became a stop along the drug-trafficking highway between producers and consumers, which the United States had a perfectly legitimate interest in closing. As the traffic grew, there was a sixfold increase in U.S. aid, yet AID officials clearly did not think it was appropriate to mention this problem in their 2016 Country Development Cooperation Strategy, or on their flamboyantly altruistic website.[2] Today's uplifters write like JFK talked—altruistically.

A CENTURY EARLIER, Progressive-era leaders sounded the same but seem to have meant it more often. Perhaps Theodore Roosevelt harbored the thought of a selfish payoff from his 1906 takeover of Cuba, for example, but no one has been able to pry it out of the archives. Certainly his interests in a canal and in excluding German gunboats reveal he was far from a pure altruist, and certainly his manly ego demanded constant massaging, but perhaps the best single document to capture his policy comes from a few days after he was sworn in as president, in a private letter to his secretary of state: "The true interest of our people, it is being more and more generally admitted, lies in helping the Latin-American countries with our more advanced industries and our characteristic forms of energy to expand into strong and flourishing communities and not in seeking to aggrandize ourselves at their expense."[3] Theodore Roosevelt was no Mother Teresa, but he belongs on the altruistic side of the continuum.

Similarly, we should have expected Woodrow Wilson to be one of the least selfish uplifters ever to enter the White House; he was, after all, a professor of political science. It is easy to be distracted by his world-class arrogance, and psychoanalysts may see something in this complex man that students of inter-American relations do not, but President Wilson appears to have been motivated primarily, albeit not exclusively, by the belief he announced so arrogantly: that the United States had a benevolent responsibility to teach Latin Americans how to elect good leaders.

And sandwiched between these fascinating giants was the plain-vanilla Taft, who seems to have meant it when he used the title "Some Instances of National Altruism" for an article explaining why he had recently named himself provisional governor of Cuba. The article's theme: "The record of the nine years since the beginning of the Spanish War, looked at from an impartial standpoint, is on the whole an unblemished record of generous, earnest effort to uplift these people, to help them on the way to self-government, and to teach them a higher and better civilization."[4]

The longer anyone observes their meetings, the more Progressives convince you of their altruism. Certainly they talked in the early 1900s like JFK talked in 1961 and AID wrote in 2016, but most of the time, in most of the cases, they were not trying to do something akin to containing communism or ending drug trafficking. They were trying to be helpful.

So why the hard power? Because aside from diplomacy there was no soft power. Only rudimentary uplifting tools were available in the early twentieth century, leaving Progressives no option other than crude protectorates.

THEN AS THE United States moved through the twentieth century, becoming the world's only true superpower, it accumulated an array of new interests to protect and promote.

Many were economic interests, most of them related to the century's extraordinary growth of production and consumption. It was a century that began with the horse and buggy and ended with interstate highways and cruise control, and in those decades a largely self-sufficient people became intimately entangled in the global economy, generally for better but sometimes for worse, as in the case of illicit drugs.

Additional new interests were related to the nation's security, of which the premier twentieth-century interest was the containment of communism. It led directly to the ultra-uplifting Alliance for Progress, an all-important moment in the creation of today's uplifting industry. Specifically, the Alliance was launched because it had become increasingly difficult for the Pentagon to protect the Cold War security interest in containing the spread of communism. Beginning with Philippine nationalists at the turn into the twentieth century, then Nicaragua's Sandinistas in the 1920s and continuing through 1950s Cuba and beyond Vietnam into the twenty-first-century Middle East and Afghanistan—through it all the Marines kept reporting that they were having difficulty protecting U.S. interests when the enemy was backed by a sympathetic citizenry. Development assistance was intended to make citizens less sympathetic to insurgents by improving their daily lives. Then they would be on our side.

Still a third interest was domestic politics, which over the course of the twentieth century slowly elbowed its way into the center of most explanations of U.S. policy toward Latin America. Since 1776 we have seen domestic politics affect foreign policy in almost every imaginable context, but almost from the beginning it has been associated with the entirely human desire to please others, especially if the others are voters. Witness the 1992 Cuban Democracy Act and the 1996 Cuban Liberty and Democratic Solidarity Act, two Hans Morgenthau laws with Adam Smith titles, both produced, not incidentally, in election years. They would hurry the downfall of Cuba's government, pleasing Cuban-American voters living in what is now the third-largest of the fifty states, with twenty-nine electoral votes. In 1900, Florida had only four electoral votes, one more than the Constitutional minimum, and the tiny handful of Cuban American voters received no special attention. In 2000, several hundred thousand Cuban American voters were outraged in April when the Clinton administration returned Elián González to Cuba, and in November vice president Al Gore lost the White House by a margin of 537 Florida votes.

The dramatically expanded scope of these three primary interests is what made it impossible for the altruists to keep up with the realists, who over the course of a century commandeered every tool on the uplifting workbench. As early as 1959 a content analysis of presidential messages and congressional debates identified five major arguments for foreign aid, four of which were related to U.S. security directly and the fifth indirectly: "Help raise living standards in the less developed areas and thus make Communist claims less attractive." Then there were ten additional minor arguments, every one of them related to the promotion of U.S. interests, including "Help provide employment for hundreds of thousands of Americans." Fifteen points for the realists, zero for the altruists.[5]

Another indicator of the realists' takeover is the evolution of how the Agency for International Development has presented itself to the recipients of development assistance. When AID was created in 1961, its legal title was "Agency for International Development."[6] Then in the early 1990s Agency officials decided that the generosity of the United States was not receiving adequate recognition and therefore was not receiving adequate gratitude. So AID became USAID. The takeover continued a decade later, in 2004, when a new generation of Agency officials announced that USAID was "undertaking a global branding effort to ensure that the U.S. government and the American taxpayer receive full credit and recognition for the billions spent each year on foreign assistance."[7]

After that, everything provided by AID, from emergency food to coffee mugs, has come with this logo:

Any departure from this logo is certain to trigger a response from AID's senior advisor for brand management, whose office has trained a posse of "branding champions," one in each overseas mission, ready to acquaint the guilty party with Section 6.1, "Clearance and Enforcement," on page 55 of the Agency's 61-page *Graphics Standards Manual and Partner Co-Branding Guide.*[8] True, §641 of the 1961 Foreign Assistance Act stipulates that "programs under this Act shall be identified appropriately overseas as 'American Aid,'" but here in the twenty-first century it cannot simply be the traditional (since 1953) handshake.

The point: Altruists never would have paused from their uplifting to prepare a branding guide, and the very last position an altruist would want the Agency to fill would be that of a Senior Advisor for Brand Management.

In 2010 this realist takeover culminated with the elevation of "development" to one of only three pillars of U.S. foreign policy—Diplomacy, Defense and Development. "The 3Ds of U.S. national security," announced the State Department; a new "central framework for American strength and influence." A few months later President Obama signed the first-ever Presidential Policy Directive on Global Development. "Development is vital to U.S. national security," explained a White House press officer; the new directive "charts a course for development, diplomacy and defense to mutually reinforce and complement one another in an integrated comprehensive approach to national security."[9]

IN THE SPECIFIC case of Honduras, the sixfold increase in development assistance between 2000 and 2016 reflected the simple fact that no one could think of a better way to stop Hondurans from serving as a drug hub, with spokes coming in from Latin America and leading out to various parts of the United States, where drug consumption and the undocumented immigration triggered by drug-related violence were issues of domestic concern and, ipso facto, of domestic politics. The sixfold increase was based upon a belief that enough soft power will eventually get the job done—that the United States can improve Hondurans to the point where they stop trafficking in drugs.

Regardless of their motive, uplifters across the altruism / realism continuum insist they are making progress, and offer elaborate proof. In 2014, for example, AID announced that "an impact evaluation released today shows the U.S. Agency for International Development's (USAID) community-based crime and violence prevention programs in Central America help residents feel safer, perceive less crime and murders, and express greater trust in policy. The three-year study, considered the gold standard of randomized control trials, was conducted by Vanderbilt University's Latin American Public Opinion Project in Honduras, El Salvador, Guatemala, and Panama."[10] Except for the fact that Vanderbilt's Latin American Public Opinion Project relied heavily upon AID to fund its own activities, which automatically took this evaluation off the gold standard, the well-respected evaluators met every other requirement of modern social science. They conducted individual interviews and focus groups, but relied primarily upon a "cluster randomized experiment"—which, they explained, "scores a 5 (the highest level) on the Maryland Scale of Accuracy in the Design of Evaluation, indicating that the findings yielded by the study should be considered strong evidence for a cause-and-effect relationship."[11]

The experiment involved surveys of residents in two types of neighborhoods, some receiving AID funding and some not receiving AID funding. The first survey was conducted in late 2011 / early 2012 and the other in late 2013—about two years apart. The survey results: When compared to neighborhoods not involved in AID's crime and violence prevention programs, in those short two years the residents of neighborhoods receiving AID assistance perceived dramatic reductions in murders, sales of illegal drugs, robberies, extortion, and gang fights. With U.S. assistance, Hondurans were improving; without U.S. assistance, they were not improving.

At about this same time, journalist Sonia Nazario returned to Honduras, where years earlier she had begun the research for *Enrique's Journey,* the story of a young boy's migration to the United States. It first appeared in 2002 as a series of articles in the *Los Angeles Times* and earned Nazario a Pulitzer

Prize. Now here in 2016 she was back in a working-class Honduran neighborhood where 194 people had been murdered in 2013. "Investments in
Honduras are succeeding," she reported—"a remarkable reduction in violence, much of it thanks to programs funded by the United States that have
helped community leaders tackle crime."

"One of the most effective tactics is the creation of neighborhood outreach centers," she continued. They were managed under AID contract by
Creative Associates International, which partnered with local civic leaders,
often evangelical Protestant ministers, to operate two hundred outreach centers in Honduras, El Salvador, Guatemala, and Panama. Nazario wrote that
"typically a church donates the building, and the United States [via Creative
Associates] remodels it and provides computers, equipment and initial funds
to hire a coordinator. The centers recruit mentors and provide vocational
training for residents and help finding jobs for them as barbers, bakers and
electricians." The payoff: "Children in that program were deemed 77 percent
less likely to commit crimes or abuse drugs or alcohol, according to Creative Associates International."

Nazario's principal illustration was a movie night at Daniel Pacheco's outreach center.

> A pastor and part-time carpenter, Mr. Pacheco picks up kids from the
> 18th Street Gang's territory as well as kids from the area controlled by its
> fiercest rival, the Mara Salvatrucha gang. Then, in swampy heat, in the middle
> of the street, he sets up a tent, projector, screen and speakers. He lines up
> plastic chairs and inflates a Scooby-Doo bouncy house.
>
> By 7:30, the night I was there, more than a hundred children were playing
> together. They shrieked with glee in the bouncy house, then settled in to
> watch "Inside Out." Finally, they lined up as a police officer handed them
> water bottles and grocery bags inscribed with 911, urging them to call the
> new emergency system to report crime. The United States provided the equip-
> ment and everything Mr. Pacheco needed for the event.

The manager of another outreach center told Nazario that "the U.S. government has been a bigger partner in change than the Honduran government."

Nazario was not uncritical, noting that "about half of the funds Congress
budgets for Honduras go to the State Department bureaucracy or American
companies paid to administer programs." One sentence was enough said

about that, however, and it was followed by this: "The test now is whether the United States can scale up from a few pilot programs to truly make a difference nationwide."[12]

We know that most development projects can be scaled up if there are funds to do so; what we do not know is whether they are sustainable. The Vanderbilt researchers were not asked to address that question, but AID personnel have been worrying for decades about sustainability, often referred to as "local ownership." The worry, of course, is related to an assumption that Washington's support for any specific project cannot continue forever. Late in the Cold War, in the mid-1980s, the Agency commissioned a 135-page study examining 212 evaluation reports and found that "only 11 percent received highly positive sustainability ratings, whereas 26 percent received strongly negative ratings."[13] Since then the pressure to demonstrate high sustainability has increased dramatically, but evaluations can be conducted in many different ways, some more convenient than others, and it is unclear whether today's sustainability level is more or less than what it was four decades ago.

PROCESS ALL THIS and then answer the question: How much of each theory explains the U.S. effort to improve Hondurans? Obviously, it is no longer a question; everyone agrees. If Hondurans had not been trafficking, and if the associated social disarray had not triggered a spike in undocumented immigration to the United States, there would have been an altruist-sized uplifting budget, about one-sixth as much—something in the neighborhood of $26 million instead of $162 million. That seems to come reasonably close to capturing the twenty-first-century relationship between uplifting altruists and uplifting realists. If dollars tell us anything about who owns the effort to improve twenty-first-century Hondurans, dollars say that one part belongs to Adam Smith and five parts belong to Hans Morgenthau.

THOUGHTFUL ALTRUISTS HAVE long understood this fact of uplifting life, and they have also understood that the realists are using them—promoting self-serving interests by employing altruists to do the hand-to-hand combat, with development assistance as their weapon. What is not understood about this grossly unbalanced relationship is why any self-respecting altruist would continue to serve as the realists' handmaiden.

No research exists on this question, but two untested hypotheses merit consideration. One is that altruists accept their subservient role because realists provide them with the means to be altruistic. Instead of having $26 million to improve Hondurans, altruists have $162 million, so who is taking advantage of whom? Nearly all altruists firmly believe that U.S. assistance will improve the recipients, even if most of the assistance is given for what they consider the wrong reason. Indeed, altruists will tell you that the 2010 "3D" designation was one of their major victories. It not only stifles budget-conscious critics who grouse about "foreign aid giveaways," but also implies that there will be new resources to battle underdevelopment.

A second hypothesis does not pussyfoot around one of the most obvious facts of all: the workers in this uplifting industry have their own interests and their own incentive structure. Specifically, today's uplifters—altruists and realists, public and private—have a deeply personal interest in being paid to fight underdevelopment. Altruists may stick it out because they need to pay the rent.

This personal-interest hypothesis may help explain a basic feature of the uplifting industry's evolution, especially in Latin America: the extraordinary expansion of the definition of what 1960s-era AID officials meant by "self-sustaining development." Look, for example, at what has happened to the promotion of good governance. First recall the 1920s, when the United States was ready to declare its mission accomplished in Nicaragua "if the forthcoming elections are conducted in a manner which leaves no room for doubt that the successful candidate has the support of a real majority of the people." While no one anticipated how long it would take to implement this policy, the policy was simplicity itself: conduct a clean election and get out.

Now jump ahead nearly a century to 2013, when Washington's democracy-promotion uplifters were ranking countries in terms of four different types of political regimes—authoritarian, hybrid, developing democracies, and consolidated democracies. What is notable? In the *consolidated* democracies, considered fortunate by most, "USAID will continue to be active in other sectors [such as] economic governance, or improvements to business regulation and commercial courts."[14]

In Costa Rica, arguably Latin America's most consolidated democracy, AID declared its mission accomplished in 1996 and announced it was leaving the country, but never really departed. In 2011 the U.S. ambassador referred to Costa Rica as a "developing-but-not-yet-developed" country, and so now the United States was "fostering innovation in governance" and helping to "improve citizen access to information." In 2016, when Central American drug trafficking was not restricted to Honduras, a different U.S. ambassador was offering the same assessment: "The challenge for Costa Rica today is to overcome the remaining barriers to achieve fully developed-country status." Two thousand sixteen was also the year AID published another of its self-congratulatory Issue Briefs, "USAID's Partnership with Costa Rica Advances Family Planning," pointing out the Agency's continued assistance "in the years since graduation."[15]

If personal self-interest helps explain why the development dog is never allowed to catch the car, then it also underscores the bureaucratic beauty of altruists and realists tuned to a common key, a harmonious symphony of uplifting performed by an elaborate ensemble of permanent uplifting institutions—an entire industry with tens of thousands of individual players who profit personally from the continuous redefinition of development to include more of everything.

It is impossible to read the first paragraph of the Introduction and not be impressed by the sheer audacity of this industry, where public and private have seamlessly combined to create a smoothly functioning political powerhouse, with branches in almost every congressional district if you include, as you should, the outsourcing contractors in so many colleges and universities.[16] Most impressive of all, this uplifting industry is based upon one of those Washington rarities, a perfect consensus. From the purest altruist to the purest realist, every member of this industry believes the United States should help to develop underdeveloped peoples. They only disagree about why.

TO BE CLEAR: No one has tested these two hypotheses or suggested what rival hypotheses need to be considered, much less has anyone estimated how the hypotheses rank in explanatory power—in the ability to explain why the altruists keep trying. While we await that research, it seems uncontroversial to recognize that Washington's altruists are human. The paycheck needs to be considered. So with an awareness that you are guessing, give personal self-interest as much weight as you see fit, but give more attention to the data collected by observing more than a century of uplifting. These data indicate that most altruists, regardless of their subservient role in the uplifting industry, are driven primarily by a belief that to them is utterly unassailable: *development assistance produces development.* With this belief we have hit the cognitive bedrock of nearly every altruist in Washington.

But even a deeply entrenched belief is not necessarily an established fact. Much depends upon what is being observed and who is doing the observation over what length of time. An altruistic observer of outreach centers in Honduras between 2011 and 2013 will insist that development assistance is producing development. Other equally altruistic observers will look at today's Honduras and wonder whether Washington's century-long uplifting effort may, on balance, have had more negative than positive consequences for the very people they have been trying to improve. Among these Doubting-Thomas altruists are many dedicated professionals who have spent an entire century tinkering with development assistance, trying everything they could think of to improve their effort to improve the recipients, adding layer after layer of projects and, in those quiet moments, struggling to stave off any doubt about their unassailable belief.

Through thick and thin, Washington's altruists have resolutely refused to surrender to underdevelopment. Fortunately, most have now lost their predecessors' godlike conceit that they can do what they will; instead they have acquired a commitment to do what they can, which is to take the realists' money and use it to act upon the one and only belief that serves as the soul of today's uplifting industry. Any observer will tell you that Washington's altruists will stop only if the realists cut off their funding. Until then, their stubborn refusal to surrender to underdevelopment suggests a nobility of character that anyone can admire. In the face of unrelenting criticism, much of it laced with undeserved contempt, they are trying to be helpful.

IT MAY BE more difficult to keep the realists engaged in Latin America, where they might conclude that Washington's uplifting is counterproductive to the protection and promotion of U.S. interests.

Recall the years that began late in the Progressive era and continued through the 1920s, when Wall Street—Dwight Morrow, Thomas Lamont, and their colleagues—began to worry that protectorates were harming the nation's economic interests. They were reacting to reports such as one from the Dominican Republic, where one admiral told another, "I have never seen such hatred displayed by one people for another, as I notice and feel here. We positively have not a friend in the land." At exactly the same time—in the same week—Secretary of State Robert Lansing was telling President

Wilson that his policy toward Mexico "is extremely distasteful to all Latin America."[17] Latin Americans who had never been the target of the Progressives' uplifting were now voicing their opposition to U.S. Marines patrolling Latin American streets, to U.S. citizens collecting Latin Americans' taxes, and, in general, to the U.S. government "protecting" Latin Americans.

Facing this reality, realists found it in their own best interest to guide the United States away from its Progressive-era commitment to uplifting. And even though economic interests appear to have been the most powerful explanation for this withdrawal, security concerns were never entirely absent. Urging that "in the future we may so act that we shall avoid mistrust by the people of South America," democracy doctor Harold Dodds warned that "the time may come when we may need their friendship much more than they need ours."[18]

The ensuing Good Neighbor and World War II years stand today as the era when U.S. interests were easiest to promote and protect in Latin America. "The American republics to the south of us have been ready always to cooperate with the United States on a basis of equality and mutual respect," FDR told a 1936 audience, "but before we inaugurated the good neighbor policy there was among them resentment and fear, because certain administrations in Washington had slighted their national pride and their sovereign rights."[19]

It is true that an impulsive Sumner Welles got the Good Neighbor years off to a false start in Cuba, but the recovery was quick and it is far more indicative of the era to recall the response by Minister Arthur Bliss Lane in 1935, when Nicaragua's president asked for advice about the selection of the country's next chief of state. "We do not 'advise' Great Britain as to how its elections or political matters should be held. Why should we so 'advise' Nicaragua?"[20] Realists had learned: no uplifting, no hard feelings.

This same concern about resentment-bred hostility resurfaced two decades later, at the beginning of the Cold War, when Washington began thinking about using foreign aid to reduce the appeal of communism. Latin Americans were asking for assistance; why not help them with their development?

Here is why not, replied assistant secretary Spruille Braden, who was not entirely a buffoon: "If we endeavor to assist another country with grants, no matter how meritorious the objectives, the recipient deep down will not like it—no one wants to be the object of charity." George Kennan, the epitome of Cold War realism and nobody's fool, said much the same thing: "Let us recognize that even benevolence, when addressed to a foreign people, represents a form of intervention into their internal affairs, and always receives, at best, a divided reception." A former member of the State Department's Policy Planning Staff nodded in agreement: "[I] doubt that assistance programs, great as their usefulness may be, are conducive to the improvement of international good feeling in the long run. There is implicit in them an almost inescapable element of degradation."[21] A year later, one of the era's most altruistic economists, Albert O. Hirschman, had this to say about JFK's Alliance for Progress: "There is some question whether we can realistically aim at becoming, by a few ringing proclamations and disbursement of some funds, the patron saint of the Latin-American social revolution." But for the sake of argument, he continued, "let us assume that it is successful; would there not then be something distasteful to the Latin Americans about our having financed social justice for them?"[22]

However, at that time most Latin American leaders were struggling to cope with their home-grown versions of Argentina's *descamisados*—the increasingly vocal urban proletariat and/or rural peasantry understood to be caught up in that revolution of rising expectations. There also was clear evidence that Cuba's revolutionary ideas were encouraging the radicalization of their reformists. Confronting these perceived threats to Latin America's existing structure of privilege, the region's leaders made it clear they did not find Washington's assistance distasteful.

That probably helps explain why the concern over resentment never amounted to much during the Cold War years. Exactly the contrary, argued the State Department's Thomas Mann in 1952: "The disparity in the amount of grant aid given to Latin America and other parts of the world has caused deep resentment in Latin America." The United States cannot "continue indefinitely to discriminate against Latin America in our foreign aid programs without incurring very serious risks of defection."[23] More aid would lead to less resentment and, not incidentally, less communism.

Once the Cold War was over, in 1991 the Congressional Research Service again warned that "aid—or, in the case of prolonged aid, dependency—can also breed resentment," but that sentence went unnoticed in Washington at a time when most Latin American governments had become accustomed to the United States helping with their improvement.[24] The best evidence of this came in the 2010 "3D" announcement that development assistance was a mechanism of power. The absence of any reaction from Latin America, positive or negative, conveyed a clear message: you in the United States have interests to protect, and to do so you have created your uplifting industry. Meanwhile, we in Latin America have our own interests to protect, and to do so we have created a dominant political culture that accepts being uplifted. You have a habit of giving, we have a habit of receiving.

WE DO NOT know if Latin Americans will ever begin to distance themselves from Washington's uplifters in order to protect their other interests, the most important of which may be their interest in self-respect. That probably was what Thoreau was thinking when he wrote that he would run for his life if he saw someone coming "with the conscious design of doing me good." Surely Latin Americans already know what Thoreau would have pointed out: that allowing an outside power to provide decade after decade of development assistance by definition brands them as underdeveloped, as second class. Surely that is why in 2010 the president-elect of Colombia told journalists, "We would like to stop being a simple country that begs for help every year."[25]

Here in our twenty-first century, with most Latin American governments imperfect only in different ways from the imperfect U.S. government, it is difficult not to wonder if Washington might be hitting an especially sensitive nerve with its political uplifting. Certainly U.S. citizens felt that nerve being pinched when a foreign power appeared to meddle in their 2016 election, and readers of the preceding chapters surely can understand why Latin Americans might see little difference between democracy promotion and political meddling. Realists will insist that this is the one area where the altruists are in command—that the United States seeks only the pleasure of seeing good governance—yet evidence to the contrary is overwhelming: since the day in 1982 when President Reagan gave his Westminster speech, Washington realists have demonstrated beyond a shadow of doubt that they are using their lion's share of the good governance budget as a tool to strengthen groups that will protect and promote U.S. interests, and to undermine groups that threaten U.S. interests.

NO ONE CAN say whether some future Latin American generation will react as Thoreau said he would react, but we do know this: the day when self-respect provokes Latin Americans to resent U.S. uplifting will be the day Washington's realists bring their soft-power altruists home, exactly as the post-Progressive realists brought their hard-power Marines home. Resentment is the last thing any realist would want to produce with development assistance. Nothing could be less in the interest of the United States.

For now, we can only be certain that the altruists, if given the money, are going to continue their relentless effort to improve Latin Americans. The same is to be expected from the realists, who are going to continue their uplifting until it is no longer in the interests of the United States. So it all depends upon Latin Americans insisting Washington's realists stop.

While we wait to see if they return the ball that has been lobbed into their court, we need to remind ourselves that inertia is almost as powerful in human relations as it is in physics. To this day the belief in Latin Americans' need for improvement, inherited from the Progressives, still governs Washington's thinking. To this day the uplifting industry, inherited from the Cold Warriors, remains superglued into Washington's foreign policy culture. Realists are still realists, altruists are still altruists, and their jointly owned uplifting industry is a wonder to behold.

Clearly, the United States has only begun its effort to improve Latin Americans.

Abbreviations

AID	U.S. Agency for International Development
APF	American Political Foundation
ARA	Bureau of American Republics Affairs, Department of State
CANF	Cuban American National Foundation
CDT	Central Democrática de Trabajadores (Chile)
CIPE	Center for International Private Enterprise
CRS	Congressional Research Service
DAI	DAI Global (formerly Development Alternatives, Inc.)
DDEL	Dwight David Eisenhower Presidential Library, Abilene, Kansas
DDRS	Declassified Documents Reference Service
DNSA	Digital National Security Archive
DOSB	*Department of State Bulletin*
DRL	Bureau of Democracy, Human Rights, and Labor, Department of State
FDRL	Franklin Delano Roosevelt Presidential Library, Hyde Park, New York
FRUS	*Foreign Relations of the United States*
FTUI	Free Trade Union Institute (later Solidarity Center)
GAO	Government Accountability Office (General Accounting Office until 2004)

GPO	Government Printing Office
HEW	Department of Health, Education and Welfare
HHL	Herbert Hoover Presidential Library, West Branch, Iowa
HSTL	Harry Truman Presidential Library, Independence, Missouri
ICA	International Cooperation Administration
IRI	International Republican Institute (earlier National Republican Institute for International Affairs)
JBUSMC	Joint Brazilian United States Military Commission
JBDC	Joint Business Development Center
JFKL	John F. Kennedy Presidential Library, Boston, Massachusetts
LBJL	Lyndon Baines Johnson Presidential Library, Austin, Texas
LC	Manuscripts Division, Library of Congress
NA	U.S. National Archives and Records Administration, College Park, Maryland
NADR	Nonproliferation, Antiterrorism, Demining, and Related Programs
NAFTA	North American Free Trade Agreement
NDI	National Democratic Institute
NED	National Endowment for Democracy
NGO	Non-Government Organization
NRI	National Republican Institute for International Affairs
NSA (1)	National Security Archive, Washington, D.C.
NSA (2)	National Student Association
NSF	National Security Files
OCB	Operations Coordinating Board
OPS	Office of Public Safety, AID
OTI	Open Technology Institute, New America
PPP	*Public Papers of the Presidents of the United States*
POF	President's Office Files
PRODEMCA	Friends of the Democratic Center in Central America
REN	Red de Empresarias de Nicaragua
RG	Record Group in the National Archives
RG 59	Record Group 59, General Records of the Department of State
RNL	Richard Nixon Presidential Library, Yorba Linda, California
Stat.	*U.S. Statutes at Large*
USAID	see AID

Notes

INTRODUCTION

1. www.usaid.gov/where-we-work/latin-american-and-caribbean/honduras (August 20, 2016).

2. Reagan, *Address to the British Parliament,* June 8, 1982, *PPP*; National Endowment for Democracy, *Annual Report 2016,* 122.

3. Email communication from the NDI's Latin America specialist, James Swigert, August 23, 2017.

4. U.S. Department of State, *Country Reports on Human Rights Practices for 2015.* In 1977, §117 of the International Development and Food Assistance Act required the Secretary of State to prepare annual human rights reports on all foreign aid recipients. In 1979, §504 of the International Development Cooperation Act broadened the scope to include reports on "all other foreign countries which are members of the United Nations."

5. Secretary Knox to Senate Committee on Foreign Relations, May 24, 1911, *FRUS* 1912, 584, 587, 593; Assistant Secretary Francis Huntington Wilson to newspaper editor William Hoster, June 24, 1911, Wilson Papers, Ursinus College. For the same assessment three years later ("there is no hope of improvement and every prospect of worse conditions unless the country is afforded decided help from without"), see memo, Boaz Long, February 10, 1914, 814.77 / 259, RG 59, NA.

6. Department of State, Bureau of Intelligence and Research, "Latin America— Current Stage of Progress in Key Socio-Economic Reforms, by Country," Research Memorandum RAR-4, September 4, 1961, NSF Regional Security, box 215A, folder "Latin America General 9/61–12/62," JFKL.

7. www.state.gov/p/wha/rt/carsi/fs/(October 28, 2015); Peter J. Meyer and Clare Ribando Seelke, "Central America Regional Security Initiative: Background and Policy Issues for Congress," CRS Report R41731, May 6, 2014.

8. Three of the other four NADR components were the traditional Economic Support Fund, Foreign Military Financing, and Development Assistance. The fourth was the more recent International Narcotics Control and Law Enforcement program.

9. Testimony of Elizabeth Hogan, AID's acting assistant administrator for Latin America and the Caribbean, before the House Appropriations Committee, Subcommittee on State, Foreign Operations, and Related Programs, February 11, 2016, typescript; White House, Office of the Press Secretary, "Fact Sheet: The United States and Central America: Honoring Our Commitments," January 14, 2016; U.S. Embassy Honduras, "Joint Communique of the Presidents of El Salvador, Guatemala, and Honduras, and the Vice President of the United States of America in Relation to the Plan of the Alliance for Prosperity in the Northern Triangle," February 24, 2016; Overseas Private Investment Corporation testimony of Assistant Secretary of State Roberta S. Jacobson before the Senate Committee on Foreign Relations, May 20, 2015, typescript.

10. The $162 million: http://beta.foreignassistance.gov/explore/country/Honduras (January 28, 2016). Gina Harkins, "Marines Set for New Mission in Troubled Central America," *Marine Corps Times* (online edition), April 13, 2015; U.S. Department of State, Office of Inspector General, Office of Inspections, *Inspection of Embassy Tegucigalpa, Honduras,* Audit ISP-I-16-21A, August 2016.

11. Kirk Bowman, *Militarization, Democracy and Development: The Perils of Praetorianism in Latin America* (University Park: Pennsylvania State University Press, 2002), 142; Marvin Barahona, *La hegemonía de los Estados Unidos en Honduras, 1907–1932* (Tegucigalpa: Centro de Documentación de Honduras, 1989).

12. Bronislaw Malinowski, *Argonauts of the Western Pacific* (London: Routledge and Kegan Paul, 1922), 25.

13. Michael Hunt, whose thoughtful work has influenced more than one generation of scholars, would prefer "ideology" to "constellation of beliefs," but ideology implies a certain coherence—Hunt defines it as "an interrelated set of convictions and assumptions"—and often there is nothing interrelated about many of the beliefs discussed in the pages that follow. Michael Hunt, *Ideology and Foreign Policy* (New Haven, CT: Yale University Press, 1987), xi.

14. Clifford Geertz, *The Interpretation of Cultures* (New York: Basic Books, 1973), 13, 25.

15. Adam Smith, *The Theory of Moral Sentiments,* 2nd ed. (1759; London: A. Millar, 1761), 1.

16. Hans Morgenthau, "A Political Theory of Foreign Aid," *American Political Science Review* 56 (June 1962): 309.

17. Roosevelt, *Special Message to Congress,* January 4, 1904.

18. John P. Mason, "A.I.D.'s Experience with Democratic Initiatives: A Review of Regional Programs in Legal Institution Building," A.I.D. Program Evaluation Discussion Paper No. 29, February 1990, identified only as "Document Order No. PN-AAX-232"; National Endowment for Democracy, *Annual Report 1985,* 7.

1. ESTABLISHING THE NEED FOR IMPROVEMENT

1. *Journals of the Continental Congress* 20 (June 1781): 705.

2. On protecting early whalers in the Pacific, see John Crane Pine, "The Role of United States Special Agents in the Development of a Spanish American Policy, 1810–1822" (PhD diss., University of Colorado, 1955), 479, 483, 484.

3. Alexis de Tocqueville, *Democracy in America,* ed. J. P. Mayer and trans. George Lawrence, enlarged 1850 ed. of 1835 first ed. (London: Fontana Press, 1994), 26, 226, 306.

4. Conversation with Joel Poinsett, January 1832, in Tocqueville's travel dairy from 1831–1832, published in English as *Journey to America,* ed. J. P. Mayer and trans. George Lawrence (London: Faber and Faber, 1959), 118–119. For Poinsett's pessimism: Poinsett to JQ Adams, November 4, 1818, Communications from Special Agents, RG 59, NA; Poinsett to Clay, October 6, 1827, in U.S. Congress, House, *Boundary—United States and Mexico,* H. Exec. Doc. 42, 25th Cong., 1st Sess., 1837, 25; Poinsett to Clay, October 12, 1825, and Poinsett to Van Buren, March 10, 1829, both Dispatches from Mexico, RG 59, NA.

5. William R. Manning, ed., *Diplomatic Correspondence of the United States, Inter-American Affairs, 1831–1860* (Washington, DC: Carnegie Endowment for International Peace, 1932–1939), 1:93 (Buenos Aires in 1832); 10:484 (Lima in 1839); 12:568 (Caracas in 1848). A second envoy to Argentina captured the gist of these early reports: "None of the South American Governments have any idea of national justice," 1:136.

6. Adams, *Address to the U.S. House of Representatives on Foreign Policy,* July 4, 1821.

7. Heman Allen to Henry Clay, February 9, 1825, Dispatches from Chile, RG 59, NA; Henry Clay to John Forbes, April 14, 1825, Instructions to U.S. Ministers, RG 59, NA.

8. James Buchanan to Albert Jewett, June 1, 1846, Instructions to Peru, RG 59, NA.

9. Instructions dated June 1 and June 3, 1848, in Manning, *Diplomatic Correspondence,* 2:4 (Bolivia) and 3:31 (Guatemala).

10. John Randolph Clay to Secretary of State Daniel Webster, June 8, 1852, and July 23, 1852, both in Manning, *Diplomatic Correspondence,* 10:589 (Peru), and 6:290n (Ecuador). John Randolph Clay was the U.S. *chargé* for both countries. Puritan John Winthrop's "City on a Hill" comment in 1630 came from the Sermon on the Mount (Matt. 5:14–15).

11. John Forsyth to Secretary of State Lewis Cass, June 17, 1858, and (for military aid) John Forsyth to Secretary of State William Marcy, November 8, 1856, both in Manning, *Diplomatic Correspondence,* 9:995 and 856. For an earlier commentary along the same line, see *Congressional Globe,* May 4, 1848, 591. William Churchwell, Special Agent of the United States to Mexico, to Secretary of State Lewis Cass, February 8, 1859, in Manning, *Diplomatic Correspondence,* 9:1027.

12. Anthony Butler to President Andrew Jackson, May 25, 1831 (Mexico), and Francis Baylies to Secretary of State Edward Livingston, August 19, 1832 (Argentina), both in Manning, *Diplomatic Correspondence,* 8:242–243 and 1:153; Henry Lane Wilson, *Diplomatic Episodes in Mexico, Belgium, and Chile* (Garden City, NY: Doubleday, Page, 1927), 13 (Chile).

13. On the U.S. culture that conditioned these envoys before their departure for Latin America, see Iván Jaksić, *The Hispanic World and American Intellectual Life* (New York: Palgrave Macmillan, 2007), 6: "All the negative characteristics ascribed to Spain were simply transferred across the Atlantic, where the element of race added even darker overtones."

14. President James Buchanan, *Message to the Senate on the Arrest of William Walker in Nicaragua,* January 7, 1858; Representative Thomas L. Anderson, *Congressional Globe,* January 10, 1859, 25th Cong., 2nd Sess., 299.

15. Andrew Carnegie, *Triumphant Democracy, Or, Fifty Years' March of the Republic* (New York: C. Scribner's Sons, 1886), 1.

16. David A. Wells, Thomas G. Shearman, J. B. Sargent, and W. G. Sumner, "Evils of the Tariff System," *North American Review* 139 (September 1884): 277. This is a compilation of four separately authored statements focused on the tariff. Here Sumner is being quoted.

17. Wells et al., "Evils of the Tariff System," 294. For one of the earliest statements of the "overproduction" argument, see Representative Gideon Tomlinson, *Congressional Record,* February 13, 1824, 1508. For an extended example of the same argument in the late nineteenth century, see U.S. Congress, House, *Report of the Secretary of the Interior,* 49th Cong., 1st Sess., 1885, H. Exec. Doc. 1, pt. 5, 281–293.

18. Senator William Drew Washburn (R-MN), *Congressional Record,* April 23, 1894, 3966.

19. Isaac Christiancy to Secretary of State James G. Blaine, May 4, 1881, Dispatches from Peru, RG 59, NA.

20. The Commission's report, dated October 1, 1885, is *Reports of the Commission Appointed under an Act of Congress Approved July 7, 1884 . . .*, H. Exec. Doc. 50, 49th Cong., 1st Sess., 1886, 24.

21. *Buenos Ayres Herald,* November 21, 1885, 1.

22. U.S. Senate, *International American Conference,* S. Doc. 232, 51st Cong., 1st Sess., 1889–1890. Part 3, a 343-page "Excursion Appendix," captures best the thinking behind the conference.

23. During this half-century, Cuba, Brazil, and Mexico took half of all U.S. exports to the region. Susan B. Carter et al., *Historical Statistics of the United States,* Millennial Edition On Line (New York: Cambridge University Press, 2006), Table Ee533–550.

24. Address at the Banquet of the American Chamber of Commerce in Paris, July 4, 1899, and Address to the Ecumenical Missionary Conference, New York, April 18, 1900, both in Benjamin Harrison, *Views of an Ex-President* (Indianapolis: Bowen Merrill, 1901), 493, 499–500.

25. *The Federalist,* no. 24, December 19, 1787.

26. Cleveland, *Annual Message to Congress,* December 8, 1885.

27. *Reports of the Commission Appointed under an Act of Congress,* 43, 55.

28. Senator John Potter Stockton (D-NH) and Senator Cornelius Cole (R-CA), *Congressional Globe,* May 1, 1872, 2963–2964.

29. President Grover Cleveland, *Annual Message to Congress,* December 6, 1886; Robert Seager II, "Ten Years before Mahan: The Unofficial Case for the New Navy, 1880–1890," *Mississippi Valley Historical Review* 40 (December 1953): 491–512.

30. Quotations of the 1876 and 1883 annual messages are in U.S. Department of the Navy, *Annual Report* of the *Secretary of the Navy for the Year 1885,* 1:xxxii–xxxiii. U.S. Congress, House, *Report of the Secretary of the Navy,* 47th Cong., 2nd Sess., 1882, 1:6. Admiral David Dixon Porter's warning: U.S. Congress, House, *Annual Report of the Secretary of the Navy, 1883,* 408.

31. Charles A. Conant, "The Economic Basis of 'Imperialism,'" *North American Review* 167 (September 1898): 326.

32. U.S. Navy General Order 325, October 6, 1884. Instruction began in 1885.

33. A. T. Mahan, *The Influence of Sea Power upon History, 1660–1783* (New York: Barnes and Noble Books, 2004 replica of 1890 original), 53, 27–28; U.S. Congress, House, *Report of the Secretary of the Navy, 1891,* 52nd Cong., 1st Sess., 1891, H. Exec. Doc. 1, pt. 3, 30–31.

34. *Report of the Secretary of the Navy, 1891,* 30–31.

35. *Address of Hon. Theodore Roosevelt before the Naval War College, Newport, R.I., Wednesday, June 2, 1897* (Washington, DC: Navy Branch, GPO), 5–6; Roosevelt, *Annual*

Message to Congress, December 3, 1906; Henry F. Pringle, *Theodore Roosevelt: A Biography* (New York: Harcourt, Brace, 1931), 167.

36. Henry Lane Wilson recalling a 1902 conversation with John Hay, in Wilson, *Diplomatic Episodes,* 84; Taft to Philander C. Knox, September 9, 1911, Taft Papers, LC. The United States gave two names, San Juan Hill and Kettle Hill, to what local residents called Las Lomas (sometimes Las Colinas) de San Juan.

37. Theodore Roosevelt, "American Ideals," *Forum,* February 1895, 749; *Address of Hon. Theodore Roosevelt,* 5–6; Roosevelt to Henry Cabot Lodge, December 27, 1895, in *Selections from the Correspondence of Theodore Roosevelt and Henry Cabot Lodge, 1884–1918,* 2 vols. (New York: Charles Scribner's Sons, 1925), 1:204–205; Charles A. Beard, *The Idea of National Interest: An Analytical Study in American Foreign Policy* (New York: Macmillan, 1934), 372.

38. "Give the prosperous man the dickens! Legislate the thriftless man into ease, whack the stuffing out of the creditors, . . . put the lazy, greasy fizzle who can't pay his debts on the altar, and bow down and worship him." "What's the Matter with Kansas?," *Emporia Gazette,* August 15, 1896, in *The Editor and His People: Editorials by William Allen White* (New York: Macmillan, 1924), 244–249. In a footnote for this 1924 collection, a mature White wrote that "the editorial represents conservatism in its full and perfect flower" (244). White eventually abandoned this wing of the Republican Party and later apologized for his intemperate comments about Kansas Populists.

39. "McKinley's Message," April 12, 1898, *Emporia Gazette,* reprinted in White, *The Editor and His People,* 304.

40. White met Roosevelt in 1897. William Allen White, *The Autobiography of William Allen White,* 2nd ed. (Lawrence: University Press of Kansas, 1990), 155–156; Henry Lane Wilson recalling a conversation with John Hay, in *Diplomatic Episodes,* 84; William E. Leuchtenburg, "Progressivism and Imperialism: The Progressive Movement and American Foreign Policy, 1898–1916," *Mississippi Valley Historical Review* 39 (December 1952): 498.

41. "McKinley's Message," April 12, 1898; "What Is to Be Will Be," *Emporia Gazette,* March 20, 1899, in White, *The Editor and His People,* 304–305; Beveridge: *Congressional Record,* January 9, 1900, 710.

42. Theodore Roosevelt, *Life of Thomas Hart Benton* (Boston: Houghton, Mifflin, 1887), 175.

43. Schurz's recall of McKinley's words after a conversation in early 1897. *Speeches, Correspondence and Political Papers of Carl Schurz,* 6 vols. (New York: G. P. Putnam's Sons, 1913), 6:271; Carl Schurz, "Manifest Destiny," *Harper's New Monthly Magazine,* October 1893, 738–745; on early anti-imperialism, especially the views of Carl Schurz, see David Healy, *U.S. Expansionism: The Imperialist Urge in the 1890s* (Madison: University of Wisconsin Press, 1970), 212–231.

44. Alfred Thayer Mahan, "The Isthmus and Sea Power," *Atlantic Monthly,* October 1893), 463; address by Senator Albert Beveridge, September 16, 1898, India-

napolis, Indiana. This address is often referred to as Beveridge's "March of the Flag" speech. The George Hoar / Orville Platt exchange: *Congressional Record,* December 19, 1898, 296–297; see also Platt to Senator Dillingham, June 11, 1903, in Louis A. Coolidge, *An Old-Fashioned Senator: Orville H. Platt of Connecticut; the Story of a Life Unselfishly Devoted to the Public Service* (New York: Knickerbocker Press, 1910), 310.

45. Henry Cabot Lodge, "Our Blundering Foreign Policy," *Forum,* March 1895, 17.

2. UPLIFTING BEGINS

1. Herbert Croly, *The Promise of American Life* (New York: Macmillan, 1909), 302. Felix Frankfurter recalled that this book "made a very deep impression on TR," and Roosevelt favorably reviewed another Croly volume: see Roosevelt, "Two Noteworthy Books on Democracy," *The Outlook,* November 18, 1914, 648–651. Felix Frankfurter, *Felix Frankfurter Reminisces* (London: Secker and Warburg, 1960), 88.

2. "Firm action": Roosevelt to Lodge, August 3, 1897, in *Selections from the Correspondence of Theodore Roosevelt and Henry Cabot Lodge, 1884–1918,* 2 vols. (New York: Charles Scribner's Sons, 1925), 1:268; "interest of civilization": Roosevelt to Henry White, March 30, 1896, in Theodore Roosevelt, *Letters and Speeches* (New York: Library of America, 2004), 629; Captain A. T. Mahan, "Strategic Features of the Gulf of Mexico and the Caribbean Sea," *Harper's Magazine,* October 1897, 690.

3. Lee to Judge [William R. Day, Assistant Secretary of State], January 12 and 13, 1898, Consular Dispatches from Havana, RG 59; Bryan quoted in *New York Times,* April 1, 1898, 1. On the accident, see Admiral Hyman Rickover's invaluable *How the Battleship Maine Was Sunk* (Annapolis: Naval Institute Press, 1995) (replica of 1976 original).

4. William Day to William McKinley, April 19, 1898, container 9, Day Papers, LC; Minister Stewart Woodford to McKinley, March 17, 1898, *FRUS* 1898, 687; Bismarck interview, May 1898, in Wolf von Schierbrand, *Germany: The Welding of a World Power* (New York: Doubleday, 1902), 352.

5. "Remember the Maine," *Emporia Gazette,* February 16, 1899, and "What Is to Be Will Be," *Emporia Gazette,* March 20, 1899, in *The Editor and His People: Editorials by William Allen White* (New York: Macmillan, 1924), 304–306, and 60 for White's subsequent regret for such comments. Major General S. B. M. Young, *Brooklyn Eagle,* August 6, 1898, 3.

6. Wood to Roosevelt, August 18, 1899, Roosevelt Papers, LC; Roosevelt to Lodge, July 21, 1899, in *Selections from the Correspondence,* 1:413–414; Cleveland to Olney, March 26, 1900, Cleveland Papers, LC.

7. McKinley, *Annual Message to Congress,* December 5, 1899; Wood to McKinley, April 12, 1900, Leonard Wood Papers, LC.

8. *Felix Frankfurter Reminisces,* 61; *From the Diaries of Felix Frankfurter* (New York: Norton, 1975), 117–118.

9. Root to Charles W. Eliot, May 4, 1900, reprinted in Philip C. Jessup, *Elihu Root,* 2 vols. (New York: Dodd, Mead and Co., 1938), 1:288. Senator Orville Platt, chair of the Senate Committee on Relations with Cuba, introduced the bill drafted by Root. The Platt Amendment is 31 Stat. 897, March 2, 1901.

10. Taft to Helen Taft, September 23, 1906, Taft Papers, LC; Wood to Roosevelt, October 28, 1901, Leonard Wood Papers, LC; Albert J. Beveridge, "Cuba and Congress," *North American Review,* April 1901, reprinted in *Congressional Record,* May 22, 1902, 5811.

11. Thomas Jefferson to Monsieur Le Roy, November 13, 1786, in *The Writings of Thomas Jefferson,* 20 vols. (Washington, DC: Thomas Jefferson Memorial Association, 1903–1904), 5:471.

12. Robert B. McAfee to Secretary John Forsyth, September 2, 1834, and James B. Bowlin to Secretary William Marcy, August 1 and October 23, 1856, both in William R. Manning, ed., *Diplomatic Correspondence of the United States, Inter-American Affairs, 1831–1860,* 12 vols. (Washington, DC: Carnegie Endowment for International Peace, 1932–1939), 5:504, 746, 786.

13. "National Duties," address before the Minnesota State Fair, September 2, 1901, in Theodore Roosevelt, *The Strenuous Life: Essays and Addresses* (New York: Century, 1902), 292–294.

14. Hay to Spooner, January 20, 1904, Letterbooks, John Hay Papers, LC.

15. Roosevelt, *Annual Message to Congress,* January 4, 1904. For a succinct government document explaining the U.S. role in separating Panama from Colombia (and Washington's subsequent expression of "sincere regrets"), see U.S. Congress, Joint Economic Committee, *Diplomatic Correspondence with Colombia in Connection with the Treaty of 1914 and Certain Oil Concessions,* S. Doc. 64, 68th Cong., 1st Sess., 1924.

16. Taft's promise: U.S. Congress, Senate, Committee on Interoceanic Canals, *Investigation of Panama Canal Matters,* 59th Cong., 2nd Sess., 1907, 3:2523. Taft's speech: December 1, 1904, *FRUS* 1904, 663–665.

17. Roosevelt to Kermit Roosevelt, November 20, 1906, in *Theodore Roosevelt Cyclopedia,* 2nd ed. (Oyster Bay, NY: Theodore Roosevelt Association, 1989), 403.

18. Roosevelt, *Annual Message to Congress,* December 5, 1905.

19. Roosevelt to F. C. Moore, February 5, 1898, Roosevelt Papers, LC; Roosevelt to Lodge, March 27, 1901, in *Selections from the Correspondence,* 1:484–485; Dexter Perkins, *The Monroe Doctrine, 1867–1907* (Baltimore: Johns Hopkins Press, 1937), 300; Walter LaFeber, *The New Empire* (Ithaca, NY: Cornell University Press, 1963), 323; Nancy Mitchell, *The Danger of Dreams: German and American Imperialism in Latin America* (Chapel Hill: University of North Carolina Press, 1999), 218; Bruce J.

Calder, *The Impact of Intervention: The Dominican Republic during the U.S. Occupation of 1916–1924* (Austin: University of Texas Press, 1984), 260n69.

20. On the early concern with Venezuela's debt, see the annual messages of President Taylor in 1849 and President Fillmore in 1852. For the 1869 takeover proposal, see Hamilton Fish to James Partridge, May 25, 1869, Instructions from the Department of State, 1801–1906, RG 59, NA. For the Garfield administration's 1881 proposal, see Blaine to Edward T. Noyes, July 23, 1881, Instructions from the Department of State, 1801–1906, RG 59, NA.

21. "Speech at Dinner of the Home Market Club, Boston, February 6, 1899," in *Speeches and Addresses of William McKinley, From March 1, 1897 to May 30, 1900* (New York: Doubleday and McClure, 1900), 192–193; "The White Man's Burden," *McClure's Magazine,* February 1899, 4; Speech to the Hamilton Club, Chicago, April 18, 1899, in *The Strenuous Life,* 19; Benjamin Harrison, *Views of an Ex-President* (Indianapolis: Bowen-Merrill, 1901), 494.

22. "Speech at Dinner," 192–193. For this same view applied to Cuba, see U.S. Senate, *The Establishment of Free Government in Cuba: Compiled by the Bureau of Insular Affairs from the Records of the War Department,* S. Doc. 312, 58th Cong., 2nd Sess., 1904; Leonard Wood, "The Military Government of Cuba," *Annals of the American Academy of Political and Social Science* 21 (March 1903): 153–182.

23. Roosevelt, *Annual Message to Congress,* December 3, 1901.

24. The U.S. flag being flown in the Philippines has "the white stripes painted black and the stars replaced by the skull and cross-bones." Mark Twain, "To the Person Sitting in Darkness," *North American Review,* February 1901, 164, 174, 176.

25. Andrew Carnegie, "The Opportunity of the United States," *North American Review,* May 1902, 611, 607.

26. *Congressional Record,* May 22, 1902, 5792–5795. A year earlier, Senator Hoar had not been opposed to the Platt Amendment; indeed, he had considered it "eminently wise and satisfactory": *Congressional Record,* February 27, 1901, 3147–3148.

27. The February 1904 arbitration decision is reprinted in U.S. Congress, Senate, *The Venezuelan Arbitration before the Hague Tribunal 1903,* S. Doc. 119, 58th Cong., 3rd Sess., 1904–1905, 106–111, 11–21.

28. Roosevelt to William Bayard Hale, February 26, 1904, and Roosevelt to Joseph Bishop, February 23, 1904, both in *The Letters of Theodore Roosevelt,* 8 vols. (Cambridge, MA: Harvard University Press, 1951–1954), 4:740, 734; Roosevelt to Theodore Roosevelt Jr., February 20, 1904, Roosevelt Papers, LC.

29. Roosevelt to John Hay, September 2, 1904, in *Letters of Theodore Roosevelt,* 4:917.

30. Francis P. Loomis, "Memorandum for the Secretary of State on the Dominican Republic," March 19, 1904, Roosevelt Papers, LC; Dillingham to Loomis, August 21, 1904, Miscellaneous Letters to the Department of State, LC. Dillingham misspelled "Santo" as "Sanot."

31. The Roosevelt Corollary was included in Roosevelt's *Annual Message,* December 6, 1904.

32. Roosevelt, *Message from the President,* February 15, 1905, *FRUS* 1905, 334; Hay to Dawson, December 28, 1904, filed out of chronological order in Instructions to the Dominican Republic, RG 59, NA (microfilm M77 / R98, frames 51–52). Loeb (Secretary to the President) to Assistant Secretary of State Loomis, February 6, 1905, bound in rough chronological order with Dispatches from the Dominican Republic, RG 59, NA.

33. There were two draft treaties, one dated January 20, 1905, and a second dated February 7, 1905. Reprinted in *FRUS* 1905, 311–312 and 342–343, respectively.

34. Steinhart to Secretary of State, September 8, 1906, in "Appendix E: Cuban Pacification," in *Annual Reports of the War Department for the Fiscal Year Ended June 30, 1906* (Washington, DC: GPO, 1906), 444–445.

35. Roosevelt to George Trevelyan, September 9, 1096, in *Letters of Theodore Roosevelt,* 5:401; Roosevelt to Henry L. White, September 13, 1906, Roosevelt Papers, LC; Roosevelt to Taft, September 26 and 28, 1906, in *Annual Reports of the War Department,* 480–481.

36. *Annual Reports of the War Department,* 456.

37. Henry Cabot Lodge to Roosevelt, September 29, 1906, in *Selections from the Correspondence,* 2:237; Albert J. Beveridge, "The Development of a Colonial Policy for the United States," *Annals of the American Academy of Political and Social Science* 30 (July 1907): 6–8; Taft to Helen H. Taft, September 22, 1906, Taft Papers, LC.

38. Roosevelt: Speech to the Harvard Union, February 23, 1907, in Theodore Roosevelt, *Presidential Addresses and State Papers* (New York: Review of Reviews, 1910), 6:1178–1179; Roosevelt to Taft, January 22, 1907, in *Letters of Theodore Roosevelt,* 5:560. Root: Address at the National Convention for the Extension of Foreign Commerce of the United States, January 14, 1907, in *Latin America and the United States: Addresses by Elihu Root* (Cambridge, MA: Harvard University Press, 1917), 275.

39. The 1907 treaty is reprinted in *FRUS* 1907, 1:307–310.

40. The report: U.S. Congress, Senate, Committee on Foreign Relations, *Statement of Prof. Jacob H. Hollander before the Committee on Foreign Relations on Wednesday, January 16, in Reference to the Debt of Santo Domingo,* 59th Cong., 1st Sess., 1906, 10; Roosevelt to the Senate, February 16, 1905, *FRUS* 1905, 335.

41. Earlier economists had served in the Philippines, and in 1900 Hollander had been sent to Puerto Rico to write the island's tax code, but with his Dominican Republic appointment he became the first such professional to be sent to an independent Latin American country.

42. Hollander's report is U.S. Congress, Senate, *Debt of Santo Domingo,* 59th Cong., 1st Sess., December 15, 1905; Jacob H. Hollander, "The Financial Difficulties of Santo Domingo," *Annals of the American Academy of Political and Social Science* 30 (July 1907): 93–103.

43. Root, Address at the National Convention, January 14, 1907, 275; Emily S. Rosenberg and Norman L. Rosenberg, "From Colonialism to Professionalism: The Public-Private Dynamic in United States Foreign Financial Advising, 1898–1929," *Journal of American History* 74 (June 1987): 60–63.

44. Jacob H. Hollander, "The Dominican Convention and Its Lessons," *Journal of Race Development* 4 (April 1914): 401; Jacob H. Hollander, "The Convention of 1907 between the United States and the Dominican Republic," *American Journal of International Law* 1 (April 1907): 295.

45. Magoon to Roosevelt, April 16, 1908, Roosevelt Papers, LC.

46. Taft to Roosevelt, September 22, 1906, Roosevelt Papers, LC; Wood to Root, February 8, 1901, Wood Papers, LC.

47. Roosevelt, *Annual Message to Congress,* December 8, 1908. The Filipino army is a rival for "first," although it was a part of the U.S. Army.

48. Beveridge, "Development of a Colonial Policy," 3.

49. Wood to Roosevelt, April 12, 1901, Roosevelt Papers, LC.

3. MONEY DOCTORS, DEMOCRACY DOCTORS, AND MARINES

1. Taft to Royal L. Melendy, April 28, 1909, Taft Papers, LC. A focus on Latin America is a narrow slice of the Taft administration. For a broader assessment, see Jonathan Lurie, *William Howard Taft: Progressive Conservative* (Cambridge: Cambridge University Press, 2011).

2. Root conversation with Philip Jessup, September 15, 1930, Jessup Papers, LC.

3. F. M. H. Wilson to William Jennings Bryan, March 16, 1913, Wilson Papers, Ursinus College. This was a time when there was neither a deputy secretary nor an undersecretary—only a counselor (for legal issues) and three assistant secretaries in numbered order. Wilson was first. To avoid confusing this Wilson with Woodrow Wilson, he will be referred to as Huntington Wilson, although Huntington was a given name, not a surname.

4. "Diplomatic Service: Conversation at Clinton Sept. 15, 1930," Philip Jessup Papers, LC; Huntington Wilson, "The Relation of Government to Foreign Investment," *Annals of the American Academy of Political and Social Science* 68 (November 1916): 301. The German ambassador in Washington characterized Huntington Wilson as "tactless and insincere." Johann von Bernstorff, *Memoirs of Count Bernstorff,* trans. Eric Sutton (New York: Random House, 1936), 111. See also T. Bentley Mott, *Twenty Years as Military Attaché* (New York: Oxford University Press, 1937), 172.

5. Huntington Wilson, undated memorandum marked "Confidential—file," probably February 1913, and intended for President-elect Wilson, Huntington Wilson Papers, Ursinus College; Henry White to Knox, October 22, 1910, 710.11 / 46, RG 59, NA.

6. Huntington Wilson, undated memorandum marked "Confidential—file."

7. "National Duties," address before the Minnesota State Fair, September 2, 1901, reprinted in Theodore Roosevelt, *The Strenuous Life: Essays and Addresses* (New York: Century, 1902), 292–294.

8. In 1841, for example, 45 percent of the ships arriving in Cuba (702 of 1,563) came from the United States. In 1899, 65 percent of U.S. residents of Cuba (4,178 of the 6,444) lived in the province of Havana. (The U.S. Army's 1899 census excluded occupying U.S. military and civilian officials.) José Vega Suñol, *Norteamericanos en Cuba* (Havana: Fundación Fernando Ortiz, 2004), 22, 24, and the table on 292.

9. Fidel Castro address celebrating the hundred-year anniversary of the beginning of the Ten Years War, October 1, 1968, http://www.cuba.cu/gobierno/discursos/.

10. The treaty, signed December 11, 1902, and ratified March 19, 1903, is 33 Stat. 2136. On this topic, see Jules Benjamin, *The United States and Cuba: Hegemony and Dependent Development, 1880–1934* (Pittsburgh: University of Pittsburgh Press, 1974).

11. The first Mexican railroad ran from Mexico City to Veracruz. Mario Gil, *Los Ferrocarrileros* (Mexico City: Editorial Extemporáneos, 1971); Fernando Cordero, *La influencia de los ferrocarriles en los cambios económicos y espaciales de México* (Stockholm: Institute of Latin American Studies, 1981); David M. Pletcher, *The Diplomacy of Trade and Investment: American Economic Expansion in the Hemisphere, 1865–1900* (Columbia: University of Missouri Press, 1998), chap. 14; Fred Wilbur Powell, *The Railroads of Mexico* (Boston: Stratford, 1921).

12. Henry Ford, *My Life and Work* (Garden City, NY: Garden City Publishing Co., 1922), 73.

13. Taft to Helen H. Taft, October 17, 1909, Taft Papers, LC.

14. Elihu Root, *Address to the Trans-Mississippi Commercial Congress, Kansas City, Missouri, Tuesday, November 20th, 1906* (Washington, DC: C. F. Sudwarth, 1906); Burton I. Kaufman, "United States Trade and Latin America: The Wilson Years," *Journal of American History* 58 (September 1971): 342–363.

15. Huntington Wilson, undated memorandum marked "Confidential—file." See also Huntington Wilson, "Relation of Government," 305; Paige Elliott Mulhollen, "Philander C. Knox and Dollar Diplomacy, 1909–1913" (PhD diss., University of Texas, 1966), 48–49, 162–164. On Taft's definition of Dollar Diplomacy, see his final *Annual Message to Congress, FRUS* 1912, x.

16. Knox to Senator Shelby Cullom, chair of the Senate Committee on Foreign Relations, May 3, 1911, *FRUS* 1912, 581. Huntington Wilson to William Hoster, June 24, 1911, Huntington Wilson Papers, Ursinus College.

17. Adee to Wilson, July 29, 1909, Numerical File 19475/86, RG 59, NA. Numerical File 19475 contains a collection of letters documenting the competition among banana companies.

18. The treaty: *FRUS* 1907, 2:692; Knox: U.S. Department of State, *Speeches Incident to the Visit of Philander Chase Knox, Secretary of State of the United States of*

America, to the Countries of the Caribbean, February 23 to April 7, 1912 (Washington, DC: GPO, 1913), 25–26. Jacob H. Hollander, "The Convention of 1907 between the United States and the Dominican Republic," *American Journal of International Law* 1 (April 1907): 214–219. On Mexico-U.S. cooperation to hold the conference, see FRUS 1907, 2:636. A year earlier the two countries had cooperated to promote conciliation between El Salvador and Guatemala, leading to the *Marblehead* agreement. See *FRUS* 1906, 1:834–866.

19. Knox to Senate Committee on Foreign Relations, May 24, 1911, *FRUS* 1912, 584, 587, 593. The original loans were made in 1867, 1869, and 1870. *FRUS* 1912, 549, 566, 570, 575, 593; W. Stull Holt, *Treaties Defeated in the Senate* (Baltimore: Johns Hopkins University Press, 1933); Dana G. Munro, *Intervention and Dollar Diplomacy in the Caribbean, 1900–1921* (Princeton: Princeton University Press, 1964), 217.

20. *FRUS* 1912, 550–572.

21. The vote of the Honduran congress, January 31, 1911, was 33 to 5. Along with the quotation above, it is discussed in *FRUS* 1912, 562, 577–580.

22. *FRUS* 1912, 562–566, 571; U.S. Department of State, *Right to Protect Citizens in Foreign Countries by Landing Forces: Memorandum of the Solicitor for the Department of State,* 3rd rev. ed. (Washington, DC: GPO, 1934), 77–78, 113, 74.

23. U.S. Department of State, *Speeches Incident,* 91–95; see also *FRUS* 1912, 626.

24. U.S. Department of State, *Speeches Incident,* 41; Huntington Wilson, "Address of the Hon. Huntington Wilson, Assistant Secretary of State, at the Third National Peace Conference, Baltimore, May 4, 1911," Huntington Wilson Papers, Ursinus College.

25. Knox to Shelby M. Cullom, June 17, 1911, 817.51/154A, RG 59, NA; U.S. Congress, Senate, Committee on Foreign Relations, *Foreign Loans,* 69th Cong., 2nd Sess., 1927, 35. A journalist closely connected to the administration wrote of this treaty: "If it fails, God help this people." William Bayard Hale, "With the Knox Mission to Central America," *The World's Work* 24 (1912): 192–193. The proposed treaty: *FRUS* 1912, 1074.

26. For the details of the receivership, see U.S. Department of State, *The United States and Nicaragua: A Survey of the Relations from 1909 to 1932* (Washington, DC: GPO, 1932), 2–17. The stabilization plan: *Monetary Reform for Nicaragua: Report Presenting a Plan of Monetary Reform for Nicaragua, Submitted to Msssrs. Brown Brothers & Company and Messrs. J. & W. Seligman & Company, by Msssrs F. G. Harrison and Charles A. Conant, April 23, 1912* (New York: W. R. Ficke, 1912).

27. Smedley Butler to Maud and Thomas Butler, March 1, 1910, and Smedley Butler to Thomas S. Butler, July 14, 1910, in *General Smedley Darlington Butler: The Letters of a Leatherneck, 1898–1931* (New York: Praeger, 1992), 75–77, 87–88. See also Butler's later "America's Armed Forces 2. 'In Time of Peace': The Army," *Current History* 4 (November 1935): 8–12. Isaac Joslin Cox, *Nicaragua and the United States, 1909–1927* (Boston: World Peace Foundation, 1927), 825–826; Edwin N. McCellan, "American Marines in Nicaragua," *Marine Corps Gazette* 6 (June 1921): 167.

28. Otto Schoenrich, "The Nicaraguan Mixed Claims Commission," *American Journal of International Law* 9 (1915): 858–865; W. W. Cumberland to Secretary of State, March 10, 1928, 817.51/1921, RG 59, NA.

29. Taft, *Annual Message to Congress,* 1912.

30. Hale, "With the Knox Mission to Central America," 334. See also Sydney Brooks, "Cuba and the Cuban Question," *North American Review* 196 (July 1912): 53.

31. Knox to John Jackson, May 6, 1911, 837.00/473, RG 59, NA.

32. Knox, "Reply to the Secretary of State of Cuba Welcoming Mr. Knox," April 11, 1912, *FRUS* 1912, 303.

33. *FRUS* 1912, 244.

34. All *FRUS* 1912, 245–253.

35. Minister, Cuba, to Department of State, June 5, 1912, 837.00/693, RG 59, NA; Taft, *Annual Message to Congress,* 1912.

36. *New York Times,* November 3, 1912, 14.

37. Address to the Southern Commercial Congress, Mobile, Alabama, October 27, 1913, Woodrow Wilson Papers, LC.

38. Arthur S. Link (who produced the 69-volume *Papers of Woodrow Wilson*), *Woodrow Wilson and the Progressive Era, 1910–1917* (New York: Harper and Brothers, 1954), 93; "Present Nature and Extent of the Monroe Doctrine, and Its Need of Restatement," June 11, 1914, *FRUS, The Lansing Papers, 1914–1920,* 2:462.

39. Woodrow Wilson, *The State: Elements of Historical and Practical Politics* (1889; Boston: D. C. Heath, 1918), 35.

40. Woodrow Wilson, "The Modern Democratic State," unpublished manuscript circa December 1885, *Papers of Woodrow Wilson,* 69 vols. (Princeton: Princeton University Press, 1966–1994), 5:63, 71.

41. Statement to the Press, March 11, 1913, reprinted in Edgar E. Robinson and Victor J. West, *The Foreign Policy of Woodrow Wilson* (New York: Macmillan, 1918), 179; *Annual Message to Congress,* December 2, 1913; *Nomination Acceptance Speech,* September 2, 1916, both *Papers of Woodrow Wilson,* 21:4, 38:134; Norman H. Davis, "A Consistent Latin American Policy," *Foreign Affairs,* July 1931, 554.

42. "Bryan on Expansion," *Literary Digest,* December 24, 1898, 739; Bryan to Woodrow Wilson, October 28, 1913, *Papers of Woodrow Wilson,* 28:456.

43. John Bassett Moore, untitled memorandum, October 21, 1913, container 92, Moore Papers, LC.

44. Undated address to the Nebraska State Association, quoted in "Distortion of Monroe Doctrine," *New York World,* August 4, 1913, 3.

45. Arthur S. Link, *Wilson: The New Freedom* (Princeton: Princeton University Press, 1956), 278.

46. The message is enclosed with Bryan to American Embassy, August 27, 1913, 812.00/8614a, RG 59, NA; Federico Gamboa to Personal Representative John Lind, August 16, 1913, Wilson Papers, LC.

47. Wilson, *Address to a Joint Session of Congress,* August 27, 1913.

48. *Papers of Woodrow Wilson,* 2:331.

49. *Papers of Woodrow Wilson,* 28:543–544.

50. The words come from the editor of the papers of Wilson's ambassador to Britain. This editor (Burton Hendrick) wrote that the U.S. ambassador to Great Britain (Walter Hines Page) told him the British envoy (William Tyrrell) had told Page that President Wilson said them—that is, Wilson to Tyrrell to Page to Hendrick—and then Hendrick to the rest of us. *The Life and Letters of Walter Hines Page,* 3 vols. (Garden City, NY: Doubleday, Page, 1923–1925), 1:204.

51. Cecil Spring-Rice to Edward Grey, May 25, 1914, Great Britain, Foreign Office, General Correspondence: Political, 1906–1953, Mexico, FO 371/2029, No. 24538, National Archives (née PRO), London.

52. Bryan to Page, November 19, 1913, 812.00/9817, RG 59, NA. All other U.S. diplomatic posts received instructions to inform their host governments of the same policy. Circular, November 7, 1913, *FRUS* 1913, 856.

53. Woodrow Wilson, Jackson Day address, Indianapolis, January 8, 1915, in *Congressional Record,* January 9, 1915, 1281–1282; address to the Democratic National Committee, December 8, 1915, *Papers of Woodrow Wilson,* 35:314.

54. Lansing to Woodrow Wilson, August 6, 1915, *Papers of Woodrow Wilson,* 34:110–112; Lansing to Edward Smith, December 5, 1919, Lansing Papers, Mudd Library, Princeton University.

55. Edith O'Shaughnessy, *Intimate Pages of Mexican History* (New York: George H. Doran, 1920), 307.

56. John Milton Cooper Jr., *Pivotal Decades: The United States, 1900–1920* (New York: Norton, 1990), 225; Cooper, *Woodrow Wilson: A Biography* (New York: Knopf, 2009), 244.

57. Boaz Long memorandum, February 10, 1914, 815.77/259, RG 59, NA.

58. Secretary of State Robert Lansing kept a "South America" notebook, and Honduras appears in mid-1917 ("Frontier dispute with Guatemala probably not to be settled until U.S. interests itself") and in late 1917 ("All factions said to be standing together against U.S.") Entries for August 29 and November 14, 1917, box 67 (microfilmed on reel 3), Desk Diaries and Notes, 1914–1920, Robert Lansing Papers, LC.

59. Charles A. Conant, "Our Mission in Nicaragua," *North American Review* 196 (July 1912): 70; U.S. Congress, Senate, Committee on Foreign Relations, *Foreign Loans,* 69th Cong., 2nd Sess., 1927, 35.

60. Press conference, July 21, 1913, *Papers of Woodrow Wilson,* 28:55–57.

61. Bryan to Wilson, August 16, 1913, *Papers of Woodrow Wilson,* 28:176.

62. Robert L. Keiser, "Treaty Negotiations: A Short History of the Negotiations regarding the Nicaraguan Canal Treaty," February 1927, ser. III, box 9, Francis White Papers, Johns Hopkins University.

63. Senator William Smith (Michigan), Senator Joseph Bristow (Kansas), Senator George Norris (Nebraska), all Republicans, quoted in *New York World,* August 4, 1913, 3; *The Spectator,* September 20, 1913, 410.

64. *Congressional Record,* July 6, 1914, 11614, 11617; see also Senator William Smith (R-Michigan), June 16, 1914, 10514; Senator Jacob Gallinger (R-New Hampshire), June 29, 1914, 11285.

65. The Economic Support Fund has had three names—initially "Defense Support," then "Security Supporting Assistance," and now "Economic Support Fund." The fund was designed for Israel in the post–World War II years, but quickly spread to assist other countries that were spending an inordinate amount of their budgets on the military. In FY2015 the Economic Support Fund accounted for 38 percent of AID funding worldwide ($5.1 billion of $13.2 billion), with the lion's share going to the Middle East.

66. Munro, "Dollar Diplomacy in Nicaragua," 233–234.

67. Bryan's instructions are reprinted Sumner Welles, *Naboth's Vineyard: The Dominican Republic, 1844–1924,* 2 vols. (New York: Payson and Clarke, 1928), 719–720; Bryan to U.S. Chargé, September 4, 1913, 839.00/860, RG 59, NA.

68. "Plan of President Wilson, Handed to Commissioners Fort and Smith, August 1914," 839.00/1582, RG 59, NA.

69. Bryan to Sullivan, April 20, 1915, *FRUS* 1915, 284–285; Admiral William S. Caperton to Rear Admiral William S. Benson, June 15, 1916, Caperton Papers, LC.

70. "Proclamation of Occupation and Military Government," November 29, 1916, 839.00/1965, RG 59, NA. For the president's authorization, see Wilson to Lansing, November 26, 1916, 839.00/1951a, RG 59, NA.

71. Wilson to Edith Bolling Galt, August 15, 1915, *Papers of Woodrow Wilson,* 34:208–209.

72. Wilson to Bryan, January 13, 1915, *Papers of Woodrow Wilson,* 3:62; Wilson to Lansing, August 4, 1915, *Papers of Woodrow Wilson,* 34:78–79.

73. Wilson instructions to the U.S. Navy, August 7, 1915, *Papers of Woodrow Wilson,* 34:122.

74. Wilson to Edith Bolling Galt, August 15, 1915, and Lansing to Wilson, August 13, 1915, *Papers of Woodrow Wilson,* 34:208–209, 183–184.

75. The September 1915 treaty (*FRUS* 1915, 449–451) was to remain in effect for ten years, but in 1917 was extended to 1936. A second agreement, reached on August 24, 1918, allowed the U.S. legation to review any proposed legislation by the Haitian legislature. The Marine's comment: U.S. Congress, Senate, Select Committee on Haiti and Santo Domingo, *Inquiry into Occupation and Administration of Haiti and Santo Domingo,* 2 vols. 67th Cong., 1st and 2nd Sessions, 1922, 1:518.

76. Robert Lansing to Rear Admiral James H. Oliver, Governor of the Virgin Islands, February 11, 1918, Chronological File, 1911–1928, box 34, Robert Lansing Papers, LC.

77. John Russell, "Memorandum concerning the Replacing of the Present Occupation of Haiti by a Legation Guard," March 21, 1919, 838.105/122, RG 59, NA. On

the behavior based upon these views, see Arthur C. Millspaugh, *Haiti under American Control, 1915–1930* (Boston: World Peace Foundation, 1931); and Paul H. Douglas, *Occupied Haiti* (New York: Garland, 1972).

78. Smedley Butler to John A. McIlhenny, June 23, 1917, *Letters of a Leatherneck*, 194–195; Butler to Franklin Delano Roosevelt, December 28, 1917, Papers as Assistant Secretary of the Navy, Personal Correspondence, folder "Bu-By," FDRL; General Eli Cole, "Conditions in Haiti," May 17, 1917, in *Inquiry into Occupation and Administration of Haiti and Santo Domingo*, 2:1783; Butler to Parents, January 27, 1918, in *Letters of a Leatherneck*, 199–200. A later Marine Commander, John Russell, wrote that "it may be taken as axiomatic that all Haitiens [*sic*] hate the Blanco." Russell, "Memorandum Concerning the Replacing of the Present Occupation of Haiti by a Legation Guard."

79. June 6, 1912, *FRUS* 1912, 256.

80. The correspondence between Washington and Havana: *FRUS* 1919, 1–3, 5, 8–9, 12, 28, 48.

81. Crowder to Secretary of State, August 30, 1919; Acting Secretary of State to Gonzales, October 23, 1919, *FRUS* 1919, 2174, 78.

82. Gonzales to Secretary of State, November 7, 1919, *FRUS* 1919, 2:80.

83. Boaz Long to Lansing, February 15, 1918, 711.13/55, RG 59, NA.

84. Boaz Long to Secretary of State, September 16, 1920, *FRUS* 1920, 2:21–22.

85. The value of Cuba's 1921 sugar crop was only 27 percent of its 1920 crop. Ramiro Guerra y Sánchez, *La industria azucarera de Cuba* (Havana: Cultural, 1940), 26. Eighteen banks, including the Banco Nacional de Cuba, with 121 branches, are listed as failing in República de Cuba, Comisión Temporal de Liquidación Bancaria, *Compendio de los trabajos realizados desde 17 de febrero de 1921, hasta 4 de agosto de 1924* (Havana: Editorial Hermes, 1924), appendix E, 119.

86. Nathaniel Davis, Acting Secretary of State, to Amlegation Havana, January 4, 1921, 837.00/1949, RG 59, NA. (*FRUS* 1921, 1:671–672 is a paraphrase.)

87. Robert E. Quirk, *An Affair of Honor: Woodrow Wilson and the Occupation of Veracruz* (Lexington: University of Kentucky Press, 1962), 2–3; Robert Lansing, *War Memoirs of Robert Lansing, Secretary of State* (Indianapolis: Bobbs-Merrill, 935), 308–309; Henry Stimson Diary, September 15, 1930, Yale University. (Available on microfilm.)

88. Butler to Thomas S. Butler, May 16, 1917, *Letters of a Leatherneck*, 193.

4. LATIN AMERICAN OPPOSITION AND THE RETREAT FROM PROTECTORATES

1. *New York Times*, August 19, 1920, 11; Frank Freidel, *Franklin D. Roosevelt* (Boston: Little, Brown, 1952–1956), 2:81–83 and 285n34; *Congressional Record*, June 19, 1922, 8943.

2. *New York Times*, August 29, 1920, 12, and September 18, 1920, 14.

3. Edward Gibbon, *History of the Decline and Fall of the Roman Empire,* pt. 6, chap. 49: "Conquest of Italy by the Franks." For a study of the late Progressive era from the perspective of the early 1920s, see Scott Nearing and Joseph Freeman, *Dollar Diplomacy: A Study of American Imperialism* (New York: B. W. Heubsch, 1925); William Edwin Diez, "Opposition in the United States to American Diplomacy in the Caribbean, 1898–1932" (PhD diss., University of Chicago, 1946); Laurence Marc Hauptman, "To the Good Neighbor: A Study of the Senate's Role in American Foreign Policy" (PhD diss., New York University, 1971), iv–v, 153; Ellen D. Tillman, *Dollar Diplomacy by Force: Nation-Building and Resistance in the Dominican Republic* (Chapel Hill: University of North Carolina Press, 2016), chaps. 5 and 6.

4. White to Hughes, November 21, 1922, enclosing Munro memorandum, "The Nicaraguan Situation," November 14, 1922, 817.00/2927, RG 59, NA.

5. Richard Olney to Secretary of State Thomas Bayard, July 20, 1895, *FRUS* 1895, 1:542–546.

6. *The Autobiographical Notes of Charles Evans Hughes* (Cambridge, MA: Harvard University Press, 1973), 269.

7. Lansing to Wilson, June 21, 1916, 812.00/18533a, RG 59, NA; Welles to Francis White, October 30, 1920, ser. 7, box 4, Francis White Papers, Johns Hopkins University; Sumner Welles, *Naboth's Vineyard: The Dominican Republic, 1844–1924* (New York: Payson and Clarke, 1928), 917.

8. "Greaser": Comment by the caretaker of Fletcher's Pennsylvania mansion: Glen L. Cump, "Henry P. Fletcher," undated at http://www.greencastlemuseum.org (January 12, 2017); Olivia Mae Frederick, "Henry P. Fletcher and United States–Latin American Policy, 1910–1930" (PhD diss., University of Kentucky, 1977), 110.

9. Dana G. Munro, untitled lectures notes, Lectures to the Foreign Service School, Department of State, May 7, 8, and 11, 1925, entry 623, RG 59, NA. For the young Munro, see his charming memoir, "A Student in Central America, 1914–1916," Publication 51, Middle American Research Institute, Tulane University, 1983.

10. Dana G. Munro, *The United States and the Caribbean Republics, 1921–1933* (Princeton: Princeton University Press, 1974), viii, 9, 12–13, 371–373. This 1974 volume tracks reliably with Munro's memos from the early 1920s.

11. Considering inflation, that $4,200 would be $101,000 in 2017, when an entry-level Foreign Service officer with White's qualifications would have been an FS-6, step 5, earning $44,969. For White's overseas postings, see 123 W 585, RG 59, NA.

12. Francis White to Undersecretary Joseph Grew, "Our Central American Policy," November 7, 1924, 711.13/65, RG 59, NA; Edward Charles Mishler, "Francis White and the Shaping of United States Latin American Policy, 1912–1933" (PhD diss., University of Maryland, 1975).

13. Samuel McRoberts, "The Extension of American Banking in Foreign Countries," *Annals of the American Academy of Political and Social Science* 36 (November 1910): 27–28; *Address by Elihu Root before the Trans-Mississippi Commercial*

Congress, Kansas City, Missouri, Tuesday, November 20th, 1906 (Washington, DC: C. F. Sudwarth, 1906), 15; *Crowded Years: The Reminiscences of William G. McAdoo* (Boston: Houghton Mifflin, 1931), 351–352.

14. Faramarz Damanpour, *The Evolution of Foreign Banking Institutions in the United States* (New York: Quorum Books, 1990), 12–13; Clyde William Phelps, *The Foreign Expansion of American Banks: American Branch Banking Abroad* (New York: Ronald Press, 1927), 85; Robert Mayer, "The Origins of the American Banking Empire in Latin America," *Journal of Inter-American Studies and World Affairs* 15 (February 1973): 61–62.

15. McAdoo, *Crowded Years,* 353; U.S. Congress, Senate, *Latin American Trade: Report of the Latin-American Trade Committee,* 63rd Cong., 3rd Sess., S. Doc. 714, January 19, 1915; John Bassett Moore, "The Pan-American Financial Conferences and the Inter-American High Commission," *American Journal of International Law* 14 (1920): 343–355.

16. Frank A. Vanderlip, *From Farm Boy to Financier* (New York: Appleton-Century, 1935), 260; McAdoo, *Crowded Years,* 351. On the Argentine loan: Paul Philip Abrahams, "The Foreign Expansion of American Finance and Its Relationship to the Foreign Economic Policies of the United States, 1907–1921" (PhD diss., University of Wisconsin, 1967), 32–33n. On similar opportunities in Chile: Fletcher to Secretary of State, August 11, 1914, 825.51/68, RG 59, NA; Ralph A. Young, *Handbook on American Underwriting of Foreign Securities,* Trade Promotion Series no. 104 (Washington, DC: U.S. Department of Commerce, Bureau of Foreign and Domestic Commerce, July 1930), 29–30.

17. "Although London remained, overall, the dominant global financial center during the 1920s, New York banks became the largest source of new funding." Emily S. Rosenberg, *Financial Missionaries to the World: The Politics and Culture of Dollar Diplomacy, 1900–1930* (Cambridge, MA: Harvard University Press, 1999), 97, 149; Burton I. Kaufman, "United States Trade and Latin America: The Wilson Years," *Journal of American History* 58 (September 1971): 342–363.

18. Norman Davis to Secretary of the Navy Edwin Denby, February 7, 1921, 837.00/1999A; Josephus Daniels to Department of State, February 9, 1921, 837.00/1999, and Davis to Amlegation Habana, February 14, 1921, 837.00/1999, all RG 59, NA.

19. Written as above, with both a capital N and an underscored *National.* Crowder to Pershing, January 30, 1923, 210.681, General Correspondence, 1917–1925, RG 407 (Records of the Office of the Adjutant General), NA.

20. Francis White, "Cuba, Panama, and South America," Lectures to the Foreign Service School, Department of State, May 13, 14, 16, and 18, 1925, entry 623, RG 59, NA.

21. Consul Clement Edwards to Acting Secretary of State, March 23, 1919, *FRUS* 1919, 2:99; Deputy General Receiver of Customs (1913–1920) John T. Vance Jr., "A Good Word for Santo Domingo," *Current History* 16 (August 1, 1922): 852; Francis

White, "Data compiled for lectures delivered by Mr. White before the Foreign Service class on May 13, 14, 15, 16, and 18, 1925, concerning certain Latin American Countries and related subjects," ser. 8, box 29, Francis White Papers, Johns Hopkins University. The number of Marines would remain above two thousand until early 1924.

22. The Navy later changed the *Guardia's* name to the *Policía Nacional Dominicana*. Military Government of Santo Domingo, *Santo Domingo: Its Past and Its Present Conditions* (Santo Domingo City, DR: Military Government of Santo Domingo, January 1, 1920), 53; *Marine Corps Gazette* 3 (September 1918): 196–197; Stephen M. Fuller and Graham A. Cosmas, *Marines in the Dominican Republic, 1916–1924* (Washington, DC: History and Museums Division, U.S. Marine Corps, 1924), 46.

23. Major Charles F. Williams, "La Guardia Nacional Dominicana," *Marine Corps Gazette* 3 (September 1918): 197–198; Military Government of Santo Domingo, *Santo Domingo,* 6.

24. Snowden to Josephus Daniels, April 17, 1919; see also Consul and Acting Chargé to Secretary of State, May 3, 1919, and Minister William W. Russell to Secretary of State, June 3, 1919, both *FRUS* 1919, 2:100, 103, 105, 118.

25. Military Government of Santo Domingo, *Santo Domingo,* 6, 54. This quotation blends two separate comments but is an accurate statement of Snowden's report. Fuller and Cosmas, *Marines in the Dominican Republic,* 53. See also Vernon T. Veggeberg, Major, U.S. Marine Corps, "A Comprehensive Approach to Counterinsurgency: The U.S. Military Occupation of the Dominican Republic, 1916–1924" (MA thesis, U.S. Marine Corps Command and Staff College, 2008).

26. *Annual Reports of the Navy Department for the Fiscal Year 1920* (Washington, DC: GPO, 1921), 342. On this period, see chap. 8 of Bruce Calder's superb *The Impact of Intervention: The Dominican Republic during the U.S. Occupation of 1916–1924* (Austin: University of Texas Press, 1984).

27. J. H. Edwards to Acting Secretary of State, March 23, 1919, *FRUS* 1919, 2:98.

28. Joseph Grew (Secretary General of the Commission to Establish Peace) to the Acting Secretary of State, April 25, 1919, *FRUS* 1919, 2:106–107, and 107–118 for Henríquez's memo.

29. *FRUS* 1919, 2:128–138.

30. Paris: April 25, 1919; Washington: September 13, 1919; both *FRUS* 1919, 2:106, 133.

31. The back-and-forth memoranda, August 8 to December 2, 1919, are reprinted in *FRUS* 1919, 2:120–144; Carl Kelsey, untitled report on Haiti and the Dominican Republic, *Annals of the American Academy of Political and Social Science* 100 (March 1922): 110–202.

32. The Junta was created in November 1919 and disbanded in January 1920. The Unión Nacional was created in March 1920.

33. Fiallo was arrested in July 1920, sentenced to three years in prison, and released in October. Secretary of State Colby to Secretary of the Navy Daniels, Sep-

tember 10, 1920, *FRUS* 1920, 2:167; Welles to Colby, October 22, 1920, sent to the President November 13, 1920, *Papers of Woodrow Wilson,* 69 vols. (Princeton: Princeton University Press, 1966–1994), 66:360. On Welles's drafting, see Colby to Wilson, November 27, 1920, 66:428. Benjamin Welles, *Sumner Welles: FDR's Global Strategist* (New York: St. Martin's Press, 1997), 65; Sumner Welles, "In Memoriam: Dr. Leo S. Rowe," *The Americas* 3 (January 1947): 365. For coverage of the episode, see *Annual Reports of the Navy Department for the Fiscal Year 1920,* 318; Executive Order 572, December 9, 1920, *FRUS* 1920, 2:169–170. Melvin M. Knight, *The Americans in Santo Domingo* (New York: Vanguard, 1928), 111–116.

34. Fabio Fiallo, "The Evacuation of Santo Domingo," *Current History* 14 (May 1921): 291–294; see also Francisco Henríquez y Carvajal, "American Rule in Santo Domingo," *Current History* 13 (March 1921): 395–399; Philip Douglass, "Americanizing Santo Domingo," *The Nation,* May 4, 1921, 663–664; Joseph Robert Juárez, "United States Withdrawal from Santo Domingo," *Hispanic American Historical Review* 42 (May 1962): 166. Fiallo later authored *The Crime of Wilson in Santo Domingo* (Havana: Arellano, 1940).

35. Woodrow Wilson to William Gibbs McAdoo, November 20, 1920, and McAdoo to Edith Bolling Galt Wilson, November 17, 1920, *Papers of Woodrow Wilson,* 66:408–409, 383–384; *FRUS* 1920, 2:136–137.

36. Colby to Daniels, November 27, 1920, *FRUS* 1920, 2:136, 138; Daniel M. Smith, "Bainbridge Colby and the Good Neighbor Policy, 1920–21," *Mississippi Valley Historical Review* 50 (June 1963): 63–65.

37. Kelsey, untitled report in *Annals of the American Academy of Political and Social Science* 100 (March 1922): 178; Snowden in his January 2, 1921, quarterly report, *FRUS* 1920, 2:155; *New York Times,* December 27, 1920, 12, and December 28, 1920, 27. Most of the financial reports during the U.S. protectorate are found in the Records of the Dominican Customs Receivership, 1904–1941, RG 139, NA.

38. Crowder, "Memorandum for Secretary [*sic*—Undersecretary Norman] Davis," July 27, 1920, 839.00/2223, RG 59, NA. Davis asked Welles to reply: Welles to Crowder, July 28, 1920, 839.00/2222, RG 59, NA. The numbering (2223 before 2222) is probably a clerical error. Ferdinand Mayer to Hughes, July 30, 1921, 839.00/2451, RG 59, NA.

39. Welles, *Naboth's Vineyard,* 906. Under pressure from Dominican leaders, the Harding Plan was revised repeatedly in 1921 and early 1922; the new administration's first plan was announced on June 14, 1921: *FRUS* 1921, 1:835–837. Welles had resigned from the Diplomatic Service in March 1922, only to be called back in late May to negotiate with Dominican leaders.

40. Calder, *The Impact of Intervention,* 248; Lieutenant Edward A. Fellowes, "Training Native Troops in Santo Domingo," *Marine Corps Gazette* 8 (December 1923): 231–232.

41. U.S. Minister to Secretary of State, May 19, 1930, *FRUS* 1930, 2:723; Henry Stimson diary, October 13, 1930.

42. Munro, *The United States and the Caribbean Republics,* 300.

43. *Autobiographical Notes of Charles Evans Hughes,* 199–201; "Observations on the Monroe Doctrine," address to the American Bar Association, Minneapolis, August 30, 1923, *American Journal of International Law* 17 (1923): 626; "The Centenary of the Monroe Doctrine," *Annals of the American Academy of Political and Social Science* III suppl. (January 1924): 6. For a judicious treatment of Harding's under-appreciated contributions, see Kenneth J. Grieb, *The Latin American Policy of Warren G. Harding* (Fort Worth: Texas Christian University Press, 1976); George Navarrete, "The Latin American Policy of Charles Evans Hughes, 1921–1925" (PhD diss., University of California, Berkeley, 1965). In addition to the actions discussed in this chapter, lower-level officials stitched together a patchwork of diplomatic successes, most of them short-lived, such as the 1923 Bucareli agreement with Mexico and the 1922–1923 Washington accord on Central America.

44. Hugh R. Wilson, *Diplomat between Wars* (New York: Longmans, Green, 1941), 174–175. Wilson was chief of State's Division of Current Information—its press officer.

45. Joseph Grew diary, in Joseph C. Grew, *Turbulent Era: A Diplomatic Record of Forty Years, 1904–1945* (London: Hammond, Hammond and Co, 1953), 668, 704; Ethan L. Ellis, "Frank B. Kellogg," in *An Uncertain Tradition: American Secretaries of State in the Twentieth Century,* ed. Norman A. Graebner (New York: McGraw-Hill, 1961), 149.

46. Knox to Nicaraguan Chargé, December 1, 1909, Records of the Division of Current Information, Confidential Publications, Information Series A, vol. 1, no. 6, RG 59, NA; Francis Mairs Huntington Wilson to Whitelaw Reid, July 1, 1910, 817.00/1147, RG 59, NA; *Congressional Record,* June 19, 1922, 8941. At the time there were 1,698 U.S. troops in Haiti.

47. Caperton testimony, May 19, 1920, U.S. Congress, Senate, Committee on Foreign Relations, *Investigation of Mexican Affairs,* 2 vols., S. Doc. 285, 66th Cong., 2nd Sess., 1920, 3215–3216.

48. White to Hughes, November 21, 1922, enclosing Munro memorandum, "The Nicaraguan Situation," November 14, 1922, 817.00/2927, and Munro to Fletcher, "Nicaraguan Situation," April 22, 1922, 817.00/2855, both RG 59, NA. For Nicaragua, Division Chief Francis White relied heavily on Munro and, later, Stokely Morgan.

49. Bryce Wood, *The Making of the Good Neighbor Policy* (New York: Columbia University Press, 1961), 32.

50. Hughes to U.S. Minister Morales, June 30, 1923, *FRUS* 1923, 2:32–434; U.S. Department of State, *Conference on Central American Affairs, Washington, December 4, 1922—February 7, 1923* (Washington, DC: GPO, 1923), 287.

51. William Kamman, *A Search for Stability: United States Diplomacy toward Nicaragua, 1925–1933* (Notre Dame, IN: University of Notre Dame Press, 1968), 5; U.S. Congress, Senate, Committee on Foreign Relations, *Foreign Loans,* 69th Cong.,

2nd Sess., 1927, 7; Charles E. Chapman, "An American Experiment in Nicaragua," *American Review of Reviews* 66 (October 1922): 405–410.

52. Acting Secretary of State to Minister in Nicaragua, December 15, 1920, *FRUS* 1920, 3:309.

53. Secretary of State to Minister John Ramer, January 18, 1923, and Ramer to Secretary of State, March 17, 1923, both *FRUS* 1923, 2:605.

54. Memorandum by the Secretary of State of a Conversation with the Nicaraguan Minister (Chamorro), September 28, 1923, *FRUS* 1923, 2:606–607.

55. On Dodds: *FRUS* 1923, 2:612–613; Hughes to Thurston, July 16, 1924, *FRUS* 1924, 2:491–492; Hughes to Ramer, February 15, 1924, *FRUS* 1924, 2:488. On Ramer ("totally unqualified for diplomacy"), see Munro, *The United States and the Caribbean Republics*, 161, 171.

56. Thurston to Secretary of State, October 28, 1924, 817.00/3196, RG 59, NA.

57. "Astonishing": Thurston to Hughes, November 5, 1924, 817.00/3222, 22, RG 59, NA; the San Juan vote: Thurston to Secretary of State, November 7, 1924, *FRUS* 1924, 2:503; Greer, "State Department Policy in Regard to the Nicaraguan Election of 1924," 460, 461.

58. Thurston to Hughes, November 5, 1924, 817.00/3222; and Francis White to Secretary of State, January 10, 1925, and Hughes to Thurston, January 16, 1925, both appended to 817.00/3222, all RG 59, NA.

59. Francis White to Secretary of State, December 3, 1924, 817.00/3222, RG 59, NA; Hughes to Thurston, December 10, 1924, *FRUS* 1924, 2:503–504.

60. White to Hughes, December 6, 1924, 817.00/3222, RG 59, NA; Hughes to Thurston, December 10, 1924, *FRUS* 1924, 2:504; Thurston to Hughes, December 12, 1924, *FRUS* 1924, 2:505–506, which reprints Solórzano's letter; Richard Millett, *Guardians of the Dynasty* (Maryknoll, NY: Orbis, 1977), chap. 2.

61. Eberhardt to Secretary of State, August 29, 1925, *FRUS* 1925, 636. On Chamorro's insistence that Colonel Alfredo Rivas acted without his approval, see his "Autobiografía (Continuación)," *Revista Conservadora del Pensamiento Centroamericano* 2 (August 1961): 145.

62. Eberhardt to Secretary of State, September 21, 1925, *FRUS* 1925, 2:638.

63. Eberhardt to Secretary of State, October 26, 1925, *FRUS*, 2:639–640; "Brief on the Validity of Decree Law of March 21, 1928," in *Report of the Chairman, American Electoral Mission in Nicaragua*, 1928, 2nd sec., box 79, Frank Ross McCoy Papers, LC; summary of Thurston report by Munro to White, December 3, 1924, attached to Thurston to Hughes, November 5, 1924, both 817.00/3222, RG 59, NA.

64. Refusal to recognize: Kellogg to Minister Salvador Castrillo, January 22, 1926, 817.00/3416, in U.S. Department of State, *The United States and Nicaragua*, 58; refusal to support Sacasa: Kellogg to Eberhardt, December 9 and 21, 1925, *FRUS* 1925, 2:642–645. Memoranda of Conversations, March 2 and 16, 1926, 817.00/3490 and 817.00/3506, both RG 59, NA.

65. Stokely Morgan to Hugh Wilson, "Activities of Adolfo Díaz during the Chamorro Regime," February 5, 1927, 817.00/4847, RG 59, NA; Chamorro, "Autobiografía," 146; Eberhardt to Secretary of State, December 24, 1925, *FRUS* 1925, 2:646. Henry Stimson diary, May 3, 1927, and Henry L. Stimson, *American Policy in Nicaragua* (New York: Charles Scribner's Sons, 1927), 65.

66. Díaz to U.S. Chargé, November 15, 1926, 817.00/4197, RG 59, NA; Douglas H. Allen to Secretary of State, January 2, 1927, 817.00/4336, RG 59, NA.

67. Francis White to Assistant Secretary of State John Cabot, August 12, 1953, ser. 2, box 11; and White to Secretary Dulles, August 14, 1953, ser. 7, box 2, Francis White Papers, Johns Hopkins University. Richard V. Salisbury, "Mexico, the United States, and the 1926–1927 Nicaraguan Crisis," *Hispanic American Historical Review* 66 (May 1986): 319.

68. Coolidge to Congress, *Congressional Record,* January 10, 1927, 1324–1336, quotations at 1326; *Congressional Record,* January 8, 1927, 1275; Raymond Leslie Buell, "The Protection of Foreign Lives and Property in Disturbed Areas," *Annals of the American Academy of Political and Social Science* 144 (July 1929): 85–96.

69. The 1927 estimate: Joseph Grew to Leo L. Rockwell, April 5, 1927, 817.00/4675, RG 59, NA; a 1928 estimate: U.S. Department of State, *A Brief History of the Relations between the United States and Nicaragua,* 2. On overall investments in Latin America, see Francis White to Sumner Welles, July 24, 1929, Francis White Papers, ser. 7, box 4, Johns Hopkins University.

70. Benjamin C. Warnick to Juan B. Sacasa, December 22, 1926, entry 164, RG 84, NA. A list of U.S. companies requesting protection in Nicaragua in 1926: Department of State, *A Brief History,* 65–70.

71. In this particular case "the people of the Bragmans Bluff Lumber Company have pretty nearly stampeded the Navy and everybody else." Henry Stimson diary, April 15, 1931.

72. Precisely $1,991,156.90. Roscoe R. Hill, *Fiscal Intervention in Nicaragua* (New York: Paul Maisel, 1933), 61.

73. Dwight W. Morrow, "Who Buys Foreign Bonds?" *Foreign Affairs,* January 1927, 232.

74. Hallgarten and Co. to Secretary of State, July 18, 1916, and William Phillips to Messrs. Hallgarten and Company, July 24, 1916, both 825.51/85, RG 59, NA; Department of State press release, March 3, 1922, *FRUS* 1922, 1:557–558. Benjamin Strong, President, Federal Reserve Bank of New York, to Secretary of State Charles Evans Hughes, June 9, 1922; and Strong to Secretary Hughes, undated but before April 20, 1922, Herbert Hoover Papers, Secretary of Commerce Files, folder "Foreign Loans, Miscellaneous, 1922," HHL.

75. Rosenberg, *Financial Missionaries to the World.*

76. Morrow, "Who Buys Foreign Bonds?" 231; Lamont to James E. Sabine of Utah, January 9, 1928, call number "bMS Am 1323 (2174)," Oswald Garrison Villard

Papers, Houghton Library, Harvard University. On the evolution of this line of thinking beginning in the nineteenth century, see Morton J. Horwitz, "The History of the Public/Private Distinction," *University of Pennsylvania Law Review* 130 (June 1982): 1423–1428.

77. Laurence Duggan for the Secretary of State, "Copy of Typical Reply to Bond-holders of Defaulted Foreign Securities," February 21, 1936, *FRUS* 1936, 5:149–150.

78. H. W. Dodds, "The United States and Nicaragua," *Annals of the American Academy of Political and Social Sciences* 132 (July 1927): 141.

79. U.S. Congress, House, *Conditions in Nicaragua. Message from the President of the United States, 10 January 1927,* H. Doc. 663, 69th Cong., 2nd Sess., 1927.

80. The *Petroleum Law of 18 December 1925* enforced and extended the presidential decrees implementing Article 27, which required President Calles to cancel the 1923 Bucareli agreements (see below). The *Alien Land Law of 23 December 1925* specified the details of Mexico's land reform, which basically outlawed foreign ownership.

81. The report: U.S. Congress, Senate, *Inquiry into Occupation and Administration of Haiti and Santo Domingo,* 67th Cong., 1st and 2nd Sessions, 1922; Borah: Speech at Carnegie Hall, May 1, 1922, reported in the *New York Times,* May 2, 1922, 2; the Senate: *Congressional Record,* June 19, 1922, 8974.

82. See, for example, *The Seminar in Mexico, a Co-operative Study of Mexican Life and Culture: Fourth Annual Session, Mexico City, July 13–August 3, 1929* (New York: Committee on Cultural Relations with Latin America, 1929).

83. On the question of not caring which party held power: Henry Stimson diary, April 7, 1927. Robert E. Olds, "Confidential memorandum on the Nicaraguan Situation," undated but noted "approximate date January, 1927," 817.00/5854, RG 59, NA.

84. On the Bucareli agreements see Rafael Trujillo Herrera, *Adolfo de la Huerta y los tratados de Bucareli* (México, D.F.: Librería de Manuel Porrúa, 1966); Asdrúbal Flores, *Protocolo secreto de los tratados de Bucareli* (México, D.F.: Galileo Ediciones, 2003); for the negotiations see *FRUS* 1923, 2:522–567.

85. Henry White to Knox, October 22, 1910, 710.11/46, RG 59, NA; Salisbury, "Mexico, the United States, and the 1926–1927 Nicaraguan Case," 322, 324.

86. Stokely Morgan, "Memorandum: Mexican Activities in Central America," December 2, 1926, 817.00/4170, RG 59 NA; Jurgen Buchenau, *In the Shadow of the Giant: the Making of Mexico's Central America Policy, 1898–1930* (Tuscaloosa: University of Alabama Press, 1996).

87. "Memorandum: The Nicaraguan Problem," December 1, 1926, 817.00/4167, 7, 11, 16, RG 59, NA. Stokely Morgan, "Re.: Situation in Nicaragua," January 24, 1927, 817.00/4868, RG 59, NA.

88. The Olds quotation is from J. Bart Campbell, "Diplomat's Propaganda Attempt Exposed," *Editor and Publisher,* December 4, 1926, 5; Wilson, *Diplomat between Wars,* 182.

89. William S. Howell Jr., "Radical and Socialist Influences in Mexico," December 14, 1926, 812.00B/134, RG 59, NA, 9.

90. *New York Times,* January 9, 1927, reprinted in *Congressional Record,* January 10, 1927, 1326–1327.

91. *Congressional Record,* January 10, 1927, 1324–1326, and separately printed as H. Doc. 633, 69th Cong., 2nd Sess., 1927. See also Secretary Kellogg to Senate Foreign Relations Committee, January 12, 1927, 817.00/4844, RG 59, NA. *Excelsior,* January 12, 1927, unnumbered "Página Editorial."

92. "Memorandum for Use Before the Foreign Relations Committee," undated but early January 1927, 817.00/4852, RG 59, NA. The transcript of Kellogg's testimony, January 12, 1927, is 817.00/4844, RG 59, NA. The two staff memos that formed the basis for Kellogg's testimony were Stokely W. Morgan, "Memorandum on the Nicaraguan Problem," December 1, 1926, 817.00/4169, and Robert Olds, "Confidential Memorandum on the Nicaraguan Situation," undated January 1927, 817.00/5854, both RG 59, NA. "Bolshevist Aims and Policies in Mexico and Latin America" was also sent as a circular to U.S. diplomatic missions in Latin America, January 27, 1927, 812.00B/16a, RG 59, NA.

93. Stokely Morgan, "RE: Situation in Nicaragua," January 24, 1927, 817.00/4868, RG 59, NA.

94. William R. Castle Jr., diary entries for December 31, 1926, and January 25, 1927, Castle Papers, Houghton Library, Harvard University. See also Undersecretary Joseph Grew, *Turbulent Era,* 704; Ellis, *Frank B. Kellogg and American Foreign Relations,* 161, 257n27, and 268n46.

95. The arbitration resolution: *Congressional Record,* January 25, 1927, 2200, with the vote (70 to 0) at 2233.

96. Stanley Robert Ross, "Dwight Morrow and the Mexican Revolution," *Hispanic American Historical Review* 38 (November 1958): 506–528, which notes that Mexico was ready to settle the property dispute. On Morrow in Mexico, see ser. 10 (Ambassador to Mexico) of the Morrow Papers at Amherst College.

97. Stimson to Coolidge, May 4, 1927, 817.00/4753, RG 59, NA; *FRUS* 1927, 3:339–348; Undersecretary Joseph C. Grew to Leo L. Rockwell, April 5, 1927, 817.00/4675, RG 59, NA.

98. Henry L. Stimson, *American Policy in Nicaragua* (New York: Charles Scribner's Sons, 1927), 16, 18, 129.

99. Morgan, "RE: Situation in Nicaragua," January 24, 1927, 817.00/4868, RG 59, NA; Stimson (via Eberhardt) to Secretary of State, May 4, 1927, 817.00/4753, RG 59, NA; the number 5,673 is from Dana Munro, *The United States and the Caribbean Area* (Boston: World Peace Foundation, 1934), 263. Wood, *Making of the Good Neighbor Policy,* 26; Virginia L. Greer, "State Department Policy in Regard to the Nicaraguan Election of 1924," *Hispanic American Historical Review* 34 (November 1954): 445–467.

100. Carleton Beals, *Banana Gold* (Philadelphia: J. B. Lippincott, 1932), 294.

101. Kellogg to McCoy, March 3, 1928, 817.00 / 5444a, RG 59, NA.

102. *Congressional Record,* April 23, 1928, 6971–6974 (King), 6974 (Norris); *Congressional Record,* January 20, 1928, 1785–1790 (Dill); William E. Borah, "What the Monroe Doctrine Really Means," *Collier's,* January 31, 1925, 25; *Congressional Record,* January 13, 1927, 1555.

103. *Congressional Record,* February 22 and 23, 1929, 4047, 4119.

104. W. W. Cumberland to Secretary of State, March 10, 1928, 817.51 / 1921, RG 59, NA. See also *FRUS* 1927, 3:434–439; U.S. Department of State, *The United States and Nicaragua,* 53–54; "Brief on the Validity of Decree Law of March 21, 1928," *Report of the Chairman, American Electoral Mission in Nicaragua, 1928, Second Section,*" box 79, Frank Ross McCoy Papers, LC; Greer, *State Department Policy in Regard to the Nicaraguan Election of 1924,* 465.

105. Stimson diary, May 3, 1927.

106. White House press release, July 2, 1927, in U.S. Department of State, *A Brief History,* 59. General McCoy's uncommonly candid reports on the election process are in boxes 79 and 80 of the Frank Ross McCoy Papers, LC.

107. Henry L. Stimson, "Bases of American Foreign Policy during the Past Four Years," *Foreign Affairs,* April 1933, 395.

108. Francis White to Undersecretary Joseph Grew, "Our Central American Policy," November 7, 1924, 711.13 / 65, RG 59, NA; Francis White to Secretary Stimson, September 5, 1930, Name and Subject Files—Stimson, Henry L., 1929–1933, Francis White State Department Records, HHL.

5. PLEDGING TO BE A GOOD NEIGHBOR

1. Senator Charles Sumner: *Congressional Globe,* December 21, 1870, 231. Pierce: *Annual Message to Congress,* December 31, 1855, and *Inaugural Address,* March 4, 1853. Roy F. Nichols, *Franklin Pierce: Young Hickory of the Granite Hills* (Philadelphia: University of Pennsylvania Press, 1931), 533.

2. Coolidge, *Annual Message to Congress,* December 4, 1928. Hoover, *Annual Message to Congress,* December 3, 1929, and *Address at the Annual Dinner of the Chamber of Commerce of the United States,* May 1, 1930.

3. Hoover, *Annual Message to Congress,* December 3, 1929.

4. W. W. Cumberland to Secretary of State, March 10, 1928, 817.51 / 1921, RG 59, NA; Cumberland to Francis White, December 24, 1927, Francis White State Department Records, Name and Subject File, Cumberland, W. W., HHL.

5. W. W. Cumberland to Secretary of State, March 10, 1928, 817.51 / 1921, RG 59, NA; Eberhardt, "Note" in Document File, February 10, 1928, 817.51A / 19, RG 59, NA; Eberhardt to Secretary of State, April 17, 1928, 817.51A / 27, RG 59, NA; Munro to

White, December 3, 1927, ser. 7, box 3, Francis White Papers, Johns Hopkins University; R. L. Keiser, "The Resident American High Commissioner and the Nicaraguan Claims Commission," February 16, 1928, 817.51A/23, RG 59, NA; Mr. Keiser to Mr. Morgan and Mr. White, "Constitution of Offices of Collector General of Customs and High Commissioner in Nicaragua," June 20, 1927, 817.51A/16, RG 59, NA; Cumberland to Francis White, December 24, 1927, Francis White State Department Records, Name and Subject File, Cumberland, W. W., HHL.

6. C. E. Nelson to A. J. McConnies, December 10, 1926, entry 164, RG 84; "Written Statement of Doctor JNO. L. Marchand [sic]," December 18, 1926, entry 164, RG 84.

7. W. W. Cumberland to Secretary of State, March 10, 1928, 817.51/1921, RG 59, NA; McCoy, "American Electoral Mission to Nicaragua. Summary of Events and Policy from Stimson Agreements to date. Revised to Sept. 1, 1928," box 79, Frank Ross McCoy Papers, LC.

8. Stimson to President Moncada, November 6 and 24, 1930, and Moncada to Stimson, November 7, 1930, FRUS 1930, 3:675–684; "Statement of Policy toward Nicaragua," February 5, 1931, FRUS 1931, 2:841–844.

9. The February 12, 1929, message requesting Captain Johnson's appointment is reprinted in U.S. Department of State, The United States and Nicaragua: A Survey of the Relations from 1909 to 1932 (Washington, DC: GPO, 1932), 115. Hanna to Secretary of State, August 15, 1930, and Chair of American Electoral Mission to Secretary of State, November 21, 1930, both FRUS 1930, 3:648–656.

10. Curtis to Cotton, February 26, 1930, FRUS 1930, 2:703–704.

11. Department of State, The United States and Nicaragua, 115–119. A lower number (182 chairs of electoral boards) is in FRUS 1933, 5:849; "Report of the Chairman, U.S. Electoral Mission to Nicaragua, 1932," undated but late 1932/early 1933, 817.00–Woodward Electoral Mission/231, RG 59, NA.

12. The Commission's report contains a selection of improvements—for example, "a Public Health and Sanitary Service, which is a model of devotion and efficiency, has been organized and maintained." FRUS 1930, 3:223–224.

13. U.S. Department of State, Report of the United States Commission on Education in Haiti, Latin American Series No. 5, 1931; Emily Greene Balch, ed., Occupied Haiti (New York: Writers Publishing Co., 1927), 125.

14. Munro's instructions, October 18, 1930, FRUS 1930, 3:255.

15. Stimson diary, November 1, 1930, microfilmed out of chronological order on reel 2.

16. Hoover, Annual Message to Congress, December 2, 1930, FRUS 1930, 1:xviii; the "Haitianization Agreement," August 5, 1931, FRUS 1931, 2:505–508. The quotation is from Munro's letter of December 24, 1958, to author Daniel B. Cooper and taken from Cooper's article, "The Withdrawal of the United States from Haiti, 1928–1934,"

Journal of Inter-American Studies 5 (January 1963): 101. Hans Schmidt, *The United States Occupation of Haiti, 1915–1934* (New Brunswick, NJ: Rutgers University Press, 1971), 232. A contemporary assessment is Raymond Leslie Buell, *The American Occupation of Haiti* (New York: Foreign Policy Association, 1931).

17. For a contrary assessment, see Alexander DeConde, *Herbert Hoover's Latin-American Policy* (Stanford: Stanford University Press, 1951).

18. Henry L. Stimson, "Bases of American Foreign Policy during the Past Four Years," *Foreign Affairs,* April 1933, 383–396; Stimson diary, November 1, 1930; see also the entry for September 16, 1930.

19. Stimson diary, November 5, 1930, and May 17, 1932.

20. *Addresses Delivered during the Visit of Herbert Hoover, President-Elect of the United States, to Central and South America, November–December 1928* (Washington, DC: Pan American Union, 1929), 3–4; see also Anon., *President-Elect Herbert Hoover's Good Will Cruise to Central and South America: This Being a Log of the Trip Aboard the U.S.S. Maryland* (San Francisco: Knight-Counihan, 1929).

21. FDR's reminiscence was dictated at the request of Vice President Henry Wallace, who was to give a speech about the administration's policy. The reminiscence is attached to GGT [Grace Tully], "Memorandum for the President," May 13, 1942, President's Secretary's File, folder "H. Wallace," box 170, FDRL.

22. Franklin D. Roosevelt, "Our Foreign Policy: A Democratic View," *Foreign Affairs,* July 1928, 585; Norman H. Davis, "A Consistent Latin American Policy," *Foreign Affairs,* July 1931, 548, 558, 548. On Roosevelt's request to Davis, see FDR to Sumner Welles (who had informed FDR of an unfavorable speech by former secretary of state Stimson), February 23, 1931, in *F.D.R.: His Personal Letters, 1928–1945,* ed. Elliott Roosevelt (New York: Duell, Sloan and Pearce, 1947–1950), 1:177. Norman Davis had served briefly as President Wilson's undersecretary of state when FDR was assistant secretary of the Navy.

23. Henry White to Knox, October 22, 1910, 710.11/46, RG 59, NA.

24. Agreement was reached that "the Governing Board will elect its President and Vice President," and that a government without an ambassador to the United States could name a special representative to the Governing Board. U.S. Department of State, *Report of the Delegates of the United States of America to the Fifth International Conference of American States, Held in Santiago, Chile, March 25 to May 3, 1923* (Washington, DC: GPO, 1924), 2, 5, 8.

25. Mexico, a neutral, did not attend the Versailles conference, nor did Costa Rica, which had declared war but was not invited because the Wilson administration, one of the powers controlling the conference, refused to recognize the unelected Tinoco government. Also absent was the Dominican Republic, ruled by the U.S. Navy since 1916, with no government of its own, although former president Francisco Henríquez y Carvajal attended as an observer without U.S. approval.

26. Sumner Welles, "In Memoriam: Dr. Leo S. Rowe," *The Americas* 3 (January 1947): 363–367; "The Latin-American Belligerents at Versailles," May 8, 1919, Private Memoranda, 1915–1922, box 63, Robert Lansing Papers, LC.

27. Latin America's "Associated Nations" were the seven that had remained neutral: Argentina, Chile, Colombia, El Salvador, Mexico, Paraguay, and Venezuela. On the Versailles conference, see U.S. Congress, Senate, Committee on Foreign Relations, *Treaty of Peace with Germany,* 66th Cong., 1st Sess., 1919. See 276 for the voting on the Covenant and 309–312 for the committee assignments.

28. Alexis de Tocqueville, *Democracy in America,* ed. J. P. May and trans. George Lawrence (London: Fontana Press, 1994), 409.

29. *Congressional Globe,* May 5, 1848, 599, and February 2, 1859, 705. Davis seemed convinced Latin Americans would consider this an improvement: "With swelling hearts and suppressed impatience they await our coming, and with joyous shouts of 'Welcome! welcome!' will they receive us."

30. *Speeches, Messages, and Other Writings of the Hon. Albert G. Brown,* ed. M. W. Cluskey (Philadelphia: Jas. B. Smith, 1859), 324, 329, 594–595.

31. José María Torres Caicedo, "Las dos Américas," reprinted in *Religión, patria y amor: Colección de versos escritos por José M. Torres Caicedo* (Paris: T. Ducessois, 1863), 457. For the "first" claim, see Arturo Ardao, *Génisis de la idea y el nombre de América Latina* (Caracas: Centro de Estudios Latinoamericanos Rómulo Gallegos, 1980), 83.

32. "El triunfo de Calibán," 1898, author's translation from Carlos Jáuregui, *Revista Iberoamericana* 64 (July–December 1998): 451–455.

33. Both quotations are from later recollections, but they capture perfectly their memos from the early 1920s. Dana G. Munro, *The United States and the Caribbean Republics, 1921–1933* (Princeton: Princeton University Press, 1974), 12–13; Dana G. Munro, "Dollar Diplomacy in Nicaragua, 1909–1913," *Hispanic American Historical Review* 38 (May 1958): 233–234; Sumner Welles, *Naboth's Vineyard: The Dominican Republic, 1884–1924* (New York: Payson and Clarke, 1928), 928–929, 823.

34. *New York Times,* December 28, 1920, 27.

35. Coolidge, *Address at the Dinner of the United Press,* New York, April 25, 1927.

36. Instructions to the U.S. delegation to Havana, January 5, 1928, *FRUS* 1928, 5:534, 574–577, 582.

37. The official report of the U.S. delegation quotes Hughes as saying "see them killed." The *New York Times,* February 19, 1928, 2, reported the term "butchered," and Hughes's biographer argues convincingly that the former secretary of state said "butchered in the jungle." Compare *Report of the United States Delegates,* 14, with Merlo J. Pusey, *Charles Evans Hughes,* 2 vols. (New York: Macmillan, 1951–1952), 2:559–560.

38. Hoover, *Address to the Gridiron Club,* Washington, DC, April 13, 1929.

39. M. J. McDermott, "Memorandum of the Press Conference, Wednesday, April 15, 1931," 817.00 Bandit Activities, 1931/55, RG 59, NA.

40. Henry L. Stimson, "Bases of American Foreign Policy during the Past Four Years," *Foreign Affairs,* April 193, 395.

41. *Addresses and Statements of the Honorable Cordell Hull . . . in Connection with His Trip to South America, 1933–1934* (Washington, DC: GPO, 1935), 34–35, 37–38.

42. Roosevelt, *Address to the Woodrow Wilson Foundation,* December 28, 1933; Roosevelt, *State of the Union Address,* January 3, 1934; Roosevelt, *Address to the San Diego Exposition,* October 2, 1935.

43. Proposed by Mexico, the "Additional Protocol Relative to Non-Intervention" was signed on December 23, 1936 and ratified by the Senate on June 29, 1937 (51 Stat. 41). It was called "Additional" because it was added to the 1933 Montevideo agreement.

44. Memorandum, Thomas C. Mann to Charles S. Murphy, Special Counsel to the President, December 11, 1952, Subject File, President's Secretary's Files, folder "Latin America," HSTL; John Cabot, "Summary of Remarks at Conference on U.S. Foreign Policy, June 4 and 5, 1953," John Cabot Papers, reel 15.

45. Guggenheim to Secretary of State, May 28, 1930, 837.00/2808; also filed as "Boo Union Nacionalista—Gul. Carlos Mendieta 1930 Political," lindh RG 59, NA

46. Guggenheim to Secretary of State, January 25, 1932, Chargé to Secretary of State, May 25, 1932, Guggenheim to Secretary of State, July 25, 1932, and Chargé to Secretary of State, September 15 and 29 and October 7, 1932, all *FRUS* 1932, 5:535–559.

47. J. H. Knox to W. Irving Glover, July 2, 1932, and Stimson to Postmaster General, July 5, 1932, both 837.00/3454, RG 59, NA.

48. Guggenheim to Secretary of State, March 22, 1932, and Stimson to Guggenheim, March 26, 1932, both *FRUS* 1932, 5:542, 545–547.

49. Charles W. Taussig, "Memorandum to Secretary Hull," March 14, 1933. *Documentary Record of Franklin D. Roosevelt Presidency* (Bethesda: University Publications of America, 2001), vol. 19, doc. 3, p. 6.

50. In 1937 Welles was promoted to undersecretary of state.

51. Ellis O. Briggs, *Proud Servant: The Memoirs of a Career Ambassador* (Kent, OH: Kent State University Press, 1998), 118–125; Undersecretary William Phillips, *Ventures in Diplomacy* (Boston: Beacon Press, 1952), 87; Grace Tully, *F. D. R. My Boss* (New York: Charles Scribner's Sons, 1949), 176; Dean Acheson, *Present at the Creation: My Years in the State Department* (New York: Norton, 1969), 12; Harold L. Ickes, *The Secret Diary of Harold L. Ickes* (New York: Simon and Schuster, 1954), 351.

52. Coolidge's handwritten note is at the top of Acting Secretary of State Joseph Grew to President Coolidge, July 6, 1925, ser. 1, file 20, microfilm reel 27, Calvin Coolidge Papers, LC, and also in Welles's personnel file: 123 W 451/75b, RG 59, NA. See also Benjamin Welles, *Sumner Welles: FDR's Global Strategist* (New York: St. Martin's Press, 1997), 114. The outside observer: Samuel Guy Inman, "The Rise and Fall of the Good Neighbor Policy," Margaret I. King Library Occasional Contributions No. 3, University of Kentucky, 1949, 3.

53. On Welles's role in FDR's 1932 presidential campaign, see Welles, *Sumner Welles,* chap. 13.

54. Sumner Welles and others, *Laurence Duggan, 1905–1948: In Memoriam* (Stamford, CT: Overbrook Press, 1948), ix; Briggs, *Proud Servant,* 124–125, 133, 404.

55. Founded in 1919, the Institute continues today to focus on educational exchanges, particularly as a contracted administrator of the U.S. government's Fulbright program.

56. Laurence Duggan, *The Americas: The Search for Hemisphere Security* (New York: Henry Holt, 1949), 212, 207.

57. *FRUS* 1933, 5:279–286.

58. Memorandum of Conversation, Welles and Secretary of State Ferrara, May 12, 1933, Welles Papers, box 175, FDRL.

59. Welles to Acting Secretary of State, June 6 and August 4, *FRUS* 1933, 5:301, 332.

60. Welles to Secretary of State, July 1 and August 9, 1933, *FRUS* 1933, 5:317, 344; Machado to FDR, September 5, 1933, and FDR to Machado, September 26, 1933, both 837.00/4062, RG 59, NA. Machado was in Canada only briefly; he lived in Miami until his death in 1939.

61. Welles to Secretary of State, July 1, August 7, 9, 12, 19, and 24, 1933, and memo of telephone conversation, Welles and Secretary of State, September 5, and follow-up dispatches, all *FRUS* 1933, 5:317–384.

62. Telephone transcript, Welles and Secretary Hull, September 7, 1933, and Welles to Secretary of State, September 7, 1933, both *FRUS* 1933, 5:386, 397–398; Cordell Hull, *The Memoirs of Cordell Hull,* 2 vols. (New York: Macmillan, 1948), 1:313 and (quoting Welles) 315.

63. Hull to Welles, September 7, 1933, *FRUS* 1933, 5:402.

64. Welles to Hull, September 8, 1933, and Secretary of State to Certain Diplomatic and Consular Missions, September 11, 1933, both *FRUS* 1933, 5:406–407, 422.

65. Welles to Secretary of State, September 5 through October 5, 1933, *FRUS* 1933, 5:388–474. See also "Relations between the United States and Cuba: Address by the Honorable Sumner Welles, Assistant Secretary of State, before the Young Democratic Club of America, District of Columbia Division, Washington, March 29, 1934," Department of State Publication No. 577, 1934. Quite different assessments are offered by Jorge Renato Ibarra Guitart, *La mediación del 33: Ocaso del machadato* (Havana: Editorial Política, 1999); Luis E. Aguilar, *Cuba 1933* (Ithaca, NY: Cornell University Press, 1972).

66. Jules Benjamin, "The New Deal, Cuba, and the Rise of a Global Foreign Economic Policy," *Business History Review* 51 (Spring 1977): 75; especially useful is Jules R. Benjamin, *The United States and Cuba: Hegemony and Dependent Development, 1880–1934* (Pittsburgh: University of Pittsburgh Press, 1977).

67. Sumner Welles, *The Time for Decision* (New York: Harper and Brothers, 1944), 198.

68. "Completely allayed": Welles, *Time for Decision,* 200. Apology: Welles via Secretary of State, "For the President . . . ," September 25, 1933, *FRUS* 1933, 5:457–458. For evidence that Welles was sincere in his support of nonintervention, see his prein-augural suggestion to FDR, February 21(?), 1933, in *Franklin Roosevelt and Foreign Affairs* (Cambridge, MA: Harvard University Press, 1969), 1:18–19.

69. Duggan, *The Americas,* 75.

70. Chargé to Secretary of State, February 5, 1930, and Francis White to Chargé, February 20, 1930, *FRUS* 1930, 3:195–197. When President Jorge Ubico tried again in 1931, the State Department simply buried his message in a file cabinet. Sheldon White-house to Secretary of State, January 29, 1931, 814.00 / 1054, RG 59, NA.

71. Welles to Hanna, May 24, 1935, and Hanna to Welles, June 3, 1935, *FRUS* 1935, 4:630–632. The yes / no vote was to amend the Constitution to permit Ubico to re-main in office. Conducted by the Guatemalan army, the voting did not allow for a secret ballot. Hanna to Secretary of State, May 14, 1935, and Chargé to Secretary of State, June 25, 1935, both *FRUS* 1935, 4:629, 634. Ubico continued in office until over-thrown by his own military in 1944.

72. Lane to Secretary, February 22, 1934, *FRUS* 1934, 5:531.

73. Laurence Duggan (?) to E. C. Wilson, "Policy of the United States towards Nicaragua," November 16, 1931, 711.7 / 253, RG 59, NA. Bryce Wood (*The Making of the Good Neighbor Policy* [New York: Columbia University Press, 1961], 46) probably was correct to indicate that the memorandum's author was Laurence Duggan, but there is no indication of that on the document. At the time Duggan's supervisor was Division Chief Edwin Wilson. Lane's request and the authorization: Lane to Secre-tary of State, May 4, 1934, and Welles to Lane, May 21, 1934, both *FRUS* 1934, 5:554.

74. Memorandum of Conversation by Willard Beaulac, October 1, 1935, and Lane to Secretary of State, October 7 and 9, 1935, both *FRUS* 1935, 4:877–883. President Sacasa's side of this story is "Cómo y por qué caí del poder," *Revista del Pensamiento Centroamericano,* no. 161 (October–December 1978): 2–32. Good coverage of the Sacasa-Somoza contest can be found in Knut Walter, *The Regime of Anastasio So-moza, 1936–1956* (Chapel Hill: University of North Carolina Press, 1993), chap. 2.

75. Memorandum of Conversation by [Division Chief] Edwin Wilson of Meeting between Federico Sacasa and Sumner Welles, October 16, 1935, *FRUS* 1935, 4:884–885.

76. Boaz Long to Robert Lansing, February 15, 1918, 711.13 / 55, RG 59, NA.

77. Secretary of State to Long, March 28, 1936 (drafted by Welles), and May 8 and 9, 1936, both *FRUS* 1936, 5:817–821.

78. The request for instructions is Corrigan to Secretary of State, January 21, 1936, *FRUS* 1936, 5:126–127. The commitment to abide by the treaty was in the instructions from Secretary of State Hughes to the U.S. Minister to Honduras, Franklin Morales, June 30, 1923, *FRUS* 1923, 2:432–434, which included an instruction to publicize the commitment as broadly as possible. On Washington's full awareness of the brutality of Maximiliano Hernández Martínez, see *FRUS* 1932, 5:613–622. On the initial U.S.

policy toward his government, see Philip F. Dur, "U.S. Diplomacy and the Salvadorean Revolution of 1931," *Journal of Latin American Studies* 30 (February 1998): 95–119.

79. For Costa Rica's earlier withdrawal, see *FRUS* 1932, 5:330–349. Somoza's constitutional disqualification was that he had married a relative of President Sacasa. Willard Beaulac, "Recommendation by the Assistant Chief of the Division of Latin American Affairs," February 18, 1936, *FRUS* 1936, 5:136–148.

80. Secretary of State to Central American Legations, April 30, 1936, *FRUS* 1936, 5:135. Corrigan to Secretary of State, July 29, 1937, and Welles ("for the Secretary of State") to Corrigan, August 13, 1937, both in *FRUS* 1937, 5:524–525.

81. Wright to Secretary of State, November 2, 1938; no decimal file number appears on the document, but Bryce Wood (*Making of the Good Neighbor Policy*, 116) gives it as 837.00/8348. The document is reproduced on microfilm reel 49 of *Confidential U.S. Diplomatic Post Records, Central America, Cuba 1930–1945, Part I: 1930–1939* (Frederick, MD: University Publications of America, 1985).

82. J. Butler Wright to Secretary of State, November 2, 1938, 837.00/8348, RG 59, NA; Second Secretary Sidney E. O'Donoghue to Secretary of State, "Reception of Batista," November 26, 1938, *Confidential U.S. Diplomatic Post Records, Central America, Cuba 1930–1945, Part I: 1930–1939*, microfilm reel 50.

83. Welles to Roosevelt, December 7, 1942, 837.001/Batista, Fulgencio/80, RG 59, NA. In 1944 Welles (*The Time for Decision*, 197) would characterize Batista as an "extraordinarily brilliant and able figure."

84. Anon. to "Prudence," April 29, 1939, on White House letterhead, Official File 432, folder "Nicaragua, 1933–40," FDRL. Somoza had requested an invitation, Welles had sought FDR's approval, and FDR placed "Visit O.K." on Welles to Roosevelt, December 12, 1938, Official File, box 432, folder "Nicaragua 1933–1940," FDRL.

85. E. M. W., "Memorandum for [Press] Secretary [Stephen] Early, April 18, 1939, Official File 432, folder "Nicaragua, 1933–40," FDRL.

86. Norweb to Secretary of State, August 21, 1939, *FRUS* 1939, 5:587, 594.

87. Briggs, *Proud Servant*, 187.

88. R. V. [*sic*] Haya de la Torre, "Los Estados Unidos Deben Defender La Democracia," *El Mundo* (Havana), February 20, 1938, 17.

6. BREAKING NEW GROUND

1. *Annual Message to Congress*, December 6, 1932.

2. Section 2(a)(1) of the Charter of the Export-Import Bank of the United States, as amended by PL 112-122, May 30, 2012. The Bank was chartered on March 8, and the first loan was signed on March 28. Carlos Hevia and Manuel Márquez Sterling were presidents for the three days between Grau and Mendieta, January 15–18, 1934.

Ellis O. Briggs, *Proud Servant: The Memoirs of a Career Ambassador* (Kent, OH: Kent State University Press, 1998), 91.

3. Memorandum of Conversation, February 2, 1934, Sumner Welles Papers, box 195, folder "Cuba, Conversations, 1933–1934," FDRL.

4. The first "Export-Import Bank of Washington, D.C." had been created on February 2, 1934 (Executive Order 6581), to finance exports to the recently recognized Soviet Union, but it had made no loans by March 8, when "The Second Export-Import Bank of Washington, D.C." was created (Executive Order 6638) and immediately made the silver loan. This "second" bank was to focus on Cuba. Congress combined the two banks in 1936, and the 1945 Export-Import Bank Act made the bank what it is today, an independent agency of the federal government.

5. For the Eximbank's initial financing, see Gardner Patterson, "The Export-Import Bank," *Quarterly Journal of Economics* 58 (November 1943): 65–68. On the Bank's early capitalization, see Charles R. Whittlesey, "Five Years of the Export-Import Bank," *American Economic Review* (September 1939): 487–502. For well-researched coverage of the U.S.-Cuba economic relationship in the early Roosevelt administration, see Jules Benjamin, "The New Deal, Cuba, and the Rise of a Global Foreign Economic Policy," *Business History Review* 51 (Spring 1977): 57–88.

6. The Duggan quotation combines two dispatches, both Duggan to Welles, February 28 and March 7, 1935, box 29, Welles Papers, FDRL; the ambassador's report is Caffery to Hull, April 2, 1934, 837.00/4964, RG 59, NA. For a flavor of Batista's puppets, see H. Max Healey, "The Impeachment and Removal of Dr. M. M. Gomez, December 1936" (MA thesis, Indiana University, 1939); R. Hart Phillips, *Cuban Sideshow* (Havana: Cuban Press, 1935), 72–73.

7. Anon., "Export-Import Bank Loans to Latin America," *Foreign Policy Reports,* June 15, 1941, 88; Eleanor Lansing Dulles, "The Export-Import Bank of Washington: The First Ten Years," *DOSB* 11 (December 3, 1944): 666.

8. McAdoo to the Secretary of State, April 4, 1938, and the response, Welles to McAdoo, April 21, 1938, both 812.6363/3696, RG 59, NA.

9. U.S. Congress, House, Committee on Foreign Affairs, *Expropriation of American-Owned Property by Foreign Governments in the Twentieth Century,* 88th Cong., 1st Sess., July 19, 1963, 10–12.

10. FDR's July 22, 1940, request to Congress: *DOSB* 3 (July 27, 1940): 41; Representative John Shafer: *Congressional Record,* February 20, 1939, 1642–1643.

11. PL 76-792, September 26, 1940, 54 Stat. 961; Dulles, "Export-Import Bank of Washington," 667.

12. The agreements, including Mexico's commitment to pay oil companies $24 million, are reprinted in *DOSB* 5 (November 22, 1941): 399–403, and *DOSB* 6 (April 18, 1942): 351–353; *New York Times,* April 22, 1942, 22.

13. Dawson to Secretary of State, March 28, 1942, *FRUS* 1942, 5:598. The "corporation" would be led by a binational committee of personnel from the host government

and the U.S. embassy. Welles to Matienzo, enclosing "Memorandum Agreement," January 27, 1942, *FRUS* 1942, 5:592–594; *DOSB* 6 (February 21, 1942): 172–173.

14. Secretary of State to the Bolivian Minister of Finance and the Bolivian Minister of National Economy, August 14, 1942, *FRUS* 1942, 5:603–607.

15. James Michael McHale, "The New Deal and the Origins of Public Lending for Foreign Economic Development, 1933–1945" (PhD diss., University of Wisconsin, 1970), 183–192; Dulles, "Export-Import Bank of Washington," 666–667.

16. Originally proposed as a railway at the first Pan-American Conference in 1889, the project was discussed as a highway at the fifth conference in Santiago in 1923, then formalized in 1937 by the Convention on the Pan-American Highway, signed by the United States and eleven Latin American countries, from Mexico to Chile. Warren Kelchner, "The Pan American Highway," *Foreign Affairs,* July 1938, 723–727.

17. Press Release, July 9, 1941, *DOSB* 5 (July 12, 1941): 19. The principal documents are in Decimal File 832.6511 for 1941, RG 59, NA.

18. Sumner Welles, *The Time for Decision* (New York: Harper and Brothers, 1944), 209, 219.

19. "An Act to Amend the Tariff Act of 1930," June 12, 1934, PL 73-315, 48 Stat. 943–945; *Congressional Record,* May 17, 1934, 8987–9016, quotation at 8988.

20. The Reciprocal Trade Agreement with Cuba, August 24, 1934, 49 Stat. 3559. Cuban exports had already enjoyed preferential access to the U.S. market under a 1902–1903 Commercial Convention.

21. United States Military Academy, *Raw Materials in War and Peace* (West Point, NY: Department of Social Sciences, U.S. Military Academy, 1947); John C. DeWilde, "Wartime Economic Cooperation in the Americas," *Foreign Policy Reports* 17 (February 15, 1942): 286–295; J. Lloyd Mecham, *The United States and Inter-American Security, 1889–1960* (Austin: University of Texas Press, 1961), 237–238.

22. On pre–New Deal lending, see Ralph A. Young, *Handbook on American Underwriting of Foreign Securities,* Trade Promotion Series, no. 104 (Washington, DC: U.S. Department of Commerce, Bureau of Foreign and Domestic Commerce, July 1930).

23. Samuel Guy Inman, *Inter-American Conferences, 1826–1954: History and Problems* (Washington, DC: University Press of Washington, D.C.,1965), 141; Inman, "Cultural Relations with Latin America," *Annals of the American Academy of Political and Social Science* 211 (September 1940): 180–185; Kenneth Flint Woods, "Samuel Guy Inman: His Role in the Evolution of Inter-American Cooperation" (PhD diss., American University, 1962); Virginia S. Williams, *Radical Journalists, Generalist Intellectuals, and U.S.–Latin American Relations* (Lewiston, NY: E. Mellen, 2001), chap. 3.

24. Inman, *Inter-American Conferences,* 140–141. The single U.S. delegate to the 1933 conference who had attended one of the two earlier conferences was J. Butler

Wright, who as a junior officer had attended the 1923 Santiago meeting as the delega-tion's secretary, not as a delegate. He had not attended the 1928 meeting. See also Spruille Braden, *Diplomats and Demagogues: The Memoirs of Spruille Braden* (New Rochelle, NY: Arlington House, 1971), 118–121.

25. Inman, *Inter-American Conferences,* 63; *Convention for the Promotion of Inter-American Cultural Relations,* in *The International Conferences of American States, First Supplement, 1933–1940* (Washington, DC: Carnegie Endowment for International Peace, 1940), 203–205.

26. Stephen Duggan, *The Two Americas: An Interpretation* (London: Charles Scribner's Sons, 1934); Duggan, *A Professor at Large* (New York: Macmillan, 1943); Justin Hart, *Empire of Ideas: The Origins of Public Diplomacy and the Transformation of U.S. Foreign Policy* (New York: Oxford University Press, 2013); Frank Ninkovich, *The Diplomacy of Ideas: U.S. Foreign Policy and Cultural Relations, 1938–1950* (New York: Cambridge University Press, 1981).

27. Rockefeller gave his 1940 plan to Hopkins on June 14; on June 15 FDR asked his secretaries of state, commerce, treasury, and agriculture to meet with him about "our economic relations Latin America," and said he was enclosing "one of many mem-oranda" he had received on the subject, presumably Rockefeller's. For the details of Hull's July 1940 Meeting of Consultation of Ministers of Foreign Affairs, including Hull's speech (p. 267) and the formal *Convention on the Provisional Administration of European Colonies and Possessions in the Americas* (56 Stat. 1273), see Document 362 in *International Conciliation,* vol. 20 (1940–1941): 267, 305–311. U.S. Office of Inter-American Affairs, *History of the Office of the Coordinator of Inter-American Affairs: Historical Reports on the War Administration* (Washington, DC: GPO, 1947), 4–6.

28. For the sequence of meetings with Roosevelt associates that eventually led Rockefeller to the Oval Office, see Geoffrey T. Hellman, "Profiles: Best Neighbor II," *New Yorker,* April 18, 1942, 22–32. For the executive branch documents creating the Office, see *History of the Office of the Coordinator of Inter-American Affairs,* 3–10 and appendix; Claude Curtis Erb, "Nelson Rockefeller and United States-Latin American Relations, 1940–1945" (PhD diss., Clark University, 1982), 12. Executive Order 8840, July 30, 1941, established a renamed Office of the Coordinator of Inter-American Affairs.

29. Emily Rosenberg, *Spreading the American Dream: American Economic and Cultural Expansion, 1890–1945* (New York: Hill and Wang, 1982).

30. Harley Notter, "German Inroads and Plans in the Other American Repub-lics," September 10, 1940, enclosed with Duggan to the Secretary, September 10, 1940, 862.20210 / 330½, RG 59, NA.

31. U.S. Congress, House, Committee on Appropriations, *National War Agencies Appropriation Bill for 1944,* 78th Cong., 1st Sess., 1943, 250; *History of the Office of the Coordinator of Inter-American Affairs,* 276.

32. Duggan, *The Americas,* 160. For propaganda by the rival Axis, see U.S. Department of War, Division of Military Intelligence, *Axis Espionage and Propaganda in Latin America* (Washington, DC: Department of War, 1946).

33. Rockefeller to Welles, November 13, 1942, box 77, and Rockefeller, response to Ambassador George Messersmith, February 28, 1941, both box 68, Welles Papers, FDRL.

34. Office for Coordination of Commercial and Cultural Relations between the American Republics, "Weekly Digest," January 6, 1941, and Rockefeller response to Ambassador George Messersmith, February 28, 1941, both box 68, Welles Papers, FDRL. Accent marks missing in originals. This office existed from August 16, 1940, to July 30, 1941, when it was replaced by the Office of the Coordinator of Inter-American Affairs.

35. For a description (and Rockefeller's defense) of the activities of the Office, see U.S. Congress, House, Committee on Appropriations, *National War Agencies Appropriation Bill for 1944,* 78th Cong., 1st Sess., 1943, 130; Darlene J. Sadlier, *Americans All: Good Neighbor Cultural Diplomacy in World War II* (Austin: University of Texas Press, 2012).

36. Adolf Berle diary, July 31, 1941, FDRL.

37. FDR to Rockefeller, March 24, 1942, in *History of the Office of the Coordinator of Inter-American Affairs,* 115–116, 282.

38. *History of the Office of the Coordinator of Inter-American Affairs,* 232.

39. Hellman, "Profiles: Best Neighbor II," 24.

40. *History of the Office of the Coordinator of Inter-American Affairs,* 63 (the personnel numbers) and 149n (the quotation). Duggan to Welles, September 30, 1940, 710.11 / 2599½, RG 59, NA; Joe Alex Morris, *Nelson Rockefeller: A Biography* (New York: Harper and Brothers, 1960), 157.

41. Rockefeller to Welles, June 2, 1942, Rockefeller to Welles, December 23, 1941, and Welles to Rockefeller, December 26, 1941, boxes 68 and 69, Welles Papers, FDRL. Portinari's most prominent U.S. work, completed in 1942 and co-funded by the Brazilian government and Rockefeller's Office, is the mural ensemble in the vestibule of the Hispanic Reading Room of the Library of Congress.

42. Duggan to Welles, December 29, 1942, box 87, Welles Papers, FDRL; Welles to Duggan, May 31, 1942, box 77, Welles Papers, FDRL; Christopher D. O'Sullivan, *Sumner Welles, Postwar Planning, and the Quest for a New World Order, 1937–1943* (New York: Columbia University Press, 2008), chaps. 2 and 8.

43. Briggs, *Proud Servant,* 354; *History of the Office of the Coordinator of Inter-American Affairs,* 184

44. *The Price of Vision: The Diary of Henry A. Wallace, 1942–1946* (Boston: Houghton Mifflin, 1973), 239. *The War Diary of Breckinridge Long: Selections from the Years 1939–1944* (Lincoln: University of Nebraska Press, 1966), 67, 210; Adolf Berle diary, February 1, 1942, FDRL. Dean Acheson believed Long was "Mr. Hull's prin-

cipal confidant." Dean Acheson, *Present at the Creation: My Years in the State Department* (New York: W. W. Norton, 1969), 13.

45. Cordell Hull, *The Memoirs of Cordell Hull,* 2 vols. (New York: Macmillan, 1948), 2:1148–1149, plus 1227–1231, 1383, 1647 for two less-important policy disagreements; Adolph Berle diary, February 1, 1942, FDRL. For a short and perhaps embellished summary of the Secretary's complaints about Welles, see *For the President, Personal and Secret: Correspondence between Franklin D. Roosevelt and William C. Bullitt* (Boston: Houghton Mifflin, 1972), 516.

46. Adolf Berle diary, January 24 and February 1, 1942, FDRL.

47. *The War Diary of Breckinridge Long,* 210, 215, 277, 324; Farley, "Memorandum," January 10, 1939, Private File, 1918–1976, box 43, James Farley Papers, LC.

48. Louis B. Wehle, *Hidden Threads of History* (New York: Macmillan, 1954), 119. The numbers cited here are useful only as a general guide, taken from the daily calendar kept by the White House staff. FDR's personal secretary, Grace Tully, recalled that Roosevelt "saw Hull or Welles daily, usually several times, plus frequent telephone calls." She also wrote that many visitors came off the record, and that for both Hull and Treasury Secretary Morgenthau the "relationship was so informal that the appointments were seldom announced." Grace Tully, *F. D. R. My Boss* (New York: Charles Scribner's Sons, 1949), 252, 286, 289.

49. Adolph Berle diary, February 1, 1942, FDRL.

50. *The War Diary of Breckinridge Long,* 324, 281; *The Diaries of Edward R. Stettinius, Jr., 1943–1946* (New York: New Viewpoints, 1975), 9.

51. Memorandum of Conversation, April 23, 1941, in *For the President, Personal and Secret,* 513–514; *The Price of Vision: The Diary of Henry A. Wallace,* 383.

52. Hull, *Memoirs,* 2:1230–1232; see also Adolph Berle diary, January 4, 1943. The FDR-Welles meeting was 11 August. Welles's August 16, 1943, resignation letter is in President's Secretary's File, box 96, FDRL; press release, *DOSB* 9 (September 25, 1943): 208.

53. *The War Diary of Breckinridge Long,* 325. Benjamin Welles, *Sumner Welles: FDR's Global Strategist* (New York: St. Martin's Press, 1997), 358; Irwin F. Gellman, *Secret Affairs: Franklin Roosevelt, Cordell Hull, and Sumner Welles* (Baltimore: Johns Hopkins University Press, 1995).

54. Henry Stimson diary, January 11, 1944, microfilmed by Sterling Library, Yale University. Welles's papers indicate a very close association with newspaper columnist Drew Pearson. See also *For the President, Personal and Secret,* 211.

55. Duggan may have lost his balance while putting on a boot—one was found on his foot, the second was on the office floor sixteen stories above. The death occurred a few days after Duggan was interviewed by the FBI about his cooperation with the Soviet Union before the Stalinist purges. On this, see John Earl Haynes and Harvey Klehr, *Venona: Decoding Soviet Espionage in America* (New Haven, CT: Yale University Press, 2008), 203; and Haynes and Klehr (with Alexander

Vassiliev), *Spies: The Rise and Fall of the KGB in America* (New Haven, CT: Yale University Press, 2010), 242.

56. In 1937 the name of the Division of Latin American Affairs had been changed to the Division of American Republics Affairs (ARA) and had reabsorbed the Division of Mexican Affairs, which had been spun off during Woodrow Wilson's administration. In 1944 the "Division" became an "Office," and in 1950 it became a "Bureau" of Inter-American Affairs. Since late 2000 the title has been Bureau of Western Hemisphere Affairs, and includes Canada.

57. Roosevelt to the presidents of Chile, Colombia, Ecuador, Paraguay, Peru, and Uruguay, January 26, 1945. As discussed below, FDR did not include Argentina, a seventh nonbelligerent. The letter to Chilean president Juan Antonio Ríos is *FRUS 1945*, 9:758–759.

58. Bowers to Secretary of State, February 2 and 5, 1945, *FRUS 1945*, 9:759–761.

59. Commercial Attaché Walter P. McConaughy memorandum, May 25, 1944, attached to Chargé Robert F. Woodward to Secretary of State, May 26, 1944, 824.00/3197, RG 59, NA. On this see Max Paul Friedman, *Nazis and Good Neighbors: The United States Campaign against the Germans of Latin America in World War II* (Cambridge: Cambridge University Press, 2003), esp. 6; U.S. Department of War, *Axis Espionage.*

60. Stettinius to Bowers, January 3, 1945, *FRUS 1945*, 9:756–757.

61. Acting Secretary of State to Bowers, February 10, 1945, and Ríos to FDR, February 14, 1945, both *FRUS 1945*, 9:768–769.

62. For Argentina's October 27, 1944, memorandum requesting the meeting, see *FRUS 1944*, 7:311–333. On Secretary Hull's opposition, see his *Memoirs,* 2:1404. FDR's "make a face" statement to Edward Stettinius, May 18, 1944, is indirect via Treasury Secretary Henry Morgenthau Jr. in a memo: "Re: CABINET," May 18, 1944, Morgenthau Diary, bk. 733, 29–31, Morgenthau Papers, FDRL.

63. On the initial U.S. effort to sidetrack Argentina's initiative and Washington's back-and-forth with Mexico, see *FRUS 1944*, 7:27–86, esp. 34–35, 82–83. On Mexico's interest in the conference, see Memorandum of Conversation, "Conference of Foreign Ministers," January 2, 1945, 710 Conference W and PW/1-245, RG 59, NA.

64. Stettinius to the President, "Suggested U.S. Policy toward Latin America," January 3, 1945, 710 Conference (W&PW)/1-345, and (FDR's agreement) February 24, 1945, 835.00/2-2445, both RG 59, NA. Adolf Berle diary, March 6, 1945. Merwin L. Bohan Oral History, June 15, 1974, HSTL: "Of all the Secretaries of State that I have known, Mr. Stettinius came as near zero as I think you can come to that symbol, frankly. I thought that I was attending a meeting of—without casting aspersions on the Rotarians—a Rotary meeting or something."

65. Dana G. Munro, "Some Notes on Latin American Policy," September 28, 1945, 710.11/9-2845, RG 59, NA.

66. Adolf Berle diary, February 27, 1945, FDRL.

67. Executive Order 9710, April 10, 1946. The subsidiary Institute for Inter-American Affairs continued to function until 1953, administering the Truman administration's Point 4 technical assistance program in Latin America.

7. TO IMPROVE OR NOT TO IMPROVE?

1. Speech in Wheeling, West Virginia, February 9, 1950, reprinted along with McCarthy's commentary in *Congressional Record*, February 20, 1950, 1952–1981, quotations at 1954.

2. Aldous Huxley, *The Doors of Perception* (New York: Harper and Row, 1963), 22–23.

3. Dwight D. Eisenhower, *Waging Peace, 1956–1961* (Garden City, NY: Doubleday, 1965), 421.

4. Thomas C. Mann to Charles S. Murphy, Special Counsel to the President, December 11, 1952, Subject File, President's Secretary's Files, folder "Latin America," 1 and 15, HSTL. Assistant Secretary of State John Cabot's June 20, 1953, performance review of Mann: "I do not know of any officer whom I would prefer to Mr. Mann to have with me at any post in the Service." *The Diplomatic Papers of John Moors Cabot* (Frederick, MD: University Publications of America, 1985), reel 14.

5. Minutes by Director of the Executive Secretariat, morning meeting, January 3, 1950, *FRUS* 1950, 2:589n.

6. Draft Report, "Briefing Material for Secretary," January 4, 1950, *FRUS* 1950, 2:589.

7. "Waging Peace in the Americas," September 19, 1949, *DOSB* 21 (September 26, 1949): 462–466, quotation at 465. Largely ignored in the U.S. press, Acheson's speech received substantial next-day newspaper coverage in Latin America, including front-page articles in *El Mercurio* (Santiago), and *Excelsior* (Mexico City), which also reprinted the entire speech, translated by the State Department, on page 11. *El Tiempo* (Bogotá) placed the story on page 8 with a prominent headline, and *La Prensa* (Buenos Aires) put it on page 2. Three of these four took the story from U.S. wire services; *El Tiempo*'s coverage was supplied directly by the U.S. Information Service (USIS).

8. Ellis O. Briggs, *Proud Servant: The Memoirs of a Career Ambassador* (Kent, OH: Kent State University Press, 1998), 246; Merwin L. Bohan Oral History, June 15, 1974, HSTL.

9. Dean Acheson, *Present at the Creation: My Years in the State Department* (New York: Norton, 1969), 257, 497.

10. Armistead I. Selden Jr., oral history, John Foster Dulles Papers, Mudd Library, Princeton University.

11. Edward G. Miller, Remarks Closing of Inter-American ECOSOC, April 10, 1950, *DOSB* 22 (April 24, 1950): 650–651. See also Miller's "Achievements of Inter-American Cooperation," October 14, 1952, *DOSB* 27 (November 3, 1952): 702–707.

12. "Briefing Material for Secretary," 591–592.

13. *FRUS* 1945, 1:389, 394, 396–397, 401, 417.

14. *FRUS* 1945, 1:417.

15. Acheson, *Present at the Creation,* 160. On the other hand, one of Braden's subordinates considered him "the kind of chief that you can bleed and die for. . . . Mr. Braden was one of the hardest working people I've ever known. He could work around the clock." Mervin L. Bohan Oral History, June 13, 1974, HSTL.

16. Spruille Braden, *Diplomats and Demagogues: The Memoirs of Spruille Braden* (New Rochelle, NY: Arlington House, 1971), 94–98.

17. *Off the Record: The Private Papers of Harry S. Truman,* ed. Robert H. Ferrell (New York: Harper and Row, 1980), 16, 23. The two men also were together on Inauguration Day, but only for the ceremonial activities, which, given FDR's fragile health, took place on the South Portico of the White House.

18. Braden to Byrnes, September 4, 1945, FRUS 1945, 9:408; U.S. Department of State, *Consultation among the American Republics with Respect to the Argentine Situation: Memorandum of the United States Government* (Washington, DC: GPO, 1946), 65–66.

19. Messersmith forwarding Secretary of State Stettinius's message to FDR, Messersmith to Department, February 22, 1945, 835.99 / 2-2245, RG 59, NA.

20. "The President's Appointments, Saturday, September 29, 1945," folder "September 1945 Daily Sheet File," Appointments File, President's Secretary's File, HSTL. The rest of the notation: "including Germany, Japan, South America, OPA etc." (OPA was the Office of Price Administration.)

21. Briggs, *Proud Servant,* 157; Ruth Alford, "Biographical Note," Messersmith Papers, University of Delaware Library Special Collections.

22. Braden to Byrnes, July 5 and September 4, 1945, *FRUS* 1945, 9:389, 408.

23. Messersmith to the President, October 23, 1946. This and an extraordinary blizzard of additional complaints about Braden, most to the secretary of state, are in Decimal File 111.12 Braden, Spruille, RG 59, NA.

24. Associated Press, "Showdown at State Department," distributed December 7 and printed December 8, 1946, in *The Standard* (Buenos Aires); Messersmith, unaddressed three-page letter but probably intended for the secretary of state, December 10, 1946, both Messersmith Papers, University of Delaware.

25. "Personal for the Ambassador, from Marshall," June 4, 1947, 7 P.M., Messersmith Papers, University of Delaware.

26. Messersmith, "Personal for the Secretary," June 5, 1947, 11 A.M., Messersmith Papers, University of Delaware.

27. Halle to Miller, December 21, 1950, *FRUS* 1950, 2:637–638.

28. One of the resolutions approved at Chapultepec had stipulated that any attack upon "an American State" was an attack upon all, and the delegates had agreed to hold a conference to produce "a treaty establishing procedures whereby such threats or acts may be met."

29. Truman, Press Conference, August 14, 1947, *PPP*.

30. Truman, *Address to the Inter-American Conference for the Maintenance of Continental Peace and Security,* September 2, 1947, *PPP*.

31. PL 66-272, June 5, 1920, 41 Stat. 1056; and PL 69-247, May 19, 1926, 44 Stat. 565.

32. Welles to Secretary of State, October 13, 1933, *FRUS* 1933, 5:484; Seldin Chapin to Laurence Duggan, July 13, 1939, 710.11 / 2403½, RG 59, NA. For slightly different numbers circa 1939, see Stetson Conn, Rose C. Engelman, and Byron Fairchild, *The Western Hemisphere: Guarding the United States and Its Outposts,* vol. 12, pt. 2 of *The United States Army in World War II* (Washington, DC: Department of the Army, 1964), 184–185.

33. Weddell to Secretary of State, March 30, 1938, *FRUS* 1938, 5:314. On the broad sweep of U.S. activities to reduce the German presence in wartime Latin America, see Max Paul Friedman's especially useful *Nazis and Good Neighbors: The United States Campaign against the Germans of Latin America in World War II* (Cambridge: Cambridge University Press, 2003); and the focused study by Stephen R. Niblo, *War, Diplomacy, and Development: The United States and Mexico, 1938–1954* (Wilmington, DE: Scholarly Resources, 1995).

34. PL 76-83, June 15, 1940, 54 Stat. 396. For details about prewar missions, see Seldin Chapin to Laurence Duggan, July 13, 1939, 710.11 / 2403½, RG 59, NA. John Child, *Unequal Alliance: The Inter-American Military System, 1938–1978* (Boulder, CO: Westview, 1980), 21.

35. "Report by the Joint Army and Navy Advisory Board on American Republics," undated but late 1943, in *FRUS* 1944, 7:90. "About $500,000,000" is the Lend-Lease estimate by Conn, Engelman, and Fairchild (*The Western Hemisphere,* 236). See also Stephen G. Rabe, "Inter-American Military Cooperation, 1944–1951," *World Affairs* 137 (Fall 1974): 133. Secretary Marshall's comment: U.S. Congress, House, Committee on Foreign Affairs, *Inter-American Military Cooperation Act,* 80th Cong., 1st Sess., 1947, 11.

36. "Meeting of the Liaison Committee, Wednesday, February 24, 1943, 2:30 P.M.," Records of the Interdepartmental and the Intra-Departmental Committees, RG 353, NA; *FRUS* 1938, 5:888–894.

37. "Meeting of the Liaison Committee, Wednesday, February 24, 1943, 2:30 P.M."

38. U.S. Congress, Committee on Appropriations, Subcommittee on War Department Appropriations, *Military Establishment Appropriations Bill for 1947,* 79th Cong., 2nd Sess., May 1946, 876; U.S. Congress, House, Committee on Appropriations, *Navy Department Appropriation Bill for 1948,* 80th Cong., 1st Sess., 1947, 1642; U.S. Congress, House, Committee on Foreign Affairs, *Inter-American Military Cooperation Act,* 80th Cong., 1st Sess., June–July 1947, 68.

39. Joint Chiefs of Staff to the Secretary of State, "Foreign Policy of the United States," March 29, 1946, *FRUS* 1946, 1:1166.

40. "Report by the Joint Army and Navy Advisory Board on American Republics," undated but late 1943, and Stimson to Hull, September 20, 1944, both *FRUS* 1944, 7:91, 120–121. See also "Instructions for Staff Conversations with Military and Naval Representatives of the Other American Republics," undated but mid-1944, *FRUS* 1944, 7:106–111; *FRUS* 1945, 9:251–259; "Draft Memorandum by the Acting Director, Office of American Republic Affairs, on Forthcoming Bilateral Staff Conversations," September 5, 1944, *FRUS* 1944, 7:118–119.

41. "Proposed Joint Statement by State, War and the Navy Department to be Approved by the President," July 7, 1945, *FRUS* 1945, 9:251–252.

42. Wallace, *The Price of Vision: The Diary of Henry A. Wallace, 1942–1946* (Boston: Houghton Mifflin, 1973), 611; Briggs to Secretary of State, December 20, 1944, *FRUS* 1944, 7:132. Three weeks later Briggs was instructed to begin discussing with the Trujillo government what its military might find useful. Stettinius to Briggs, January 8, 1945, *FRUS* 1944, 7:133.

43. The failed effort to pass this legislation is explained by Chester J. Pach Jr., "The Containment of U.S. Military Aid to Latin America, 1944–49," *Diplomatic History* 6 (Summer 1982): 225–243. The Surplus War Property Act of 1944 was used to provide some aid during the early postwar years. *FRUS* 1945, 9:254.

44. Acting Secretary of State Acheson to Secretary of War Patterson and Secretary of the Navy Forrestal, March 19, 1947, *FRUS* 1947, 8:106.

45. Patterson to Acheson, March 27, 1947, and Forrestal to Acheson, March 31, 1947, *FRUS* 1947, 8:108, 111.

46. Minutes of Meeting of Secretaries State, War, and Navy, May 1, 1947, *FRUS* 1947, 8:114; *Inter-American Military Cooperation Act,* June–July 1947, 9.

47. "Arms Policy for Other American Republics," November 4, 1947, *FRUS* 1947, 8:126.

48. The Mutual Defense Assistance Act of 1949, PL 81-329, October 6, 1949, §408(e); *DOSB* 21 (August 8, 1949): 188; Rabe, "Inter-American Military Cooperation," 141–142.

49. A typical military assistance agreement: *DOSB* 26 (March 3, 1952): 336–338. A typical administration budget justification: U.S. Department of State, Department of Defense, and International Cooperation Agency, *The Mutual Security Program, Fiscal Year 1959, A Summary Presentation, February 1958* (Washington, DC: Department of State et al., 1958), 29.

50. PL 77-671, 56 Stat. 662, July 20, 1942.

51. Willard Beaulac to Assistant Secretary John Cabot, March 20, 1953, *Diplomatic Papers of John Moors Cabot,* reel 15.

52. Pedro A. Villoldo, *Latin American Resentment: Why They Spat Upon the Vice-President* (New York: Vantage Press, 1959), 49; U.S. Congress, House, Committee on

Foreign Affairs, Subcommittee on Inter-American Affairs, *Report on United States Relations with Latin America,* 86th Cong., 1st Sess., May 12, 1959, 3. For the State Department's defense of the award, see U.S. Congress, Senate, Committee on Foreign Relations, *Executive Sessions of the Senate Foreign Relations Committee (Historical Series),* vol. 10, 85th Cong., 2nd Sess., 1958, 249; for the embassy's defense, see *FRUS 1952–1954,* 4:1674–1676.

53. *DOSB* 14 (May 19, 1946): 859–860; *Congressional Record,* May 6, 1946, 4518, which includes the draft bill; message of May 23, 1947, *DOSB* 16 (June 8, 1947): 1122.

54. U.S. Congress, Senate, Special Committee to Study the Foreign Aid Program, *Foreign Aid Program: Compilation of Studies and Surveys,* S. Doc. 52, 85th Cong., 1st Sess., 1957, 1521–1535.

55. For the details of this meeting, see Document 362 in *International Conciliation* 20 (1940–1941), Hull's comment at 267.

56. The Havana meeting was 21–30 July; FDR's executive order was 16 August. Hull had an advantage Truman lacked: the creation of the Office had been in the planning stages for some time, before Rockefeller's involvement. Office of Inter-American Affairs, *History of the Office of the Coordinator of Inter-American Affairs* (Washington, DC: GPO, 1947), with FDR's executive order printed in the appendix, 280; on the planning, see 3–10.

57. Article 25 of the "Final Act of the Third Meeting of Foreign Ministers," *DOSB* 6 (February 7, 1942): 134; Stephen G. Rabe, "The Elusive Conference: United States Economic Relations with Latin America, 1945–1952," *Diplomatic History* 2 (Summer, 1978): 279–280, 285.

58. Foreign Minister Ezequiel Padilla's address and the ceremonial opening address by President Manuel Ávila Camacho are published in *Hacia la organización de la nueva paz* (Mexico, D.F.: Secretaría de Relaciones Exteriores, 1945), 28. A part of Padilla's address is reprinted in U.S. Department of State, *Report of the Delegation of the United States of America to the Inter-American Conference on Problems of War and Peace* (Washington, DC: GPO, 1946), 7. Padilla's "gardens" *("jardines")* may have been a reference to preschools *(jardines infantiles).*

59. U.S. Department of State, *Report of the Delegation of the United States of America to the Inter-American Conference on Problems of War and Peace* (Washington, DC: GPO, 1946), 86, 121.

60. Marshall's address: *DOSB* 18 (April 11, 1948): 469–473, quotations at 470, 472; Roy R. Rubottom Jr., Oral History, February 13, 1990, Association for Diplomatic Studies and Training, Arlington, VA, 5; see also Sumner Welles, "Bogota's Lesson," *Washington Post,* April 20, 1948, 11.

61. Briggs, *Proud Servant,* 176, 183. A copy of the January 28, 1942, contract between the U.S. Defense Supplies Corporation and the *Instituto Cubano de Estabilización de Azúcar* is in folder "Correspondence Diplomatic 1942 S-We," box 9, Spruille Braden Papers, Columbia University.

62. José Figueres, "Point Four . . . A Latin American View," *Central America and Mexico* 1 (April 1953): 6–7.

63. Eugene Ysita, "The National Economy of Uruguay—Part I," *Commercial Pan America,* April 1948, 13.

64. Edward G. Miller Jr., "Remarks at Closing of Inter-American ECOSOC," April 19, 1950, *DOSB* 22 (April 24, 1950): 650–651.

65. Edward G. Miller Jr., "Inter-American Relations in Perspective," March 22, 1950, *DOSB* 22 (April 3, 1950): 521–523.

66. Memorandum of Telephone Conversation, February 26, 1953, Dulles Papers, Seeley Mudd Library, Princeton University.

67. The report is reprinted in *DOSB* 29 (November 23, 1953): 695–717, emphasis in original. *Diplomatic Papers of John Moors Cabot,* reel 15, contains Cabot's scribbled diary of the trip. Eisenhower, *State of the Union Address,* January 7, 1954.

68. C. Douglas Dillon Oral History, May 2, 1972, Rare Book and Manuscript Library, Columbia University, 30, 35.

69. Commission on Foreign Economic Policy, *Report to the President and the Congress,* H. Doc. 290, 83rd Cong., 2nd Sess., January 23, 1954, 9.

70. Dwight D. Eisenhower, *Waging Peace, 1956–1961* (Garden City, NY: Doubleday, 1965), 424; U.S. Department of State, *Tenth Inter-American Conference, Caracas, Venezuela, March 1–18, 1954, Report of the Delegation of the United States of America with Related Documents* (Washington, DC: GPO, May 1955).

71. Thomas C. Mann to Charles S. Murphy, Special Counsel to the President, December 11, 1952, Subject File, President's Secretary's Files, folder "Latin America," 24, HSTL.

72. Thomas C. Mann to Charles S. Murphy, December 11, 1952, 23, President's Secretary File, folder Latin America, HSTL.

73. In 1999 Guatemala's Historical Clarification Commission issued its report, *Guatemala: Memoria del Silencio,* indicating that 83 percent of the more than 200,000 killed were indigenous Mayan and that "state forces and related paramilitary groups were responsible for 93% of the violations." Later that year President Clinton flew to Guatemala to issue what amounted to an apology for the U.S. role.

74. Peurifoy's testimony, October 8, 1954, *DOSB* 31 (November 8, 1954): 690–696; the declassified CIA documents: www.cia.gov/library/readingroom/collection/guatemala.

75. Basically a transfer of cash, "Defense Support" was an early term for "Security Supporting Assistance," which became today's "Economic Support Fund." U.S. Congress, Senate, Special Committee to Study the Foreign Aid Program, *Foreign Aid Program: Compilation of Studies and Surveys,* S. Doc. 52, 85th Cong., 1st Sess., 1957, 1522–1538; Press release, October 30, 1954, *DOSB* 31 (November 8, 1954): 696; Memorandum of Conversations, Department of State, Washington, April

28–29, 1955, "Current Situation in Guatemala and Projected Aid Program," *FRUS* 1955–1957, 7:71–75.

76. "Report of the Vice President on Latin American Trip, Memorandum of Discussion at the 240th Meeting of the National Security Council," *FRUS* 1955–1957, 6:618; Eisenhower, *Waging Peace*, 426.

77. *Tenth Inter-American Conference, Caracas, Venezuela, March 1–18, 1954, Report of the Delegation of the United States*, 65–66, 133, 157.

78. Henry F. Holland, "A Preview of the U.S. Position at the Rio Conference," Address to the Pan American Society of New York, October 27, 1954, *DOSB* 31 (November 8, 1954): 684–690.

79. "Memorandum for the Record," September 7, 1954, White House Office Files, NSC Series, Briefing Notes Subseries, Office of the Special Assistant for National Security Affairs: Records, 1952–1961, box 12, folder "Latin America, U.S. Policy toward (3) 1954–60," DDEL.

80. George M. Humphrey, "Economic Cooperation in the Americas," *DOSB* 31 (December 6, 1954): 863–869.

81. Minutes, NSC Meeting, December 21, 1954, *FRUS* 1952–1954, 2:838; "Memorandum of Discussion at the 237th Meeting of the National Security Council, Washington, February 17, 1955, *FRUS* 1955–1957, 6:4–5.

82. Eisenhower to George Humphrey, March 27, 1957, Ann Whitman File, Administrative Series, box 21, folder "George M. Humphrey (4)," DDEL.

83. C. Douglas Dillon Oral History, 29, 35–36.

84. Memorandum, Deputy Assistant Secretary Snow to Secretary of State, August 22, 1957, *FRUS* 1955–1957, 6:525–526.

85. C. Douglas Dillon Oral History, 27.

86. The Committee's papers are located in National Archives Record Group 353.2.

87. Dean Acheson, "Aid to Underdeveloped Areas as Measure of National Security," Statement before the Senate Committee on International Relations, March 30, 1950, *DOSB* 22 (April 10, 1950): 533.

88. The Technical Cooperation Administration was established on October 27, 1950, to administer the Point 4 programs authorized under the Foreign Economic Assistance Act of 1950 (June 5, 1950, 64 Stat. 207). The TCA absorbed Rockefeller's 1940s-era Institute of Inter-American Affairs, which initially served as the TCA's subunit responsible for Latin America.

89. Jonathan B. Bingham, *Shirt-Sleeve Diplomacy: Point 4 in Action* (New York: John Day, 1953), 5–7. Bingham sat on the altruistic side of the altruism–realism continuum and would subsequently serve nine terms in the House of Representatives; Edwin McCammon Martin, *Kennedy and Latin America* (Lanham, MD: University Press of America, 1994), 29.

90. FOA [Foreign Operations Administration] Mission Post to FOA [illegible], June 2, 1954, "Foreign Post Differential Questionnaire," entry UD 181, box 18, RG 469, NA.

91. Archived documents variously refer to Patterson as the "Director of U.S. Operations Mission," as "Chief of Field Party," as "Office Director," and as "Country Director." See entry UD 181, boxes 24 and 26, RG 469, NA.

92. Figueres, "Point Four," 5. In the United States of the 1950s, few officials disagreed with the State Department's Thomas Mann, who dismissed structuralism as "largely an emotional rationalization of their own political, economic and social failures." Thomas C. Mann to Charles S. Murphy, December 11, 1952, 8.

93. Milton Friedman, "Schools at Chicago," *University of Chicago Magazine,* August 1974, 11; also available in *The Indispensable Milton Friedman,* ed. Lanny Ebenstein (Washington, DC: Regnery, 2012), 25–36. Two academic observers, both highly respected Latin Americanists, noted that "one reason that the University of Chicago was originally considered appropriate for this project was that it represented in the intellectual world a strongly libertarian philosophy in economics." Richard N. Adams and Charles C. Cumberland, "The Economics Project of the University of Chicago and the Catholic University of Chile," 1960, entry P236, box 4, folder "University Assistance," RG 469; also published as one chapter of *United States University Cooperation in Latin America: A Study Based on Selected Programs in Bolivia, Chile, Peru, and Mexico* (East Lansing: Institute of Research on Overseas Programs, Michigan State University, 1960).

94. The initial three-year contract implementing the Chicago-Católica agreement came after the TCA had been absorbed by the Foreign Operations Administration (FOA), and after the FOA had been renamed the International Cooperation Administration (ICA). "International Cooperation Administration in Chile," August 12, 1957, entry P232, box 18, folder "Program Development 1952–1957," and "Personnel on Board USOM/Chile," April 8, 1958, entry P232, box 27, folder "Reports—Personnel, 1956–1959," both RG 469. For a typical Chicago-Católica renewal, this one for $150,000, see "Contract Status Report December 1959," entry 469, box 24, folder "Reports—Contract Status," RG 469, NA.

An indispensable study using both U.S. and Chilean documents is Juan Gabriel Valdes, *Pinochet's Economists: The Chicago School in Chile* (Cambridge: Cambridge University Press, 1995). See also Manuel Delano and Hugo Traslavina, *La herencia de los Chicago Boys* (Santiago: Ediciones del Ornitorrinco, 1989); Anil Hira, *Ideas and Economic Policy in Latin America* (Westport, CT: Praeger, 1998). The initial contract, which was between the ICA and the University of Chicago, is probably located somewhere in the woefully disorganized Record Group 469, which also lacks a useful finding aid. The figure used here is from Valdes, who mentions $350,000 on p. 126 and $375,000 on p. 138.

95. Bureau of Intelligence and Research, Department of State, "Latin American Political Stability and the Alliance for Progress," January 17, 1962, *FRUS 1961–1963,*

12:85. Roger Hilsman Jr., the INR assistant secretary of state at the time, had an undeserved reputation as an altruist.

96. Note the Hans Morgenthau realist title: "Aid to Underdeveloped Areas as a Measure of National Security," Statement before the Senate Committee on Foreign Relations, March 30, 1950, *DOSB* 22 (April 10, 1950): 552–555.

97. John M. Cabot, Luncheon address to the New York Export Managers Club, March 17, 1953, *DOSB* 28 (March 30, 1953): 462.

98. Milton Eisenhower's 1963 book, *The Wine Is Bitter: The United States and Latin America* (Garden City, NY: Doubleday), is a faithful reproduction of the thinking underlying his reports. The 1959 report is *DOSB* 40 (January 19, 1959): 89–105. U.S. Congress, House, "U.S. Foreign Aid. Its Purposes, Scope, Administration, and Related Information. Prepared by Legislative Reference Service, Library of Congress," H. Doc. 116, 86th Cong., 1st Sess., June 11, 1959, 85.

8. CUBA DETERMINES THE ANSWER

1. *Revolución,* January 3, 1959, 4. Unless indicated otherwise, all quotations of Castro speeches are from http://www.cuba.cu/gobierno/discursos/.

2. Wayne S. Smith, *The Closest of Enemies: A Personal and Diplomatic Account of U.S.-Cuban Relations since 1957* (New York: W. W. Norton, 1987), 42.

3. *Meet the Press,* April 19, 1959 (www.nbcnews.com/video/meet-the-press /38212466). Castro's comment regarding military advisers was made during an address to the Havana Lions Club, January 13, 1959.

4. Senator Russell Long and Representative James Fulton, both quoted in *New York Times,* April 18, 1959, 10.

5. "Memorandum of a Conference with the President," March 17, 1960, and "Memorandum of a Telephone Conversation . . . ," March 19, 1960, both *FRUS* 1958–1960, 6:861–863, 866. Mikoyan had arrived for his ten-day visit six weeks earlier, on February 4.

6. Dwight D. Eisenhower, *Waging Peace, 1956–1961* (Garden City, NJ: Doubleday, 1965), 525; Karl E. Mundt, "How Cuban Freedom Really Was Won," *Reader's Digest,* August 1960, 168.

7. Embassy to Department of State, March 13, 1959, 737.00 / 3-1359, RG 59, NA.

8. "Transfer: January 19, 1961, Meeting of the President and Senator Kennedy," January 19, 1961, folder "Kennedy, John F. 1960–61 (2)," box 2, Augusta-Walter Reed Series, Post-Presidential Papers, DDEL.

9. Radio address, April 23, 1961, and speech, Havana, May 1–2, 1961; Speech, Havana, July 26, 1961, in *Revolución,* July 28, 1961, 1. The Marxist-Leninist declaration was in a Havana speech, December 2, 1961.

10. U.S. Department of State, Department of Defense, and International Cooperation Administration, *The Mutual Security Program, Fiscal Year 1959, A Summary Presentation, February 1958* (Washington, DC: Department of State et al., 1958), 112; JFK, *Message to Congress,* March 14, 1961, *DOSB* 44 (April 3, 1961): 477. The quotation used in this chapter's epigraph is from a campaign speech in Portland, Oregon, September 7, 1960. For the jumble of AID's predecessor organizations, see the National Archive's helpful finding aid for Record Group 469 (Records of the U.S. Foreign Assistance Agencies, 1948–1961).

11. U.S. Congress, House, *U.S. Foreign Aid: Its Purposes, Scope, Administration, and Related Information,* prepared by the Legislative Reference Service, Library of Congress, H. Doc. 116, 86th Cong., 1st Sess., June 11, 1959, 84, 94.

12. George W. Ball, *The Past Has Another Pattern* (New York: W. W. Norton, 1982), 183.

13. Max F. Millikan and Walt W. Rostow, "Notes on Foreign Economic Policy," May 21, 1954, in *Universities and Empire: Money and Politics in the Social Sciences during the Cold War,* ed. Christopher Simpson (New York: New Press, 1998), 41.

14. Ibid., 43. Millikan was an economics professor who in 1951–1952 took a leave to work with the CIA, then returned to MIT as director of its new CIA-funded Center for International Studies. Rostow was an MIT professor of economic history. On the MIT-CIA ties, see the memoir of MIT's president, James R. Killian Jr., *The Education of a College President* (Cambridge, MA: MIT Press, 1985), 67–68.

15. *Congressional Record,* August 17, 1951, 10290.

16. W. W. Rostow, *The Stages of Economic Growth* (Cambridge: Cambridge University Press, 1960), 6. The book was originally presented as a series of lectures at Cambridge University. An earlier, coauthored version: Max F. Millikan and W. W. Rostow, *A Proposal: Key to an Effective Foreign Policy* (New York: Harper and Brothers, 1957), chap. 5.

17. Rostow, *Stages of Economic Growth,* chap. 2.

18. William N. Parker review in *American Economic Review* 50 (December 1960): 1058–1059; Goran Ohlin, "Reflections on the Rostow Doctrine," *Economic Development and Cultural Change* 9 (July 1961): 648–655, quotations 649, 650, 651.

19. John H. Coatsworth, *Walt W. Rostow: The Stages of Economic Stagnation* (Ann Arbor, MI: Radical Education Project, [1967?]), 16.

20. Harry Schwartz, "Nations Have Their Phases," *New York Times,* May 8, 1960, BR [Book Review] 6; J. A. Livingston, "Red Growth Explained in Rostow Fatalism," *Washington Post,* June 10, 1961, B22.

21. Millikan and Rostow, *A Proposal,* 54.

22. U.S. Congress, Senate, Special Committee to Study the Foreign Aid Program, *Foreign Aid Program: Compilation of Studies and Surveys,* 85th Cong. 1st sess., S. Doc. no. 52, 70.

23. Ball, *Past Has Another Pattern,* 3.

24. Rostow to Mann, "Reflections and Recommendations on Brazil," September 7, 1964, NSF, Country File, box 10 (1 of 2), folder "Brazil vol. 5, 9 / 64–11 / 65," LBJL.

25. Rostow to the President, "The Idea of an Economic Development Decade," March 2, 1961, POF, Staff Memos, box 64a, folder "Rostow, Walt W. 11 / 60–2 / 61," JFKL.

26. Adam Smith, *The Theory of Moral Sentiments,* 2nd ed. (1759; London: Printed for A. Millar, 1761), 1.

27. Kubitschek's letter and Eisenhower's reply, May 28 and June 5: *DOSB* 28 (June 30, 1958): 1090–1091; Richard N. Goodwin, *Remembering America: A Voice from the Sixties* (Boston: Little, Brown, 1988), 159.

28. U.S. Congress, House, Committee on Foreign Affairs, *International Coopera-tion Administration Replies to Criticisms of the Foreign Aid Program,* 85th Cong., 1st Sess., March 14, 1958, 6, 24, 50.

29. Milton Eisenhower's initial report to the President, August 1, 1958: *DOSB* 39 (August 25, 1958): 309–310. The full report was presented in late December.

30. The *aide-mémoire,* August 9, 1958, is reprinted in Council of the OAS, Special Committee to Study the Formulation of New Measures for Economic Coopera-tion, *Volume L Report and Documents, First Meeting, Washington, D.C., November 17–December 12, 1958* (Washington, DC: Organization of American States, 1959), 29–31. The minutes of the Dulles-Kubitschek meeting and related materials are *FRUS* 1958–1960, 5:696–710, Dulles letter at 700–701.

31. "Statement of U.S. Policy toward Latin America," NSC 5902 / 1, February 16, 1959, *FRUS* 1958–1960, 5:92.

32. *Joint Statement of the President and President Kubitschek of Brazil,* Feb-ruary 23, 1960, *PPP.*

33. Act of Bogotá, September 13, 1960, reprinted in *DOSB* 43 (October 3, 1960): 537–540; Christopher Darnton, "Asymmetry and Agenda-Setting in U.S.–Latin American Relations: Rethinking the Origins of the Alliance for Progress," *Journal of Cold War Studies* 14 (Fall 2012): 55–92; Stephen G. Rabe, *Eisenhower and Latin America: The Foreign Policy of Anti-Communism* (Chapel Hill: University of North Carolina Press, 1988), 149; Thomas Tunstall Allcock, "The First Alliance for Progress? Re-shaping the Eisenhower Administration's Policy toward Latin America," *Journal of Cold War Studies* 16 (Winter 2014): 88.

34. PL 86-735, 74 Stat. 869, September 8, 1960.

35. Adolph Berle diary, July 14 and November 25, 1960, FDRL.

36. Goodwin, *Remembering America,* 162, 134.

37. Bruce L. R. Smith, *Lincoln Gordon: Architect of Cold War Foreign Policy* (Lexington: University Press of Kentucky, 2015), 216, 455n12, coverage of the Berle task force at 219–223. Gordon claimed authorship of the report's economic chapter: Oral History interview, July 10, 1969, 34, LBJL.

38. *Navigating the Rapids, 1918–1971: From the Papers of Adolf A. Berle* (New York: Harcourt Brace Jovanovich, 1973), 725–726; the full report is in box 1074, Pre-Presidential Papers, JFKL.

39. "Alliance for Progress: A Program of Inter-American Partnership, Statement Developed at the Foreign Policy Clearing House Conference of Cambridge, Massachusetts Faculty Club of Harvard University, December 19, 1960," Willard Beaulac Papers, box 1, folder 18, Georgetown University Library.

40. *Address by President Kennedy at a White House Reception for Latin American Diplomats,* March 13, 1961, *DOSB* 44 (April 3, 1961): 471–474.

41. Cable, August 8, 1961, *FRUS* 1961–1963, 12:48n. Dillon's speech is *DOSB* 45 (August 28, 1961): 356–360.

42. Chester Bowles diary, January 1962, folder 155, box 392, Chester Bowles Papers, Sterling Memorial Library, Yale University.

43. George R. Marotta to Bundy, "OCB Latin America Working Group Meeting, February 2," NSF Regional Security, box 215, folder "Latin America, General 1/61–2/61," JFKL. The Eisenhower-era OCB was abolished in February 1961.

44. Arthur M. Schlesinger Jr., "Good Fences Make Good Neighbors," *Fortune,* August 1946, 131–135, 161–171; see also Arthur M. Schlesinger Jr., *A Thousand Days: John F. Kennedy in the White House* (Boston: Houghton Mifflin, 1965), 170–175, 186–205.

45. Schlesinger to the President, June 27, 1961, *FRUS* 1961–1963, 12:29.

46. Goodwin to JFK, September 28, 1961, *FRUS* 1961–1963, 12:65; Kennedy, NBC News Interview by Ray Scherer, April 11, 1961, JFKL.

47. Assistant Secretary Edwin McCammon Martin, *Kennedy and Latin America* (Lanham, MD: University Press of America, 1994), 29; Schlesinger, *A Thousand Days,* 193; Schlesinger, Oral History, November 4, 1971, LBJL; CIA: Jacob D. Esterline Oral Interview, November 10–11, 1975, 49, DNSA (nsarchive.gwu.edu/bayofpigs /esterlineinterv.pdf); FSO: Raymond Thurston Oral History, June 9, 1970, 14, JFKL; dissertation writer: Ralph Nicholas Hoffman Jr., "Latin American Diplomacy: The Role of the Assistant Secretary of State, 1957–1969" (PhD diss., Syracuse University, 1969), 350; McGeorge Bundy Oral History, Special Interview 1, March 30, 1993, LBJL.

48. Chester Bowles diary, June 3, 1961, Chester Bowles Papers.

49. Chester Bowles, two letters, of December 12, 1972, and February 22, 1973, attached to Bowles Oral History, JFKL.

50. Mann to Secretary Rusk, February 15, 1961, *FRUS* 1961–1963, 10:95; Mann oral history, Interview 1, 21, LBJL. A balanced reassessment is Thomas Tunstall Allcock, "Becoming 'Mr. Latin America': Thomas C. Mann Reconsidered," *Diplomatic History* 38 (November 2014): 1017–1045.

51. Bundy to the President, February 18, 1961, *FRUS* 1961–1963, 10:107; Meeting April 4, 1961, summarized by General David Gray, "Memorandum for Record: Summary of White House Meetings," May 9, 1961, *FRUS* 1961–1963, 10:185.

52. Schlesinger to JFK, June 27, 1961, *FRUS 1961–1963*, 12:29; JFK statement at press conference, June 28, 1961, *PPP*.

53. Chester Bowles diary, January 1962, Chester Bowles Papers.

54. Goodwin to the President, September 10, 1963, *FRUS 1961–1963*, 12:147; Goodwin, *Remembering America*, 211–215.

55. Robert R. Woodward Oral History, November 4, 1968, 14, LBJL; Chester Bowles, *Promises to Keep: My Years in Public Life, 1941–1969* (New York: Harper and Row, 1971), 311. Although the Bureau of American Republics Affairs (ARA) had been renamed the Bureau of Inter-American Affairs in 1949, many continued to refer to it as ARA until well into the 1970s.

56. Martin, *Kennedy and Latin America*, v; White House Staff Files of Dorothy Davies, box 412, folder "Assistant Secretaries of State," JFKL. This folder also contains a helpful biosketch of Robert Woodward; Goodwin, *Remembering America*, 216.

57. Memorandum for the President, McGeorge Bundy, "The Under Secretaryship [*sic*] for Latin American Affairs and Ed Martin," December 9, 1963, NSF, Memos to the President, box 1, folder "McGeorge Bundy, 11/63–2/64, vol. 1," LBJL.

58. Adlai E. Stevenson, "The Alliance for Progress: A Road Map to New Achievements," *DOSB* 45 (August 21, 1961): 313.

59. See, for example, Rusk's speech April 25, 1962, *DOSB* 46 (May 14, 1962): 787–794.

60. Edwin M. Martin, "Address to the Institute of World Affairs, University of Southern California, in Pasadena," December 4, 1962, Teodoro Moscoso Papers, ser. 6, Speech File, 1956–1964, box 10, folder "Speech Materials, 11/62–12/62," JFKL. See also Martin, "Cuba, Latin America, and Communism," address to the Los Angeles World Affairs Council, September 20, 1963, *DOSB* 49 (October 14, 1963): 581; Martin, *Kennedy and Latin America*, 2.

61. Testimony, January 12, 1965, U.S. Congress, Senate, Committee on Foreign Relations, *Executive Sessions of the Senate Foreign Relations Committee together with Joint Sessions with the Senate Armed Services Committee*, Historical Series, vol. 17, 89th Cong., 1st Sess., 1965, 164, 173.

62. Ibid., 751, 760, 785–785; Mann to W. Marvin Watson [LBJ's informal chief of staff], December 16, 1965, NSF, Country File, Latin America, box 2, folder "Latin America Vol IV [1 of 2], 7/65–8/66," LBJL.

9. LOSING PANACHE, ENTRENCHING INSTITUTIONS

1. W. W. Rostow, *The Diffusion of Power: An Essay in Recent History* (New York: Macmillan, 1972), 424; Edwin M. Martin, *Kennedy and Latin America* (Lanham, MD: University Press of America, 1994), 460; William D. Rogers, *Twilight Struggle:*

The Alliance for Progress and the Politics of Development in Latin America (New York: Random House, 1967), 226.

2. Exchange between Assistant Secretary Lincoln Gordon and Representative Otto Passman, in U.S. Congress, House, Subcommittee of the Committee on Appropriations, *Hearings on Foreign Operations and Related Agencies: Economic Assistance,* 90th Cong., 1st Sess., 1968, pt. 2, 1198–1199.

3. Martin to Rusk, December 2, 1963, *FRUS* 1961–1963, doc. 721 in microfiche supplement to volumes 10 / 11 / 12.

4. Telephone conversation, December 2, 1963, folder "December 1963 [1 of 3] Chrono File," box 1, Recordings and Transcripts of Telephone Conversations and Meetings, JFK Series, LBJL.

5. Bundy, Memorandum of Conversation with the President, February 19, 1964, *FRUS* 1964–1968, 31:11.

6. Desmond FitzGerald to Joseph Burkholder Smith, in Smith, *Portrait of a Cold Warrior* (New York: G. P. Putnam's Sons, 1976), 384; Ray Cline oral history, May 31, 1983, *The Cuban Missile Crisis, 1962: A National Security Archive Document Set,* doc. 3309; John Crimmins Oral History, May 10, 1989, LBJL; Harvey Summ Oral History, March 5, 1993, Foreign Affairs Oral History Project, Association for Diplomatic Studies and Training, Arlington, VA.

7. Nixon to Haldeman, Erlichman, and Kissinger, March 2, 1970, *FRUS* 1969–1972, 1:204–206.

8. Robert A. Hurwitch, *Most of Myself: An Autobiography in the Form of Letters to His Daughters,* 2 vols. (Santo Domingo, Dominican Republic: privately printed by Editora Corripio, November 1990), 2:264–265, emphasis in original. Hurwitch was an unusually prominent deputy assistant secretary of state for Latin America during the Nixon-Ford years.

9. John Bartlow Martin, *Overtaken by Events: The Dominican Crisis from the Fall of Trujillo to the Civil War* (New York: Doubleday, 1966), 727–730.

10. PL93-189, 87 Stat. 714, December 17, 1973.

11. Title IX is §106 of PL 89-583, 80 Stat. 800, September 19, 1966. On the gestation of Title IX, see John Richard Davidson, "The Implementation of the Political Development Goals of the Alliance for Progress" (PhD diss., University of Wisconsin, 1976).

12. *National Security Action Memorandum No. 177,* August 2, 1962, NSF, Meetings and Memoranda Series, National Security Action Memoranda, JFKL.

13. U.S. Congress, Senate, Committee on Foreign Relations, *Executive Sessions of the Senate Foreign Relations Committee, Together with Joint Sessions with the Senate Armed Services Committee,* Historical Series, vol. 17, 89th Cong., 1st Sess., 1965, made public September 1990, 152. In 1962 an Inter-American Police Academy had been opened in the Canal Zone, but it closed its doors once the Georgetown facility was operating. The National Archives records of the Inter-American Police Academy are in Record Group 286.3.4.

14. U.S. Agency for International Development, *FY1966 Annual Report to the Congress* (Washington, DC: AID, 1967), 38; U.S. Congress, Senate, Committee on Foreign Relations, Subcommittee on Western Hemisphere Affairs, *United States Policies and Programs in Brazil,* 92nd Cong., 1st Sess., May 1971, 3–51.

15. *United States Policies and Programs in Brazil;* U.S. Congress, House, Committee on Foreign Affairs, Subcommittee on International Organizations and Movements, *Torture and Oppression in Brazil,* 93rd Cong., 2nd Sess., December 11, 1974; Amnesty International, *Report on Allegations of Torture in Brazil* (1973); American Committee for Information on Brazil, *Terror in Brazil: A Dossier* (1970). A most helpful guide to this topic is James N. Green, "Clerics, Exiles, and Academics: Opposition to the Brazilian Military Dictatorship in the United States, 1969–1974," *Latin American Politics and Society* 45 (April 2003): 87–117.

16. U.S. Joint Chiefs of Staff, "Response to National Security Study Memorandum #68: The Military Establishment of Latin America—as of August 1969," undated but October 1969, 364.

17. U.S. Congress, House, Committee on Foreign Affairs, Subcommittee on Asian and Pacific Affairs, *The Treatment of Political Prisoners in South Vietnam by the Government of the Republic of South Vietnam,* 93rd Cong., 1st Sess., September 13, 1973, 20–21.

18. §112 of the Foreign Assistance Act of 1973, PL 93-189, 87 Stat. 716, December 17, 1973, which exempted the FBI (whose Police Training School dated from 1935) and the Drug Enforcement Agency.

19. AID, *Congressional Presentation for FY1988,* 205A, and Congressional Presentation for FY1989, 202; U.S. Congress, House, Committee on Foreign Affairs, *The Private Enterprise Initiative of the Agency for International Development,* 101st Cong., 1st Sess., September 1989, 11, 63. This initiative would be followed by the first Bush administration's Partnership for Business Development.

20. Bush, *Address to the American People,* September 5, 1989, *PPP.*

21. Bush, press conference, December 19, 1991, *PPP.* This had been the policy of President Bush's predecessor, Ronald Reagan: "We don't have any dealings with Cuba. If they'd ever like to rejoin the civilized world, we'd be very happy to help them." *Question and Answer Session with Editors and Broadcasters,* April 16, 1982, *PPP,* 484.

22. Rostow to Rusk, January 6, 1961, and Rostow to The President, February 24, 1961, both POF Staff Memos, box 64A, folder "Rostow, Walt 10 / 60–2 / 61," JFKL. President Kennedy, *Address at a White House Reception for Latin American Diplomats,* March 13, 1961, *PPP.* Lansdale's rambling lecture, "Civic Action," is attached to Rostow's February 24 memo.

23. Joint Chiefs of Staff (Lyman Lemnitzer) to the President, "Actions of Latin America to be taken by the Military Establishment," November 9, 1961, NSF Regional Security, box 215a, folder "Latin America General 9 / 61–12 / 62," JFKL; Department of Defense, Joint Chiefs of Staff, "Military Actions for Latin America," undated but

November 1961, NSF, Departments and Agencies, box 276, folder "DOD, JFK, vol. 1, Military Actions for Latin America," 38–39, 43, JFKL.

24. Benjamin H. Read to McGeorge Bundy, "Latin American Military Aid," September 2, 1964, NSF, folder "National Security Action Memoranda: NSAM 297, Latin American Military Aid," box 4, LBJL, 4.

25. Adlai E. Stevenson, "The Alliance for Progress, a Road Map to New Achievements," *DOSB* 45 (August 21, 1961), 311–316.

26. U.S. Congress, House, Committee on the Judiciary, *Analysis of the Philosophy and Public Record of Nelson A. Rockefeller, Nominee for Vice President of the United States,* 93rd Cong., 2nd Sess., October 1974, 125–126.

27. U.S. Congress, House, Committee on Foreign Affairs, *The International Development and Security Act,* 87th Cong., 1st Sess., 1961,431; Anon., "Military Actions for Latin America," undated but November 1961, NSF, Departments and Agencies, box 276, folder "DOD, JCS, vol. 1 Military Actions for Latin America," 1, JFKL; U.S. Congress, House, Committee on International Relations, Subcommittee on Inter-American Affairs, *Arms Trade in the Western Hemisphere,* 95th Cong., 2nd Sess., June–August 1978, 74.

28. U.S. Congress, Senate, Committee on Foreign Relations, *Foreign Assistance Act of 1962,* 87th Cong., 2nd Sess., 1962, 420; Joint Chiefs of Staff, "Response to National Security Study Memorandum #68," 21.

29. For the case of Honduras, which was typical, see Matías H. Funes, *Los deliberantes: El poder militar en Honduras* (Tegucigalpa: Guaymuras, 1995); Leticia Salomón, *Política y militares en Honduras* (Tegucigalpa: Centro de Documentación de Honduras, 1989); Kirk Bowman, *Militarization, Democracy and Development: The Perils of Praetorianism in Latin America* (University Park: Pennsylvania State University Press, 2002), 141–180; Robert H. Holden, "The Real Diplomacy of Violence: United States Military Power in Central America, 1950–1990," *International History Review* 20 (May 1993): 283–322.

30. For the basic documents, accompanied by a helpful commentary, see James G. Hershberg and Peter Kornbluh, eds., "Brazil Marks 50th Anniversary of Military Coup," National Security Archive Briefing Book No. 465, April 2, 2014, http://nsarchive.gwu.edu/brazil/; Anthony W. Pereira, "The U.S. Role in the 1964 Coup in Brazil: A Reassessment," *Bulletin of Latin American Research,* June 2016, online only.

31. A transcript of this taped conversation, April 3, 1964, is in Michael R. Beschloss, ed., *Taking Charge: The Johnson White House Tapes, 1963–1964* (New York: Simon and Schuster, 1997), 306. LBJ made his "good week" comment to the press on April 4, 1964. Ambassador Lincoln Gordon to Secretary of State, April 10, 1964, NSF, Ralph A. Duggan, box 391, folder "Brazil 12 / 61–9 / 64 and undated," JFKL.

32. U.S. Congress, *United States Policies and Programs in Brazil,* 52–53.

33. Vernon Walters oral history, April 21, 1970, DDEL. On the U.S.-Brazil relationship during World War II, see Neill Lochery, *Brazil: The Fortunes of War: World*

War II and the Making of Modern Brazil (New York: Basic Books, 2014); Rubem Braga, *Crônicas da Guerra na Itália,* 3rd ed. (Rio de Janeiro: Record, 1985).

34. Vernon Walters Oral History, April 21, 1970, DDEL.

35. Vernon A. Walters, *Silent Missions* (Garden City, NY: Doubleday, 1978), 374–377, 381–382, 391, 253, 44.

36. U.S. Congress, Senate, Committee on Foreign Relations, *Nomination of Lincoln Gordon to Be Assistant Secretary of State for Inter-American Affairs,* 89th Cong., 2nd Sess., February 7, 1966, 44.

37. U.S. Congress, House, Committee on Foreign Affairs, *Inter-American Military Cooperation Act,* 80th Cong., 1st Sess., June and July 1947, 68.

38. Joint Chiefs of Staff, "Response to National Security Study Memorandum #68," 13–14; on this topic, see David F. Schmitz, *Thank God They're on Our Side: The United States and Right-Wing Dictatorships, 1921–1965* (Chapel Hill: University of North Carolina Press, 1999), 268–282.

39. Carlos Gustavo Poggio Teixeira, *Brazil, the United States, and the South American Subsystem* (Lanham, MD: Lexington Books, 2012), 78–80, 91; Gaddis Smith, *The Last Years of the Monroe Doctrine, 1945–1993* (New York: Hill and Wang, 1994), 119.

40. Rostow to Thomas Mann, "Reflections and Recommendations on Brazil," September 7, 1964, NSF: Brazil, NSF, Country File, box 10 (1 of 2), folder "Brazil, vol. 5, 9 / 64–11 / 65," LBJL; U.S. Central Intelligence Agency, Office of Current Intelligence, "Plotting against Goulart," March 8, 1963, OCI No. 0503 / 63, POF Country Series, Brazil, box 112, JFKL.

41. On the Communist Party and its history of democratic electoral competition, see Federico G. Gil, *The Political System of Chile* (Boston: Houghton Mifflin, 1966), 280–281; on the party's non-Leninist early history, see Fernando Alegría, *Recabarren* (Santiago: Antares, 1938). On National Security Adviser Henry Kissinger's conception of the party, see U.S. Congress, Senate, Committee on Foreign Relations, Subcommittee on Multinational Corporations, *Multinational Corporations and United States Foreign Policy,* 93rd Cong., 1973, pt. 2, 542–543.

42. Joint Chiefs of Staff, "Response to National Security Study Memorandum #68," 129, 130, 144.

43. *New York Times,* September 11, 1974, 14. Quoting an unnamed source, the *Times* reporter may or may not have captured Kissinger's exact words, but subsequent events indicate that it captured his thinking and behavior and that of President Nixon.

44. Headquarters to Station, September 27, 1970, doc. 7 in Peter Kornbluh, *The Pinochet File* (New York: New Press, 2003); Lubna Z. Qureshi, *Nixon, Kissinger, and Allende: U.S. Involvement in the 1973 Coup in Chile* (Lanham, MD: Lexington Books, 2009).

45. On the murder of General René Schneider: U.S. Congress, Senate, Select Committee to Study Governmental Operations with Respect to Intelligence Activities,

Alleged Assassination Plots Involving Foreign Leaders: An Interim Report, 94th Cong., 1st Sess., November 20, 1975, 225–255, esp. 235–236. On the Nixon "scream" order: "Meeting with the President on Chile at 1525," September 15, 1970, Kornbluh, *The Pinochet File,* unnumbered page 36.

46. Tanya Harmer, *Allende's Chile and the Inter-American Cold War* (Chapel Hill: University of North Carolina Press, 2011), 252–253, 255–256, 272.

47. Ford, press conference, September 16, 1974, *PPP.*

48. Department of State, Memorandum of Conversation, June 8, 1976, Santiago, Chile, DDRS.

49. Bell: U.S. Congress, Senate, Committee on Appropriations, *Foreign Assistance Appropriations, 1965,* 89th Cong., 2nd Sess., 1964, 82; Mann, Commencement Address, University of Notre Dame, June 7, 1964, *DOSB* 50 (June 29, 1964): 995–1000; Symington: *Executive Sessions of the Senate Foreign Relations Committee, Together with Joint Sessions with the Senate Armed Services Committee,* 993.

50. Johnson, *Remarks upon Receiving an Honorary Degree at the University of Denver,* August 26, 1966, *PPP.*

51. Donald M. Fraser, "New Directions in Foreign Aid," *World Affairs* 129 (January–March 1967), 245, 250.

52. §106 of PL 89-583, 80 Stat. 800, September 19, 1966.

53. James Buchanan to John Appleton, June 1, 1848, in *Diplomatic Correspondence of the United States, Inter-American Affairs, 1831–1860,* ed. William R. Manning (Washington, DC: Carnegie Endowment for International Peace, 1932–1939), 2:4, James Buchanan to Elijah Hise, June 3, 1848, at 3:31; James Buchanan to Richard Rush, March 31, 1848, in U.S. Congress, House, H. Doc. 551, 56th Cong., 2nd Sess., 1906, 1:124–125.

54. Jefferson to Pinckney, December 30, 1792, in *The Writings of Thomas Jefferson* (Washington, DC: Thomas Jefferson Memorial Association, 1903–1904), 9:7–8; *An Address, Delivered at the Request of the Committee for Arrangements for Celebrating the Anniversary of Independence, in the City of Washington on the Fourth of July, 1821, upon the Occasion of Reading the Declaration of Independence by John Quincy Adams* (Cambridge: Hilliard and Metcalf, 1821), esp. 32. On this topic, see Willem Theo Oosterveld, *The Law of Nations in Early American Foreign Policy: Theory and Practice from the Revolution to the Monroe Doctrine* (Leiden: Brill Nijhoff, 2016), 180; and http://founders.archives.gov/documents/Jefferson/01-24-02-0776.

55. Peru: William Seward to Alvin P. Hovey, March 8, 1866, and Hovey to Seward, April 16, 1866, *DOSB* 71 (November 18, 1974): 685. Mexico: Assistant Secretary Frederick Seward to John W. Foster, May 16, 1877, Instructions to Mexico, RG 59, NA.

56. John Bassett Moore to Woodrow Wilson, May 15, 1913, *The Papers of Woodrow Wilson* (Princeton, NJ: Princeton University Press, 1966–1994), 27:437–438; Wilson to Lansing, November 26, 1916, 839.00 / 1951a, RG 59, NA.

57. Dana G. Munro, *The United States and the Caribbean Republics, 1921–1933* (Princeton: Princeton University Press, 1974), 381; Henry L. Stimson, "Bases of American Foreign Policy during the Past Four Years," *Foreign Affairs,* April 1933, 395; see also *FRUS* 1930, 1:387.

58. Laurence Duggan, *The Americas: The Search for Hemisphere Security* (New York: Henry Holt, 1949), 201, 203.

59. Schlesinger to JFK, March 10, 1961, *FRUS* 1961–1963, 12:14; Robert C. Hill, "Confidential Report and Suggestions on Latin America," n.d. but late 1960 or early 1961, Robert Hill Papers, Dartmouth College Library, Hanover, NH. Secretary of State Dean Rusk's announcement of an aid cutoff to the Dominican Republic and Honduras is *DOSB* 49 (October 21, 1963): 624. See also President Kennedy's press conference, October 9, 1963: "Dictators are the seedbeds from which communism ultimately springs up." Theodore C. Sorensen, *Kennedy* (New York: Harper and Row, 1965), 535.

60. U.S. Peace Corps, *Who's Working Where: A Catalogue of Peace Corps Volunteer Skills* (Washington, DC: Peace Corps, 1964), 11, 13, 28.

61. AID, "Report to the Congress on the Implementation of Title IX," May 10, 1967. On the early discussions regarding implementation of Title IX, see Brian E. Butler, "Title IX of the Foreign Assistance Act: Foreign Aid and Political Development," *Law and Society Review* 3 (August 1968): 115–152.

62. Mann, "Commencement Address, University of Notre Dame," 1000.

63. Taped Oval Office conversations No. 523-4 with Charles Bluhdorn, June 6, 1971, and No. 490-14, with Admiral Thomas Moorer and David Packard, May 4, 1971, RNL.

64. Harkin remarks in *U.S. Policy on Human Rights in Latin America (Southern Cone): A Congressional Conference on Capitol Hill* (New York: Fund for New Priorities in America, 1978), 75–76.

65. Reagan, *Address to the British Parliament,* June 8, 1982, *PPP*. PL 98-164, November 22, 1983, 97 Stat. 1039.

66. Hans Morgenthau, "A Political Theory of Foreign Aid," *American Political Science Review* 56 (June 1962): 308.

10. THE EVOLUTION FROM ECONOMIC TO POLITICAL IMPROVEMENT

1. USAID, "Latin America and the Caribbean," www.usaid.gov (January 2009).

2. http://www.usaid.gov,/; U.S. Congress, House, Committee on Foreign Affairs, Subcommittee on the Western Hemisphere, *U.S. Policy toward Latin America in 2009 and Beyond,* 111th Cong., 1st Sess., February 4, 2009, 2.

3. For the similarity between Cold War and post–Cold War programs, compare Larry Q. Nowels, *Foreign Aid: Budget, Policy, and Reform,* CRS Issue Brief IB89014,

updated January 27, 1989; and Curt Tarnoff and Larry Nowels, *Foreign Aid: An Introductory Overview of U.S. Programs and Policy,* CRS Order Code 98-916, updated January 19, 2005.

4. C. Douglas Dillon Oral History, May 2, 1972, 69–70, Rare Book and Manuscript Library, Columbia University. Dillon placed much of the blame on the recipients: "Even now [in 1972] there is a great deal to wish for in terms of recipients handling their aid programs sensibly."

5. www.aid.gov (July 6, 2005).

6. On what post–Cold War policymakers inherited, see U.S. Congress, House, Committee on Foreign Affairs, *U.S. Foreign Aid in a Changing World: Options for New Priorities,* 102nd Cong., 1st Sess., February 1991, 21.

7. Oxfam America, *Smart Development: Why US Foreign Aid Demands Major Reform,* 2008, 11. For a helpful discussion of these numbers, see Dianne E. Rennack and Susan G. Chesser, *Foreign Assistance Act of 1961: Authorizations and Corresponding Appropriations,* CRS Report R40089, July 29, 2011.

8. The clean 280 pages (with neither footnotes nor annotations) as of February 10, 2018: https://legcounsel.house.gov/Comps/Foreign%20Assistance%20Act%20Of%20 1961.pdf. The original law is 75 Stat. 424–465.

9. The numbers come from several sources: USAID, *Response to Congress: Choice of Appropriate Mechanism to Carry Out USAID Mission,* undated but early 2015. (This 85-page document is divided into two parts, with the pages numbered separately. "Report One" primarily provides tabular data, and page 1 contains the number [3,146] of direct-hire personnel. "Report Two" gives the numbers about Institutional Support Contractors doing administrative work. U.S. Congress, House, Committee on Foreign Affairs, *Report of the Task Force on Foreign Assistance,* 101st Cong., 1st Sess., February 1989, 194; Alison Stanger, *One Nation under Contract: The Outsourcing of American Power and the Future of Foreign Policy* (New Haven, CT: Yale University Press, 2009), 119, 128; Curt Tarnoff and Marian Leonardo Lawson, "Foreign Aid: An Introduction to U.S. Programs and Policy," CRS Report R40213, April 9, 2009, 29.

10. On 1950s outsourcing, see U.S. Congress, Senate, Special Committee to Study the Foreign Aid Program, *Foreign Aid Program: Compilation of Studies and Surveys,* Senate Doc. 52, 85th Cong., 1st Sess., 1957, 1527.

11. Fowler was a second speaker at JFK's *Remarks at the Signing of a Contract to Aid Electrification of Underdeveloped Countries,* November 1, 1962, *PPP.*

12. USAID, *Response to Congress.* For additional staffing data, see Stanger, *One Nation under Contract,* 119, 132; *Report of the Task Force on Foreign Assistance,* 101st Cong., 1st Sess., February 1989, 184; Tarnoff and Lawson, "Foreign Aid"; U.S. GAO, *Government Contractors: An Overview of the Federal Contracting-Out Program,* GAO-T-GGD-95-131, March 29, 1995. For a case study with helpful details about the outsourcing process, see U.S. GAO, *Aid to Nicaragua: Status of U.S. Assistance to the*

Democratically Elected Government, May 1991, GAO / NSIAD-91-183, May 1991. AID's management of funding agreements is specified in a set of procedure manuals with one name: "Automated Directives System" (ADS). ADS chap. 302 deals with direct contracting. https://www.usaid.gov/who-we-are/agency-policy/about-ads.

13. FHI 360 *Annual Report,* 2014, 4. In 2014, AID outsourced another $85 million to an FHI spin-off, FHI Development 360. Combined, the two organizations were AID's fourth-largest vendor. https://www.usaid.gov/results-and-data/budget-spending/top-40-vendors.

14. For a brief assessment of the incentive structure inherent in private-sector contractors, see Clark C. Gibson, Krister Andersson, Elinor Ostrom, and Sujai Shivakuman, *The Samaritan's Dilemma: The Political Economy of Development Aid* (New York: Oxford University Press, 2005), 231–232.

15. *Wall Street Journal,* March 30, 2007, A1.

16. Stanger, *One Nation under Contract,* 110, 119, 131–132; Susan B. Epstein and Matthew C. Weed, "Foreign Aid Reform: Studies and Recommendations," CRS Report R40102, July 28, 2009, 12; Thomas Carothers, *Revitalizing Democracy Assistance: The Challenge of USAID* (Washington, DC: Carnegie Endowment for International Peace, 2009), 20–21, 25; Rubén Barríos, *Contracting for Development: The Role of For-Profit Contractors in U.S. Foreign Development Assistance* (Westport, CT: Praeger, 2000), 2.

17. An assessment of these early efforts is William A. Douglas, *Developing Democracy* (Washington, DC: Helfref, 1972), 166–167. Researchers will save weeks of time by first reading Elizabeth Cohn, "Idealpolitik in U.S. Foreign Policy: The Reagan Administration and the U.S. Promotion of Democracy" (PhD diss., American University, 1995).

18. Charles E. Lindblom, "The Science of 'Muddling Through,'" *Public Administration Review* 19 (Spring, 1959): 79–88, quotations at 84, 86, emphasis in original.

19. Charles E. Lindblom, "A New Look at Latin America," *Atlantic Monthly,* October 1962, 81–86, quotations at 85–86.

20. Fulbright: U.S. Congress, Senate, Committee on Foreign Relations, *Executive Sessions of the Senate Foreign Relations Committee, Together with Joint Sessions with the Senate Armed Services Committee,* Historical Series vol. 17, 89th Cong., 1st Sess., 1965, 987. The *Ramparts* ads appeared on February 14, 1967, in the *New York Times* at p. 31 and in the *Washington Post* at p. A9.

21. *Los Angeles Times,* February 26, 1967, B3; Cord Meyer, *Facing Reality: From World Federalism to the CIA* (New York: Harper and Row, 1980), 86–103. Meyer was chief of the CIA's Covert Action Staff and then assistant deputy director for plans.

22. Philip Agee, *Inside the Company: CIA Diary* (New York: Stonehill, 1975).

23. President Johnson's directive and the brief Katzenbach Committee report are reprinted in the *Weekly Compilation of Presidential Documents* 3 (April 3, 1967): 556–558; Angus Mackenzie, *Secrets: The CIA's War at Home* (Berkeley: University of California Press, 1997), 25.

24. U.S. Department of State (?), "Democracy Promotion Programs Funded by the U.S. Government: A Report to the Senate Foreign Relations Committee and the House Foreign Affairs Committee of the U.S. Congress, as Requested in PL 103-236, Section 534," n.d. but 1994, available at http://pdf.usaid.gov/pdf_docs/Pcaaa756.pdf (February 8, 2018). Elizabeth Cohn and Michael J. Nojeim, "Promoting Democracy," in *U.S.–Latin American Policymaking: A Reference Handbook* (Westport, CT: Greenwood Press, 1995), 466.

25. The following pages rely heavily upon the George E. Agree Papers at the Manuscript Division of the Library of Congress and upon Cohn's "Idealpolitik in U.S. Foreign Policy."

26. Freedom House, "Credo of Support," July 20, 1965; "Johnson Is Backed by Freedom House on Vietnam Policy," *New York Times,* July 21, 1965, 3.

27. M. Pinto-Duschinsky, "Foreign Political Aid: The German Political Foundations and Their US Counterparts," *International Affairs* 67 (January 1991): 33–63.

28. John C. White to Agree, July 12, 1978, and Bill Brock to Agree, September 7, 1978. See also Agree to Samuel P. Huntington, February 3, 1978. All three in box 2 of George Agree Papers, LC.

29. Press release draft, October 15, 1979; "American Political Foundation," undated description of activities used with fund-raising letters.

30. Samuels to Agree, February 7, 1980, Agree Papers, box 2, LC. Samuels, "Project Proposal: A Comprehensive Policy Response to Expanding U.S. Interests in the Third World," attached to Agree to Samuels [*sic*], February 15, 1980, box 1, folder "APF Correspondence," Agree Papers, LC. Samuels's oral history, October 22, 1991, focuses largely on Africa: Association for Diplomatic Studies and Training Foreign Affairs Oral History Project, available online through the Library of Congress.

31. Agree to Samuels, February 15, 1980, Agree Papers, box 2, LC.

32. Brock, Manatt, and Richardson to President Reagan, June 4, 1982, Agree Papers, box 2, LC.

33. Robert Pee, *Democracy Promotion, National Security and Strategy: Foreign Policy under the Reagan Administration* (New York: Routledge, 2016), 91.

34. Reagan, *Address to the British Parliament,* June 8, 1982, *PPP.* Robert C. Rowland and John M. Jones, *Reagan at Westminster: Foreshadowing the End of the Cold War* (College Station: Texas A&M University Press, 2010), contains a chapter, "The Drafting of the Westminster Address," that leaves many questions unanswered.

35. The initial proposal was submitted to AID attached to a letter from Agree to the Agency's administrator, Peter McPherson, August 27, 1982, Agree Papers, box 2,

LC. The grant letter is from AID's L. E. Stanfield to Agree, December 1, 1982. An annual budget for the President's "Unanticipated Needs" was authorized by PL 95-570, November 2, 1978, 92 Stat. 2449. When the Foundation had spent the $300,000 and had not yet completed its work, AID provided another $100,000. U.S. GAO, "Events Leading to the Establishment of the National Endowment of [*sic*] Democracy," Report GAO/NSIAD-84-121, July 6, 1984, 6–7.

36. U.S. Congress, Senate, Committee on Finance, *Nomination of Michael A. Samuels,* 99th Cong., 2nd Sess., February 4, 1986.

37. National Security Decision Directive 77, January 14, 1983, https://fas.org/irp /offdocs/nsdd/nsdd-077.htm.

38. GAO, "Events Leading," 3, 10, 13, 51. The feasibility study was released on April 18, 1983. A draft, "The Democracy Program's Initial Recommendations: A Summary," undated but early 1983, indicates that very little of the work specified in the August 27, 1982, proposal to AID had been done. Box 2, folder "National Endowment for Democracy, 1983, 1984," Agree Papers, LC.

39. The Republicans subsequently changed the name of their institute to the International Republican Institute (IRI), and the AFL CIO's institute subsequently became the American Center for International Labor Solidarity and then today's Solidarity Center.

40. PL 98-164, November 22, 1983 (authorization), and PL 98-166, November 28, 1983 (appropriation).

41. NED, *Annual Report 2014,* 116; NED, *Annual Report 2015,* 136.

42. Carl Gershman interview in *El Mercurio* (Santiago, Chile), January 10, 1988, D6–D7.

43. Representative Sanders: *Congressional Record,* June 22, 1993, 13594. The House debate (in which newcomers did not participate) is *Congressional Record,* June 22, 1993, 13590–13596. For the views of the NED's severest critic in the 1990s, Representative Paul Kanjorski (D-PA), see 13590.

44. *Congressional Record,* July 28, 1993, 17558, 17551, 17545.

45. Ibid., 17554, 17550. The 2002 Federal Election Campaign Act prohibits any foreign national from contributing, donating, or spending funds in connection with any federal, state, or local election. §303 of PL 107-155, 116 Stat. 81, March 27, 2002. See http://www.fec.gov/pages/brochures/foreign.shtml for the constraints on foreign campaign contributions.

46. *Congressional Record,* July 28, 1993, 17520–17583, quotations at 17553 and 17582, vote at 17583.

47. Ibid., 17552 and 17568. See also "Democracy Promotion Programs Funded by the U.S. Government," 14; U.S. Congress, Senate, Committee on Foreign Relations, *Nongovernmental Organizations and Democracy Promotion: "Giving Voice to the People,"* Committee Print 109-73, 109th Cong., 2nd Sess., December 22, 2006, 87.

48. Of these amounts, about a quarter (23.6 percent in 2016) goes to administrative expenses—"internal support services" of the NED and "indirect expenses" of the four core grantees.

49. PL 99-93, August 16, 1985, 99 Stat. 432; U.S. Congress, House, Committee on Foreign Affairs, Subcommittees on Human Rights and International Organizations and on International Operations, *Authorizing Appropriations for Fiscal Years 1992–93 for the Department of State, the U.S. Information Agency, the Voice of America, the Board for International Broadcasting and for Other Purposes,* 102nd Cong., 1st Sess., February, March, and April 1991, 1192.

50. William E. Brock to Charles Z. Wick, January 26, 1984, DNSA. Representative Dante Fascell had served only briefly as chair of the NED's board of directors.

51. U.S. Department of State, Office of Inspector General (OIG), *Management Assistance Report: Oversight of Grants to the National Endowment for Democracy* (AUD-SI-15-35, June 2015). The first two audits: OIG, *Audit of the National Endowment for Democracy Use of Department of State FY 2006–FY 2014 Grant Funds* (AUD-SI-16-05, November 2015) and OIG, *Audit of the National Endowment for Democracy and Its Core Institutes Use of Grant Funds during FYs 2015 and 2016* (AUD-FM-18-24, January 2018).

52. Author's interview with Barbara Haig, June 14, 2016, Washington, DC.

53. The Board's by-laws stipulate a minimum of thirteen and a maximum of twenty-five members, who serve a maximum of three 3-year terms. It meets quarterly to approve or reject grant proposals, with most of the large grants going to the four core grantees, who then make their own grants to U.S. and foreign organizations. Before each meeting the NED's regional experts meet to vet each proposal, and the four core grantees are given an opportunity to withdraw proposals that are not likely to be approved. The regional experts attend the board meetings and present the grant proposals to the Board.

54. *Congressional Record,* September 22, 1983, 24290, 25308. Senator Helms's proposal to kill the authorizing legislation was defeated, 42 to 49.

55. Barbara Conry, "Loose Cannon: The National Endowment for Democracy," Cato Foreign Policy Briefing No. 27, November 9, 1993.

56. Carl Gershman, "The World according to Andrew Young," *Commentary,* August 1, 1978, 23. Jeane J. Kirkpatrick, "U.S. Security and Latin America," *Commentary,* January 1981, 36. For a follow-up, see Gershman's "The Andrew Young Affair," *Commentary,* November 1979, 25–33.

57. Thomas Carothers, *Critical Mission: Essays on Democracy Promotion* (Washington, DC: Carnegie Endowment for International Peace, 2004), 147.

58. John R. Schott, "A New Dimension in US Foreign Aid?," *Foreign Service Journal* 47 (March 1970): 19, 21.

59. U.S. GAO, *Foreign Affairs and Defense Agencies Funds and Activities—1991 to 1993*, GAO / NSIAD-94-83, January 1994, 1, 4; U.S. Congress, House, *State, Foreign Operations, and Related Programs Appropriations Bill*, 2018, 115th Cong., 1st Sess., July 2017, 8.

60. https://www.state.gov/s/d/rm/rls/dosstrat/2007/html/82952.htm (February 2, 2018).

61. Michele Wozniak Schimpp, "AID and Democratic Development: A Synthesis of Literature and Experience," Center for Development and Evaluation, AID, May 1992.

62. Obama, *Remarks at the Palacio de la Moneda Cultural Center, Santiago, Chile*, March 21, 2011, *PPP*.

63. USAID, *USAID Strategy on Democracy, Human Rights, and Governance*, June 2013, 29.

11. PROMOTING GOOD GOVERNANCE

1. Since 1974 the President has been required to approve each covert operation by signing a written "finding" that the operation is important to national security, and then to provide "timely notice" of each operation to the appropriate committees of Congress. In this case, parts of the February 1, 1981, finding were redacted when declassified; the less-redacted quotation here is from "Memorandum of Notification," March 24, 1983, to the National Security Planning Group, DDRS doc. CK3100254268.

2. Tom Barry, *Central America Inside Out* (New York: Grove Weidenfeld, 1991), 404. NED *Annual Report 1984*, 17–18. The amount in 1985 was $60,000. NED *Annual Report 1985*, 44.

3. NED *Annual Report 1985*, 46.

4. All data are for fiscal years and from NED annual reports. The amount for 1986 excluded a $330,000 grant to Freedom House for use in Central America generally.

5. *Los Angeles Times*, March 5, 1985, 1; U.S. Congress, House, Committee on Foreign Affairs, *The Mining of Nicaraguan Ports and Harbors*, 98th Cong., 2nd Sess., 1984. For a short but revealing introduction to U.S. undercover activities in early 1980s Nicaragua, see Jacqueline Sharkey, "Back in Control," *Common Cause Magazine*, September–October 1986, 28–39.

6. TC ["The Courier—Robert Owen] to BG ["Blood and Guts"—Oliver North], "Overall Perspective," March 17, 1986, NSA.

7. JTP (Janine Perfit) to KES (Keith Schutte), "Nicaragua," August 11, 1989, facsimile published in William I. Robinson, *U.S. Intervention in the Nicaraguan Elections and American Foreign Policy in the Post–Cold War Era* (Boulder, CO: Westview

Press, 1992), 249–251. The IRI had not yet changed its name from the National Republican Institute for International Affairs (NRI).

8. Robinson interview with Atwood, November 1987, quoted in Robinson, *U.S. Intervention in the Nicaraguan Elections,* 48; NED *Annual Report 1984,* 40.

9. NED, *Annual Report 1990,* 43. For Nicaragua, the NED had two funding sources almost from the beginning: its congressional appropriation and grants from AID and the State Department. Of the 1990 funding for Nicaragua—$7,209,535—95 percent came from an AID grant, not from the NED's annual congressional appropriation. The $32 million: U.S. General Accounting Office, *Promoting Democracy: National Endowment for Democracy's Management of Grants Needs Improvement,* Report GAO / NSIAD-91-162, March 1991, 39.

10. *New York Times,* March 16, 1986, E26. On the NED's ties to PRODEMCA, see Secretary of State to U.S. Embassy, Managua, April 4, 1985, DNSA.

11. §210, PL 99-93, 99 Stat. 431.

12. Elizabeth Cohn and Michael J. Nojeim, "Promoting Democracy," in *U.S.–Latin American Policymaking: A Reference Handbook,* ed. David W. Dent (Westport, CT: Greenwood Press, 1995), 468.

13. Joshua Muravchik, *Exporting Democracy: Fulfilling America's Destiny* (Washington, DC: AEI Press, 1991), 210. For a list of UNO-affiliated grantees, see U.S. Congress, House, Committee on Foreign Affairs, Subcommittees on Human Rights and International Organizations and on International Operations, *Authorizing Appropriations for Fiscal Years 1992–93 for the Department of State, the U.S. Information Agency, the Voice of America, the Board for International Broadcasting and for Other Purposes,* 102nd Cong., 1st Sess., February, March, and April, 1991, 1198.

14. Rep. George Miller, *Congressional Record,* October 4, 1989, 23282. On the newsprint issue, see John Spicer Nichols, "*La Prensa:* The CIA Connection," *Columbia Journalism Review,* July 1, 1988, 34–35.

15. Smedley Butler, Address to the Pittsburgh Builders Exchange, December 5, 1929, reported in the *New York Herald Tribune,* December 7, 1929, 11.

16. U.S. Congress, Senate, Committee on Foreign Relations, *Nongovernmental Organizations and Democracy Promotion: "Giving Voice to the People,"* Committee Print 109-73, 109th Cong., 2nd Sess., December 22, 2006, 60; U.S. Congress, *Authorizing Appropriations for Fiscal Years 1992–93,* 568, 580.

17. McCoy, "American Electoral Mission to Nicaragua: Summary of Events from Stimson Agreements to date, revised to Sept. 1, 1928," n.d. but September 1928, box 79, folder "Nicaragua Electoral Mission Correspondence, Reports, 1921–1932," Frank Ross McCoy Papers, LC.

18. The "Dire Emergency Supplemental Appropriations . . . Act," PL 101-302, 25 May 1990, 104 Stat. 213. U.S. Government Accounting Office, *Aid to Nicaragua: Status of U.S. Assistance to the Democratically Elected Government,* GAO / NSIAD-91-183, May 1991, 3, 5, 22, 34.

19. Knox to American Chargé, August 15, 1912, *FRUS* 1912, 315; Henry L. Stimson, *American Policy in Nicaragua* (New York: Charles Scribner's Sons, 1927), 94.

20. USAID FY1998 Congressional Presentation Document, www.info.usaid .gov/publs/cp98/lac/countries/ni.htm (October 1997).

21. U.S. Department of State, *Congressional Budget Justification, Department of State, Foreign Operations, and Related Programs, Fiscal Year 2016*, 156.

22. U.S. Department of State, *Congressional Budget Justification, Department of State, Foreign Operations, and Related Programs, Fiscal Year 2017*, 178. Given what was happening in neighboring Honduras and to a lesser extent in Nicaragua, $32.88 million was spent in FY2017, 30 percent of it for democracy, human rights, and governance.

23. www.ned.org/region/latin-america-and-caribbean/nicaragua-2014/(March 2016); http://cipe.org/search/google/nicaragua/(August 2017).

24. U.S. Congress, Senate, Select Committee to Study Governmental Operations with Respect to Intelligence Activities, *Covert Action in Chile, 1963–1973*, 94th Cong., 1st Sess., 1975, 1, 9.

25. Richard Nixon, *The Memoirs of Richard Nixon* (New York: Gosset and Dunlap, 1978), 489.

26. Alexander M. Haig Jr. to The President, "Our Policy toward Chile," February 16, 1981, facsimile reprinted in Peter Kornbluh, *The Pinochet File: A Declassified Dossier on Atrocity and Accountability*, updated version (New York: New Press, 2013), 450.

27. "Tuve una conversación muy agradable con el Presidente," and "me pareció un hombre muy serio, muy honorable, y muy agradable." *El Mercurio* (Santiago), August 7, 1981, A20. On U.S. policy during this period from a contemporary Chilean perspective, see Heraldo Muñoz and Carlos Portales, *Una amistad esquiva: Las relaciones de Estados Unidos y Chile* (Santiago: Pehuén, 1987), chap. 3.

28. Amembassy Santiago to SecState Washington, "Ambassador Kirkpatrick's Visit to Santiago: Overview," August 10, 1981, DNSA.

29. Amnesty International, "Amnesty International Calls on World Public to Press for End to Killings and Torture in Chile," September 9, 1981. Amnesty International's *Annual Report 1982* (for events of 1981), 118–122, details the Pinochet government's torture methods.

30. Susan Kaufman Purcell in Mark Falcoff, Arturo Valenzuela, and Susan Kaufman Purcell, *Chile: Prospects for Democracy* (New York: Council on Foreign Relations, 1988), 65.

31. Tony Motley to the Deputy Secretary, "U.S. Policy toward Chile," December 20, 1984, facsimile in Kornbluh, *The Pinochet File*, 453–454; on the issue of supporting "moderates" when challenged by "radicals," especially in labor unions, see William I. Robinson, *Promoting Polyarchy: Globalization, US Intervention, and Hegemony* (New York: Cambridge University Press, 1996), 175–193.

32. Shultz to the President, "U.S. Policy Seeks Peaceful Transition to Chile Based on Broad National Consensus," September 3, 1985, facsimile in Kornbluh, *The Pinochet File,* 455; "Prepared Statement by the Assistant Secretary of State for Inter-American Affairs before a Subcommittee of the House Banking, Finance and Urban Affairs Committee," December 5, 1985, in U.S. Department of State, *American Foreign Policy, 1985, Current Documents,* 1086–1090, quotation at 1087.

33. James Theberge, *Russia in the Caribbean* (Washington, DC: Center for Strategic and International Studies, Georgetown University, 1973); Theberge, *Soviet Seapower in the Caribbean* (New York: Praeger, 1972); Theberge, *The Soviet Presence in Latin America* (New York: Crane, Russak for NSIC, 1974).

34. The 1980 Constitution was approved in a special referendum. For the plebiscite details, see Articles 27 and 28 of the Transitory Provisions.

35. "No hizo otra cosa que hacer propaganda política contra el gobierno para destruirlo. . . . A ese señor no le digo adiós ni hasta luego." *La Epoca,* November 28, 1988, 9.

36. NED, *Annual Report 1985,* 13, 42, 45.

37. This estimate is from Robinson, *Promoting Democracy,* 175.

38. *El Mercurio* (Santiago, Chile), January 10, 1988, D7.

39. U.S. Congress, House, Committee on Foreign Affairs, Subcommittee on International Operations, *Authorizing Appropriations for Fiscal Years 1990–91 for the Department of State, the U.S. Information Agency, the Voice of America, the Board for International Broadcasting and for Other Purposes,* 101st Cong., 1st Sess., March 1989, 231.

40. *Congressional Record,* July 28, 1993, 17548.

41. NED *Annual Report 2014,* 68–73.

42. *Toast by the Vice President to the President of Cuba, Havana (National Palace),* folder "RN's Toast to the President of Havana, Cuba—National Palace," box 2; ser. 361: Briefing materials, Nixon's Statements, Staff Memos, General Correspondence. January–April 1955: Pre-Presidential Papers of Richard Nixon (Laguna Niguel): subseries B: 1955 Trip to Central America and the Caribbean, RNL.

43. Bundy in "Cuba Meeting—Wednesday, February 19, 1964," Memorandum for the Record, 19 February 1964, *FRUS 1964–1968,* 31:11. The memo's language reveals the drafting hand of Bundy's aide Gordon Chase, whose favorite adjective was "nasty."

44. Fourth debate of the presidential candidates, October 21, 1960, http://www.presidency.ucsb.edu/ws/index.php?pid=29403.

45. *Interview with NBC Owned and Operated Television Stations,* November 20, 1991, *PPP.*

46. PL 104-114, 110 Stat.785, March 12, 1996, §205, §206, and §109(a)(3); *Remarks at a Freedom House Breakfast,* October 6, 1995, *PPP,* 1459.

47. U.S. Commission for Assistance to a Free Cuba, *Report to the President* (Washington, DC: U.S. Department of State, 2004).

48. U.S. Government Accountability Office, *U.S. Democracy Assistance for Cuba Needs Better Management and Oversight,* GAO Report 07-147, November 2006, 37; *Miami Herald,* November 15, 2006, A24.

49. The 2010 U.S. census indicated that most of the nation's 1,785,547 Cuban Americans resided in the state with the third-largest number of electoral votes, and that 1,370,335 were now U.S. citizens.

50. In his settlement of *United States of America v. Felipe E. Sixto,* the defendant admitted that he "engaged in especially intricate conduct that facilitated the commission and concealment of a scheme to defraud CFC and USAID." United States District Court for the District of Columbia, *United States of America v. Felipe E. Sixto,* Criminal No. 08-345 RBW, December 19, 2008. Calzon did not use an accent mark on his last name.

51. http://www.ned.org/region/latin-america-and-caribbean/cuba-2014/; NED *Annual Report 2014,* 9; NED *Annual Report 2015,* 81; NED *Annual Report 2016,* 121.

52. Barbara Haig interview with author, Washington, DC, June 4, 2016.

53. https://www.facebook.com/events/1301568479869661/.

54. Over time it became increasingly difficult to keep AID's legacy grants separate from the NED grants, because both AID and the State Department's Bureau of Democracy, Human Rights, and Labor were regularly giving the NED special "Cuba" grants that were in addition to the NED's congressional appropriation.

55. www.echocuba.org (June 6, 2016).

56. Obama, *Address to the Cuban American National Foundation,* Miami, 23 May 2008, *PPP.*

57. *Statement by the President on Cuba Policy Changes,* December 17, 2014; *State of the Union Address,* January 20, 2015, *PPP.*

58. Obama, *Remarks at the Gran Teatro de la Habana Alicia Alonso,* Havana, Cuba, March 22, 2016, *PPP.*

59. *Address of Provisional Governor William Howard Taft, Opening Day Exercises of the National University of Havana,* October 1, 1906, reprinted in *Annual Reports of the War Department for the Fiscal Year Ended June 30,* 1906 (Washington, DC: GPO, 1906), 541–542.

60. *Address to the 7th Congress of the Communist Party,* April 16, 2016, http://lademajagua.cu/discurso-de-raul-en-la-clausura-del-7mo-congreso-del-pcc/and http://en.granma.cu/cuba/2016-04-18/the-development-of-the-national-economy-along-with-the-struggle-for-peace-and-our-ideological-resolve-constitute-the-partys-principal-missions.

61. U.S. Department of State, *Congressional Budget Justification, Department of State, Foreign Operations, and Related Programs, Fiscal Year 2016,* Appendix 3, 385.

62. *Presidential Policy Directive—United States–Cuba Normalization,* October 14, 2016, https://www.federalregister.gov/documents/2017/10/20/2017-22928/strengthening-the-policy-of-the-united-states-toward-cuba. In the same document the President twice said "State will ensure democracy programming is transparent."

63. https://www.usaid.gov/results-and-data/budget-spending/top-40-vendors (April 20, 2017).

64. United States District Court for the District of Columbia, "Alan Gross and Judy Gross, Plaintiffs, v. Development Alternatives, Inc . . . , and The United States of America, Defendants." C.A. No. 12-1860, filed March 15, 2013.

65. "DAI never saw a penny of that," insisted a knowledgeable DAI official; "anything and everything that was secured from that action went toward the settlement with the Gross family." Author's email correspondence with DAI's Steven O'Connor, October 4, 2017. The DAI-AID dispute was adjudicated by the Civilian Board of Contract Appeals, created by the 1978 Contract Disputes Act (PL 95-563, 92 Stat. 2383). Lodged within the General Services Administration, it is responsible for resolving contract disputes between contractors and government agencies.

66. U.S. Agency for International Development, Office of Inspector General, *Review of USAID's Cuban Civil Society Support Program,* Review Report No. 9-000-16-001-S, December 22, 2015, http://pdf.usaid.gov/pdf_docs/PBAAD880.pdf.

67. "Eight Facts about ZunZuneo," posted by Matt Herrick, AID Spokesperson, April 7, 2014, https://blog.usaid.gov/2014/04/eight-facts-about-zunzuneo/(12 February 2017).

68. Alberto Arce, Desmond Butler, and Jack Gillum, "US Secretly Created 'Cuban Twitter' to Stir Unrest," Associated Press, April 4, 2014.

69. "Eight Facts about ZunZuneo," AID Press Release, April 7, 2014; "The Right Call in Cuba," *Washington Post,* April 7, 2014, A14.

70. *Atlantic Monthly,* July / August 2012.

71. https://www.newamerica.org/(May 16, 2016).

72. "U.S. Underwrites Internet Detour around Censors," *New York Times,* June 12, 2011, A1. Meinrath directed the Institute while also serving as vice president of New America, and subsequently accepted a professorship at Pennsylvania State University.

73. https://commotionwireless.net/about/faq/(May 11, 2016).

74. Tracey Eaton, https://alongthemalecon.blogspot.com.

75. http://www.miamiherald.com/news/nation-world/world/americas/article1963203.html#storylink=cpy. See also http://www.huffingtonpost.com/anya-landau-french/pbs-news-hour-responds-to_b_804189.html.

76. The claim of Cuba expertise, subsequently removed: https://www.newamerica.org/our-people/emily-parker/(March 23, 2017); "Why Cuba Needs the Internet," *Politico,* December 22, 2014; http://emilyparkerwrites.com (June 2017).

77. http://www.politico.com/magazine/story/2014/12/en-cada-barrio-internet-113751.

78. F. Scott Fitzgerald, *The Great Gatsby* (1925), chap. 6.

CONCLUSION

1. $35,819,268 (1994), $23,028,000 (1995), $21,208,200 (1996), $29,548,000 (1997), $23,411,204 (1998), or a total of $133,014,672 divided by 5 = $26,602,934. https://explorer.usaid.gov/reports.html (October 4, 2017). Hurricane Mitch devastated Honduras in October 1998, just as the 1999 fiscal year was beginning, and humanitarian relief (not development assistance) increased substantially during Fiscal Years 1999 and 2000.

2. AID's 2016 Country Development Cooperation Strategy: https://www.usaid .gov/honduras/cdcs. Website: usaid.gov / where-we-work / latin-american-and-caribbean / honduras (both January 20, 2016). AID was slightly more candid when asking Congress for money: U.S. Department of State, *Congressional Budget Justification, Foreign Operations, Appendix 1, Fiscal Year 2016*, 421–429.

3. Roosevelt to Secretary of State John Hay, October 8, 1901, in *The Letters of Theodore Roosevelt* (Cambridge, MA: Harvard University Press, 1951–1954), 3:166.

4. *National Geographic,* July 1907, 438. But note Taft's economic interest in protecting U.S. investors: Taft to Helen Taft, October 17, 1909, Taft Papers, LC.

5. U.S. Congress, House, *U.S. Foreign Aid. Its Purposes, Scope, Administration and Related Information. Prepared by Legislative Reference Service, Library of Congress,* H. Doc. 116, 86th Cong., 1st Sess., June 11, 1959, 84.

6. After congressional authorization, which mentioned no name (§621, PL 87-195, September 4, 1961), the Agency was created by Executive Order 10973, November 3, 1961, 27 *Federal Register* 10469.

7. USAID, *U.S. Agency for International Development Primer: What We Do and How We Do It,* revised (Washington, DC: USAID, January 2006), 8.

8. The Branding Guide, revised February 2016: https://www.usaid.gov/branding/ gsm (November 10, 2017). In addition to the branding guide, page 25 of AID's *Automated Directives System (ADS),* chap. 320.3.8, "Branding and Marketing" (Partial Revision Date: 01 / 02 / 2015), stipulates punishment for "major or chronic noncompliance." See also USAID, "USAID Branding Initiative: Redefining the Image of America," undated, http://pdf.usaid.gov/pdf_docs/Pdacn483.pdf (November 24, 2017).

9. President of the United States, *National Security Strategy,* May 2010. The quotation is from the State Department's unveiling of this new strategy document: http:// www.state.gov/s/d/rm/rls/perfrpt/2010/html/153715.htm (July 7, 2016) White House Press Release, September 22, 2010.

10. USAID Press Office, "Study Affirms Impact of USAID Prevention Approach to Crime and Violence in Central America," October 30, 2014.

11. "Impact Evaluation of USAID's Community-Based Crime and Violence Prevention Approach in Central America: Regional Report for El Salvador, Guatemala, Honduras and Panama," October 2014, 15, https://www.usaid.gov/node/131331.

12. Sonia Nazario, "No Longer the Most Violent Place on Earth," *New York Times,* August 14, 2016, SR1. This was a lengthy article in the Sunday opinion section.

13. John Kean et al., *Analysis of Institutional Sustainability Issues in USAID 1985–86 Project Evaluation Reports* (Washington, DC: U.S. Agency for International Development, March 1987), vii.

14. Secretary of State Charles Evans Hughes to Minister John Ramer, February 15, 1924, *FRUS* 1924, 2:488; USAID, *USAID Strategy on Democracy, Human Rights, and Governance,* June 2013, 29.

15. 2011: Ambassador Anne Slaughter Andrew, "Striving for Developed Status: Costa Rica and the United States' 21st Century Engagement," *The Ambassadors Review,* Spring 2011, 12–15. 2016: http://costarica.usembassy.gov/usassistance.html and http://www.state.gov/r/pa/ei/bgn/2019.htm (both June 29, 2016). Also beta.foreignassistance.gov (August 3, 2016). USAID, "Issue Brief: USAID's Partnership with Costa Rica Advances Family Planning," May 2016. On earlier announced "graduations" of other countries (Brazil, Colombia, Paraguay, Uruguay) that lasted briefly or never began, see U.S. Congress, House, Committee on Foreign Affairs, Subcommittee on Inter-American Affairs, *Foreign Assistance Legislation for Fiscal Year 1982,* 97th Cong., 1st Sess., 1981, pt. 1, 297–299, and pt. 2, 125.

16. For a contrary view based upon unconvincing district-level data, see Robert K. Fleck and Christopher Kilby, "Foreign Aid and Domestic Politics: Voting in Congress and the Allocation of USAID Contracts across Congressional Districts," *Southern Economic Journal* 67 (January 2001): 598–617.

17. Admiral William S. Caperton to Rear Admiral William S. Benson, June 15, 1916, Caperton Papers, LC; Lansing to Wilson, June 21, 1916, 812.00/18533a, RG 59, NA.

18. H. W. Dodds, "The United States and Nicaragua," *Annals of the American Academy of Political and Social Science* 132 (July 1927): 141.

19. Address at Chautauqua, New York, August 14, 1936.

20. Lane to Secretary of State, October 9, 1935, *FRUS* 1935, 4:883.

21. Spruille Braden, Address to the Executive Club of Chicago, September 13, 1946, reprinted in *DOSB* 15 (September 22, 1946): 541; George F. Kennan, *Realities of American Foreign Policy* (Princeton: Princeton University Press, 1954), 57; Louis J. Halle, *American Foreign Policy: Theory and Reality* (London: George Allen and Unwin, 1960), 173–174.

22. Albert O. Hirschman, "Second Thoughts on the 'Alliance for Progress,'" *The Reporter,* May 25, 1961, 21–22. On Hirschman and his impact on a generation's thinking, see Jeremy Adelman's superb *Worldly Philosopher: The Odyssey of Albert O. Hirschman* (Princeton: Princeton University Press, 2013).

23. Memo, Thomas C. Mann to Charles S. Murphy, Special Counsel to the President, December 11, 1952, p. 32, Subject File, President's Secretary's Files, folder "Latin America," HSTL.

24. U.S. Congress, House, Committee on Foreign Affairs, *U.S. Foreign Aid in a Changing World: Options for New Priorities,* 102nd Cong., 1st Sess., February 1991, 18.

25. President-elect Juan Manuel Santos quoted in *New York Times,* June 21, 2010, A10.

Index

Spanish names are alphabetized according to common usage; for example, Zelaya rather than Santos Zelaya, and Menocal rather than García Menocal.

Malinowski, Bronislaw, 5

Manifest Destiny, 16, 24, 105. *See also* Annexation of Latin American territory; Roosevelt, Theodore

Mann, Thomas C., 186–187, 302, 349n4; Johnson administration, 222, 228, 234, 238; Kennedy administration, 213–214, 216–217

Marines, U.S., 71–72, 112; Cuba, 65, 78; Dominican Republic, 84, 87; Haiti, 64–65, 110–111; Honduras, 4; Nicaragua, 51, 87, 92, 107–108, 130. *See also* Navy, U.S.; Protectorates

Marshall, George, 172, 174, 178, 182, 184

Marshall Plan, 172–173, 184, 201

Martin, Edwin, 214–216, 219, 227, 243–244

Martínez, Bartolomé, 89–90

Mas Canosa, Jorge, 267, 279

McAdoo, William, 76–77, 140

McBain, Howard, 126

McCarthy, Joseph, and McCarthyism, 163–164, 186, 276

McCoy, Frank, 104, 108, 269

McKinley, William, 23–24, 27–29, 33–34, 41, 55

Mendieta, Carlos, 138, 144

Menocal, Mario García, 66–68

Messersmith, George, 169–172

Mexican Revolution, 47, 54–55, 96–97, 146

Mexico, 26, 46–47, 113; Central America, 88, 92–100; Great Depression, 140–142; Mexican-American War, 15–16, 116; Investments, U.S., 46–47, 95, 97, 101, 113; U.S. assessment of Mexicans, 15–16; Woodrow Wilson policy, 56–58, 72–73, 300–301

Meyer, Cord, 250–251

Military assistance, 16, 173–180, 185, 187, 195, 225–234, 241; Brazil, 175, 228–231; Chile, 231–234; civic action, 225–234; Cuba, 41, 179–180; Lend-Lease, 174; Nicaragua, 225, 267; transfer of U.S. values, 179–180, 226–231. *See also* Constabularies

Miller, Edward, 184

Modernization Theory, 200–206

Moncada, José María, 104, 108–109

Money Doctors, 40, 50–51, 60, 63, 107, 246, 288

Monroe, James, 13

Monroe Doctrine, 11, 22, 32, 44, 85, 111, 173, 199; Roosevelt Corollary, 36, 45

Morales Carrión, Arturo, 208

Morgan, Stokely, 97–98, 100, 102

Morgenthau, Hans, 7, 210, 240, 290. *See also* Realism

Morgenthau, Henry, 138–139

Morrow, Dwight, 93–94, 101, 300

Moscoso, Teodoro, 208

Munro, Dana, 74–75, 85, 87, 113, 118, 161, 236; in Haiti, 110–111

National Democratic Institute (NDI), 2, 255, 266–267, 274

National Endowment for Democracy (NED), 2, 8, 41, 240–241, 249–262; Board of Directors, 259–260; Chile, 271–276; Congressional oversight, 256–258; Cuba, 279–280, 282; Executive branch oversight, 258–259; funding, 254–256, 258; Honduras, 2, 8; leadership, 259–261; legislative history, 251–256; Nicaragua, 253, 256, 264–271. *See also* Democracy promotion; Gershman, Carl; Outsourcing

National Republican Institute for International Affairs. *See* International Republican Institute

National Security Council (NSC), 190, 207, 267

National Student Association, 250–251

Navy, U.S., 13–14, 19–22, 30–31, 43, 59, 62–63, 67–68, 77–78, 83–84. *See also* Dollar Diplomacy; Marines, U.S.

Nazario, Sonia, 295–297

New America (formerly New America Foundation), 286–288

Nicaragua: 1920s, 71–72, 87–104, 106–109, 119, 298; 1930s, 109, 301; Cold War, 223, 256, 268; post–Cold War, 264–271; Police assistance, 223; Progressive era, 50–52, 60–61; U.S. conflict with Mexico, 92, 95–101. *See also* Agency for International Development (AID/USAID); Iran-Contra Scandal; National Endowment for Democracy (NED); Sandinistas

Nixon, Richard, 188, 198, 220–221, 276–277; Chile, 231–234, 271; South America trip (1958), 195, 206; support of dictators, 238

Non-Intervention, U.S., 15, 119–122, 219. *See also* Hoover, Herbert; International Conferences of American States; Roosevelt, Franklin D. (FDR)

Nonproliferation, Antiterrorism, Demining and Related Programs (NADR), 4

North, Oliver, 255, 266

Obama, Barack, 3–4, 243, 271, 294; Cuba, 278–288; democracy promotion, 263, 271, 283–287

Obregón, Álvaro, 99, 113